Political passion

MANCHESTER
UNIVERSITY PRESS

Politics, culture and society in early modern Britain

General editors

PROFESSOR ANN HUGHES
DR ANTHONY MILTON
PROFESSOR PETER LAKE

This important series publishes monographs that take a fresh and challenging look at the interactions between politics, culture and society in Britain between 1500 and the mid-eighteenth century. It counteracts the fragmentation of current historiography through encouraging a variety of approaches which attempt to redefine the political, social and cultural worlds, and to explore their interconnection in a flexible and creative fashion. All the volumes in the series question and transcend traditional interdisciplinary boundaries, such as those between political history and literary studies, social history and divinity, urban history and anthropology. They contribute to a broader understanding of crucial developments in early modern Britain.

Political passions

Gender, the family and political argument in England 1680–1714

RACHEL WEIL

Manchester
University Press
Manchester and New York

distributed exclusively in the USA by St. Martin's Press

Published by Manchester University Press
Oxford Road, Manchester M13 9NR, UK
and Room 400, 175 Fifth Avenue, New York, NY 10010, USA
www.manchesteruniversitypress.co.uk

Distributed exclusively in the USA by
Palgrave, 175 Fifth Avenue, New York NY 10010, USA

Distributed exclusively in Canada by
UBC Press, University of British Columbia, 2029 West Mall,
Vancouver, BC, Canada V6T 1Z2

British Library Cataloguing-in-Publication Data
A catalogue record for this book is available from the British Library

Library of Congress Cataloging-in-Publication Data
A catalog record for this book is available from the Library of Congress

ISBN: 0 7190 8124 6 paperback

ISBN 13: 978 0 7190 8124 8

First published 1999 by Manchester University Press

First digital, on-demand edition produced by Lightning Source 2010

FOR LAWRENCE STONE
1919–1999

Contents

———◆———

Acknowledgements

Parts of Chapter 3 were published in Lois G. Schwoerer (ed.), *The Revolution of 1688–89: Changing perspectives* (Cambridge, Cambridge University Press, 1992), and are produced with the permission of Cambridge University Press.

Significant financial support was provided by Princeton University, Hull Memorial publication fund of Cornell University, Cornell University, the American Association of University Women, and my parents.

Specific references in Chapters 3 and 4 were provided by Lois Schwoerer and Henry Horwitz, respectively. Frances Harris generously shared her vast knowledge of the Blenheim papers and other archives. Tom Cogswell, Cynthia Herrup, Ann Hughes, Itsie Hull, Larry Klein, and an anonymous reader for Stanford University Press read and commented helpfully upon various drafts of the entire manuscript; Dan Baugh, Penny Becker, Sandra Greene, Itsie Hull (again), Harold Mah, Larry Moore, Virangini Munasinghe, Mary Beth Norton, and Michael Steinberg offered advice and encouragement in dealing with some especially troublesome sections of it. Rose Weil helped to clean up the prose. I am also grateful to Gerard M.-F. Hill for meticulous copyediting.

Other debts are harder to name. Steve Pincus has been a great friend, a font of wisdom, and a superb reality check. Peter Lake's contributions to this book are impossible to categorize but very real. Graduate school at Princeton in the 1980s was, despite the stress, a rewarding experience, and my friends from those days who made it so challenging but kept it so human know who they are. I feel incredibly lucky that my mother and brothers are among my best friends.

I have had excellent teachers. For nurturing my interest in early modern England and in feminist scholarship, I thank Bill Vanech, David Underdown, Susan Amussen, Natalie Davis, and Joan Scott. But my greatest teacher was my dissertation adviser, Lawrence Stone. When he wrote the word 'nonsense' in the margins of my draft, he was usually right. He kept me honest, and so this book is for him.

Rachel Weil
Ithaca, New York

Abbreviations

BL | British Library.
Bodl. | Bodleian Library.
Bohun, *PP* | 'Preface' by Edmund Bohun to Robert Filmer, *Patriarcha: or the natural power of kings* (R. Chiswell, 1685). Citations are by part and section numbers.
Burnet, *HOT* | Gilbert Burnet, *History of his own time*, 2nd edn enlarged, 6 vols (Oxford, Oxford University Press, 1833).
Hamilton diary | *The diary of Sir David Hamilton, 1709–14*, ed. Philip Roberts (Oxford, Clarendon Press, 1975).
HRO | Hertfordshire Record Office.
Locke, *TT* | John Locke, *Two treatises of government*, ed. Peter Laslett (Cambridge, Cambridge University Press, 1991). Citations are by treatise and section numbers.
Manley, *Novels* | *The novels of Mary Delarivière Manley*, ed. Patricia Koster, 2 vols (Gainesville, Florida, Scholars' Facsimiles and Reprints, 1971).
MGC | *The Marlborough–Godolphin correspondence*, ed. Henry L. Snyder, 3 vols (Oxford, Clarendon Press, 1975). Citations given by letter number.
Patriarcha | Robert Filmer, *Patriarcha and other political writings*, ed. Johann P. Sommerville (Cambridge, Cambridge University Press, 1991).
POAS | George de F. Lord *et al.* (eds), *Poems on affairs of state: Augustan satirical verse, 1660–1714*, 7 vols (New Haven, Connecticut, Yale University Press, 1963–75).
Tyrrell, *PNM* | [James Tyrrell], *Patriarcha non monarcha. The patriarch unmonarch'd* (Richard Janeway, 1681).

Throughout, the place of publication is London, unless otherwise specified. The year is taken to begin on 1 January. Seventeenth- and eighteenth-century spelling and punctuation has been standardized, except in book titles.

Introduction

———————

In March, 1702, Susanna Wesley wrote to Lady Yarborough to ask her help in a terrible situation. One night at family prayers, her husband, Samuel, had noticed that Susanna 'did not say "Amen" to his prayer for K[ing] W[illiam] as I usually do to all others'. In response to this expression of political defiance, Samuel 'kneeled down and imprecated the divine vengeance upon himself and all his posterity if he ever touched me more or came into a bed with me before I had begged God's pardon and his for not saying "Amen" to his prayer for the k[in]g'. Susanna tried to persuade him otherwise:

> I've unsuccessfully represented to him the unlawfulness and unreasonableness of his oath: that the man in that case has no more power over his own body than the woman over hers: that since I'm willing to let him quietly enjoy his opinions he ought not to deprive me of my little liberty of conscience.[1]

True to his word, Samuel 'that night forsook my bed to which he has been a stranger ever since'. He made arrangements to separate from his wife and six children by enlisting as ship's chaplain on a man-of-war.

The conflicts about political legitimacy and loyalty that had divided England after the Revolution of 1688 were at the heart of the Wesleys' quarrel. Susanna's refusal to pray for King William reflected her sympathies for the deposed King James. It is therefore not surprising that Lady Yarborough referred Susanna to George Hickes, one of the nonjuring clergymen deprived of office after the Revolution of 1688 for refusing to swear an oath of allegiance to the new regime. Significantly, George Hickes and Susanna Wesley both described the problem in terms of oaths. Susanna wanted to know whether Samuel, having sworn such a rash oath, was now nonetheless bound to keep it, since she deemed it 'a fearful thing to fall into the hands of the living God, or to trifle with the divine vengeance'.[2] Hickes assured her that Samuel's oath was 'wholly contrary to the prior obligation of his marriage promise, and the relative duties of a husband resulting from thence. It was perjury of him to make it, and it will be perjury for him to persist in the performance of it'.[3] These remarks on perjury were especially pointed because Samuel had taken an oath of allegiance to the new regime: his abandonment of his lawful wife echoed his abandonment of his lawful king, James II, and in each case the new oath violated a previous, unbreakable one. Samuel thereby offended not merely his sovereign or his wife, but God.

Samuel Wesley also interpreted the the quarrel in political terms, but in a very different way. For him, the issue was the threat that Susanna's disobedience posed to order in *both* the family and the state. The two were inextricably intertwined. What Susanna saw as 'my little liberty of conscience' was, for Samuel, not just an affront to William III's authority, but an 'injury' to himself.[4] His view was entirely conventional. By the terms of virtually any political theory circulating in late Stuart England, split political loyalty in a family could be taken to compromise the husband's authority by giving his wife an alternative standard of duty, and to compromise the king's authority by making the husband an inadequate representative of it. Even those theorists who held that government was based on a contract between ruler and ruled thought that women and children gave their consent to live under a government *through* their husbands and fathers. From that perspective, Susanna's political dissent undermined the marriage bond. In a possibly apocryphal version of the story, the Wesleys' son John reported that Samuel had declared, 'if we have two kings, we must have two beds'.[5] If Susanna did not abide by the decision of the bishops of York and Lincoln, the members of the (juring) Anglican establishment to whom Samuel wanted to refer the case, then (Susanna reports) Samuel would 'do anything rather than live with a person that is the declared enemy of his country, which he believes himself obliged to love before all the world'.[6]

As this story shows, men and women in the late seventeenth and early eighteenth centuries readily made connections between the family and the state, marriage vows and political allegiance, husbands and kings. Political events often took on the character of a family drama writ large. The role of Mary of Orange in the Revolution of 1688 was variously excoriated as the epitome of patricidal rebellion or praised as an example of conjugal obedience, while the pathetic spectacle of an heir defrauded of his rightful inheritance was at the centre of the exclusion crisis in 1680 and the scandal surrounding the allegedly fraudulent birth of the Prince of Wales in 1688. To affirm or deny the justifiability of resistance and revolution involved making claims about domestic violence, rape, adultery and divorce. Stories about marriage accrued layers of political meaning in the writings of the diehard tory and early feminist, Mary Astell, in the scandal novels of Delarivière Manley, and in the parliamentary divorce trials of the 1690s. The presence of two queens on the throne during the period 1680–1714 made the paradoxical nature of female authority in a patriarchal society a central problem in representations of royal power, both positive and negative. Questions of gender thus entered the political arena in many different ways.

The shared mental habit of connecting the family and the state did not produce consensus about the nature of the family, nor about the nature of political authority. As the Wesleys' quarrel suggests, conflicts about the one were played out in terms of conflicts about the other. In what ways these conflicts were played out, and with what consequences for how people in late Stuart England thought about politics and about gender, is the question that drives this book. The answers ought to be of interest both to historians of gender (concerned with sex–gender system, at whatever level of expression) and to historians of politics (concerned with struggles for control of the instruments of state, whatever they conceive they are, and whatever kind of struggle they look at).

Historians of gender and historians of politics traditionally have different perspectives and little contact. One of the greatest challenges in writing this book has been to cross the divide between two distinct realms of historical enquiry in a way that enriches both, without condescending to either. Fortunately, historians in each field do ask some of the same questions. How was the unequal distribution of power legitimated in the eyes of the people who found themselves at the lower end of the power hierarchy? Was early modern society held together by a consensus about the proper order of things, or riven by conflict? How was this conflict expressed? At a methodological level, how can a historian detect it?

It will not be possible, however, to map conflicts about gender, or between genders, onto political conflict in any straightforward manner. Political conflict, power struggles between gendered individuals, and clashes of ideas *about* gender, marriage or the family were distinct phenomena. The Wesley story illustrates the differences: Susanna and Samuel Wesley were openly in conflict about who was the rightful king; they may well have been in conflict over power in their marriage; they did not actually express directly conflicting *ideas* about marriage, although each emphasized a different element in the set of ideas that they held in common. Because historians of gender and historians of politics have different ways of categorizing and locating significant divisions, the insights of one field cannot simply be imported into the other. The dialogue between the two will benefit from methodological explicitness. Hence, some discussion of my own assumptions, categories of analysis, methods and sources is in order.

GENDER AS A CATEGORY OF HISTORICAL ANALYSIS

'Gender' (or even 'the woman question') was not a topic of discussion in late Stuart England, as it is in late twentieth-century academia. This is not to say that late Stuart people had nothing to say about female monarchs, female favourites, female literary hacks, the permissibility of divorce, polygamy, domestic violence, the mental and physical differences between men and women, the role of midwives, the system of inheritance to the throne and to property via male primogeniture, or the sexual double standard. Twentieth-century feminist scholars, including myself, would probably agree that the issues on this list are connected somehow under the rubric of 'gender', or 'the sex–gender system', even if we do not agree on exactly how the connections work. But it is entirely possible that a person in late seventeenth-century England would not see these issues as being connected. Or rather, each item on the list might for her be connected much more closely to items *not* on our list than to other items that *are* on that list.

Moreover, 'women' was not always a useful term for political and social categorization in our period. In discussions of property rights, for example, the relevant division was not between women and men, but between married women and other adults (single women, single men, married men). Similarly, a seventeenth-century person might be mystified to find twentieth-century scholars asking questions about the role of women in late Stuart political life, and the attitudes of contemporaries towards it. What seventeenth-century people thought of a legitimate female monarch was a far cry from what they thought of a scheming female favourite. They might condemn female rioters, but condemn male rioters as well (unless, of course, they were rioting for a good cause). The women who entered the political sphere were differentiated by class, role, and party. Late Stuart people did not have an opinion on 'women' in the political (or public) sphere *per se*.

Views of gender did not exist as a codified, coherent entity.[7] This insight allows us to understand better the process by which political debates affected ideas about marriage, women, and the family (that is, about aspects of what we call gender). In a set of ideas about gender that consists of relatively freestanding parts, each idea may be more malleable, at the level of each part, than in a set of ideas in which the elements are tightly integrated. People in late Stuart England were apparently willing to modify their notions about the meaning of gender in accordance with political circumstances. The prospect of putting Mary of Orange on the throne by herself in 1688 elicited strong objections ostensibly based upon the principles that a wife cannot be superior to her husband and that women are incapable of governing; but when Anne was crowned in 1702, there was no protest, despite the fact that she, too, was a married woman. The difference between the two cases lay in the political context, not the sex of the royal heir. Opinions about the justifiability of divorce were determined in part by the high political stakes involved in the most important divorce case considered by Parliament in the 1690s, that of the Duke and Duchess of Norfolk. The line between the family and the state, or between the public and the private, was drawn in different ways in different political contexts. Thus, politics was an arena in which ideas about gender, or relevant to the social construction of gender, were shaped and transformed.

WHIGS AND TORIES

Unlike 'gender', the terms 'whig' and 'tory' *were* recognizable to people in late Stuart England. But political historians of the period disagree among themselves about the depth of the division between whigs and tories, the nature of their ideological positions, and whether it is best to conceptualize political conflict in terms of whig and tory, or in some other way (for example, through a court vs. country division, or around rival patronage networks).[8] The uncertainty of historians in itself tells us something of importance about the nature of late Stuart political culture. Distinct and conflicting ideologies are harder to locate in this period than they are in, say, revolutionary France because late Stuart society put a premium on consensus. This is not to say that there were not profound ideological conflicts. However, proponents of each side expressed conflict not by articulating distinct, competing principles, but by seeking to appropriate for themselves the symbols and values upon which everyone theoretically agreed. Thus, both whigs and tories were in favour of the rule of law and abhorred popery. The trick, as far as the makers of political argument were concerned, was to show that one's own side was the one that truly held those values, while the other side was just pretending to hold them.

This style of conducting political arguments meant that whig–tory divisions, while profound, came about in a piecemeal fashion, developed as a process over time, and meant different things at different times. They were articulated around specific issues rather than abstract principles. By the end of Anne's reign, whigs were identified with a set of discrete positions: they were sympathetic to the rights of religious dissenters and believed that the nation should fight the the War of the Spanish Succession to the bitter end. Tories feared that the Church of England was in danger, and thought that the war should be financed differently, and ended sooner. Also, whigs and tories had somewhat different accounts of what had happened in 1688: tories, while supporting the Glorious Revolution, tended to explain it in ways that were reconcilable with their cherished principle of 'passive obedience'. Whigs used other arguments. While these differences serve as a rough guide to party identification, it must be remembered that there was room for disagreement within parties, and movements of individuals between parties. Whether it is possible to identify an ideological loadstone that would confer internal coherence on the collection of discrete positions that each party took remains debatable.

Attention to the role of gender in political argument may help political historians to understand better the differences, or lack thereof, between whigs and tories. First, the processes by which whig and tory identities developed did not take place solely within the realm of politics. Men and women in late

Stuart England took political affairs with an extraordinary passion and seriousness (the Wesleys were typical in this respect) because they were able to make political ideas meaningful in the context of their lives. Much insight into what the experience of political conflict was like can be gained by looking at political ideology in conjunction with some other dimension of experience about which people felt strongly. Gender is a particularly apt choice. The story of the Wesleys' quarrel suggests that it was precisely because notions of political legitimacy and obligation could be translated by men and women into guidelines for behaviour in marriage (albeit not in any straightforward or predictable way) that these political notions commanded credence and loyalty.[9]

Attention to the role of gender in political argument can also force historians to think more clearly about the relationship between rhetorical strategy and fundamental principle, and about the nature of ideological division and consensus. If late Stuart society discouraged the clear articulation of ideological differences with respect to the political order, it was even more averse to the expression of conflicting views of the gender order. Contemporaries were in favour of the 'well-ordered family'. The challenge that faces the historian of gender is to discover what, within this broad consensus, the 'well-ordered family' meant to different people. The techniques appropriate to this task may prove useful to historians looking for other kinds of divisions as well.

Whig and tory discourses on the family provide an instructive case study in the significance of ideological difference. Although the two groups did not have obviously distinct views of what constituted a well-ordered family, they did have different rhetorical tendencies and mental habits. Tories liked to talk about order and authority, while whigs concerned themselves with property, population growth and economic productivity. For tories, therefore, the family was a site where order was established and maintained. For whigs, it was a place where children were produced and cared for, and through which property was transferred. There was not necessarily a conflict between these two ways of thinking. Given half a chance, everyone was in favour of all of the above. But the difference in emphasis could result – under certain circumstances – in opposing opinions on a particular aspect of gender and family relations. Under other circumstances, however, the differences were obscured. Therefore, a study of how, when and why differences between whigs and tories about aspects of the sex–gender system emerged and subsided can shed light on the larger questions about the nature, significance, and expression of party differences during this period.

WOMEN, LIBERALISM AND POLITICAL MODERNITY

The peculiarities of late Stuart modes of conceptualizing gender and party politics, as discussed above, should not blind us to the relevance of this study to broader questions about women, liberalism and political modernity. They do, however, require an approach to these questions somewhat different from that taken by other scholars who have considered the relationship of gender and politics in both England and Europe over the course of the long eighteenth century.

The convergence of several intellectual and political agendas allowed the relationship between gender and politics to become the subject of historical enquiry in a number of fields during the 1980s and 1990s. Historians of women (or gender), no longer satisfied with merely adding women to the historical record, began to ask how their scholarship could change the writing of 'mainstream history', as it was taught in textbooks and introductory courses.[10] Political historians, hoping to overcome the perceived narrowness and elitism of their sub-field, broadened their concerns to include 'political culture' and 'politics out of doors'. For feminist historians of the long eighteenth century, present political concerns made the overlap between gender and politics an especially enticing subject. Modern liberal democracy had failed to give women full equality in the family or even in the state; perhaps the cause of that failure lay in its founding moments. Accordingly, many feminist scholars examined the American, French, and Glorious revolutions, as well as Locke, the enlightenment, and occasionally 'classical republicanism' to see how they affected status of women, the laws respecting women and the family, or women's ability to engage in political activity.[11] To connect the histories of gender and of politics (at any level) was in itself a political act for many of these scholars; it posed an audacious challenge to the very divisions between public and private, the personal and political, which many feminists have considered to be one of the mechanisms whereby a liberal-democratic but nonetheless patriarchal polity has justified the exclusion of women.

Late Stuart England has been, oddly, both central and peripheral to this new field of enquiry. As will be seen, John Locke has been a crucial figure even for historians of the French Revolution; Carole Pateman's feminist critique of Lockeian contract theory in *The sexual contract* (1988) is one of the most frequently cited texts among scholars interested in the relationship between gender and politics at all stages of the long eighteenth century – as the period 1688 to 1815 (or even 1832) is often called. It should not surprise us to find scholars ready to assume that what happened in England around 1688 was roughly comparable to what happened on the continent around 1789, since within many historiographical paradigms England in the seventeenth century is widely understood to represent the 'first road to modernity'. Indeed, 'political modernity' is a useful term for denoting what is common both to late Stuart English and late eighteenth-century continental contexts: the presence of a language of political rights, theories of political legitimacy seen as ascending from the people rather than descending from higher authority, a 'public sphere' (or an ideal of one) in which issues central to the national interest are subjected to critical, reasoned debate, and an insistence (at the institutional and rhetorical level) on the necessity of distinctions between the public and the private and the dangers of confusing the two.

Yet, the volume of work on gender and politics in late Stuart England is quite small, compared to the volume of work on the same subject for eighteenth-century France. This study fills a gap, asking questions analogous to those asked by historians in other fields concerned, broadly, with the implications of political modernity for women. What was the impact of the Revolution of 1688 upon ideas about gender and the family? What relative support for – or subversion of – the existing sex–gender system was offered, respectively, by whig and tory political ideologies? How were attitudes towards the place of women in political life shaped by political ideologies and political events?

The paucity of systematic scholarship on the relationship of gender and political ideology in late Stuart England makes it hard to offer an overview of historiographical controversy on the subject. Nonetheless, it is possible to tease out from existing literature some diametrically opposing stories about the significance of the Revolution of 1688 (or more broadly, political modernity) for women. The first, most powerfully presented by Lawrence Stone's *Family, sex and marriage* (1977) was a synthesis of whig political history, modernization theory, and family history. Stone argued that over the course of the long eighteenth century, an unquestioning acceptance of patriarchal authority – no matter how brutal – was replaced by 'affective individualism', a new vision of the family where the individuality, choices and emotional needs of all members were respected. Although the Revolution of 1688 did not cause this transformation, Stone thought that the demise of patriarchalist political theory and the rise of the Lockeian idea of the social contract certainly assisted this change – or perhaps reflected it.[12] Family relationships were taken to alter in tandem with political and social relations in the direction of greater equality and individual liberty.

Stone's account came under fire from several directions. Historians of the family questioned his neatly contrasting 'before' and 'after' pictures: they argued that conjugal relationships in the earlier period were not so frigid as Stone had made them out to be, that parents in the earlier period loved their children more than Stone allowed, and that the differences between the eighteenth and seventeenth centuries that Stone emphasized had more to do with the rise of sentimental rhetoric than with the genuine transformation of feelings and expectations.[13]

Meanwhile, the combination of whig political history and sociological modernization theory upon which Stone had implicitly relied was undermined by revisionist historians of England, who in various ways questioned the status of the Revolution of 1688 as a sign of the emergence of modern, liberal attitudes toward government. J. P. Kenyon, in his influential *Revolution principles* (1977), argued that Lockeian contract theory played only a tiny role in defences of the Glorious Revolution, the supporters of which were anxious not to be seen as habitual revolutionaries.[14] Other revisionist-identified political historians have emphasized the importance of religious issues and anti-Catholicism (both of which can be construed as traditional, non-modern, backward-looking concerns) in both the ideology of exclusionist whigs and in the Revolution of 1688.[15]

Revisionists have had less to say about whether the family, gender relations, or the social structure were changing; they have been largely uninterested in social history. But J. C. D. Clark, the most extreme exponent to date of the revisionist view, has challenged Stone's narrative of social and familial change, arguing that the English remained committed to patriarchalist and divine-right political doctrines, a hierarchical social order based on paternalism and deference, and patriarchy in the family, until 1832.[16]

Stone's interpretation of the period has been challenged from a completely different angle by feminist historians and theorists, who have produced what I will call for convenience the 'anti-liberal feminist narrative'. Where Stone saw liberalism and political modernity as somehow beneficial for women, anti-liberal feminists see them as not better and perhaps worse.

Carole Pateman's *The sexual contract* provides a starting point for the anti-liberal feminist case. Pateman argues that the transition from Filmerian patriarchalism to Lockeian liberalism was simply a putting of old wine into new bottles. Both patriarchalism and liberalism protected men's right to women as sexual property, but did so by different means. Patriarchalism put the relationship between fathers and sons at the centre of its story: men have power over their sons because they beget them. This scenario, Pateman argues, ignores or suppresses the fact that men must have power over women before they can have power over children: a man can only say that his children are his own because he has a sexual monopoly on his wife. Liberalism also rendered men's possession of women invisible, because Locke conceptually separated the family and the state. The subordination of women within the family was thereby preserved, but now defined as natural rather than political. In this sense, liberalism has been worse for women than patriarchalism because it makes it impossible to talk about 'private life' or family relationships in political terms; power, when invisible, is easier to abuse.[17]

Pateman's analysis built upon – and has resonated in – many realms of feminist scholarly enquiry. Her emphasis on the deleterious effects of the private–public division in Locke echoes an older historiographical narrative about the impact of capitalism (which was, in this narrative, closely tied to liberalism): as the home and workplace were separated, middle-class women were physically relegated to the home, and their activities explicitly defined as domestic, non-economic, and private.[18] The work of Jurgen Habermas has provided a vehicle whereby the narrative of social historians about women's exclusion from the economic sphere has been transformed into a narrative about women's exclusion from the 'public sphere' of political debate and action.[19] Amongst literary critics, a plethora of studies of tory women writers (including Margaret Cavendish, Jane Barker, Anne Finch, Aphra Behn, Mary Astell, and Delarivière Manley) has given weight to Pateman's suspicion that liberalism had little to offer women.[20]

This is not to say that the anti-liberal feminist narrative is monolithic. There are important differences, for example, between those who identify the liberal logic of contracts and individualism as being inherently in some way detrimental to women, and those who criticize liberals for having historically failed to extend the logic of contract far enough into the domestic arena.[21] Some scholars distinguish the enlightenment, which they see as having liberating potential, from forms of political liberalism that exclude women;[22] others place the blame for the exclusion of women not so much on liberalism but on the allegedly more misogynist tradition of 'classical republicanism'.[23]

There is not one version of the anti-liberal feminist narrative, then: there are many. However, despite the diversity of chronological frames, analytical categories, and modes of explanation used by anti-liberal feminist historians of the long eighteenth century, the work of each has tended to lend authority to the work of all, creating the impression that they form a coherent whole. The sense of unity is conveyed by Sarah Maza, who seamlessly joins Pateman's critique of seventeenth-century contract theory to an account of the expulsion of women from the public sphere in later eighteenth-century France:

> Whatever the social origins of this reaction against the presence of women in the public sphere, its ideological roots must no doubt be connected to the rise and dissemination of contractual theories of government. Eighteenth-century lawyers, well-versed in the classic texts of seventeenth-century natural law, assumed that government and society originated in the free covenanting of rational beings; women, assumed to be by nature neither free nor rational, were not a party to this contract. Hence, as Carole Pateman has pointed out, the classic paradigm of the social contract nearly always implied a secondary contract that subjected women to their husbands: 'What it means to be an "individual", a maker of contracts and civilly free, is revealed by the subjection of women within the private sphere'.[24]

This present book takes issue with some of the assumptions and conclusions present in the passage quoted above, and in the anti-liberal feminist narrative more generally. The relationships among contract theory, the bifurcation of the public and the private, and the exclusion of women from political life are not, I will argue, as direct as Maza suggests. First, the political ideologies and arguments of the late seventeenth century did not carry an inevitable, inherent politics of gender. Part I of this book will demonstrate the diversity of views that existed within each political or ideological camp, whether whig or tory, contractarian or 'patriarchalist'. Notions about gender, women and the family became attached to a party ideology or political argument in different ways by different people, depending in part on the choices of political actors, in part on political circumstances. As I will try to show in Part II, a variety of contingent events – the birth of the Prince of Wales in 1688, the joint settlement of the crown upon a married couple, the Norfolk divorce – shaped and redirected the ways in which such connections were made. The drawing of the boundary between public and private was a similarly contingent and variable phenomenon. Part III, which explores the legitimation and delegitimation of women as political actors, challenges the assumption (ubiquitous in many anti-liberal feminist accounts) that the public and private were unambiguously separated, in either a conceptual or spatial sense, at a precise moment in the eighteenth century. It will be argued here, by contrast, that the public–private divide was itself the object of struggle, a rhetorical construct which was deployed in kaleidoscopically shifting ways to a variety of ends; in this process, moreover, women were participants as well as objects.[25]

The goal here, however, is not simply to refute the anti-liberal feminist narrative, much less to replace it with the whig or revisionist one. Because this book is specifically about seventeenth-century England and not, say, eighteenth-century France, it will not directly challenge the conclusions of historians working in other fields; there is no reason to expect that our findings will all be the same. Indeed, one might explain the fact that this study will *not* locate distinct and coherent whig and tory ideologies of gender, and will *not* show women to have been unable to legitimate their participation in political life, simply by noting that late Stuart England represents only a partial and incomplete case of 'political modernity'. But at the very least, this book raises questions that will force scholars in other fields to be more precise about the specificity or generalizability of their own accounts.

SOURCES

Late Stuart persons confidently assumed the existence of a relationship between families and states, fathers and kings. On what grounds can we, as twentieth-century scholars, make the same assumption? What do we think that the relationship is, and how would we demonstrate it? These questions have produced no scholarly consensus, as a brief survey of a few recent works will readily show.

For Sarah Hanley, the existence of the family–state analogy in early modern France points to a deeper, structural connection between political and familial organization, a 'family–state compact' whereby the absolutist state literally depended upon and promoted patriarchal authority within the family.[26] For Susan Amussen, by contrast, the analogy drawn in seventeenth-century England between the family and state was ideological and artificial rather than structural and organic: it allowed defenders of social and political hierarchies to link those hierarchies to a far more uncontested patriarchal order.[27] Carole Pateman offers yet another perspective: for her, the family *is* what is at stake in political theory, since both patriarchalism and contract theory are seen as different methods of justifying men's control over the bodies of women.[28] Lynn Hunt, agreeing with Pateman that political ideas can be about sex, but seeking to break free of Pateman's conviction that the triumph of patriarchy was inevitable, emphasizes the fact that the struggle for sexual control during the French Revolution was not hidden (as it is in Pateman's account), but magnified: participants in the Revolution tried to imagine a new political and social order through anxiety-producing images of radical disruption in the family, images which took on a life of their own. What the structure or logic of that life was, however, and what it had to do with 'real' families and gender relations or with political conflicts, is left an open question in Hunt's account.[29]

Faced with this diversity of approaches, I have tried rigorously to limit my claims to those appropriate to the available sources. This book is a study of political argument, broadly defined to include 'high' political theory, polemical tracts, satires, scandal novels, lampoons, and private correspondence. Had it been possible systematically to gain access to further cases like that of the Wesleys, cases which provide evidence about the role that political argument played in actual marriages, more of them would appear here. Given the difficulty of finding such sources, it has been necessary to focus instead on how people who constructed political argument in this period deployed notions of gender, the family and marriage in those arguments. The cases have been selected by following the logic of political circumstances, looking for debates, events and crises in which people making political arguments might be likely to discuss the questions of gender.

The advantage of using political argument as a source is that it gives us, in the most direct form, access to the ways in which concerns about gender became intertwined with concerns about politics. We do not need to postulate an *a priori* connection between them; it is enough that they are present in the same text. We may not know how the sex–gender system was connected in a structural way to the political system, or how 'gender ideology' as a whole is connected to 'political ideology' as a whole. But we can safely say that X idea about gender and Y political argument are connected by a particular writer in a particular text, for a reason that we may be able to deduce if we understand the context of the polemic and know what the writer was trying to achieve. Thus, the fact that a writer chose to connect them will always be a starting point of any analysis. Such a method confines us to dealing with the surfaces of texts, and with the relationship of texts to other texts. This approach is legitimate, as long as we are honest about its limitations and consequences.

These proceed from the simple fact that political argument is argument.[30] It is words and images put together to persuade an audience of something. Political argument is obviously not a transparent reflection of social reality. It may not even reflect ideological, mental or cultural reality. Insofar as implicit or explicit assertions about women, marriage, divorce, inheritance, the family and so on can be culled from a political argument, they do not necessarily indicate a passionate commitment to those views on the part of the author (although they are probably not total distortions either). They are in the text because the author thinks they will help make the argument. Much of what Locke says about the family in the *Treatises* can be explained by the exigencies of replying to Filmer, for example.

Moreover, political argument may be the place where authors are *least* likely to say something startling or unconventional about marriage, women, and the family, even if they really think it. A study of political argument will readily uncover the points of consensus in late Stuart society. Neither whigs nor tories in the 1690s, in their eagerness to proclaim themselves the party of sexual order, had anything good to say about fornication or adultery. Neither side was enthusiastic about the rights of wives or the possibility of equality in marriage, and both assumed that property should be in the hands of men. The range of ideas expressed about gender within the context of political (or politicized) debates may have been narrower than in other media. If one is trying to persuade an audience of the rightness of one's cause, why risk controversy? Thus, for example, it is possible to find texts from our period that deal with polygamy or polyandry in a sympathetic way; but with the exception of Dryden's *Absalom and Achitophel*, there are few political polemics which do so. Most of the unconventional thinking about gender for this period remained in manuscript.

If we saw only consensus, this study would be a bit dull. But within this predictable consensus, there were nuances and differences in emphasis. Some people defined familial order in terms of the authority of husbands, others in terms of the authority of fathers. Some people thought that the passage of property from a man to the heirs of his own loins could be guaranteed by allowing men to divorce adulterous wives; others thought it could be facilitated by allowing illegitimate children to inherit; and still others saw the epistemological uncertainty at the heart of paternity as inevitable. Some people defended the sexual double standard whereby female adultery was more harshly condemned than male adultery; some did not. Some talked about queens as if they were subject to all of the vulnerabilities and character flaws of the female sex, whereas others regarded them as fundamentally different from other women. The range of what one could think about the nature of gender, marriage and the family was thus wider than it at first appears to be.

The fact that so many political debates in this period became entangled with debates about gender may have made the existence of a range of possibilities more obvious to contemporaries. It is therefore important to ask whether people in late Stuart England may have in fact used political debate as an arena in which to argue about gender. What women did with political ideology is of particular interest because it sheds light on how they understood and manipulated political ideas and arguments in ways that helped them to negotiate their place in the world as gendered individuals. Thus, some portion of this book is devoted to cases where the maker of a political argument was herself a woman. This is not to say that men did not count as 'gendered individuals', that they were always happy with their lot as men, or that their opinions about the gender order were transparent or uninteresting. But the case can be made that in the very act of engaging in political argument, and legitimating their right to speak on matters of political importance, women were implicitly saying something about their place in society as women. On occasion, they had things to say explicitly on this subject as well.

Thus, this study will ask some of the traditional 'women's history' questions about women's agency, their capacity for self-assertion within a patriarchal social order, the possibilities available to them for calling that order into question. These questions are not only inherently important, but are highly relevant to the political historians' question of what caused people to have a stake (material, emotional, psychological) in the political arguments they embraced.

What women had to say, and how they deployed political ideas and arguments to say it, is often surprising. Nothing in this study will give us room to say that some political ideologies are 'better' for women than others. The story of Susanna and Samuel Wesley, with which we began, calls the categories of pro- or anti-feminist, of progressive and regressive, into question. To whom would we assign which label? Susanna Wesley appears to have combined the impulse toward obedience and suffering with a demand for 'liberty of conscience' and reciprocal obligation in marriage. Samuel held the 'progressive' position that marriage was dissoluble while at the same time upholding the 'patriarchalist' or 'traditional' equation of royal, divine and husbandly authority. Each was in a way subversive of the existing sex–gender system; each in a way was not. We will not come out of this with a heroine. We will learn that straightforward subversiveness is hard to find, and that partial, problematic subversiveness came from unexpected places.

This book is organized as a set of linked case studies rather than as a linear narrative, for reasons that should be clear from the preceding discussion. First, this is because gender was not a category that seventeenth-century persons would recognize: they did not generate sources or organize archives systematically to cover 'gender' as a topic. It seems wise to let the form of the book reflect the way in which our knowledge of 'gender' in late Stuart England actually comes to us, that is, in parts. This will invite – rather than prematurely foreclose – further discussion of how the parts are related.

Moreover, the case-study approach allows us to examine closely the contexts in which arguments were made. Whigs and tories took ideas about aspects of gender on board as part of their argument in concrete, specific situations. In order to describe the gender ideology of whigs and tories, or Williamites and Jacobites, we must look at what happened when purely theoretical statements (say, about the origins of sovereign power) intersected with more specific agendas in particular circumstances, in ways that might force a party to embrace specific ideas about gender (or aspects thereof) for strategic reasons. To make matters more complicated, we should remain aware of the possibility that people engaged in political argument might have their own ideas about aspects of gender, and might trim their political argument accordingly.

Although each chapter in this book deals with a very different topic, they all address similar questions about the dynamics of political argument, the processes by which it becomes connected to arguments about gender, and the relationship between the ideas about gender that are invoked in the context of political argument and ideas about gender invoked in discussions of something else. Why did people who were engaged in political arguments bother to talk about what we would call gender in the first place? Was there something about late Stuart political culture that particularly encouraged people to invoke notions of gender in the course of political argument? When notions of gender were invoked in political arguments, did this produce a debate *about* gender? Or were only the least controversial notions invoked? Did uncontroversial notions become controversial *when* – and because – they were invoked in the context of political argument? These questions should be of equal interest to historians of gender and to historians of politics; they provide a ground upon which dialogue between the two fields becomes possible and fruitful.

NOTES

1 Robert Walmsley, 'John Wesley's parents: quarrel and reconciliation', *Proceedings of the Wesley Historical Society* 29 (Sept 1953), p. 52. See also E. Gordon Rupp, *Religion in England, 1688–1791* (Oxford, Clarendon Press, 1986), pp. 25–6.

2 Walmsley, 'John Wesley's parents', p. 52.

3 *Ibid.*, p. 55. On the non-jurors and oaths, see Mark Goldie, 'Tory political thought 1689–1714' (Ph.D. dissertation, Cambridge University, 1977), ch. 6.

4 Walmsley, 'John Wesley's parents', p. 54.

5 *Ibid.*

6 *Ibid.*

7 Hence, this book does not attempt to outline a system of gender ideology. Significant attempts to do so include Lawrence Stone, *The family, sex and marriage in England 1500–1800* (New York, Harper & Row, 1977); Anthony Fletcher, *Gender, sex and subordination in England 1500–1800* (New Haven, Yale University Press, 1995); Margaret Sommerville, *Sex and subjection: attitudes to women in early-modern society* (Arnold, 1995). It is worth noting that the first two of these explicitly characterize the period 1680–1714 as a moment of flux and transition; the last-named does so implicitly by ending in 1700. See also Robert Shoemaker, *Gender in English society, 1650–1850: the emergence of separate spheres?* (Longman, 1998) for a synthesis of recent work.

8 A recent summary of the state of debate is Tim Harris, *Politics under the later Stuarts* (New York, Longman, 1993). On the validity of party distinctions in the exclusion crisis, see Jonathan Scott, *Algernon Sidney and the Restoration crisis, 1677–1683* (Cambridge, Cambridge University Press, 1991); for a response, see Tim Harris, 'Party turns? or, whigs and tories get off Scott free', in *Albion* 25 (1993), and Gary S. De Krey, 'The first Restoration crisis' and Richard L. Greaves, 'The Restoration in turmoil', in the same issue. See also Mark Knights, *Politics and opinion in crisis, 1678–81* (Cambridge, Cambridge University Press, 1994). For court–country vs. whig–tory conceptualizations of political conflict in William's reign, see David Hayton, 'The "country" interest and the party system, 1689–c.1720', in Clyve Jones (ed.), *Party and management in parliament, 1660–1784* (Leicester, Leicester University Press, 1984); Dennis Rubini, *Court and country, 1688–1702* (Rupert Hart-Davis, 1967); Henry Horwitz, *Parliament, policy and politics in the reign of William III* (Manchester, Manchester University Press, 1977). An excellent overview of historiography on party conflict in Anne's reign is Geoffrey Holmes, *British politics in the age of Anne*, rev edn (Hambledon Press, 1987), both old and new introductions. On the persistence of party conflict after Anne's reign, compare J. H. Plumb, *The growth of political stability in England, 1675–1725* (Macmillan Press, 1967); Linda Colley, *In defiance of oligarchy: the tory party, 1714–1760* (Cambridge, Cambridge University Press, 1982).

9 Some models for an enquiry into politics through the lens of gender include Lynn Hunt, *The family romance of the French Revolution* (Berkeley, University of California Press, 1992); Ann Hughes, 'Gender and politics in Leveller literature', in Susan Amussen and Mark Kishlansky (eds), *Political culture and cultural politics in early modern England* (Manchester, Manchester University Press, 1995); Cynthia Herrup, 'The patriarch at home: the trial of the second Earl of Castlehaven for rape and sodomy', *History Workshop Journal* 41 (1996).

10   The ambition of feminists to change mainstream history was expressed most eloquently and influentially by Joan Scott, 'Is gender a useful category of historical analysis?' in her book *Gender and the politics of history* (New York, Columbia University Press, 1988).

11   Works examining the overlap beteeen gender and politics include Mary Beth Norton, *Liberty's daughters: the revolutionary experience of American women, 1750–1800* (Boston, Little, Brown & Co., 1980); Linda Kerber, *Women of the republic: intellect and ideology in revolutionary America* (Chapel Hill, University of North Carolina Press, 1980); Ruth Bloch, 'The gendered meanings of virtue in revolutionary America', *Signs* 13 (1987); Hunt, *Family romance*; Joan Landes, *Women in the public sphere in the age of the French revolution* (Ithaca, New York, Cornell University Press, 1988); Dorinda Outram, *The body in the French revolution: sex, class and political culture* (New Haven, Connecticut, Yale University Press, 1989); Dorinda Outram, '*Le langage male de la vertu*: women and the discourse of the French revolution' in Peter Burke and Roy Porter (eds), *The social history of language* (Cambridge, Cambridge University Press, 1987); Dena Goodman, *The republic of letters: a cultural history of the French enlightenment* (Ithaca, New York, Cornell University Press, 1994); Suzanne Desan, '"War between brothers and sisters": inheritance law and gender politics in revolutionary France', *French Historical Studies* 20:4 (1997); Isabel V. Hull, *Sexuality, state and civil society in Germany, 1700–1815* (Ithaca, New York, Cornell University Press, 1996); Carole Pateman, *The sexual contract: aspects of patriarchal liberalism* (Stanford, Connecticut, Stanford University Press, 1988); Lois Schwoerer, 'Women and the Glorious Revolution', *Albion* 18 (1986); Mary Shanley, 'Marriage contract and social contract in seventeenth-century English political thought', *Western Political Quarterly* 32 (1979); Hughes, 'Gender and politics in Leveller literature'; Hannah Pitkin, *Fortune is a woman: gender and politics in the thought of Niccolò Machiavelli* (Berkeley, University of California Press, 1984). See also works cited in notes 18–20 below.

12   Stone, *Family, sex and marriage*, especially pp. 239–44, 265–6.

13   Important critiques include Lois G. Schwoerer, 'Seventeenth-century Englishwomen: engraved in Stone?', *Albion* 16 (1984); E. P. Thompson, 'Happy families', *Radical History Review* 20 (1979); Eileen Spring, 'The family, strict settlement, and the historians', in G. R. Rubin and David Sugarman (eds), *Law, economy and society, 1750–1914* (Professional Books, 1984).

14   John P. Kenyon, *Revolution principles: the politics of party, 1689–1720* (Cambridge, Cambridge University Press, 1977). Kenyon may have overstated the case: cf. Mark Goldie, 'The Revolution of 1689 and the structure of political argument', *Bulletin of Research in the Humanities* 83 (1980).

15   See, for example, Jonathan Scott, 'England's troubles: exhuming the popish plot', in Tim Harris *et al.* (eds), *The politics of religion in Restoration England* (Oxford, Basil Blackwell, 1990), and his *Algernon Sidney and the Restoration crisis*, ch. 12. See also Tony Claydon, *William III and the godly revolution* (Cambridge, Cambridge University Press, 1996). Another kind of revisionist reading is Robert Beddard, 'The unexpected whig revolution of 1688', in Robert Beddard (ed.), *The revolutions of 1688* (Oxford, Clarendon Press, 1991).

16   J. C. D. Clark, *English society, 1688–1832* (Cambridge, Cambridge University Press, 1985), esp. pp. 83–6.

17   Pateman, *The sexual contract*, esp. pp. 82–94.

18 The earliest articulation in modern times of this view, that in the period 1680–1714 a woman's place was seen as only in the home, is Alice Clark, *The working life of women in the seventeenth century* [1919], ed. M. Chaytor and J. Lewis (Routledge, 1982); a recent expression of the same view is Bridget Hill, *Women, work and sexual politics in the eighteenth century* (Oxford, Basil Blackwell, 1990). Amanda Vickery, 'From golden age to separate spheres?: a review of the categories and chronology of English women's history', *Historical Journal* 36 (1993) both summarizes and savages the 'separation of spheres' thesis, in part on grounds that historians find it occurring in too many different periods. See also Margaret R. Hunt, *The middling sort: commerce, gender and the family in England 1680–1780* (Berkeley, University of California Press, 1996).

19 Landes, *Women in the public sphere*; Outram, '*Le langage male*'; Goodman, *Republic of letters*.

20 Important discussions of the usefulness of tory ideology to women writers include the essays in Janet Todd (ed.), *Aphra Benn studies* (Cambridge, Cambridge University Press, 1996); Carol Barash, *English women's poetry, 1649–1714: politics, community and linguistic authority* (Oxford, Clarendon Press, 1996); Catherine Gallagher, 'Embracing the absolute', *Genders* 1 (1988); Ruth Perry, 'Mary Astell and the feminist critique of possessive individualism', *Eighteenth Century Studies* 23 (1990); Joan Kinnaird, 'Mary Astell and the conservative contribution to English feminism', *Journal of British Studies* 19 (1975); Hilda Smith, *Reason's disciples* (Urbana, University of Illinois Press, 1982); Paul Monod, 'The politics of matrimony: Jacobitism and marriage in eighteenth-century England', in Eveline Cruikshanks & Jeremy Black (eds), *The Jacobite challenge* (Edinburgh, John Donald, 1988).

21 Examples of those who see liberalism as harmful to women are Perry, 'Mary Astell', and Gallagher, 'Embracing the absolute'. The other view, that contractual ideas did not sufficiently penetrate liberal thinking on domestic life, is expressed in Susan Staves, *Married women's separate property in England, 1660–1833* (Cambridge, Mass., Harvard University Press, 1990) and Elizabeth Fox-Genovese, 'Property and patriarchy in classic bourgeois political theory', *Radical History Review* 4:2 (1977).

22 Examples of contributions which see the enlightenment as potentially emancipatory for women, include Hull, *Sexuality, state and civil society in Germany, 1700–1815*, and Carole Pateman, 'Women's writing, women's standing: theory and politics in the early modern period' in Hilda Smith (ed.), *Women writers and the early modern British political tradition* (Cambridge, Cambridge University Press, 1998).

23 That liberalism and republicanism were distinct ideologies was influentially argued by J. G. A. Pocock, in *The Machiavellian moment: Florentine political thought and the Atlantic republican tradition* (Princeton, New Jersey, Princeton University Press, 1975) and his *Virtue, commerce and history* (Cambridge, Cambridge University Press, 1985), chs 2, 3. More recently, the usefulness of the distinction has been challenged by Alan C. Houston, *Algernon Sidney and the English republican heritage in England and America* (Princeton, New Jersey, Princeton University Press, 1991). Republicanism is emphasized, for example, in Pitkin, *Fortune is a woman*, in Bloch, 'The gendered meanings of virtue', and (implicitly) in much of the work on the French Revolution, especially Landes, *Women in the public sphere* and Outram, '*Le langage male*'.

24 Sarah Maza, 'The diamond necklace affair revisited', in Lynn Hunt (ed.), *Eroticism and the body politic* (Baltimore, Johns Hopkins University Press, 1991), p. 84. The quotation is from Pateman, *The sexual contract*, p. 11. See also Sarah Maza, *Private lives and public*

affairs: the causes célèbres of prerevolutionary France (Berkeley, University of California Press, 1993), pp. 321–2.

25 The instability of the public–private divide is emphasised in John Brewer, 'This, that and the other: public, social, and private in the seventeenth and eighteenth centuries', in Dario Castiglione and Lesley Sharpe (eds), *Shifting the boundaries: transformation of the languages of public and private in the eighteenth century* (Exeter, University of Exeter Press, 1995). See also Lawrence E. Klein, 'Gender and the public/private distinction in the eighteenth century: some questions about evidence and analytic procedure', *Eighteenth Century Studies* 29 (1995); Dena Goodman, 'Public sphere and private life: towards a synthesis of current historiographical approaches to the old regime', *History and Theory* 31 (1992).

26 Sarah Hanley, 'Engendering the state: family formation and state building in early modern France', *French Historical Studies* 16 (1989). See also her 'The monarchic state in early modern France: marital regime government and male right', in Adrianna Bakos (ed.), *Politics, ideology and the law in early modern Europe* (Rochester, New York, University of Rochester Press, 1994).

27 Susan Amussen, *An ordered society: class and gender in early modern England* (Oxford, Basil Blackwell, 1988).

28 Pateman, *The sexual contract.*

29 Hunt, *Family romance.*

30 Note on terminology: by 'political argument' I mean arguments that assist political actors to achieve political ends, conventionally understood. I do not use 'political' as a synonym for 'of or pertaining to power', but rather as meaning 'of or pertaining to power exercised through the mechanisms and institutions of the state'. Political struggle is the struggle between people and groups to control those mechanisms. Political argument is the means by which they enhance their chances of doing so by persuasion, and/or legitimate the fact that they have done so. It is itself part of political struggle.

   When I say 'gender politics' I mean of or pertaining to power relations organized around gender.

Part I

The family in political writing
during the exclusion crisis

Chapter 1

Patriarchalism, politics
and the family

Between 1679 and 1681, the whigs tried several times in Parliament to pass a bill excluding Charles II's Catholic brother (James, Duke of York) from the throne of England. Their efforts reflected the widespread belief that James, if allowed the crown, would destroy English liberties, sell out the country to Louis XIV, and violently persecute the protestant religion. The temptation to alter the succession was particularly strong because the eldest of Charles II's many illegitimate children, the staunchly protestant Duke of Monmouth, provided an attractive alternative to his uncle.[1]

Whether the legitimate heir could be deprived of his hereditary right to the throne was only one of the many interlocking layers of controversy that erupted in the exclusion crisis. Anxieties about the prospect of 'popery and arbitrary government' under the future King James might not have led to attempts at exclusion had they not been aggravated by mounting suspicions about the pro-French, Catholic and absolutist leanings of the present King Charles. These were further aggravated when the king sought to prevent the passage of an exclusion bill by dissolving Parliament. He undermined the independence of the judiciary, attacked town corporations through a *quo warranto* campaign, and caused divine-right ideology to be systematically proclaimed from the pulpits and in the press. After 1681, he embarked on the same project of rule without Parliament as had his father, Charles I. The threat of absolutism was matched, however, by that of overweening parliaments and rebellious rabbles. As the whigs resorted to public demonstrations and petitioning campaigns, tory supporters of the government stirred up memories of the terrible things that had happened in the 1640s and 1650s, when Parliament had similarly presumed to dictate to a monarch. The exclusion crisis was thus as much about the origins and limits of sovereign power as it was about who would inherit the throne. For this reason, it forms a watershed in the history of English political thought, providing the context for

John Locke's *Treatises of government* and Algernon Sidney's *Discourses concerning government*.

The exclusion crisis also provoked a public discussion about the purpose of the family and the nature of power within it. The controversy over succession to the crown plugged into, and drew energy from, a wider set of debates about primogeniture, entailment, and the laws regulating marriage and legitimacy. Anti-exclusionist writers argued that the rules of succession which entitled the Duke of York to inherit from his brother were inviolable, in accordance with divine, natural and fundamental English law.[2] On the other side, pamphleteers found ways to deny the crown to the Duke of York by criticizing or reinterpreting the laws concerning marriage, divorce and inheritance. One author, for example, argued that Charles II ought to be able to divorce his barren consort, Catherine of Braganza, in order to obtain a legitimate heir.[3] Others wishfully imagined that Monmouth was already legitimate, spreading the story that as a youth Charles had secretly married Monmouth's mother, Lucy Walter.[4] William Lawrence (about whom we will hear more later) took a different approach, arguing that it did not matter whether Charles had married Lucy Walter, because illegitimate children always had a right to inherit from their fathers. The debate on succession connected the personal to the political; or so the tory Edmund Bohun assumed when he remarked dismissively of his whig opponent, James Tyrrell, 'Surely this gentleman is a younger brother he has such an aversion for primogeniture'.[5]

The family also became caught up in political debates because it had been, since the time of Aristotle, a terrain upon which questions of political power could be discussed. During the English civil war, royalists and parliamentarians made reference to divorce and domestic violence when arguing about whether subjects could depose or resist a monarch, and accused one another of undermining familial order.[6] This mode of argument persisted in the Restoration.[7] Among the tracts published by Charles II's government in an effort to defend royal prerogative during the exclusion crisis was *Patriarcha*, a manuscript treatise written before or during the civil war by the royalist Robert Filmer, which dramatically proclaimed the intimate relationship between political and familial authority by identifying the origin of all sovereign power in the paternal power, or 'fatherly right', of Adam.[8] As is well known, Filmer became the favourite target of the more theoretically-orientated whig writers, such as John Locke, Algernon Sidney, James Tyrrell and Thomas Hunt. Their attack on Filmer was, inevitably, an attack on what they took to be Filmer's view of the family, and in particular of the power of fathers.

Thus, tracts and treatises during the exclusion crisis wound up being saturated with commentary on the family. Did this mean that the ideological conflict between whigs and tories translated into conflicting views of gender and family relationships? To what extent did the whigs' radical political ideas encourage, or draw upon, new ways of thinking about the family?

Before attempting to answer these questions, two *caveats* are in order. First, while it is tempting to assume that ideological conflicts will produce contrasting views of the family, these contrasts may turn out to be less stark than expected. The whig and tory writers considered in this and the next chapter were all male, and arguably shared the same stake in a gendered system of familial power. They did not, with the possible exception of William Lawrence, advocate changing laws or cultural norms that governed familial relationships. As propagandists, they appealed to convention, presenting themselves as the upholders of a universally accepted familial and sexual order rather than as innovators.

Second, we must avoid discussing differences between whigs and tories solely in terms of the contrast between Locke and Filmer. Locke represents only one of a range of possible ways in which whigs talked about the family; moreover, he was separated from Filmer not merely by ideology but by at least forty, and possibly sixty, chronological years.[9]

The remainder of this chapter will address several questions which must be answered if we are to provide an adequate account of the relationship of gender to political ideology in the exclusion crisis. First, what was considered 'conventional thinking' about the family in the late seventeenth century? And therefore, when were writers on either side playing to the crowd, and where were they breaking with accepted norms? Second, what did Filmer's notorious works actually say about the family? And what was the relationship between what Filmer said and what whigs attacked? Third, what was the relationship between Filmer's opinions on politics and the family, and those of tories actually writing during the exclusion crisis? Another important question – what Locke's relationship was to other whigs writing in the exclusion crisis – will be addressed in the next chapter.

LATE SEVENTEENTH-CENTURY DISCOURSES ON THE FAMILY

> I say all practical principles or opinions by which men think themselves obliged to regulate their actions with one another, as that men may breed their children, or dispose of their estates as they please, ... that polygamy and divorce are lawful or unlawful: these opinions and the actions following from them [are] things indifferent.   John Locke, 'An essay concerning toleration'(1667)[10]

When John Locke wanted to provide examples of beliefs and behaviours that would fall into the category of 'things indifferent' (that is, things about which God had given no positive command but which for the sake of social peace were subject to regulation by the magistrate) he hit upon the subjects that concern us in this chapter: inheritance, childrearing, polygamy and divorce!

Locke recognized that practices regarding such matters could vary across cultures; and while he accepted the need to make laws about them, he did not see such laws as based on foundations firmer than those of 'convenience'. As this suggests, there was by no means absolute consensus as to what was morally right and wrong with respect to Locke's list of subjects.

Locke's very choice of subjects, however, helps to delineate a cluster of issues which came to loom large in discussions of the family during the late seventeenth century. Any such discussion primarily revolved around two problems: first, how to organize the transfer of property in families over time, and second, how to ensure an expanding and productive population. These were perceived to be connected to one another, and together they shaped thinking on a host of issues. Late seventeenth-century writers were fascinated by the question of how systems for organizing sexuality, determining paternity, transferring estates and caring for children would affect morality and society. These concerns were not entirely new, although some aspects of what will be discussed below – the development of new conveyancing techniques, and the rise of a commercially-orientated 'political arithmetic' that located the source of wealth in people rather than land – have been associated specifically with this period.[11] But significantly, these concerns were not present in Filmer's works, whereas they had a powerful impact on the *political* writings of the later seventeenth century. They opened up issues concerning the organization of the family, and the nature of power within it, that the writers discussed here found difficult to resolve.

INHERITANCE

It is hard to overestimate the centrality of inheritance to the way that people in the seventeenth century understood relationships between spouses, parents, children, siblings and other kin. Although the arrangements for the transfer of property across generations made in wills and marriage settlements were expressed in notoriously arcane jargon, both men and women of the property-holding classes had a surprisingly strong grasp of the relevant legal terminology. The author of a 1732 handbook on law written specifically for a female audience expected his reader to comprehend a sentence like:

> A man is seised of lands in fee, and hath issue two daughters, and makes a gift in tail to one of them, and then dies seised of the reversion in fee, which descends to both sisters, the donee, or her issue, is impleaded, she shall not pray in aid of the other co-parcener, either to recover *pro rata*, or to deraign the warranty paramount.[12]

It was around issues of property settlement that people in seventeenth-century England engaged with questions of love, obligation, justice, and power in the family. Family estates connected the fates of individuals together;

one person's economic future hinged upon another's death, or luck at marriage or childbearing. Emotional bonds and predicaments were figured in terms of property and bequests. Joan Thirsk has noted that as the practice of primogeniture spread amongst the English gentry in the seventeenth century it was accompanied by an angry literature protesting the harsh treatment of the neglected younger sons.[13] John ap Robert's popular and much reprinted *The younger brother his apologie* conveys the emotional intensity of such literature. The elder brother squandering the family estates that he undeservedly inherited is, says ap Robert, a 'civil monster' who

> consumes the womb of his family (viper-like) wherein he was born: and without all remembrance of his obligement to the dead (whom, as having his being from them, he ought to honour) or respect to the living (to whom he should be a comfort) devours in some sort, them of his own species, society and blood: all which, the cannibals do not.[14]

Brotherhood was only one of the familial relationships rendered fraught and complicated by the evolving strategies of the propertied classes to ensure the perpetuation of estates.

More important for our purposes is the effect of these developments upon images of the father. Sometimes, fathers were demonized in the contemporary literature on primogeniture. James Harrington, who likened the 'flinty custom' of primogeniture to the common treatment of newborn puppies ('take one, lay it in the lap, feed it with every good bit, and drown five!'), blamed the practice on the 'cruel ambition' of the father who foolishly sought immortality by raising 'a golden pillar for his monument, though he have children, his own reviving flesh'.[15] But, as the passage from John ap Robert quoted above suggests, fathers (and ancestors) could be seen as the victims of the custom. Paternal power was potentially diminished by the development of conveyancing techniques (strict settlement and entailment) which secured the integrity of a family estate by allowing the owner to determine how the estate was to be settled in future generations; a father would be unable to discipline his children by threatening disinheritance, since such an act was now out of his power.[16]

Lacking leverage over his heirs and bound by the planning of a distant ancestor, the male head of household was further vulnerable to betrayal by his wife. The sad plight of men whose wives became pregnant while committing adultery was a prominent theme in the literature of the period: these husbands lost not only masculine authority (to be cuckolded was a sign that one could not control one's family) but also the right to pass their estate on to the children of their own loins. As we will see below, reformers who argued in favour of permitting divorce on grounds of adultery almost always pointed out that female adultery had especially serious ramifications because of its implications for the inheritance property, amounting essentially to a form of theft.

Critics of inheritance practices in England may have been encouraged by the knowledge that alternatives existed elsewhere. Travel literature was an important resource for thinking about the family. There was nothing new in this kind of writing. It had been popular since the sixteenth century, and in the years before the exclusion crisis both new works and reprints (as well as compendia that recycled previously published material) continued to pour from the presses.[17] From these, readers could learn that inheritance practices, as well as marital arrangements, varied across cultures. Amongst the natives of Virginia, for example, the kingdom descends 'not to [the king's] sons, but first to his brethren, and after their decease to his sisters, and to the heirs of his eldest sister'.[18] In China, 'the king hath one wife, but many Concubines, whose children inherit if the lawful wife be barren'.[19] Thomas Herbert explained that because in South Asian societies 'it was the custom that the *Bracman* had the first nights company with the bride, supposing the ground of better value by that holy seed', the king, 'to make sure work used to confer his command upon his sister's issue; assured it seems that she was of his blood and they of his [blood] by consequence'.[20]

Readers of travel literature would also learn that the English practice of considering the husband of the mother to be the father of the child was not universal. There were many different ways of attributing paternity, of apportioning responsibility for the care of children, and of deciding who the legitimate heir would be. In Malabar, some women 'have six or seven husbands, fathering their children on which of them she pleaseth best'.[21] In Benin, there was a class of widows, called '*regetairs* or nurses', belonging to the king, who 'considering they need not stand in fear of a husband, choose as many single men as they like, to whom they prostitute themselves at pleasure: and when any of them prove with child, and bear a son, they are free from paying of tribute; but if they have a girl, it becomes the king's due to dispose of'.[22]

Although the tone of these accounts ranged from the proto-ethnographic and sympathetic to the sensationalist and derogatory, they all endowed their readers with the empowering knowledge that cultural practices varied. John ap Robert noted that 'in the matter of succession, or the claims of inheritance' he could find 'no one country observing the form held by another', suggesting that 'nature never set down as a law, that those fortunes should be left to the elder brother or younger, or to any one in particular, or to all'.[23] Algernon Sidney, as we will see later, made much of the variation of inheritance practices across cultures in order to challenge the God-givenness of primogeniture as a system for deciding who should inherit the throne.

THE 'INCREASE OF MANKIND'

The need to increase the number of people preoccupied late seventeenth-century social thinkers. As Joyce Appleby has noted, 'the most significant change of opinion about the poor was the replacement of the concern about overpopulation at the beginning of the seventeenth century with fears about a possible loss of people at the end'. Economic thinkers believed that a larger population would lead to greater national wealth.[24] This assumption also lay behind William Petty's development of the science of 'political arithmetic', a method of analysing economic issues mathematically in terms of the relationship between land and population. Petty's thesis, that 'labour is the father and active principle of wealth, as lands are the mother', was clearly echoed (even in its colourfully gendered language) in Locke's explanation of how private property comes into being. When a man gathers nuts from 'nature's common store', Locke tells us in the *Second treatise*, it is the act of gathering itself that makes them his: 'That labour put a distinction between them and common. That added something more to them than nature, the common mother of all, had done, and so they became his private right'.[25] Land that is left uncultivated, Locke asserts, is mere waste; therefore, 'numbers of men are to be preferred to largeness of dominions'.[26]

The notion that the increase of mankind is the ultimate good could lead thinkers to ask whether the existing organization of sexual relations was the best way to achieve population growth. William Petty's unpublished papers on 'the multiplication of mankind' contain a number of bold speculations. In a paper entitled 'about the increase of mankind', he advocates compassion for women who bear children out of wedlock, recommending 'that no woman be punished for bearing a child, but left to God, her own conscience, and honour'. Petty also suggests taxing the public to finance direct payments to women (*not* to their husbands) both as a reward for bearing children and to defray the expenses of lying in. Moreover, although he does not reject marriage 'in the present way', he suggests that men and women might engage instead in 'short marriages', or 'covenants'. These were to be agreements concerning '1. the time of cohabitation 2. the allowance to the woman 3. the disposal of the children and the power of inheritance, portion, name etc'. They could be 'dissolved in six months, in case of no conception, to be proved by proper signs; otherwise to continue till the delivery of the woman'. Men and women 'may cohabit upon any covenant they please, which the magistrate shall see well performed'. Finally, paternity might be a matter of judicial concern, but women should be shielded from the prying eyes of the public: 'a woman is not bound to declare the father, but to the officer who was privy to the contract'.[27]

Like the critics of primogeniture discussed above, Petty may have been influenced by travel literature.[28] His unpublished essay on 'Californian marriages' describes a complex system of polygamy and polyandry that he believed to be practised among the natives of the American northwest. In California, he tells us, one 'great man' (known as the 'hero', and 'excelling in strength, nimbleness, beauty, wit, courage, and good senses') was given a sexual monopoly on four 'ingenious healthy women' while at the same time 'one great rich woman had five men at her command, and was absolute mistress of them all'. Lest the creative energies of the five men were underused, they were given in turn 'one woman in common to them all', although 'none of the said five men meddled with the common woman without leave of the mistress, and unless she had no need'. Amongst the advantages, 'the hero and the mistress have their full and choice of venery', 'the increase of children will be great and good', and 'no controversy about jointure, dower, maintenance, portion etc.'.[29]

John Locke, too, was led by his interest in the increase of mankind to question conventional notions of sexual morality. His diary contains several entries describing plans for an imaginary society, 'Atlantis'. In one, Locke proposes that 'he that is already married may marry another woman with his left hand ... the ties, duration and conditions of the left hand marriage shall be no other than what is expressed in the contract of marriage between the parties'.[30] Writing in his commonplace book on the subject of 'vice and virtue', he questions the necessity of marriage in its existing form:

> Thus, for a man to cohabit and have children by one or more women, who are at their own disposal, and when they think fit to part again, I see not how it can be condemned as a vice, since nobody is harmed, supposing it done amongst persons considered as separate from the rest of mankind.[31]

There were limits, however, to how far, and how publicly, Locke was willing to speculate. The free sexual exchange that he imagined possible among 'persons considered as separate from the rest of mankind' was 'a vice of deep dye' in the context of most societies,

> For if a woman, by transgressing those bounds which the received opinion of her country or religion, and not nature or reason, have set to modesty, has drawn any blemish on her reputation, she may run the risk of being exposed to infamy and other mischiefs, among the least of which is not the danger of losing the comforts of a conjugal settlement, and therewith the chief end of her being, the propagation of mankind.[32]

The same rationale for conventional morality was repeated in the *Second treatise*: the 'main intention of nature, which willeth the increase of mankind and the continuation of the species' could only be attained by 'the distinction of families, with the security of the marriage bed'; sodomy, adultery and incest were particularly 'aggravated' sins because they frustrated nature's intent.[33]

The increase of mankind was thereby redomesticated within a monogamous conjugal bond.

Petty's published writings, like Locke's, were far tamer than his manuscripts. His *Observations on the bills of mortality* (1676), for example, illustrates how the logic of political arithmetic could be used to argue *against* polygamy. Here, Petty uses the fact that males outnumbered females in the city of London to show 'that the Christian religion, prohibiting polygamy, is more agreeable to the law of nature, that is, the law of God, than Mohametism, and others that allow it: for one man his having many women, or wives, by law, signifies nothing, unless there were many women to one man in nature also'. Petty also invokes the medical commonplace of his day that a woman copulating with more than one man would be less likely to conceive, so as to explain 'why the law is, and ought to be so strict against fornications and adulteries: For, if there were universal liberty, the increase of mankind would be but like that of foxes [who copulate without restriction but produce few offspring] at best'. He concludes that 'it is no wonder why states, by encouraging marriage and hindering licentiousness, advance their own interest as well as preserve the laws of God from contempt and violation'.[34] A belief that population growth was the intention of nature could thus be reconciled with conventional morality. Indeed, there was nothing new in this. As Margaret Sommerville points out, thinkers had long speculated about whether alternative sexual arrangements, especially polygamy, would lead to greater reproduction; and then concluded in the negative.[35]

Even so, a concern with the increase of mankind played a more central and subversive role in late seventeenth-century thought than it had previously. The stakes were higher or at least more overtly political: Locke was committed to the expansion of population not simply because he accepted as a truism – as did all Christian thinkers – that the purpose of marriage was reproduction, but because he was deeply involved in imperial and economic affairs.[36] Furthermore, although Petty and Locke conformed to tradition by endorsing monogamy, they were not traditional in their willingness to raise other issues: the possibility of 'short marriage', a non-punitive approach to women who bore children out of wedlock, and an awareness that the sexual double standard was cultural rather than natural.

Locke and Petty speculated, moreover, not just on how to produce large numbers of children, but on how to produce healthy, flourishing children as well. Locke's interest in this aspect of population growth is particularly obvious. John Marshall, in his study of Locke's social and ethical thought, stresses Locke's commitment to an ethical system based on the obligation of every human being to care for and preserve God's creation. This 'ethic of care' tied together Locke's interest in agricultural experiment, his gentlemanly sense of an obligation to charity and liberality, the centrality of the right to self-preservation in his political theory, and his interest in education. The obligation of parents to care for children was one aspect, but a particularly powerful one, of Locke's ethical system.[37]

Locke was not alone in this emphasis on care. Lawrence Stone and J. H. Plumb have both noted the rise of negative attitudes towards corporal punishment over the long eighteenth century, and suggested that (in Plumb's words) the 'autocratic, indeed ferocious' attitude of the seventeenth century was replaced by a gentler approach to children.[38] It is hard to say how deeply the change in attitude ran, or whether it was as dramatic a change as Stone and Plumb make it out to be. The actual feelings of parents for their children are notoriously hard to discover.[39] For our purposes, however, the evidence of discursive shifts noted by Stone and Plumb is sufficient. As we will see below, the idea that the family existed for the benefit of children (rather than for the benefit of fathers, or the keeping of order) became so deeply rooted in the writings of whig thinkers that it was assumed rather than defended; it was not, in fact, even denied by tories.

FILMER, PATRIARCHALISM AND PATRIARCHY

To what extent the concerns described above were of particular importance to whigs (as opposed to tories) remains to be seen. They were strikingly absent, however, from the political writings of Robert Filmer. It is of course a commonplace in the history of political thought that Filmer and his whig critics disagreed about the family. The whigs did much to call attention to the differences. For a suitably horrifying image of what he took to be the logical consequences of Filmer's concept of 'fatherly right', Locke turned to Garcilasso de la Vega's account of the Incas of Peru. In some provinces, Locke informed his readers, they were 'so liquorish after man's flesh' that the men begat children upon female captives taken in war, and 'choicely nourished [them] ... till about thirteen years old they butchered and ate them, and they served their mothers after the same fashion, when they grew past childbearing, and ceased to bring them any more roasters'.[40] Locke further deduced that Filmer would sanction adultery, incest, and sodomy, as well as the castration, sale, and exposure of children to the elements, because the Bible and ancient history gave precedents for such behaviour.[41]

However, I would suggest that the differences between Filmer and the whigs had less to do with their views about the family than with the questions they asked about the family and with its function as part of their respective polemics.[42] For whigs in the exclusion crisis, the family was the institution in which children were produced and cared for, and (as a means to these two ends) through which property was transferred between generations. Filmer used the family to make a point about order: it was the site on which he raised and answered (in the negative) the question of whether anyone could avoid being subject to a higher authority.

Filmer's argument was simple. He sought to refute what he perceived to be the common and dangerous opinion that 'mankind is naturally endowed and born with freedom from all subjection, and at liberty to choose what form of government it please'. This opinion implied that all existing governments had originally been established by consent, 'at the discretion of the multitude'.[43] On the contrary, Filmer argued, no one had ever been born free. God had given to Adam, the first man, absolute and unconditional dominion over the world, over Eve, and over Eve's offspring. This absolute power had since been fragmented spatially (that is, the world was now broken up into several distinct governments) and had been transferred from one ruler to another in many different ways, but it remained the same kind of power. Filmer called this power the 'right of fatherhood', or 'fatherly right'.

Filmer's concept of 'fatherly right' is abstract and maddeningly elusive. It is by no means clear, for example, what it has to do with the power of fathers in actual families, or even with Adam's power as a father. Although Filmer associates 'fatherly right' with the original dominion of Adam over the earth and mankind, he cites at least two sources for Adam's authority that are not related to the power of fathers over children, but rather to the power of husbands over wives, or of humans over animals. The first is God's curse on Eve in *Genesis* 3:16 ('thy desire shall be to thy husband and he shall rule over thee') which Filmer takes to be the origin of political power.[44] The second cited authority is God's blessing to man in *Genesis* 1:28, enjoining him to 'have dominion over the fish of the sea, and over the fowl of the air, and over every living thing that moveth upon the earth'.[45]

Neither of these passages says anything about paternal power *per se*. Elsewhere, however, Filmer equates rulership and actual fatherhood. He asserts that 'creation made man prince of his posterity', and draws on biblical history to demonstrate that the first kings were heads of families and 'eldest parents'.[46] He cites examples of the absolute power of fathers over their children in the ancient world: the Romans let fathers execute their children, Judah condemned his daughter-in-law Thamar to death.[47] Moreover, 'there is no nation that allows children any action or remedy for being unjustly governed [by their father]'.[48] In this sense, the reason that humans are born in subjection is not merely because they are born subject to the holder of Adam's original power but because they are born subject to their own fathers.

> I see not then how the children of Adam, or of any man else, can be free from subjection to their parents. And this subjection of children is the only fountain of all regal authority, by the ordination of God himself.[49]

But of course, kings are not really the fathers of their people, and Filmer knows it. He indicates, for example, that the power of magistrates supersedes the power of fathers to put their children to death. It is important to him that 'the power of a father over his child gives place to and is subordinate to the power of the magistrate' because it proves that the power of magistrates is as natural as the power of fathers.[50] In fact, it is (and was) possible to read Filmer as a subversion of the powers of actual fathers in favour of the powers of kings.

The ambiguity in Filmer's notion of 'fatherly right' is the source of controversy amongst present-day historians about Filmer's typicality as a royalist thinker, his relationship to a wider tradition of 'patriarchalism', and the significance of his thought (or of patriarchalism more broadly) with respect to relations of power within the family. In the first serious treatment of the subject, Gordon Schochet has placed Filmer within a broad stream of 'patriarchalism', which he defines not as a single idea but as a cluster of analytically distinct but related notions: that hierarchies in nature, the state and the family are divinely ordained, that they are therefore in some sense analogous to one another, that they depend on one another, that obedience to kings can be justified in the same way as obedience to fathers (through the commandment 'honour thy father'), and that once upon a time fathers and kings were the same.[51] These notions, he argues, were widely shared by most seventeenth-century political thinkers, functioning often as unconscious habits of mind rather than as fully defended theories. Their pervasiveness can be attributed to actual social experience. The seventeenth-century English family 'was indeed an authoritarian institution that was well-suited to be the basis of an absolutist political doctrine, and ... for the vast majority of Englishmen in this period, the patriarchal justification of the duty to obey the state was an accurate translation of their regular experiences into political terms'.[52] Thus, Schochet describes Filmer as both a 'patriarchalist' political theorist and as a proponent of 'patriarchy' as a social institution.

Some historians, however, have questioned Schochet's account of how patriarchalist political theory was related to social practices and institutions. In *The patriarch's wife*, Margaret Ezell uses Filmer's unpublished manuscript – to which she gives the title 'In praise of the vertuous wife' – to argue that, when he turned his mind to domestic relationships as he himself experienced or hoped to experience them, Filmer accorded to women a great deal of autonomy and power within the household. His ideal woman was by no means an inferior, but a trusted second-in-command to her husband, credited with abilities and talents and expected to use them. It is precisely the fact that 'patriarchalism' was so flexible in practice, Ezell speculates, that made it acceptable in theory.[53]

Ezell further suggests that women could be empowered by tensions within and elements of patriarchalist theory. The power of the patriarch in the patriarchalist ideal of the household comprised two elements: the power of a parent over his children and the power of a husband over his wife. Patriarchalist theorists did not usually bother to distinguish between the two, since both forms were in practice combined in the person of the male head of household. However, insofar as patriarchalism upheld *parental* authority, it could be marshalled as a justification of the power of women as mothers within the household.[54] Mary Beth Norton, in her study of colonial North America, has pushed this point even farther. The 'Filmerian world view', she notes, held all kinds of hierarchies, of status and age as well as gender, to be natural and God-given. This meant that women of high status, especially widows or 'fictive widows' who headed households, were held worthy of exercising political power.[55] Unlike Schochet, then, Ezell and Norton detect possibilities for the empowerment of some women within Filmerian political thought.

Despite their differences, Norton and Ezell nonetheless share Schochet's belief that Filmer was part, even a paradigmatic part, of a 'patriarchalist' theoretical mainstream. Some historians of political thought, however, have questioned that assumption. R. W. K. Hinton has argued that Filmer's work can be read as a negation of patriarchalist logic. Hinton contrasts Filmer with a 'true patriarchalist' like Bodin. The latter, Hinton explains, was interested in enhancing the power of actual fathers alongside that of kings, because 'he saw himself as living in a society of infinite chaos where there was plenty of room for both kings and fathers to have more power at the same time'. The role of Bodin's 'patriarchal' king was therefore to defend the power of fathers over their families. Significantly, this meant that Bodin was able to distinguish kings from fathers, treating their respective powers as similar but not identical. Filmer, by contrast, went a step farther than Bodin by equating kings and fathers. He thus, Hinton argues, failed to sidestep the fundamental dilemma: 'if kings are fathers, fathers cannot be patriarchs ... patriarchal kings and patriarchal fathers are a contradiction in terms'.[56] As a result, Filmer magnified the power of kings at the expense of fathers: 'Filmer's ultimate statement on fathers and rulers – though he did not make it – was that between them a great gulf was fixed. Rulers were sovereign, fathers nothing: rulers had all power, fathers had none'.[57]

Whether one accepts Hinton's reading or not, the important point is that Filmer's views on familial relations can be interpreted in different ways because he said so little about them. Whig writers, by contrast, were refreshingly concrete. They treated fatherhood (or parenthood) as a particular relationship that could not be abstracted or transferred. 'To expect relative duties without relation, is most unnatural', wrote the whig Thomas Hunt: the duty of parents toward children was so personal 'that it cannot be transferred, or permitted absolutely to any other person by the parents; nor can any challenge a right, or discharge the father from it, or require the same affection, submission and reverence that is due from a child to his father'.[58] This non-transferability was itself often the point. As we will see below, Algernon Sidney expressed moral outrage over the system of hereditary succession to the throne and over the patriarchalist metaphor of king-as-father by complaining that these substituted 'chimerical' for actual fathers. Similarly, William Lawrence was obsessed with the difference between 'true' (biological) and 'false' (legal) fathers. John Locke and James Tyrrell were less bothered by the problem of biological truth. However, they shared the conviction that fatherhood must be a concrete, particular relationship. Tyrrell argued that parental power could not be transferred to kings, because even 'if parents are to be trusted with this absolute power over their children, because of the natural affection they are always supposed to bear them; then princes ought not to be trusted with it, since none but parents themselves can have this natural affection towards their children'.[59]

This refusal to let familial relations stand as metaphors for political relations does not mean that the whigs removed the family from political thought; rather, they inserted it into political argument in a different way. When whig theorists wrote about the family, they believed that they were writing about 'real' families and not just using the family as a metaphor for something else. The family itself became an object of concern for them in a way that it was not for Filmer.

The differences between the whigs and Filmer emerge most sharply around the problem of paternal identity. Whig writers made much of the fact that men could not, by definition, be certain that they were the biological fathers of the children who were reputed to be their own. Sidney used this fact to criticize the system of hereditary succession to the throne. Tyrrell invoked it to refute 'some writers' who 'think they have done sufficiently when they tell us, that the father hath an absolute dominion over his child, because he got it, and is the cause of its being',[60] But although Filmer was ostensibly the target of the books by Tyrrell and Sidney in which these criticisms were made, the criticisms could not with any justice be levelled at Filmer (which explains why Tyrrell refers vaguely only to 'some writers'). Filmer himself never argued that kings had to succeed to the throne by primogeniture through the male line. Rather, he imagined that the crown could be transferred in many different ways:

> It skills not which way kings come by their power, whether by election, donation, succession or by any other means, for it is still the manner of government by supreme power that makes them properly kings, and not the means of obtaining their crowns.[61]

Nor did Filmer claim that fathers had absolute power over their children because they literally begot them. This second point may be controversial, because it contradicts Carole Pateman's well-known exegesis of Filmerian patriarchalism. Pateman takes Filmer's statement that 'God at the creation gave the sovereignty to the man over the woman, as being the nobler and principle agent in generation' to mean that Filmer thought that Adam had power over his children because he appeared to generate them by himself. By imagining that men gave birth autogenously, Filmer and the patriarchalists obscured the role of women in reproduction and hence hid the fact that men needed to possess women through marriage in order to obtain power over their 'own' children.[62] Filmer, however, did not actually say – in the passage that Pateman quotes – that men have power over children because they beget them. There is no reason to suppose that he would have found such an argument polemically helpful. If he did not worry about whether a king was literally a father, it is logical to suppose that he did not need not worry if a father was literally a (biological) father: his point was about the quality of authority rather than how a ruler came to have it. Moreover, because Filmer was concerned with what children owed to their father, he would not have wanted to set limits as to which people could be considered 'children'. The power of a 'father' is enhanced by having people conventionally labelled as his 'children', whether they are biologically his children or not.

Thus, the question of whether a father was the biological parent of his child was of little concern to Filmer. Quite the contrary. In his *Observations concerning the original of government*, Filmer responded to Hobbes' comments on the uncertainty of paternal identity by saying that legal paternity is sufficient:

> As to the objection [by Hobbes], that 'it is not known who is the father to the son but by the discovery of the mother', and that 'he is son to whom the mother will, and therefore he is the mother's', the answer is, that it is not at the will of the mother to make whom she please the father, for if the mother be not in possession of a husband, the child is not reckoned to have any father at all; but if she be in the possession of a man, the child notwithstanding whatsoever the woman discovereth to the contrary it is still reputed to be his in whose possession she is. No child naturally or infallibly knows who are its true parents, yet he must obey those that in common reputation are so, otherwise the commandment of 'honour thy father and thy mother' were in vain, and no child bound to the obedience of it'.[63]

The difference between whig theorists and Filmer was not, then, that Filmer assumed that paternal identity was knowable and the whigs did not. Rather, it was that Filmer had a framework and set of concerns which made the uncertainty of paternal identity irrelevant. Although whigs loved to mock Filmer by enumerating the difficulties attendant upon finding the direct lineal heir of Adam ('for ought I know to the contrary', sneered Tyrrell, 'the author's footman may be the man'),[64] they were attacking a straw man. The fact that they did insist on raising an issue that was not important to Filmer suggests that it was important to them rather than to him. For the whigs, fatherhood was not a metaphor but a specific relationship. Although they did not believe that fatherhood was necessarily a biological fact, the problematic nature of biological paternity was, for them, worth thinking about.

THE FAMILY IN TORY WRITING DURING THE EXCLUSION CRISIS

The whigs and Filmer were thus, in a sense, talking past one another. What, then, of the tory polemicists of the 1680s? Did they continue to treat the family, as Filmer had, in abstract, metaphorical terms? Or did they, like their contemporary whig opponents, concern themselves with the concrete relations of power and obligation arising from the material and reproductive functions of the family as an institution? Did they make the claim that fathers had power over children because they were the 'nobler agent in generation?'

A key difference between Filmer and the tories of the 1680s is that the latter had to deal with the problem of succession to the throne. Although Filmer himself had never pushed the claim that royal power was conferred by indefeasible hereditary succession, one might expect tories in the 1680s to care more. It is extremely interesting, therefore, that they hedged their bets on the sacred status of primogeniture. Biblical justification for primogeniture could be found in the promise of God to Cain that his brothers would obey him. The fact that Charles II dated his reign from 1649 (rather than from his coronation in 1660) indicated that he had automatically become king upon his father's death, in accordance with divine law, even when there was no English coronation ceremony to confirm his title.[65] But the divinely decreed origin of indefeasible hereditary right to the throne was not as high on the tory agenda as we might expect. Strict principles of primogentiure were dangerous to tories because, arguably, they supported the rights of Monmouth, the King's eldest son, more powerfully than they did those of York, who was only Charles's brother; precisely this argument (as we will see below) was made by the whig lawyer William Lawrence.

Moreover, the assertion that the Duke of York's right to the throne was established by God was less useful to the tories than the claim that it was 'lawful', that is, in accordance with the fundamental laws of England. Many tory writers argued that indefeasible hereditary right to the crown was part of the constitution, so much so that it could not be changed by Parliament, or even by the king himself. Edmund Bohun, although at some points appearing to defend the principle of *jure divino* primogeniture, casually dismissed as irrelevant a challenge from Algernon Sidney to show that any given prince was descended from the eldest son of Noah through a line of eldest sons. Descent from Noah might indeed entitle a prince to 'universal monarchy' (that is, rulership of the world), Bohun admitted, but nobody had yet claimed it, and (the italics are mine) 'it is reasonable that all princes should in the mean time enjoy what they are in *lawful possession* of, till this heir of Noah hath ma[de] out his pedigree and title, and then they may consider further of it'.[66]

The defence of James's hereditary right in terms of English law rather than divine decree gave the tories a tremendous advantage in the propaganda war.[67] It enabled them to paint themselves as the party best suited to defend the constitution and fundamental law of England. It followed that they, and not the whigs, were the party of liberty and property. The tory author of *A letter to a friend, reflecting upon the present condition of this nation* baldly accused the whigs of hypocrisy:

> Give me leave to ask all the vehement sticklers for liberty and property [the whigs], what they mean by those terms? Is it not to be under the protection of reasonable, known and determinate laws, that we may have other measures of our duties and punishments, other measures of what we may call ours, than the will of imposers. If it be (which no doubt they must confess) let them show by what known and determinate laws the Duke [of York] hath forfeited the inheritance, which a known determinate law hath given him.[68]

The Filmerian emphasis on absolute, undivided sovereign power was thus softened in the tory writing of the 1680s by constitutionalist rhetoric. But this 'tory constitutionalism' is only part of the story.[69]

Tories continued to hold absolutist views of the origins of law and the limits of monarchical power. John Nalson, who of all tory writers sounded the most 'Lockeian' in his passionate defence of property rights, law and Magna Carta against the whig threat, also believed that these came from the king – hardly a view Locke would have endorsed.[70] As the exclusionists embarked on popular demonstrations and petitioning campaigns and as Charles II defended his brother by proroguing and dissolving the Parliament, tories defended the God-givenness and absoluteness of royal prerogative against the theory that sovereign power originated in the people. The tory defence of prerogative could occur at the expense of tory arguments about indefeasible hereditary right. One tory pamphleteer, to indicate the God-given character of royal power, chose to deploy the marriage metaphor in a way that implied that kings might indeed be elected: just as (italics mine) 'a woman by her *choice and consent* designeth a husband, but the marital power and dominion is only from God. So that you clearly see that *a human act may design* the person of the king, but the power is from God alone'.[71] Similarly, the author of *Two great questions determined* (1680) upheld the absolute powers of the prince and the subject's duty of passive obedience; he also, however, denied that hereditary succession was divinely ordained, and argued that because the king was indeed above the law he could change the succession at will.[72]

Tories thus held somewhat contradictory positions on the relative importance of royal prerogative against that of indefeasible hereditary right, and were unclear as to whether such indefeasible hereditary right rested on man-made law or divine decree. The internal tensions were also evident in the mixed reactions of tories to the 'limitations scheme' proposed by Charles II himself, whereby James would succeed to the throne but be bound by statutory restraints on his authority. Because this 'limitations scheme' would rescue the principle of indefeasible hereditary succession to the throne at the expense of royal prerogative, some tories regarded it as more 'republican' than exclusion itself; others found it a reasonable solution to the problem of a popish successor.[73] Had Charles II wanted to alter succession by fiat, tories might well have split into two groups, one supporting the 'law' of hereditary succession and the other upholding the superiority of the king to the law itself. But because the king opposed exclusion, tories did not have to choose between the various strands of tory argument.

The very combination of absolutist and constitutionalist elements in tory writing made it broadly appealing, but at the expense of theoretical precision.[74] One tory pamphleteer vaguely assured readers that he did not mean to endorse 'despotical sovereignty, an absolute power, such as the great Turk this day exercises over his subjects', but only 'royal, paternal sovereignty, as we and our ancestors have lived long, and happily under;' he did not define the difference between the two forms of power.[75] Edmund Bohun's defence of Filmer against the criticism of James Tyrrell was similarly confusing. He complained that Filmer had been unfairly misrepresented by the whigs, who 'make the people believe Sir Robert Filmer was for an absolute monarchy *jure divino*, so that no other government can be lawfully exercised nor the least limitations set to it, without sacrilege, and diminution of that sovereignty which is derived from no less an original than God himself'. But why, exactly, this constituted a misrepresentation was left unexplained; indeed, Bohun went on to state a position virtually identical to the one which he maintained the whigs had falsely accused Filmer of having: England was a monarchy 'depending upon none but God almighty. Nor can any power on earth set the least limitation to it against the consent of the proper monarch'.[76]

The presence of both constitutionalist and absolutist elements in tory ideology, and the tension between them, shaped the ways in which tories deployed ideas about the family in their political writing. Just as they could sound like whigs in their defences of liberty and property, so too they could sound like whigs in their paeans of praise to the family as the site of care and nurturance. Tories used ideas about the family to help them smooth over the internal contradictions of their position. At the same time, tories writing on the family in the 1680s had, in crucial respects, more in common with Filmer than with their whig opponents.

The rhetorical similarities between tories and whigs are evident in tory accounts of the purpose of family, society and government. These institutions existed not to punish sin but for human good, self-preservation and material well-being. As Edmund Bohun explained, 'man coming naked and helpless into the world, and having need of many things for his well being in it, can not subsist well but in society'.[77] Governments were only viable if they allowed men 'to preserve themselves ... by uniting with the rest for their support and protection'.[78] John Nalson agreed: 'whoever will trace society and government to their first original, will easily be convinced, that it was that love which naturally all men have for themselves, and their own happiness, which first invited them into mutual combinations'.[79] Not surprisingly, tories defied whig stereotypes of them in their accounts of the nature of paternal power. The whig picture of Filmer as an enslaver of children or subjects was misleading, Bohun declared, since 'according to Sir R's principles, princes are bound to treat their subjects as their children, and it is not the nature of mankind to make their offspring slaves'.[80]

Tories could strengthen their image as proponents of loving, nurturing families by defining themselves against the notorious figure of Thomas Hobbes. Here they had an advantage not available to Filmer. Hobbes was the perfect target; his belief that the state of nature was a state of war was repellent to everyone, including whigs. Moreover, Hobbes had applied this principle to the family, outrageously maintaining that fathers (and in a state of nature, mothers) had power over their newborn infants because the infants had implicitly consented to be subject to the parent in return for not being murdered or left to starve.[81] Thanks to Hobbes, tory writers were able to associate *all* contractarian views with atomism and violence (and conversely, to link loving familial relationships to tory anti-contractarian principles).

John Nalson dramatically invoked the 'old fable of Cadmus in Ovid' to describe the Hobbesian distopia of equality and mutual hostility. Hobbes would

> suppose all mankind to be like the harvest sprung from the serpent's teeth; unnatural sons of the earth, born in arms; and immediately like fabulous knights-errant, entering upon martial actions, and a mutual combat and slaughter of one another: For there is no such thing as equality by the state of nature; but the father by the very priority of a natural cause must be superior to his children.[82]

Nalson's deft mythological allusion crystallized the tory argument about the family. Because a father is superior, we are not, as Hobbes would have it, like Cadmus's dragon's teeth, in a perpetual contest for power against our fellow human beings; rather, we are naturally united by love. But this love cannot subsist without the presence of an undivided, undisputed authority. So God, in His wisdom, spared human beings the need to decide amongst themselves who was in charge. Edmund Bohun pointed out that if God had created Adam and Eve at once, 'it could not have been known which of these two were to command, and which to obey;' worse, their children 'could as little have told which of the parents they should have obeyed in case of a difference betwixt them two'.[83] God had made a point of creating Adam first in order to avoid such disputes. Passive obedience to authority, familial or political, was necessary because if people believed that they could resist authority they would perpetually seek reasons to do so, leading to a state of total war.

Thus, one did not need to accept an arcane or controversial reading of the *Genesis* narrative in order to appreciate tory arguments against resistance. Common sense, and the ever-present memory of the civil war, supported their claims. It is a sign of tory confidence, then, that tories did not feel compelled to discuss the family with much rigour or detail. The author of *A letter to a friend shewing from scripture* apparently felt he had sufficiently addressed the nature of familial relationships with one flippant, dismissive passage:

> If all power be originally in the people, then it will by consequence follow, that the lawful authority of a father over his children, and a husband over his wife, are derived from the children and wife, and the children and wife in some cases may resume their power ... and their native liberty: If our author will aver so, he is to be cudgelled, not to be answered.[84]

What else was there to say? Whig writers, as we shall see in the next chapter, had to put much more intellectual energy into refuting this argument than the tories did into making it.

The only tory (that I have found) to embark in the 1680s upon systematic, extended discussions of familial relationships was Edmund Bohun, who defended Filmer against polemical attacks by both Algernon Sidney and James Tyrrell. The pressure of responding to whig critics forced Bohun to be far more explicit than Filmer had been about the precise nature of power within the family; in effect, he filled in the blanks left by Filmer's rather cursory treatment. Yet, Bohun is an exception that proves the rule. Like Filmer, he appeared uninterested in the situation of actual, contemporary families. Indeed, he admitted that his description of the relations of Adam, Eve and their children was irrelevant to the experience of people in the present, since the civil law restrained the power that fathers had claimed in their original, natural state.[85]

Bohun also, like Filmer, treated paternity as an abstract concept, applicable in all relationships between superiors and subordinates. Tyrrell was wrong, he insisted, to deny that kings could feel for their people the same 'natural affection of a father' for his children, for God 'has in his hands the hearts of all princes, and endows them with such affections as he thinks fit, not only towards the people in general but towards each particular person'.[86] Paternity was so widely transferable, in fact, that Bohun used it (in a way that might have fascinated Freud) to describe all other relationships within the family. Accordingly, he dismissed the distinction – dear to the hearts of whig theorists – between paternal and conjugal power.[87] 'Adam having no superior but God, Eve owed him a filial subjection as well as [the children]'.[88] Because Eve was created out of Adam, 'Adam was a kind of father to his wife. That marital, as well as all other power, might be founded in paternal jurisdiction'.[89]

Not surprisingly, Eve's role as a mother went completely ignored in Bohun's account. He made no reference to maternal or parental power that would have complicated the equation of conjugal and paternal power. His conflation of the conjugal and the paternal did not, however, depend on the myth that Adam was solely responsible in a biological sense for the generation of his children. He entirely sidestepped the need to make Adam a parent of his children by invoking the civil-law maxim by which the mother's status was passed to her children, so that 'if Eve was subject to Adam by the will of God, her children were so too; for they could not in the life of the father be in a better state than their mother'.[90] Alternatively, Adam's power could be derived merely from the fact that he was created first. If God had wanted people to be equal, he would have indicated this by creating many of them at once. Again, the subjection of Eve and the subjection of the children were based on the same thing, 'for if a priority of being gave Adam power over his wife, it gave him much more so over his children'.[91]

Paradoxically, Bohun's emphasis on the identical – and identically hierarchical – quality of all familial and political relationships made possible a feminist critique of whig assumptions about marriage and gender. Because whigs (as will be seen below) assumed that power hierarchies originated in consent, they needed to explain why the power of husbands was justifiable in practical or natural terms. Locke's admission that since 'the rule must be placed somewhere, it naturally falls to the man's share as the abler and stronger' epitomized whig attempts to reconcile the principles of equality and consent with the fact of male domination.[92] Tories, because they could explain male authority simply with reference to divine decree, had no need to offer no such rationalizations. Bohun rejected any assumption that men ruled because they were abler and stronger than women, since it might 'happen that the woman has a little more wit than her husband', or that she might 'happen to be the stronger of the two'.[93] He also ridiculed the idea that a woman would willingly consent to be 'absolutely subject' to her husband (as Tyrrell imagined she might), as this was 'as extravagant a bargain as ever entered into the thoughts of any man'.[94]

George Hickes, another tory theorist, asked in a similar spirit why whig writers who located original sovereignty in the people failed to include women in the category of 'people' who could consent to government:

If men only have an interest in the supreme power, by whose order and authority, or by what Salic law of nature were women excluded from it, who are as useful members of the commonwealth, and as necessary for human societies, as men are? Who gave men authority to deprive them of their birthright, and set them aside as unfit to meddle with government; when histories teach us, that they have wielded sceptres as well as men, and experience shows, that there is no natural difference between their understandings and ours, nor any defects in their knowledge of things, but what education makes?[95]

Hickes and Bohun thus turned the assertion that women were obliged to obey their husbands by divine decree into a radical critique of the notion that men deserved power by their own merits, or because women had consented to it; their argument foreshadowed, and perhaps influenced, the tory feminist Mary Astell twenty years later.

UNRESOLVED QUESTIONS IN WHIG POLITICAL THOUGHT

There was an appealing coherence and simplicity to the tory position. The whigs were at a comparative disadvantage: they were forced to explain how it was possible to combine the natural freedom of individuals with hierarchy within families and still maintain peace. It was a problem that they never quite solved. Reliance on a ludicrously stereotyped version of Filmer gave the whigs an illusion of clarity and unity (*we* do not eat our children). But as we shall see in the next chapter, there was much ambiguity, and a wide range of opinion, in how whigs handled issues of power and its limits within the family.

Acknowledging the problematic nature of biological paternity also raised some difficult issues for whig writers. Was it a bad thing that men could not know for certain that their children were truly their biological progeny? The whig attitude depended to an extent on what issue they were considering. When they were discussing the nature of paternal power, the fact that paternal identity was uncertain worked to their advantage. Locke and Tyrrell were both quick to point out that adoptive fathers had as much power as natural ones. This supported, in their eyes, the larger argument that it was the responsibility of caring for children, however acquired, that conferred authority on the care-giver. The uncertainty of paternal identity was also not a problem for most whigs when they were discussing the principle of hereditary succession to the throne. Most of the whigs (with the exception of William Lawrence) were – in the context of the exclusion crisis – content to see that principle undermined, and pointing out that paternal identity was uncertain helped to undermine it. They were far more committed, however, to the principle of hereditary succession to private property. Here, an acknowledgement that paternity was uncertain could be more threatening.

The gender politics involved in the problematization of paternal identity were complex. The admission that paternity was unknowable played up the role of women in reproduction. It therefore exposed the fact that men are only fathers because they control women, and thereby forced onto the whig agenda questions about the particular character of the power of husbands over wives. On the other hand, the problematization of paternal identity exploited and intensified cultural anxieties about the capacity of women to undermine men's authority and control over property by foisting bastards upon unwitting husbands. In that sense, it could justify the notion that women needed to be disciplined.

What I have described here is not a coherent ideology, but rather a set of pressures, influences and concerns that raised more questions than they answered. Although whigs appeared united in their repudiation of Filmer, they held diverse views on the significance of biological paternity, inheritance, and the limits of paternal and husbandly authority. Not every whig writer discussed in the next chapter took up every issue, but the issues were all linked to whig political arguments, and cropped up in more than one place. To fully understand the position of an individual whig thinker on any of these issues requires a detailed and contextualized discussion of his political thought and agenda.

NOTES

1 This account follows closely that of Mark Knights, *Politics and opinion in crisis, 1678–81* (Cambridge, Cambridge University Press, 1994). If J. R. Jones's *The first whigs* (Oxford, Clarendon Press, 1961) placed too much emphasis on the solitary issue of exclusion, Jonathan Scott's *Algernon Sidney and the restoration crisis, 1677–1683* (Cambridge, Cambridge University Press, 1991) tendentiously eliminates it.

  About terminology: I have allowed myself to refer to 'whigs' and 'tories', albeit in full awareness that each term is problematic. Knights eschews 'whig' and 'tory' because he believes that since the parties emerged as a *result* of the exclusion crisis, it would be anachronistic to use party labels with reference to things occurring before it was over. But Knights' preferred designations, 'loyalist' and 'oppositionist' create more problems than they solve, since virtually everyone at the time claimed to be loyal in some sense to king and country. 'Exclusionist' and 'anti-exclusionist' will not do either, for reasons well explained by Knights and Jonathan Scott. I use 'whig' and 'tory' as the least of the available evils; they should be taken as loose but convenient ideological designations, and do not necessarily denote membership in a 'modern' party organization (but cf. Jones, *First whigs*). I use 'exclusion crisis' to describe the events of 1678–81 because it is recognizable; Knights' preferred term, 'succession crisis', would otherwise do equally well.

2 For an overview, see Howard Nenner, *The right to be king: the succession of the crown of England, 1603–1714* (Chapel Hill, University of North Carolina Press, 1995), chs 5, 6.

3 *Two great questions determined by the principles of reason and divinity* (Richard Janeway, 1681).

4 [Robert Ferguson], *A letter to a person of honour, concerning the King's disavowing the having been married to the Duke of Monmouth's mother* [1680]; [Robert Ferguson], *A letter to a person of honour concerning the black box* [1680].

5 Bohun, *PP*, I.64.

6 Examples of the growing literature on the significance of gender in English political discourse before or during the civil war include: Mary Shanley, 'Marriage contract and social contract in seventeenth-century English political thought', *Western Political Quarterly* 32 (1979); Dagmar Freist, 'The king's crown is the whore of Babylon: politics, gender and communication in mid-seventeenth-century England', *Gender and History* 7:3 (1995); Susan Wiseman, '"Adam, the father of all flesh", porno-political rhetoric and political theory in and after the English civil war', in James Holstun (ed.), *Pamphlet wars: prose in the English Revolution* (Frank Cass, 1992); Ann Hughes, 'Gender and politics in Leveller literature', in Susan Amussen and Mark Kishlansky (eds), *Political culture and cultural politics in early modern England* (Manchester, Manchester University Press, 1995); Cynthia Herrup, 'The patriarch at home: the trial of the second Earl of Castlehaven for rape and sodomy', *History Workshop Journal* 41 (1996); Frances Dolan, *Dangerous familiars: representations of domestic crime in England, 1550–1700* (Ithaca, Cornell University Press, 1994); Belinda Peters, '"That immaculate robe of honour": marriage in seventeenth century English political thought' (Ph.D. dissertation, University of California at Irvine, 1996).

7 See, for example, Susan Owen, *Restoration theatre and crisis* (Oxford, Clarendon Press, 1996), ch. 5; Susan Greenfield, 'Aborting the "mother plot": politics and generation in *Absalom and Achitophel*', *ELH* 62 (1995); Steven Zwicker, 'Virgins and whores: the politics of sexual misconduct in the 1660s' in Conal Condren and A. D. Cousins (eds), *The political ideology of Andrew Marvell* (New York, Scolar Press, 1990); Paul Hammond, 'The king's two bodies: representations of Charles II' in Jeremy Black and Jeremy Gregory (eds), *Culture, politics and society in Britain 1660–1800* (Manchester, Manchester University Press, 1991); Rachel Weil, 'Sometimes a sceptre is only a sceptre' in Lynn Hunt (ed.), *The invention of pornography* (New York, Zone, 1993); Harold Weber, *Paper bullets: print and kingship under Charles II* (Lexington, University of Kentucky Press, 1996); Julia Rudolph, 'Rape and resistance: women and consent in seventeenth-century English legal and political thought', *Journal of British Studies* (forthcoming).

8 For Filmer's place in the exclusion crisis, see Mark Goldie, 'John Locke and Anglican royalism', *Political Studies* 31 (1983); cf. James Daly, *Sir Robert Filmer and English political thought* (Toronto, University of Toronto Press, 1979). See also Alan C. Houston, *Algernon Sidney and the republican heritage in England and America* (Princeton, Princeton University Press, 1991), ch. 2.

9 On the dating of Filmer's works, see Johann P. Sommerville's introduction to *Patriarcha*, pp. xxxii–xxxvii.

10 *Political writings of John Locke*, ed. David Wootton (New York, Mentor, 1993), p. 191. (Hereafter Locke, *Political writings*).

11 On conveyancing, see H. J. Habbakuk, 'Marriage settlements in the eighteenth century', *Transactions of the Royal Historical Society*, 4th ser., 32 (1950), and his 'The rise and fall of English landed families', *Transactions of the Royal Historical Society*, 5th ser., 29 (1979). On commercially-orientated conceptions of wealth, see the suggestive remarks by Steve Pincus, 'Neither Machiavellian moment nor possessive individualism:

commercial society and the defenders of the English commonwealth', *American Historical Review* 103:3 (1998). See also Joyce Appleby, *Economic thought and ideology in seventeenth-century England* (Princeton, Princeton University Press, 1978); Charles Webster, *The great instauration: science, medicine and reform 1626–1660* (Duckworth, 1975).

12 *A treatise of feme coverts: or, the lady's law* (1732), p. 20.

13 Joan Thirsk, 'Younger sons in the seventeenth century', *History* 54 (1969), pp. 358–77.

14 [John ap Robert], *The younger brother his apologie* (Oxford, Henry Hall, 1671), pp. 35–6. According to Thirsk, 'Younger sons', the first known edition is 1618; it was reprinted in 1624, 1634 and 1641.

15 James Harrington, *The commonwealth of Oceana* [1656], ed. J. G. A. Pocock (Cambridge, Cambridge University Press, 1992), p. 109.

16 On these developments, see H. J. Habbakuk, 'Marriage settlements' and his 'The rise and fall of English landed families'. For their effect on paternal power, see Ralph Houlbrooke, *The English landed family 1450–1700* (Longman, 1985), pp. 231–2.

17 See Edward G. Cox, *A reference guide to the literature of travel: the new world* (Seattle, University of Washington Publications in Language and Literature, 1938).

18 Samuel Clarke, *A true and faithful account of the four chiefest plantations of the English in America* (Robert Clavel, 1670), p. 11.

19 G. Meriton, *A geographical description of the world*, 3rd edn (William Leake, 1679), p. 213.

20 [Thomas Herbert], *Some years travels into diverse parts of Africa and Asia the great*, 4th edn (R. Everingham, 1677), p. 337.

21 Meriton, *Geographical description*, p. 201.

22 John Ogilby, *Africa* (Thomas Johnson, 1670), p. 472.

23 ap Robert, *The younger brother*, pp. 6–7.

24 Appleby, *Economic thought*, pp. 135–7.

25 Locke, *TT*, II.28.

26 *Ibid.*, II.42; see also II.40–1, I.33. For Locke's interest in political arithmetic, see Karen Iverson Vaughn, *John Locke, economist and social scientist* (Chicago, University of Chicago Press, 1980).

27 *The Petty papers: some unpublished writings of Sir William Petty from the Bowood papers*, ed. Marquess of Lansdowne, 2 vols (Constable, 1927), vol. 2, ch. 13.

28 On non-monogamy, see Meriton, *A geographical description*, p. 229; [Herbert], *Some years travels*, p. 339; Lancelot Addison, *The present state of the Jews* (William Crook, 1676), p. 70.

29 *Petty papers*, vol. 2, ch. 13.

30 His diary entries describing this utopian society are printed in John Locke, *Political essays*, ed. Mark Goldie (Cambridge, Cambridge University Press, 1997), p. 256. The entry is dated 15 July 1678.

31 Locke, *Political writings*, pp. 241–2. The entry is dated 1681.

32 *Ibid.*

33 Locke, *TT*, II.59.

34 *The economic writings of Sir William Petty*, ed. Charles H. Hull, 2 vols (Cambridge, Cambridge University Press, 1899), 2:374–8.

35 Margaret Sommerville, *Sex and subjection: attitudes to women in early modern society* (Arnold, 1995), pp. 150–61.

36 For Locke's involvement in imperial and economic affairs, see James Tully, 'Rediscovering America: the *Two treatises* and aboriginal rights', in *An approach to political philosophy: Locke in contexts* (Cambridge, Cambridge University Press, 1993), and works cited therein.

37 John Marshall, *John Locke: resistance, religion and responsibility* (Cambridge, Cambridge University Press, 1994), pp. 169, 177, 293, 297 and *passim*.

38 J. H. Plumb, 'The new world of children in eighteenth-century England', *Past and Present* 67 (1975); Stone, *The family, sex and marriage in England 1500–1800* (New York, Harper & Row, 1977), pp. 439–40.

39 Linda Pollock, *Forgotten children: parent–child relations from 1500–1900* (Cambridge, Cambridge University Press, 1983).

40 Locke, *TT*, I.57; see also I.58.

41 *Ibid.*, I.59.

42 But cf. Gordon Schochet, 'The significant sounds of silence: the absence of women from the political thought of Sir Robert Filmer and John Locke', in Hilda Smith (ed.), *Women writers and the early modern British political tradition* (Cambridge, Cambridge University Press, 1998).

43 *Patriarcha*, p. 2.

44 *Ibid.*, pp. 138, 145 [from *The anarchy of a limited or mixed monarchy*].

45 Filmer, *Observations on Aristotle's Politics* and *The original of government*, in *Patriarcha*, pp. 236, 217–18.

46 *Patriarcha*, p. 6, pp. 7–11.

47 *Ibid.*, pp. 18–19, p. 7.

48 *Ibid.*, p. 35.

49 *Ibid.*, p. 7.

50 *Ibid.*, p. 12. Filmer assumes here that if the power of magistrates were only conventional it could never supersede what is 'natural'.

51 Gordon Schochet, *Patriarchalism in political thought: the authoritarian family and political speculation and attitudes especially in seventeenth-century England* (New York, Basic Books, 1975), ch. 1.

52 *Ibid.*, p. 64.

53 Margaret J. M. Ezell, *The patriarch's wife: literary evidence and the history of the family* (Chapel Hill, University of North Carolina Press, 1987), chs 5–6; Filmer's essay 'In praise of the vertuous wife' is printed on pp. 117–203.

54 *Ibid.*, p. 139. See also Susan D. Amussen, *An ordered society: gender and class in early modern England* (Oxford, Basil Blackwell, 1988), pp. 59–60.

55 Mary Beth Norton, *Founding mothers and fathers: gendered power and the forming of American society* (New York, Alfred A. Knopf, 1988), esp. section III.

56 R. W. K. Hinton, 'Husbands, fathers and conquerors, part I', *Political Studies* 15 (1967), pp. 291–300, at p. 294.

57 *Ibid.*, pp. 299–300.

58 Thomas Hunt, *Mr. Hunt's postscript for rectifying some mistakes in some of the inferiour clergy* (1682), p. 72.

59 Tyrrell, *PNM*, p. 22.

60 *Ibid.*, p. 14.

61 *Patriarcha*, p. 44.

62 Carole Pateman, *The sexual contract: aspects of patriarchal liberalism* (Stanford, Stanford University Press, 1988), p. 87. The quotation is from Filmer's *Observations concerning the original of government*, in *Patriarcha*, p. 192.

63 *Patriarcha*, p. 192. The argument to which Filmer responds is in Thomas Hobbes, *De cive: the English version*, ed. Howard Warrender (Oxford, Clarendon Press, 1983), p. 123 (ch. 9, section 3).

64 Tyrrell, *PNM*, p. 45.

65 See, for example, E. F., *Letter from a gentleman of quality in the country, to his friend, upon his being chosen a member to serve in the approaching Parliament* (1679); *Great and weighty considerations relating to the D. or successor of the crown* (1679), p. 2; [John Brydall], *The white rose: or, a word for the house of York* (1680); Bohun, *PP*, I.64 and I.69. These arguments are well described in Nenner, *Right to be king*, pp. 109–14, 123–5.

66 [Edmund Bohun], *A defence of Sir Robert Filmer against the mistakes and misrepresentations of Algernon Sidney, esq.* (Walter Kettilby, 1684), p. 16.

67 Tim Harris, *London crowds in the reign of Charles II: propaganda and politics from the Restoration until the exclusion crisis* (Cambridge, Cambridge University Press, 1987).

68 *A letter to a friend reflecting upon the present condition of this nation* (1680), pp. 4–5. See also *An answer to Pereat Papa* [1681], p. 2; *Great and weighty considerations* [1679], p. 7; [John Nalson], *The character of a rebellion, and what England may expect from one* (Benjamin Tooke, 1681), pp. 7–10; [John Nalson], *The complaint of liberty and property* (Robert Steele, 1681).

69 The 'constitutionalism' of the tories is affirmed by Daly, *Sir Robert Filmer* but cf. Goldie, 'John Locke and Anglican royalism'.

70 [Nalson], *The character of a rebellion*, pp. 8–14.

71 *A letter to a friend. Shewing from scripture, fathers and reason, how false that state-maxim is, royal authority is ... in the people* (1679), p. 6. For the same metaphor, see George Hickes, *A discourse of the sovereign power* (1682), p. 3. See also Belinda Peters, 'That immaculate robe of honour', pp. 62–4.

72 *Two great questions determined by the principles of reason and divinity* (Richard Janeway, 1681); for other tory pamphlets holding that a change in the succession, while neither advisable nor just, might be lawful, see Roger L'Estrange, *The case put concerning the succession*, 3rd edn (Henry Brome, 1680), and *A letter to a friend reflecting upon the present condition of this nation* (1680), pp. 3–4.

73 Knights, *Politics and opinion*, pp. 32–4, 87–90, 99–101, 299, 329. For a tory tract expressing optimism that Parliament and the law will restrain a popish king from ruining the protestant religion, see *Great and weighty considerations*, p. 2.

74 Houston, *Algernon Sidney*, p. 95.

75 *A letter to a friend, shewing from scripture*, p. 8.

76 Bohun, *PP*, I.5. See also I.6–7.

77 *Ibid.*, I.17.

78 *Ibid.*, I.63.

79 John Nalson, *The common interest of king and people* (Jonathan Edwin, 1678), p. 5.

80 Bohun, *PP*, I.12. See also Bohun, *A defence of Sir Robert Filmer*, pp. 13–14.

81 Thomas Hobbes, *Leviathan*, chapter 20.

82 Nalson, *The common interest*, p. 6.

83 Bohun, *PP*, I.20–1.

84 *A letter to a friend shewing from scripture*, p. 7. The whig author attacked here is unidentified.

85 Bohun, *PP*, I.67.

86 *Ibid.*, I.51.

87 *Ibid.*, I.27.

88 *Ibid.*, I.31.

89 Bohun, *A defence of Sir Robert Filmer*, p. 13.

90 Bohun, *PP*, I.31.

91 *Ibid.*, I.37.

92 Locke, *TT*, II.82.

93 Bohun, *PP*, II.41, II.42. See also I.20.

94 *Ibid.*, II.43.

95 Hickes, *A discourse of the sovereign power*, p. 22.

Chapter 2

Four whig political writers

Feminist political theorists seeking to understand the implications of the liberal political tradition for women have, understandably, concentrated their attention upon its founder, John Locke.[1] This chapter, however, concerns not the gender politics of liberalism in the abstract but the gender politics of whig political thought *circa* 1680–81. It asks what it was possible to think about gender, power and the family from a whig political perspective.

As it is impossible within the scope of one chapter to examine the massive body of literature produced by whigs between 1679 and 1682, I have chosen to concentrate on four whig writers who dealt explicitly with problems of gender, power and the family in their political writing. Three of them (Algernon Sidney, James Tyrrell, and John Locke) are well-known as political theorists, and all produced lengthy critiques of Filmer's *Patriarcha*. The fourth, William Lawrence, stands out for producing whig propaganda in the form of a treatise upon the regulation of marriage. My choice of subjects is admittedly somewhat arbitrary. However, since the purpose of the chapter is to underscore the lack of consensus among whig political thinkers about the nature of power within the family or its place in political thought, the inclusion of more examples would further strengthen the case.

The reader is warned, then, that this chapter will not provide a neat definition of a 'whig ideology of gender'. Nor will it attempt to characterize whig ideology as a whole as damaging or beneficial to women. Taken as a group, whig writers offered a number of different kinds of challenges to the laws, practices, and ideologies surrounding the family: individual whigs can be found criticizing practices of coverture or primogeniture, proposing that wives and children might have the right to resist abuse, treating paternity as a social construct rather than a natural fact, and describing marriage as a contract based on consent. But the gender politics of these challenges (that is, their consequences for relations of power between men and women) could cut in more than one direction. In some cases, whig ideology promoted the freedom of women as individuals; in others, it played into male anxieties about women's power. Often it did both.

An awareness of the lack of consensus among whigs makes it possible to read Locke with more historical sensitivity, allowing us to see what choices he made among a range of available positions. Such an approach will illuminate the nature and sources of Locke's most famous contribution to whig argument, his distinction between the family and the state. I shall argue in this chapter that the family–state distinction was not the majestic centrepiece of a coherent intellectual system. Rather, it was an *ad hoc*, somewhat confused, and not consistently deployed response to a series of conundrums that presented themselves when Locke put his mind to making arguments about relations of power within the family, arguments that would support his position on relations of power in the state. These conundrums become more visible when Locke is viewed against the background of his whig contemporaries, who faced the same challenges.

ALGERNON SIDNEY[2]

Women and children are patriarchs; and the next in blood, without any regard to age, sex, or other qualities of mind or body, are fathers of as many nations as fall under their power.[3]

This is how Algernon Sidney described the logical consequences of Sir Robert Filmer's political theory. As an accurate description of what Filmer actually thought, it is at best dubious. Filmer, as we saw, did not emphasize the rights of the 'next in blood' to inherit crowns. But casting Filmer as a defender of indefeasible hereditary right allowed Sidney to put forward an outrageous paradox: in a system of hereditary succession, women and children can become 'patriarchs'. Patriarchalism (defined by Sidney as a doctrine of hereditary succession) may thus undermine patriarchy (the power of fathers over children and husbands over wives). The theme of Filmer as the destroyer of patriarchy and therefore of the natural order of society runs throughout Sidney's work, and is responsible for much of its emotional power.

Filmer, Sidney thinks, threatens real paternal authority by setting up 'chimerical fathers' (that is, kings) to supplant natural ones.[4] Sidney chooses to take Filmer's equation of fathers and kings literally in order to render it perverse. For example, picking up on Filmer's acknowledgement that kingship by conquest can be legitimate, Sidney suggests that this would, in Filmer's language, make the conqueror the 'son' of the ruler he conquered, and therefore a parricide: 'Filmer alone is subtle enough to discover that Jehu, by extinguishing the house of Ahab, drew an obligation of looking on him as his father'.[5] Sidney revels in the incestuous possibilities of patriarchalist metaphors:

> If Claudius was the father of the Roman people, I suppose the chaste Messalina was
> the mother, and to be honoured by virtue of the same commandment ['honour thy
> father and mother']: But when [*sic*] I fear that such as met her in the most obscure
> places, were not only guilty of adultery, but of incest.[6]

Filmer is thus a violator rather than an upholder of the natural order; he
'delights in monsters'.[7]

Sidney's perception that hereditary monarchy and patriarchalist metaphors
are somehow obscene must be placed in the context of his larger political
preoccupations. Sidney is often described by scholars as a 'classical republican' or 'neo-Harringtonian'.[8] Although the identifying content and even the
distinct existence of that tradition remain a matter of debate, some aspects of
Harrington's thought were important in shaping Sidney's.[9] First, Sidney as a
younger son responded to Harrington's virulent hatred of primogeniture (the
reader will recall the remark about drowning puppies quoted in the last
chapter). Second, Sidney was preoccupied, like Harrington, with the problem
of change and corruption.

According to Harrington, the government had collapsed in 1640 because of
an imbalance between the structure of landholding and the structure of
political authority. The previous concentration of land, and hence military
power, in the hands of the landed nobility had formed the basis for the ancient
'gothic' constitution (essentially a monarchy with the king dependent upon,
and reined in by, a powerful nobility). Now, however, land had progressively
fallen into the hands of commoners, rendering the ancient constitution
obsolete. It was necessary to bring 'empire' (that is, power based on property)
into line with 'authority' (that is, the constitution), or vice versa.

Sidney did not adopt all aspects of Harrington's analysis.[10] But Harrington's
notion that different political systems were appropriate to different situations
supplied Sidney with a comparative, almost anthropological approach to many
aspects of his argument. For example, he catalogued the variety of systems of
succession across cultures to prove that no single one is divinely ordained. The
same method allowed him to treat the conventions of marriage and legitimacy
as socially constructed and politically contingent.

Sidney also took from Harrington an interest in the problem of how to keep
a polity healthy over time; this, for Sidney, did not require stasis, but rather the
capacity to respond creatively to changing circumstances. From this perspective, hereditary succession to the throne was the epitome of both instability
and stagnation. Far from providing continuity, it left a nation vulnerable to the
whims of the fools, madmen, women, and children who happen to inherit the
throne. Moreover, legitimate succession was no guarantee of stability because
the concept of legitimacy itself was flawed. Rules of succession varied across
cultures, and no matter how well defined a nation's laws might be, there was
still room for ambiguity and human choice. For example, 'we often see that

marriages which have been contracted, and for a long time taken to be good, have been declared null', as in the case of Henry of Navarre and Marguerite de Valois. Likewise, 'bastards may be thought legitimate, and legitimate sons bastards'.[11] No people, Sidney asserts, would be

> so careless of their most important concernments, as to leave them in such uncertainty, and simply to depend upon the humour of a man, or the faith of a woman, who besides their other frailties have been often accused of suppositious births: and men's passions are known to be so violent in relation to the women they love or hate, that none can safely be trusted with those judgements.[12]

Marriage and legitimacy are thus legal and political concerns, not natural facts. Reliance upon hereditary succession to provide smooth political transitions creates more disputes than it resolves.

On all of these grounds, Sidney found hereditary monarchy repellent. Moreover, he tied his criticism of it to his defence of political equality and popular sovereignty against Filmerian absolutism. The problem of how authority is transferred from one generation to the next is central to Sidney's argument against patriarchalism as a political theory. Sidney has no trouble accepting the patriarchalist scenario of original sovereign authority residing in Adam or Noah. He regards paternal power, both in the beginning of society and in real families, as legitimate and natural. He balks, however, at the notion that paternal authority can be inherited from a father by one of his sons. A brother cannot assume a position of authority over his own brethren, for 'no man can be my father but he that did beget me; and it is absurd to say that I owe that duty to one who is not my father, which I owe my father, as to say he did beget me, who did not beget me'.[13]

> Having proved, that the right of fathers is from nature and incommunicable, it must follow, that every man doth perpetually owe all love, respect, service, and obedience, to him that did beget, nourish, and educate him, and to no other under that name. No man can therefore claim the right of father over any, except one that is so; no man can serve two masters; the extent and perpetuity of the duty which every man owes to his father, renders it impossible for him to owe the same to any other: this right of the father cannot be devolved to the heir of the father ... no man can owe to his brother that which he owed to his father, because he cannot receive that from him which he had from his father.[14]

Sidney's objection to primogeniture rests, then, upon the claim that what is appropriate in the relationship between father and son is not appropriate in relations among brothers. If fatherhood is incommunicable, then all sons must inherit equally.

Brotherhood for Sidney is thus both the metaphor for, and the supposed origin of, political equality. He draws an idealized picture of the Israelites as brothers. 'We cannot find a more perfect picture of freemen living together than Abraham and Lot'. The same goes for their descendants: 'there was no lord, slave, or vassal; no strife was to be among them: they were brethren'.[15]

It is precisely because Sidney believes that fatherhood is incommunicable that he can reconcile his vision of fraternal equality with an endorsement of paternal authority. Although he always invokes brotherhood as a political metaphor ('by nature we are all brethren')[16] he refuses to challenge the power of fathers,

> for the question is not concerning the power that every householder in London hath over his wife, children and servants; but whether they are all perpetually subject to one man and family; and I intend not to set up their wives, prentices and children against them.[17]

Indeed, Sidney is even willing to complain that the laws of England give children too much 'equality' with their fathers, 'from which proceed many ill effects'.[18] Sidney thus employs Harringtonian modes of explanation to reconcile paternal authority and fraternal equality. Change over time (the rise of a new generation) necessitates a change in the structures of authority; the equality of sons does not invalidate the father's rule, but rather confirms it as absolute and incommunicable. Ironically, the scepticism and cultural relativism implicit in Harringtonian thought were put to the service of the patriarchal familial order.

WILLIAM LAWRENCE[19]

William Lawrence provides a fascinating point of comparison with Algernon Sidney. Whereas the two writers share a wholly positive view of paternal power (and worry about threats to it), they differ radically on the question of hereditary succession. Whereas Sidney criticized hereditary succession to the throne on the grounds that it subverted the natural, hierarchical, patriarchal order of families, Lawrence upheld hereditary right but criticized relations of power within actual families.

Lawrence's *Marriage by the moral law of God vindicated* (1680) is not a formal work of political theory, nor a response to Filmer's *Patriarcha*. Alone amongst the texts considered here, it is the one that seems to be more about the family than about politics. Lawrence is in some ways the most willing of all the writers discussed here to question the existing family and gender order. Indeed, as Mark Goldie has noted, he exaggerates its evils to radicalize his case.[20] It may, in fact, be the absence of overt polemical content that frees Lawrence of the necessity of presenting himself as a conventional thinker on issues of gender.

Nonetheless, it is appropriate to treat Lawrence as a whig exclusionist writer. He combined the virulent anti-Catholic sentiment that energized much of the exclusion movement with a reverence for 'liberty' and 'property', both of which are allegorized as female figures on the title page of *Marriage by the moral law of God*. There is, moreover, some evidence that Lawrence's books were financed by the Earl of Shaftesbury.[21] Lawrence's argument that marriage is constituted by the act of sexual union itself and not by a formal ceremony involving a priest, and that therefore all children can be considered the legitimate children of their fathers and have a right to inherit from them, was directly applicable to the case of the Duke of Monmouth, Charles II's eldest and 'illegitimate' son. The relevance of his argument to Monmouth's claims is even clearer in the next volume that Lawrence published in the same year, *The right of primogeniture in succession to the kingdoms of England, Scotland and Ireland*, which promised on its title page to prove 'that to compass or imagine the death, exile or disinheriting of the King's eldest son is high treason' and to answer 'all objections against declaring him [Monmouth] a protestant successor'. He thus brought together several disparate ideological elements within the whig exclusionist coalition (anti-popery, concerns for property, support for Monmouth) and joined them to his own apparently idiosyncratic ideas about the reform of laws regarding marriage, bastardy, and inheritance to form an apparently seamless whole.

Lawrence's 'anti-Popery' requires some explanation. At one level, it was just that, directed literally against Catholics like the Duke of York. But, like the 'hot Protestants' of the Elizabethan and early Stuart Church, and like the dissenters of the Restoration, Lawrence's anti-popery was also directed at the insufficiently reformed aspects of the Church of England: its courts, its bishops, and its clergy.[22] Using the classic rhetoric of Protestant reform, Lawrence claimed to uphold the original 'moral law of God' derived from the scriptures against all other codes. He indicted not only the laws of Muslims, Jews and pagans but also the ecclesiastical laws of the Church of England, dubbing them the 'popish canons' on grounds that they reflected a Roman Catholic influence that had never been shaken off at the Reformation.

In this opinion, Lawrence was not alone. A similar argument had already been made during the Roos divorce case, which was heard in the House of Lords in 1669. A small but vocal minority of clergymen had invoked Matthew 5:32 ('whosoever shall put away his wife, saving for the cause of fornication, causeth her to commit adultery') to support the legality of divorce *a vinculo* (that is, a complete dissolution of marriage) on grounds of adultery. The existing prohibition on all divorce (that is, except divorce *a mensa et thoro*, without the right of the injured party to remarry) was characterized by them as a popish doctrine. 'I know not why they should be called the Church of England, that join with the Council of Trent, and plead so much to uphold it', wrote John Cosin, one of the two bishops to support Roos's bill for divorce in the House of Lords.[23] Lawrence sharply differed from Bishop Cosin and his ilk, however, in that he singled out for opprobrium not merely popish laws, but the power of priests and bishops.

Although the emotional force of *Marriage by the moral law of God* derives from a specifically anti-Catholic mythology regarding the lewdness and greed of Catholic priests, the actual target is the power of *all* clergy over marriage. Lawrence juxtaposes 'marriage by the moral law of God' with marriage defined by the 'ceremonial law'. The former is defined by the sexual union of the parties, the latter by the exchange of vows before a priest. Whereas by the moral law of God the validity of a marriage is determined by the parties involved, who are the only ones who know for certain whether a marriage has taken place, the 'popish canons' put the power to decide whether a marriage occurred in the hands of an external authority, the priest. This means that legal marriages do not necessarily reflect sexual 'truth'. Lawrence is particularly concerned with how this discrepancy affects definitions of legitimacy and bastardy. Because the laws assume that any child born within wedlock is legitimate, regardless of whether the husband is the biological father or not, they have the effect (and the choice of words is not accidental here) of 'transubstantiating the children of the wife into the children of the husband'.[24] The crucial distinction for Lawrence is thus between the certainty of private experience, upheld by the moral law of God, and the inauthenticity of the public record, which the ceremonial law maintains.

The privileging of the public fiction of marriage over its sexual truth, according to Lawrence, threatens property rights and political order. It gives priests and bishops the final say in determining the succession of kingdoms. The failure to recognize the claims of the Duke of Monmouth simply because Charles II had not formally married Monmouth's mother, Lucy Walter, is obviously the case in point. The law of entails, which constrains men to pass on property to their so-called 'legitimate' children, and gives them no choice about which children will inherit, is also a particular bugbear for Lawrence. He uses it to symbolize the destruction of patriarchy by conspiracy of priests and women. In his imaginary history, 'the first form of government instituted in families by God and nature', was overthrown by 'the priests of Priapus and Venus', who

> for the forementioned ends of satisfying their own lust, covetousness, and ambition first prohibited all marriage except by a priest in a temple, then entailing all estates to the heirs, lawfully begotten of the body of the woman married by the priest, and the priest to be judge both of the marriage, and the lawful begetting; by this the priest ... got a greater dominion over the woman and the children, than the husband or father, for he [the husband] was not to be judge whether the wife or children were his, but the priest ... and thereby the hierarchy of the priest, the gynarchy of the wife, and paedarchy of the sons, necessarily arising from such principles, turned the poor patriarch out of doors, and took his goods, when, and as they pleased.[25]

In this manner the law of entails becames 'a screen to adulteries and adulterous successions, and thereby [the priests'] power over women, without which no sacerdotal empire can subsist'.[26]

The link between popery and femininity, so evident in the passage above, is a standard theme in anti-Catholic propaganda of the seventeenth century; it is therefore not surprising that there is a strong misogynist element in Lawrence's work. However, to read *Marriage by the moral law of God* simply as a case of misogyny put to the service of anti-popery is to miss its most interesting ingredients. Alongside his portrait of women as exploiters of men, Lawrence also develops an analysis of women's exploitation by men, both outside and inside marriage.

The plight of unmarried women is, for Lawrence, the obverse of the privilege of adulteresses. The ceremonial law, he argues, 'encourages fathers to deflower virgins, and when got with child, to desert both the mother and the child'.[27] 'Whereas by the unquestionable law of God, if the greatest peer lie with a beggar, whom he may lawfully marry, and get her with child, he lawfully makes her his wife'.[28] In declaring that there is no such thing as a bastard, that all children are entitled to inherit from their natural fathers and each woman can consider herself the wife of the man with whom she has had intercourse, Lawrence implicitly takes the side of seduced and abandoned women and challenges the sexual double standard. Significantly, he does not question the veracity of unmarried mothers' claims about the identity of the fathers of their children.

We may regard Lawrence's views on this subject as in one sense traditional. They hearken back to the practices of churchwardens and poor-relief commissioners, who questioned unmarried mothers about the paternity of their children in the hope of holding the biological father financially responsible for his offspring. In another sense, they are prophetic: they look forward to the writings of the French feminist Olympe de Gouge, who in her *Declaration of the rights of woman* (1791) argued that the liberty of free speech was one of the most precious rights of woman, 'since that liberty assures the recognition of children by their fathers. Any female citizen thus may say freely, I am the mother of a child which belongs to you'.[29] But however we label these views, they are significantly different from those of his fellow whigs. James Tyrrell, for example, believed that 'no man is obliged to take care of or breed up a bastard, because the mother, if she had her liberty of keeping what company she pleased, can never morally assure him that the child is his'.[30] Locke, as we saw in Chapter 1, assumed that the 'security of the marriage bed' is necessary for the raising of children. Lawrence is unusual among whigs in his belief that marriage is not necessary to organize the transfer of property between generations.

Lawrence also subverts existing socio-sexual arrangements in his critique of the legal doctrine of coverture (that is, as Blackstone put it, that 'the husband and wife are one person in law, and that person is the husband'). The same anti-Catholic metaphor unites this critique to his argument about legitimacy. Just as the law of legitimacy 'transubstantiates' the children of the wife into the children of the husband, so too the law of coverture conflates the identities of the wife and husband, 'transubstantiating' the woman into the man. This time, however, the transubstantiation is largely at the woman's expense. Although Lawrence is careful to point out that a woman might gain from coverture by being able to run up debts in her husband's name, he dwells at length on how coverture renders women vulnerable. Women in marriage 'lose all the right of propriety in their own goods to the husband ... as if they had been bought by him for slaves at a market'.[31] A woman has no legal recourse against her husband if he abuses her. Worse, if another man ravishes her, she cannot take action without her husband's help; this, Lawrence points out, means that a husband might allow his wife to be raped in return for money. Finally, the law of coverture 'encourageth vile persons to rob the noble and rich of their daughters, and makes the city of London so insecure for young ladies, that few great fortunes escape from being betrayed to persons unworthy of them'.[32]

Lawrence ends with an eloquent plea that women's legal personhood within marriage be recognized:

> Whereas it is well known men and women of all estates and conditions, if they have not been before a priest in a temple, will live forty years together in one house and dare not rob, beat, or injure one another, because they have liberty to sue for damage, which benefit this sottish sacrament of priests, and lawyers, gives not persons transubstantiated. A law would be thought very absurd and unjust, which should enact, that no man or woman should sue one another in the commonwealth; what horrible wickednesses and villainies would be committed by the two sexes, one against another ... But men and their wives are chained together, and cannot avoid the injuries of one another; and have no remedy unless they have the same liberty too for injury and propriety of their own, as all other subjects have, and not compelled to live as outlaws, deprived of benefit of law.[33]

Lawrence thus makes a strong case for recognizing the separate identities of the parties within marriage, rather than subsuming them in a single identity. It is ironic that, in the name of protecting the patriarchalist principle of hereditary succession, he should offer more of a challenge to the gender and familial order than does the 'anti-patriarchalist' Algernon Sidney. It is even stranger that in his insistence that a man and his wife in marriage are separate people he proves to be more 'contractarian' than the political contractarians, Tyrrell and Locke. To them we now turn.

JAMES TYRRELL[34]

James Tyrrell's *Patriarcha non monarcha. The patriarch unmonarch'd* has one of the catchiest titles of any work of political theory written in the late seventeenth century. For all that, the book is rarely discussed by scholars. This is all too understandable. Reading Tyrrell's text is a maddening experience. His train of thought is often difficult to follow, full of ambiguities and apparent contradictions. Moreover, as David Wootton has pointed out, irregularities in the book's pagination indicate that Tyrrell changed his mind sometime during the process of printing.[35] This analysis of Tyrrell's treatment of the family will put those ambiguities and contradictions centre stage, and thus call attention to Tyrrell's ambivalence both about the status of the family within political argument and the way in which power within the family ought to be distributed and regulated. Tyrrell's confusion is both a product of his larger polemical strategy and a reflection of the debates surrounding the family that were discussed in Chapter 1.

Unlike Sidney and Lawrence, Tyrrell is more concerned with the character of political authority than with the mechanisms by which it is transferred. He is also, of all the whigs considered here, the one most prone to treat the family as an analogy for the state. A discussion of power in the family plays a prominent but elusive role in Tyrrell's book. Its status in the argument is not clear. On the one hand, Tyrrell asserts that kings and fathers are separate, and that there is no paternal origin of kingly power because fathers cannot transfer their paternal power to anyone else.[36] On the other hand, the family serves in *Patriarcha non monarcha* as model for the state. If a father cannot brutalize his children, Tyrrell argues, a king cannot do so to his subjects. In making this leap, Tyrrell plays into the very family–state analogy he claims to reject.

This two-pronged approach might be explained as the work of an unsystematic thinker who, in constructing an argument against Filmer, uses every possible argument indiscriminately. But it is hard not to suspect that Tyrrell is driven to talk about the family beyond the call of polemical wisdom; it is as if, having taken up the family polemically, he cannot let it go. His treatment of the family does not always help his case and is not entirely coherent. Why, then, does he bother with it?

Tyrrell's discussion of the family is best understood as an aspect of his effort to establish himself as a 'moderate'. As Peter Lake has argued, 'moderation' was a key term of legitimation in seventeenth-century political and religious discourse; it was claimed by people of all persuasions. They could do so, of course, because the definition of 'moderation' was subjective: what one considered moderate depended upon where one marked the extremes.[37]

Tyrrell's claims to moderation are conspicuous in *Patriarcha non monarcha*. The book's frontispiece sports a picture of Charles II; to emphasize his loyalty,

Tyrrell states in the preface that his book is directed as much against 'those who would destroy this ancient government, and set up a democracy amongst us', as against defenders of absolutism, 'since I know not which is worse, to be knawn to death by rats, or devoured by a lion'.[38] However, the nature of Tyrrell's *political* moderation remains unclear. The historian David Wootton has argued, legitimately, that – in comparison to Locke – Tyrrell was moderate, in the sense that his work offered no justification for revolution.[39] At the same time, it is hard to give a positive content to Tyrrell's moderation. For one thing, he is rather vague about actual political institutions, structures and situations. Moreover, Tyrrell's claims to moderation cannot be treated at face value. For example, the fact that Tyrrell picks 'democracy' to represent one of two extremes – and it is important to remember here that democracy was considered extreme by Locke as well – might indicate that he wants to push the 'centre' as far to the left as possible; that is, he needs to posit the existence of radical democrats in order to make himself look moderate. In any case, it is significant that the Tory writer Edmund Bohun read Tyrrell, despite his claims to moderation, as covertly sanctioning revolution (see below). For Bohun, of course, Filmer was a 'moderate' who had been unfairly labelled an absolutist extremist![40]

'Moderation' is an elusive category, both for the historian and for Tyrrell himself. The well-ordered family, however, seems to provide Tyrrell with a terrain on which he can put forward his claims to moderation in a more sure-footed way. By describing proper relationships in families, in a way that does not give 'an extravagant power to parents on the one hand to abuse their power, or a privilege to children on the other side to be stubborn or disobedient to their parents'[41] he can make the elusive political middle ground seem easily grasped in terms of everyday experience and common sense. He can establish conservative credentials, showing both a commitment to hierarchy and a faith that those who wield power have the good of their subjects at heart; at the same time, he can assert that the good of subjects is the natural limit to power. For Tyrrell, the family is 'good to think with'.

On second thoughts, the family turns out not to be so good to think with. Characteristically, Tyrrell's writing grows ever more convoluted when he discusses power in the family. There are two broad areas of difficulty in Tyrrell's writing on the family. The first arises from his treatment of the problem of domestic violence. The second arises from the fact that he treats wifehood as if it were analogous to slavery. In both areas, Tyrrell raises more questions than he answers about the proper nature of familial relationships.

The most striking feature of *Patriarcha non monarcha* is its stark and frequent acknowledgement of the existence of violence within families. Paternal power, Tyrrell asserts, is justified because and insofar as it promotes the good of the family. But what if it ceases to be benevolent? Like Locke,

Tyrrell calls up images of paternal savagery which can be metaphorically associated with Filmerian absolutism. But whereas Locke locates this paternal savagery in far away Peru, Tyrrell perceives it close to home. In Tyrrell's *Bibliotheca politica* (1692), a treatise cast in the form of a dialogue, the Williamite Freeman asks if a wife has a right to resist if her husband tries to kill her; when his Jacobite opponent, Meanwell, responds that such cases 'rarely happen', Freeman exclaims:

> Rarely happen! I see you are not very conversant at the Old Bailey, nor at our country assizes; where if you please to come, you may often hear of cases of this nature.[42]

He then goes on to chide Meanwell: as a lawyer in the church courts, surely Meanwell has seen plenty of suits brought by wives for separation, and cannot doubt but that 'husbands do often use their wives so ill, that it is not to be endured'.[43] Thus, the violence that Tyrrell wants us to imagine occuring in families is not meant to be taken as purely hypothetical.

Patriarcha non monarcha contains a dramatic catalogue of paternal abuses. The danger of fathers injuring their children is greater than that of children becoming over-enthusiastic about their own rights:

> for looking on themselves as having an absolute and unquestionable power over them, and that they may deal with them as they please, [fathers] are apt to think themselves slighted and disobeyed by their children, perhaps on very light occasions; and their passion often rises to that height (as not considering the follies and inconsiderateness of youth) that they may, if choleric or ill-natured, strike them with that which may either kill them, or else cripple or maim them; perhaps out of an immoderate anger, or being weary of them, murder them on purpose.[44]

Tyrrell also considers less drastic threats to a child's well-being: Suppose, for example, that

> Adam had been so cruel and unnatural (as some fathers are) and being sensible of the profit he received from his sons labours, would never have given them leave to have left his family, and have set up for themselves, nor to have had anything of their own, but (only allowing them and their wives a bare subsistence) have kept them like slaves as long as they lived?[45]

Tyrrell's discussion of violence leaves him with a problem, however. Having convinced his readers of the undesirability of absolute paternal authority, he has not explained what is to stop a father from exercising it. He appears to believe that children and wives have something like a right of resistance against paternal or conjugal abuse. For example,

> no man will deny but it is lawful for children to hold, nay bind their mad or drunken parents, in case they cannot otherwise hinder them from doing mischief, or killing either themselves, their mothers or brethren.[46]

Likewise, if a father 'should go about to violate his son's wife in his presence or to kill her, or his grandchildren, I suppose he may as lawfully use the same means for their preservation ... as he might for his own'.[47] The threat, however, need not be as dire as rape or murder:

> suppose the husband in such a [mad or drunken] fit should command his wife to deliver him a sum of money which she had in her keeping, when she was morally sure that he would presently play it or otherwise squander it away; will any rational man affirm that a wife may not deny to deliver her husband his own money in such circumstances?'[48]

At the same time, Tyrrell needs to show himself as firm supporter of patriarchal authority. Denying that there can be two heads of a family, he asserts that except in unusual cases where the husband cannot govern, 'the wife in all matters peculiar to the marriage-bed, and in all other things that relate to the well-ordering of the family, is obliged to submit her will to that of her husband'.[49] Moreover, the husband can enforce this submission through physical punishment, 'as I do not deny but perhaps it may be lawful for the husband, as head of the family, in some cases, if the wife prove palpably obstinate and disobedient to his reasonable commands, and will not hearken to reason, to compel her by correction'.[50]

Can Tyrrell posit a right of resistance to abuse without, ultimately, under-mining the authority he claims to uphold? Tyrrell's attempts to resolve this dilemma lead him into further quandaries and make for confusing reading. As the tentativeness of the last quotation (loaded as it is with qualifiers like 'perhaps', 'may', and 'in some cases') might suggest, Tyrrell is hunting for limits. The 'good of the family' might be taken to provide a criterion for distinguishing legitimate from illegitimate violence – except that Tyrrell never tells us who gets to decide what the 'good of the family' is. Alternatively, Tyrrell at times distinguishes between extreme violence, which as seen above can be resisted, from non-extreme violence which must be suffered passively. Although children, he asserts, have the right to defend their lives from their father's unjust violence, 'yet I would not be here understood to give children this right of resisting upon any less occasion ... For we are obliged by the law of Christ to bear smaller injuries from others, much more from a father'.[51] But on the other hand, we might also recall that some of the cases in which Tyrrell has said that the patriarch might be disobeyed (for example, when a father prohibits his son from marrying, when a husband demands money from his wife for gambling) do not involve the threat of death or injury.

It is virtually impossible to combine these assertions into a coherent account of who has the right to do what to whom in the family. Tyrrell never tells us how we know what the 'good of the family' is, or how to draw the line between injuries that may be resisted and those that must be borne. The tory

Edmund Bohun, in his preface to the 1685 edition of Filmer's *Patriarcha*, homed in on Tyrrell's vagueness concerning the question of judgement. Thus, Tyrrell's seemingly unproblematic notion that mad and drunk husbands can be legitimately resisted provokes a question from Bohun: 'Suppose they [a husband and a wife] should mutually charge each other with madness or drinking too much, who should judge betwixt them?'[52] Bohun thought that Tyrrell offered a covert justification of revolution: how could all of these instances in which Tyrrell encourages subordinates to consider resistance (rather than passive suffering) *not* also encourage political rebellion?

The conclusions that Bohun derives from Tyrrell's work are precisely the ones that Tyrrell tries to avoid. Tyrrell bends over backwards to avoid sanctioning revolution, or even the subversion of hierarchical authority. To do so, he relies upon the manipulation of language. His attempt to redefine the resistance of wives and children to abuse in such a way that it does not need to be considered an attack on patriarchal authority is a case in point. When a son defends himself from an attack by his father, Tyrrell explains, he is not usurping paternal authority because he is not presuming to act as his father's 'superior'. He is merely exercising a right to self-preservation, which he has as an equal to his father: 'if a son have any right to defend himself in what belongs to him from the unjust violence of his father, he doth not act as his superior; but in this case as his equal, as he is indeed in all the rights of nature, considered only as a man'.[53]

> Suppose a son cannot otherwise preserve his own life, or that of his mother, or brothers from the rage of his mad or drunken father; but by holding him, or binding him, if need be; I suppose no reasonable man will deny the lawfulness of this action; and yet this power over his father's person is not authoritative, or civil, but moral, and which the son does exercise not as superior to his father, but as a rational creature obliged by the laws of nature, to preserve his own being, and to endeavour the good preservation of his parents and relations, not against paternal authority (which is always rational, and for the good of the family) but brutish, irrational force: which God gives every man a right to judge of.[54]

Moreover, although the passage quoted above makes no mention of resistance stronger than 'holding' or 'binding', Tyrrell says elsewhere that if the father is accidentally killed in such a struggle, 'I think his blood is upon his own head'.[55] Notions of divine providence are invoked to explain that if such a son injures his father, he could be said to have functioned as the instrument of God's punishment of his father: 'For God may sometimes appoint those for the instruments of his justice, who otherwise do injury to the person punished; as in the case of Absalom's rebellion against his father David'.[56]

One can see why Bohun was worried. Tyrrell preserves the principle of patriarchal authority largely through a play on words that make challenges to that principle acceptable because they are called something else. Yet, Bohun's verdict that Tyrrell intends covertly to undermine patriarchal authority is not entirely valid. The fact that Tyrrell bends over backwards to reconcile the principle of self-preservation with the inviolability of paternal authority suggests the depth of his commitment to the latter.

The fact that Tyrrell chooses to discuss wives and slaves in the same breath prompts similarly contradictory thoughts about the nature of his commitment to the principle of familial hierarchy. The equation of slaves (or servants) and wives is implicit in the structure of *Patriarcha non monarcha*. Slaves and wives are discussed next to one another in the same section of the book.[57] Moreover, Tyrrell's discussion of marriage is permeated by the language of slavery. This in itself is striking. As Margaret Sommerville points out, it was a cliché in the early modern period that a wife was different from a slave or servant.[58] One may, then, interpret the very fact that he equates them as a subversive feminist statement. Insofar as his choice to discuss marriage and slavery together dictates that he acknowledges the element of power (rather than love or reciprocity) in the marital relationship, such a judgement is fair. But the equation does not in itself proceed from a desire to question the gender order. Indeed, Tyrrell finds a way to justify the fact that wives can be treated as slaves, and that both wives and slaves are treated rather badly.

Why, then, does Tyrrell emphasize the analogy between wives and slaves? His choice is dictated by the fact that he wants to distinguish both relationships from that of fatherhood. What marriage and slavery have in common, he tells us, is the fact that in both cases the male head of household has power over other individuals through his position *as* head of household, rather than as a father *per se*. Thus, if we want to know how Tyrrell treats wifehood and slavery, we have to know how he treats fatherhood.

Tyrrell begins his discussion of fatherhood by setting up a tory straw man. He refers vaguely to 'some writers' who think fathers have absolute power over their children because they beget them.[59] This is of course easy to refute. He triumphantly invokes the fact that paternal identity is uncertain, and that fatherhood cannot exist without the institution of matrimony:

> It is evident that this power of fathers over their children, can only take place in a state of wedlock; as to children got out of marriage, it is uncertain who is their father: who can only be known by the declaration of the mother; and she sometimes cannot certainly tell her self.[60]

Similarly,

> [If] the man being master of his wife, is by the contract so likewise of her issue: Then it follows, that this power of the father does not commence barely from generation, but is acquired from the contract of marriage.[61]

The observation that paternity requires marriage helps Tyrrell to argue that the power of fathers does not come from generation, but exists so that they can care for their children. It cannot be a power over life and death because fathers cannot be said to give their children life. Tyrrell may also want to suggest that fatherhood cannot be considered the original political relationship, because it requires a prior relationship (marriage) in order to exist.

Ironically, in refuting a tory straw man, Tyrrell has come close to the position that, as we saw, was actually held by Filmer himself. Tyrrell seems to be aware that Filmer's arguments about Adam's power over Eve and her children did not hinge upon the fact that Adam was a father, but rather on the fact that he had power over Eve, and *therefore* over her children.

> The author [Filmer] seems to found this power [of the patriarchs over their families] upon ... God's ordinance there should be civil government, because *Gen. 3:16* God ordained Adam to rule over his wife, and her desire was to be subject to his; and that as hers, so all theirs that should come out of her'.[62]

Moreover, Tyrrell takes the point on board:

> Since this power of Adam over Eve and her children, cannot be pretended to belong to him as a father, but as a master of a slave, and those that shall be descended from her; it were worth while to enquire, what power a father or master of a family can claim separate from any commonwealth (as we will suppose these patriarchs were).[63]

Tyrrell's gleeful acknowledgement of the fact that paternal identity is uncertain thus commits him to the position that a man is, in some sense, 'master' of his wife. For this reason, he puts wives and slaves into the same category.

Tyrrell insists, however, that wifehood and slavery are both contractual relationships. He thereby distinguishes his own position from Filmer's. Having recognized that the power of a father over his children must come through a husband's position as 'master of his wife', he is willing to suggest that the terms of that mastery are subject to negotiation. Indeed, he imagines that women might have authority over their offspring:

> I see not why it might not be so agreed by the contracts, that the father should not dispose of the children without the mother's consent: since we see it often so agreed in the marriages of sovereign princes, who are always supposed to be in a state of nature in respect to each other.[64]

This is not to say, however, that Tyrrell relishes the idea of sole maternal power. It is probably no accident that the two women whom he cites in *Patriarcha non monarcha* as examples of sovereign princes who contracted to retain control over their children are Mary Tudor and Mary Queen of Scots, figures who would have been highly unpopular with a seventeenth-century Protestant audience! Likewise, the unmarried woman exercising power over her offspring is not presented as a figure to be admired. Tyrrell makes fun of Bodin's claim that fathers have the right to put their children to death by pointing out that 'upon Bodin's principle, women that murder their bastards would have a good time on't, because having no husbands, they would have full power over the life of their children'.[65] Thus, the unmarried infanticidal mother is the *reductio ad absurdum* of Bodinian principles.

Tyrrell is thus ambivalent about the power which women might have if they did not contract to give it away. The same ambivalence surfaces again in the broader discussion of slaves and of wives. In each case, Tyrrell begins by emphasizing the flexible nature of the contract which establishes slavery and wifehood. He then, however, finds a way to deny to slaves and wives the exercise of the rights that he has just theoretically conferred upon them. Tyrrell's discussion of slavery is clearly motivated by his larger political agenda. By reassuring his reader that even slavery can be seen as a relationship in which the master's power has natural limits, he can show that there are natural limits to the power of kings as well. He affirms that because slavery is a personal contract, a slave cannot be sold by his master to another, or bequeathed to his master's heirs.[66] Likewise, if a slave is denied 'liberty' (from fetters) and the 'enjoyment of the ordinary comforts of life' (which are never specified), then 'I believe there is no sober planter in Barbados (who are most of them the assignees of slaves taken in war) but will grant such a slave may lawfully run away if he can'.[67]

Is this statement meant as a tribute to the fairmindedness of the planters, or as a subtle justification for resistance? The question cannot be resolved from Tyrrell's text itself. The characteristic and disturbing feature of Tyrrell's work is the elusiveness of its moral thrust. Tyrrell acknowledges that in real life slaves are not treated in accordance with his model. He handles this fact by making a distinction between the laws of nature and the 'civil law' (by which he means the laws of particular commonwealths). Thus, Tyrrell argues, 'though it is true that the cruelty and avarice of diverse nations hath proceeded so far, that slaves are reckoned amongst household goods, and are ordered not so much by command, as by the force of an absolute dominion and property: yet this is not from the law of nature, but the civil law of that particular commonwealth'.[68] Clearly, there is a discrepancy between the laws of nature on the one hand, and existing laws and institutions on the other. But what he wants to make of the discrepancy is unclear. Tyrrell never explains whether the 'law of nature' is normative; it is therefore hard to know whether he means to criticize existing institutions and practices which fail to conform to the workings of natural law as he describes it, or whether he simply accepts the fact that the law of nature and the laws of particular commonwealths may differ.

Tyrrell's discussion of marriage follows the same pattern. Here again, he makes the point that in a state of nature there can be no 'absolute dominion' (in the sense of a licence for the husband to do anything to his wife, even to kill her) because such power is not necessary to the purposes of marriage. He then, however, provides a conceptual loophole that explains how a husband might acquire a right to kill his wife. The wife might consent to conditions harsher than what the laws of nature require:

> I grant, that if she made it part of her bargain to be so absolutely subject to [her husband] that he might command her in all things as a slave, and make her her do what work he pleased to appoint, and that he may either turn her away or put her to death if he find her embezzling his goods or committing adultery; the woman in this case is bound by her contract, as another servant, who makes herself so by her own act or consent.[69]

Moreover, in real life the wife's consent to the hard bargain does not have to be personal. The same absolute power 'may likewise be conferred by the civil laws of particular commonwealths. Thus it is murder for a man in England to kill his wife taken in the very act of adultery, but it is not so in Spain, Italy, and most other countries'. [70]

Did Tyrrell mean his account of slavery and wifehood according to the 'law of nature' to provide a standard by which to judge and criticize existing laws and institutions? Or did he mean to justify the fact that in real life (that is, by the existing laws of particular nations) things are worse for wives and slaves than the law of nature would make them? Ultimately, it is impossible to tell. In his ambiguous text there is material supporting both readings. But even if Tyrrell wanted to refrain from criticizing existing institutions of marriage (and slavery), his book continually offers the reader an opportunity to do so. *Patriarcha non monarcha* seems to strain at its own boundaries and subvert its own conclusions. In comparison to Locke, however, two features of the book stand out: the fact that Tyrrell acknowledges the existence of violence in the family, and the fact that Tyrrell acknowledges the fact that paternal identity is uncertain. As we have seen, these points raise issues for Tyrrell that he does not fully resolve. It is striking that Locke manages to avoid such problems.

LOCKE AND TYRRELL COMPARED: PATERNAL BENEVOLENCE

> Fathers will be as apt to kill and maim their children, as children their fathers. (James Tyrrell)[71]

> God hath woven into the principles of humane nature such a tenderness for their offspring, that there is little fear that parents should use their power [of commanding and chastising] with too much rigour: the excess is seldom on the severe side, the strong bias of nature drawing the other way. (John Locke)[72]

> It may be objected that an enraged father may abuse the power which he has over the life and property of his children ... But if a father is not out of his mind, he will

never be tempted to kill his own child without cause ... The affection of parents for their children is so strong, that the law has always rightly presumed that they will do only those things which are of benefit and honour to their children. (Jean Bodin)[73]

David Wootton has recently suggested that Locke drafted his *Second treatise* after having read Tyrrell's *Patriarcha non monarcha*.[74] While his proposal is not essential for the analysis presented here, it would help to explain Locke's uncanny ability to sidestep the problematic issues over which Tyrrell stumbled. For example, Locke's famous claim that the family and the state were distinct allowed him to avoid having to define (as Tyrrell so awkwardly did) the limits of authority and resistance within families. Yet, on closer reading, the smooth surface that Locke presents is not so stable as it appears. The family–state distinction rests on shaky foundations (joint authority), is asserted rather than proven, and is invoked at moments of stress in the argument. It is hardly the majestic centrepiece of a coherent intellectual system from which all other ideas logically radiate.

The connections and differences between Tyrrell and Locke can be seen in their respective discussions of fatherhood. Both sharply contrast Filmer's enthusiasm for paternal tyranny with their own ethos of paternal or parental care. The care of offspring, they assert, is a natural parental instinct and a duty to God. For Tyrrell, 'both the instinct of nature and the law of reason dictate, that they [parents] are obliged to take care of and provide for that child, which they as subordinate causes have produced; as being those on whom God has imposed this duty'.[75] Locke writes that 'the nourishment and education of their children, is a charge so incumbent on parents for their children's good, that nothing can absolve them from taking care of it'.[76]

But Locke, unlike Tyrrell, never questions the idea that fathers or parents are naturally benevolent. All of Tyrrell's hypothetical scenarios of fathers murdering their children and raping their son's wives disappear from Locke's work; he does not mention familial violence, except when he is caricaturing Filmer. As the quotations printed at the head of this section demonstrate, Locke simply assumes that fathers are benevolent. Ironically, his view is closer to the absolutist Bodin's than to the contractarian Tyrrell's!

Moreover, Locke *cannot* question the assumption that fathers are naturally benevolent because that assumption is deeply embedded in the social and political arguments of the *Two treatises*. Paternal benevolence provides Locke not merely (as it did for Tyrrell) with a model for the purposes and limits of political authority, but with the critical link in a series of arguments about property, inheritance, conquest, and the relationship of the family and the state.

The natural benevolence of fathers, for example, is central to Locke's justification of the inheritance of property. Inheritance poses a problem for Locke because it sits uneasily with his famous account of how private property was established. In the beginning, Locke has told us, the earth was held in common by all mankind; the individual comes to own a piece of it by mixing his labour with it (rather than, as Filmer said, because he got it at the will of the king, who got it from God via the original grant to Adam or Noah). Obviously, the person who has inherited property did not gain it by mixing his labour with it. Acknowledging the discrepancy, Locke asks how children 'come by this right of possessing, before any other, the properties of their parents upon their decease?' Why does this property 'not return again to the common stock of mankind?' He answers that the inheritance of property by children is a natural right, which springs from the God-given character of parental love.

> God planted in men a strong desire also of propagating their kind, and continuing themselves in their posterity, and this gives children a title, to share in the property of their parents, and a right to inherit their possessions ... Men being by a like obligation bound to preserve what they have begotten, as to preserve themselves, their issue come to have a right in the goods they are possessed of.[77]

The existence of a natural right to inherit, once established, does much useful work for Locke. Along with his account of the invention of money,[78] the assertion that children have a natural right to inherit from their parents helps Locke to overcome the awkward discrepancy between his initial claim that property is acquired by labour and the obvious fact that many agricultural labourers in seventeenth-century England did not own the land upon which they toiled.

Moreover, many of the political arguments in the *Two treatises* hinge upon the claim that the inheritance of property is a natural right. Take, for example, Locke's denial that conquest can establish political authority. Even in the case of conquest in a just war, Locke argues, the conqueror only acquires a dominion over the lives and property of the individuals who made war against him. He cannot become a permanent ruler because this right does not extend to the lives and property of the innocent children of the guilty individuals:

> the [justly conquered] father, by his miscarriages and violence, can forfeit but his own life, but involves not his children in his guilt or destruction. His goods, which nature, that willeth the preservation of all mankind as much as is possible, hath made to belong to the children to keep them from perishing, do still continue to belong to his children.[79]

Even more importantly, the existence of a child's natural right to inherit allows Locke to make a strategically crucial distinction between the inheritance of property and the inheritance of political power.

> The right a son has to be maintained and provided with the necessaries and conveniences of life out of his father's stock, gives him a right to succeed to his

father's property for his own good, but this can give him no right also to succeed to the rule, which his father had over other men.[80]

This distinction in turn helps Locke, in the context of the exclusion crisis, to undercut the God-givenness of the Duke of York's indefeasible hereditary right to the throne without undermining (as the tories would have it) the property rights of English subjects. Moreover, it provides Locke with an alternative to Filmer's reading of biblical history. The 'birthright' which descended to the first-born sons of the patriarchs, says Locke, was only an entitlement to a larger share of the parents' goods, and not (as Filmer would have it) to political power.[81]

We can see now why Locke would want to avoid Tyrrell's hypothetical discussions of domestic violence: if paternal benevolence was something other than natural, it is not natural that children inherit their father's property; much of Locke's conceptual edifice would thereby crumble. It is not surprising, then, that Locke simply says less than did Tyrrell about how relationships in families work. Unlike Tyrrell, Locke resists the impulse to consider every possible scenario that might arise in the life-cycle of a family, and thereby occludes certain problems about the nature of power within it.

The difference between Locke and Tyrrell is evident in their respective accounts of the stages by which a child comes to maturity. Tyrrell divides the process into three periods. There is infancy, a time of 'imperfect judgement, or before the child comes to be able to exercise his reason'. Such a child is properly under the 'absolute dominion' of his parents. In the next stage, a child is of 'perfect' and 'mature' reason, but continues as part of his father's family and (with the usual maddening imprecision) 'they are still under their father's command, and ought to be obedient to it in all actions which tend to the good of their father's family and concerns'. In the third stage, the child leaves his father's house: while the obligation of gratitude to parent's continues, 'they are in all actions free, and at their own dispose'.[82]

Locke, by contrast, recognizes only two categories, which correspond to the first and third stages of Tyrrell's account. There is nonage, in which a child is so devoid of understanding that he needs a parent to understand and will on his behalf, so much so that he cannot even be considered unfree because he has no will of his own: 'Whilst he [the child] is in an estate, wherein he has not understanding of his own to direct his will, he is not to have any will of his own to follow: He that understands for him must will for him too'. And there is adulthood: when he arrives at the age of reason, 'the estate that made his father a freeman, the son is a freeman too'.[83] Locke says little about the intermediate step. He imagines maturation as a gradual process: the 'bonds of this subjection are like the swaddling clothes they are wrapped up in ... age and reason, as they grow up, loosen them till at length they drop quite off, and leave a man at his own free disposal'.[84]

But Locke passes over the situation of the adolescent who is only half-wrapped in swaddling clothes, the youth who (in Tyrrell's account) does possess reason but is nonetheless subject to his father. It is not hard to see why Locke does this. It is when the youth is in the transitional stage that it is easiest to imagine him engaging in reasonable resistance to paternal authority; and it is in recognizing that possibility that Tyrrell, as we saw, raised questions that he could not resolve about the legitimacy of resistance within families. By condensing and telescoping his description of the life-cycle of a family, Locke is able to ignore problematic questions about nature of paternal power over reasonable children.

Similarly, Locke sidesteps questions about the nature of conjugal authority by eliminating important aspects of Tyrrell's argument. As we saw, Tyrrell treated the husband–wife relationship as a variation upon the master–slave relationship; this approach was necessitated, moreover, by his acknowledgement that a man's relationship to his children is indirect, and occurs only through his relationship with his wife. Locke declines to take on board the insights and questions about conjugal authority that are generated by Tyrrell's acknowledgement that paternity is indirect, and paternal identity problematic. In this sense, he is the one seventeenth-century thinker about whom Carole Pateman is right: Locke may not believe in autogenous male generation, but he does ignore the problematic character of paternal identity.

Locke's deproblematization of paternal identity comes, ironically, at the very moment in the text where he seems to be elevating the role of women in reproduction. Feminist scholars favourably disposed toward Locke often contrast Locke with Filmer by pointing out that Locke, unlike Filmer, included mothers in the category of 'parent'.[85] If biology counts as a source of authority over children, Locke asserts, then mothers must be at least the equals of fathers: 'For whatever obligation nature and the right of generation lays on children, it must certainly bind them equal to both concurrent causes of it'.[86]

When it is put into textual and inter-textual context, however, this passage must be read as something less than an enhancement of women's power in the family. First, although the mother's role in biological generation is asserted, the importance of biological generation as a source of authority is undercut. Locke's remarks are presented as if for the sake of argument: if generation confers authority, then mothers have authority. But does it? Locke raises doubts: in I.54, for example, he reminds us that the real creator of children is God rather than parents. In the *Second treatise*, he cites the case of adoptive fathers of abandoned children to show that paternal power does not depend upon biological paternity.[87]

Second, when read in the context of what other seventeenth-century thinkers have said about maternity and paternity, Locke's emphasis on the roughly equal share of both parents in biological reproduction is remarkable not for its inclusion of the mother, but for its inclusion of the father. As we saw, Tyrrell and Sidney, for different reasons, both made much of the fact that biological paternity, unlike biological maternity, is always uncertain; Filmer himself did not deny this fact. It is striking, therefore, that at the moment when Locke asserts the important contribution that mothers make to the biological production of children, he likewise takes the father's contribution as a given.

If the difference between Locke and Filmer is that Locke includes the mother as an equal partner in generation (recall that Filmer had named the father as the 'nobler agent'), the difference between Locke and other whigs is that Locke includes the father as a partner at all. Of all the whig thinkers discussed in this chapter, Locke seems to be the least interested in making a sustained argument about the inherent unknowability of paternal identity. Although he demonstrates in passing an awareness that in some situations (for example, 'that part of the world where one woman hath more than one husband at a time') it would be impossible to have paternal power because one could never establish paternal identity,[88] Locke is more interested in the fact that children have two parents than in the fact that they can be certain of the identity only of one.

Locke's purpose in calling attention to the two parents in reproduction is not simply to deny the fact that the biological paternity of a particular father is unprovable. As we shall see, the duality of parenthood is important to a larger argument about the difference between parental and sovereign authority. Nonetheless, the effect of Locke's discovery – that authority over children is 'parental' rather than 'paternal' – is to make fatherhood a less problematic relationship for him than it is for Tyrrell. Tyrrell's picture of the family might be described as a linear chain of authority that runs from the father to the mother to the children; or, in the absence of marriage, simply from the mother to the children. Women always have a direct and immediate authority over their offspring, whereas men have a direct and immediate authority only over their wives.

While Tyrrell does not approve of sole maternal authority, it is for him a theoretical possibility. In Locke's model, by contrast, both the father and the mother have direct authority over the children. Instead of a single line of authority running from top to bottom, Locke gives us a two-sided triangle:

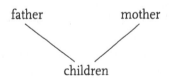

As is clear from this diagram, Locke's image of the family does not indicate the flow of power in the relationship between husband and wife. And this is precisely the point: by imagining the link between father and child to be direct rather than indirect, Locke can discuss paternal authority without reference to conjugal authority. He can avoid calling attention to the questions about power between the sexes and within marriage in the way that Tyrrell (albeit perhaps reluctantly) had done in both *Patriarcha non monarcha* and *Bibliotheca politica.*

Locke's chapter on 'Adam's title to sovereignty by subjection of Eve' in the *First Treatise* is the exception which proves the rule. Because the purpose of the chapter is to refute Filmer's claim that monarchy was established by God's curse on Eve in *Genesis* 3.16 ('in sorrow thou shalt bring forth children; and thy desire shall be to thy husband, and he shall rule over thee'), it is inevitable that Locke will focus on the nature of power within marriage. He drops the issue, however, after an inconclusive discussion.

Locke starts by asserting that God's curse on Eve in *Genesis* 3.16 does not have the status of a command but is merely a prediction of what usually happens. He notes that the phrase, 'in sorrow thou shalt bring forth children' has never been interpreted to mean that a woman ought not to avoid pain in childbearing if she can help it.[89] Similarly, in the second part of the curse, God 'only foretells what should be woman's lot, how by his providence he would order it so, that she should be subject to her husband, as that we see that generally the laws of mankind and the customs of nations have ordered it so; and there is, I grant, a foundation in nature for it'.[90] As an endorsement of marital equality as an ideal, this seems rather mealy-mouthed: if God did not order women to be subject, the arrangements that make them so are divinely ordained! In any case, Locke goes on to hedge his bets. He acknowledges in the next paragraph that even if God's words to Eve can be taken 'as a law to bind her and all other women to subjection', and 'if these words give any power to Adam', it can only be a conjugal rather than political power.[91]

It is interesting that Locke's drawing of the line between political and conjugal power comes at the end rather than the beginning of his discussion of *Genesis* 3.16. The invocation of the family–state distinction occurs at the very moment when his discussion of the family has become awkward. As part of his larger argument against Filmer, the move is entirely appropriate: Locke is able to strip *Genesis* 3.16 of political significance by distinguishing between the family and the state. He is not obligated to decide what it says about the family. But then, why discuss the family at all? The fact that Locke raised the question of whether the subjection of wives to husbands is God-given suggests that he found it important but not conveniently resolvable. Unlike Tyrrell, however, Locke has a way out: the family–state distinction. One wonders if it was constructed for precisely this purpose.

THE FAMILY–STATE DISTINCTION

Locke devotes far less detailed discussion to actual relationships in families than did Tyrrell. Two aspects of his conceptual framework make this possible. First, Locke is far more insistent than Tyrrell that the family and state are different from each other. This means that far less is at stake in his account of authority within the family. Second, Locke posits the existence of joint authority between parents in the family. This has the effect of flattening out what in Tyrrell's work was presented as a finely graded hierarchy of authority and responsibility within the home. Locke therefore does not have to wrestle with what it means to say that a wife is a sort of second-in-command to her husband, subordinate to him but almost as responsible as he is for the good of her children; he just asserts that she has equal authority. These two aspects of Locke's conceptual framework are connected: the fact that parental authority is shared by two people is for him the clinching argument that it is different from sovereign power, which by definition must reside with a single entity.

Together these two concepts (joint parental authority and the family–state distinction) provide the sword that allows Locke to cut the Gordian knot into which Tyrrell had twisted his arguments around questions of power in the family. Yet, if they help Locke to avoid some of the intellectual difficulties that faced Tyrrell, they create some of their own. Locke's use of these concepts is ultimately less straightforward and rigorous than his rhetoric would make one think.

Because the claim that parental authority is joint authority is so crucial to Locke's ability to establish the family–state distinction, it is worth examining carefully. Some difficulties are immediately obvious. For one thing, Locke does not sustain the claim consistently. In Chapter Seven of the *Second treatise*, for example, we learn that when a conflict arises between the husband and wife concerning 'things of their common interest and property', 'it therefore being necessary, that the last determination , that is, the rule, should be placed somewhere, it naturally falls to the man's share, as the abler and the stronger'.[92] Moreover, Locke offers no positive description of what joint parental authority would be like. This is not, perhaps, surprising. Given Locke's view that parental power actually involves understanding and willing on behalf of a child, it is hard to see how it could be shared by two people unless they had one understanding and will.

As Carole Pateman and Teresa Brennan have pointed out, it is at the very moment when he starts to talk about the nature of the authority exercised over a child that Locke slips into using the word 'paternal', and speaks in terms of fathers and sons: 'When he comes to the estate that made the father a freeman, the son is a freeman too;' 'If this made the father free, it shall make the son free too;' 'a child is free by his father's title, by his father's understanding'.[93] Locke's use of male terms in his discussion of authority stands in marked contrast to the sex-neutral language to which he returns when he takes up the subject of 'honour', which he distinguishes from obedience because children owe it to their parents all of their lives. The difference in language is evident even in the space of a single sentence. For example, 'the *subjection* of a minor places in the *father* a temporary government which terminates with the minority of the child: and the *honour* due from a child places in the *parents* a perpetual right to respect, reverence, support and compliance'.[94] Locke thus re-includes women in the 'honour' due to parents at the very moment when he distinguishes 'honour' from obedience to authority. The inclusion of women at that point serves to sharpen the distinction, for Locke puts a particular stress on the honour due to mothers when he is demonstrating that one can honour someone without having to obey her. The clinching example, for Locke, is that 'the honour due to parents, a monarch on the throne owes his mother, and yet this lessens not his authority, nor subjects him to her government'.[95]

Thus, although the claim that parents have joint authority over their children is the theoretical foundation for the family–state distinction, Locke fails to sustain it rigorously throughout the *Two treatises*. What does this inconsistency tells us about the nature of the family–state distinction?

The family–state distinction is considered one of Locke's most important contributions to political theory. He asserts it boldly at the opening of the *Second treatise*, where he proclaims his intention to show 'that the power of a magistrate over a subject, may be distinguished from that of a father over his children, a husband over his wife, and a lord over his slave'.[96] But the family–state distinction at some points in Locke's work becomes difficult to grasp. The problem is especially evident in Locke's discussion of conjugal society, in II.80–83. This section deserves careful examination, as it seems to both establish and undermine the differences beween magistrates and husbands.

Let us work backwards. Locke ends his discussion of marriage by forcefully asserting that the husband's power is not 'political'. The 'first societies', he has told us earlier in the chapter, were between man and wife and were antecedent to the formation of political society.[97] The opening statement of II.83 that a magistrate does not 'abridge' the husband's authority supports this larger point. If the magistrate were seen to 'abridge' the husband's authority (take over a bit of it) then it would mean that the power of a magistrate was originally *in* the husband, which would support Filmer's argument about the familial origins of political power.

> For all the ends of marriage being to be obtained under politic government, as well as in the state of nature, the civil magistrate doth not abridge the right, or power of either [the husband or wife] naturally necessary to those ends, *viz.* procreation and

mutual support and assistance whilst they are together; but only decides any controversy that may arise between man and wife about them.[98]

The ultimate proof that Locke offers for his conclusion that conjugal society is fundamentally different from political society is the fact that the husband does not need to possess the power of life and death over his wife for 'conjugal society' to exist:

> If it were otherwise, and that absolute sovereignty and power of life and death naturally belonged to the husband, and were necessary to the society between man and wife, there could be no matrimony in any of those countries where the husband is allowed no such absolute authority. But the ends of matrimony requiring no such power in the husband, the condition of conjugal society put it not in him, it being not at all necessary to that state.[99]

The introduction of the distinction between having and not having the power over life and death at the very end of the dicussion is worth pondering. It follows two paragraphs (II.82–83) in which Locke has tried to show that a husband is 'far from an absolute monarch' over his wife by sorting out who has the right to what in a marriage, and how far these rights are negotiable. His attempts, as we will see, are extremely confusing and contradictory. One might therefore take Locke's abrupt introduction of the 'life and death' issue as an effort to salvage a distinction that he has failed to establish in some other way.

Locke has difficulty in establishing not only the distinction between a husband and an 'absolute monarch', but even that between a husband and a 'civil magistrate'. The problem becomes evident when we note the contradiction between the first line of II.83 (where Locke says that the civil magistrate does not 'abridge' the power of either husband or wife but only 'decides any controversy which may arise' between them) and Locke's statement in II.82 that husbands have the right to decide controversies between spouses:

> But the husband and wife, though they have but one common concern, yet having different understandings, will unavoidably sometimes have different wills too; it therefore being necessary, that the last determination, that is, the rule, should be placed somewhere, it naturally falls to the man's share, as the abler and stronger.[100]

Alongside his contradictory statements about who is to judge in controversies between spouses over matters of their 'common concern', Locke creates confusion over just what these matters might be. The distinction between what is of common concern (or 'things of their common interest and property') and things that are the wife's 'peculiar right' runs through paragraph II.82, and is central to Locke's case that a husband is not an 'absolute monarch' over his wife. Having established the man's right to the 'last determination' or 'rule', Locke backtracks:

But this [man's right to rule] reaching but to things of their common interest and property, leaves the wife in full and free possession of what by contract is her peculiar right, and gives the husband no more power over her life, than she has over his. The power of the husband being so far from that of an absolute monarch, that the wife has, in many cases, a liberty to separate from him; where natural right or their contract allows it, whether that contract be made by themselves in the state of nature, or by the customs and laws of the country they live in.[101]

If Locke is relying upon the distinction between 'things of their common interest and property' and things that are a wife's 'peculiar right' to mark the limits of the husband's authority (that is, to say that the husband has power over the former but not the latter), he fails to explain how to make the distinction.

It is especially unclear whether children are to be regarded as being of 'common concern' (or 'common interest and property'). One is led to believe that they are, since Locke has told us that the entire *raison d'être* of matrimony is procreation and the care of children. The fact that humans take longer to grow up than do animals explains why human marriages last longer than those of other species.[102] When Locke famously suggests in II.81 that human marriages need not last for life, but might be 'made determinable either by consent, or at a certain time, or upon certain conditions, as well as by any other voluntary compacts', he seems to mean that this can only happen after the basic purpose of matrimony has been served, that is, 'where procreation and education are secured, and inheritance taken care of'.[103] This would suggest that by definition, children are of 'common concern'. However, if children are of common concern, *and* if husbands have authority over things of common concern, Locke has contradicted his own claim that parents have joint authority over children.

It may be, however, that children are not of common concern, since Locke (ignoring the restriction on divorce that he set forth in II.81) concludes his discussion of the right of wives to separate from their husbands with the observation that 'the children upon such separation fall to the father or mother's lot, as such contract does determine'.[104] This would imply that power over and responsibility for children might be the wife's peculiar right. If this is the case, however, then there would be no reason for children to be raised by married couples at all, which would undermine Locke's assertion that raising children is the purpose of marriage.

To all of these difficulties of interpretation presented by Locke's account of conjugal society, we must add another: what, exactly, does Locke mean by the assertion that the husband is 'far from an absolute monarch?' Is the husband's authority being distinguished from *all* political authority, or just absolute political authority? Given that Locke intends to say that the family and the state are different, we should choose the first reading. But if that is what he means to say, he isn't saying it effectively. As we saw, the distinction he makes in II.83 between the power of the husband and that of the magistrate is undermined by II.82. Moreover, if we look at nature of the wife's subjection as Locke describes it in II.82, it sounds suspiciously like a description Locke might give of the nature of the subject's contractual subjection to a monarch in liberal political society: it is, in other words, a contractual subjection in which authority is granted only over a limited set of things, and which leaves the subordinate in full and free possession of what is his or her own. The passage seems to draw on the family–state analogy even as it rejects it.

The more one ponders these problems, the more Locke's invocation in II.83 of the power of life and death as the thing that clearly distinguishes conjugal from political power looks like a desperate effort to rescue a distinction which he has failed to establish in the discussion preceding it. But even this move does not make the distinction between the family and state completely clear and foolproof.

Tyrrell's experience with the same argumentative strategy is, as always, instructive. In *Patriarcha non monarcha*, Tyrrell similarly argues that because the power of life and death is unnecessary for the purposes for which marriage exists, the husband does not have it, and therefore is different from a monarch. Typically, Tyrrell finds it necessary to expand and qualify. He goes on, for example, to note that in some situations, in the absence of a higher authority, a husband might have to punish his wife with death. This, for Tyrrell, doesn't compromise the argument because the husband is doing it in his capacity of master of the family, rather than husband.[105] Locke, typically, refrains from such inconvenient elaborations, and never asks whether a husband might execute his wife for crimes in the absence of a higher power. Yet, Locke is not entirely consistent in his claim that the power over life and death has no place in the family. In the *First treatise*, he allows power over life and death to creep into family relationships by pointing to a passage in *Proverbs* to establish the jointness of parental authority; here, an injunction to both parents to put an offending child to death shows that 'here not the father only, but father and mother jointly, had power in this case of life and death'.[106]

The family–state distinction is neither effectively proven nor consistently employed in Locke's *Two treatises*. A recognition of this is important for several reasons. First, it helps to explain the radically divergent interpretations of his work offered by feminist critics. For example, Mary Shanley has made a case for reading Locke as a feminist, praising him as the first contractarian political thinker to push the family–state analogy to its logical conclusion: if the political contract is voluntary and terminable, the marriage contract must be so as well.[107] Carole Pateman, as we saw in the Introduction, has a more jaundiced view of Locke which condemns him for *separating* the family and the state. Logically, Shanley and Pateman cannot both be right, but each has textual warrant for her position. Indeed, Locke's discussion of conjugal society in II. 80–83 can be used to support either one. For Shanley, this is the section where Locke permits divorce, since as long as 'procreation and education are secured ... there is no necessity in the nature of [the marriage compact], nor the ends of it, that it should always be for life'. For Pateman, this section establishes the family–state distinction.

A productive approach to Locke might begin not by choosing between the positions of Pateman and Shanley but by asking what it is about Locke's writing that it supports such diametrically opposing claims. The answer, as I have suggested, is that the family–state distinction was itself unstable. It is best understood as a contingent, strategic rhetorical move made by writers to solve particular problems, rather than as a social, cultural or political event (as in the phrase, 'the family and state were separated'). The interesting historical question to ask, then, is not 'what did Locke's separation of the family and state cause to happen?' but rather, 'to what conundrums faced by Locke (or any other writer) was the claim that the family and state were distinct a helpful response?'

By asking why the family–state distinction was helpful to Locke, we can locate the points of confusion in Locke's thinking about power in the family. He emerges from this chapter more ambivalent about, and bothered by, such issues than is usually acknowledged by his feminist critics or his feminist defenders. Locke's ambivalence must in turn be related to the unresolved problems confronting whig thinkers that were discussed in the previous chapter.

Despite the bad reputation of whig political theory amongst some feminist scholars, it did have the potential to subvert patriarchal structures by putting the questions of power in the family onto the agenda of political argument; this was in part because whigs found it important to acknowledge rather than to hide the problematic nature of paternity. Even Locke, who used the family–state distinction to sidestep the most vexing problems that plagued Tyrrell, did at least devote space to defining the terms of the marriage contract. True, he abandoned his discussion of Eve's subjection, and of the rights of married women with respect to things of 'common concern', before he got to the point of questioning the justifiability of male power. But even he could not avoid the questions.

The subversive possibilities of whig theory, however, were dampened by the Revolution of 1688, which gave whigs both the opportunity and the need to proclaim themselves the party of familial as well as political order. The transformation of whig and tory ideologies in light of changing circumstances during the 1690s is the subject of Part II.

NOTES

1 The feminist literature on Locke and women includes Carole Pateman, *The sexual contract: aspects of patriarchal liberalism* (Stanford, Stanford University Press, 1988); Teresa Brennan and Carole Pateman, '"Mere auxiliaries to the commonwealth": women and the origins of liberalism', *Political Studies* 27 (1979); Mary Shanley, 'Marriage contract and social contract in seventeenth-century English political thought', *Western Political Quarterly* 32 (1979); Melissa Butler, 'Early liberal roots of feminism: John Locke and the attack on patriarchy', *American Political Science Review* 22 (1978); Ruth Perry, 'Mary Astell and the feminist critique of possessive individualism', *Eighteenth Century Studies* 23 (1990); Lorenne M. G. Clark, 'Who owns the apples in the garden of Eden?' in Lorenne M. G. Clark and Lynda Lange (eds), *The sexism of social and political theory: women and reproduction from Plato to Nietzsche* (Toronto, University of Toronto Press, 1979); Elizabeth Fox-Genovese, 'Property and patriarchy in classic bourgeois political theory', *Radical History Review* 4:2 (1977).

2 For Sidney in the context of the exclusion crisis, see Alan C. Houston, *Algernon Sidney and the republican heritage in England and America* (Princeton, Princeton University Press, 1991); Blair Worden, 'The commonwealth kidney of Algernon Sidney', *Journal of British Studies* 24 (1985); Jonathan Scott, *Algernon Sidney and the Restoration crisis, 1677–1683* (Cambridge, Cambridge University Press, 1991).

3 Algernon Sidney, *Discourses on government* [1698], 3 vols (New York, Richard Lee, 1805), 1:311 (I.intro). Chapter and section numbers are given from here onwards in parentheses.

4 *Ibid.*, 1:417 (I.18).

5 *Ibid.*, 3:80 (III.16).

6 *Ibid.*, 1:425 (I.19).

7 *Ibid.*, 1:392 (I.15).

8 The identification of Sidney with 'classical republicanism' or 'neo-Harringtonianism' is made, for example, by J. G. A. Pocock in *The Machiavellian moment: Florentine political thought and the Atlantic republican tradition* (Princeton, Princeton University Press, 1975) pp. 421–2, 507; see also Blair Worden, 'Classical republicanism and the puritan revolution', in Hugh Lloyd-Jones, *et al.* (eds), *History and imagination* (Duckworth, 1981).

9 A symptom of the problem, as Alan Houston rightly points out, is that Sidney is in fact barely mentioned in Pocock's work on the Machiavellian or republican tradition; see Houston, *Algernon Sidney*, p. 4 n.5. The hallmarks of the 'classical republican' tradition are variously defined; compare Worden, 'classical republicanism' to Pocock, *Machiavellian moment*, and to Pocock, 'Machiavelli, Harrington and English political ideologies in the eighteenth century' in his *Politics, language and time* (New York, Atheneum, 1971). Houston in *Algernon Sidney* has questioned the sharp dichotomy drawn by Pocock and others between republicanism and liberalism. For biographical details linking Sidney directly and indirectly to Harrington during the Commonwealth, see Blair Worden, 'Commonwealth kidney', and Jonathan Scott, *Algernon Sidney and the English republic 1623–1677* (Cambridge, Cambridge University Press, 1988).

10 Houston emphasizes important differences between Harrington and Sidney; see *Algernon Sidney*, pp. 120, 160, 177.

11 Sidney, *Discourses*, 2:52 (II.7).

12 *Ibid.*, 3:122 (III.8).

13 *Ibid.*, 1:396 (I.16).

14 *Ibid.*, 2:395–6 (III.1).

15 *Ibid.*, 2:20 (II.5).

16 *Ibid.*, 1:359 (I.9).

17 *Ibid.*, 2:74–5 (II.9).

18 *Ibid.*, 2:404 (III.1).

19 The only serious treatment of Lawrence is Mark Goldie, 'Contextualizing Dryden's Absalom: William Lawrence, the laws of marriage, and the case for King Monmouth', in Donna B. Hamilton and Richard Strier (eds), *Religion, literature and politics in post-reformation England, 1540–1688* (Cambridge, Cambridge University Press, 1996).

20 Goldie, 'Contextualizing Dryden's Absalom', pp. 217–18.

21 See W. O. Furley, 'The whig exclusionists', *Cambridge Historical Journal* 14 (1957); Mark Knights, *Politics and opinion in crisis, 1678–81* (Cambridge, Cambridge University Press, 1994), pp. 162, 263; Goldie, 'Contextualizing Dryden's Absalom'.

22 Goldie characterizes Lawrence as an 'erastian presbyterian' and *Marriage by the moral law of God* as a 'belated essay in puritan anti-formalism', in Goldie, 'Contextualizing Dryden's Absalom', p. 213. For Restoration examples of attacks on Anglicanism as 'popery', see Mark Goldie, 'Danby, the bishops and the whigs' in Tim Harris *et al.* (eds), *The politics of religion in restoration England* (Oxford, Basil Blackwell, 1990).

23 John Cosin, *Bishop Cozen's argument, proving that adultery works the dissolution of a marriage* [1669].

24 [William Lawrence], *Marriage by the moral law of God vindicated* (1680), p. 72.

25 *Ibid.*, p. 77.

26 *Ibid.*

27 *Ibid.*, p. 80. By 'fathers' Lawrence means fathers of the child, not fathers of the virgins.

28 *Ibid.*, p. 91.

29 The *Declaration of the rights of woman* is printed in Darline Gay Levy *et al.*, *Women in revolutionary Paris, 1789–1795* (Urbana, University of Illinois Press, 1979), p. 91.

30 Tyrrell, *PNM*, pp. 13–14.

31 Lawrence, *Marriage*, p. 67.

32 *Ibid.*, p. 70.

33 *Ibid.*, p. 71.

34 The only full-length study of Tyrrell is Julia Rudolph, 'Revolution by degrees: the whig theory of resistance' (Ph.D. dissertation, Columbia University, 1995). I am grateful to Dr Rudolph for letting me see this work. See also J. W. Gough, 'James Tyrrell, whig historian and friend of Locke', *Historical Journal* 19 (1976); David Wootton's introduction to *The political writings of John Locke* (New York, Mentor, 1993). Hereafter Locke, *Political writings*.

35 Locke, *Political writings*, pp. 58–60.

36 Tyrrell, *PNM*, pp. 101–2.

37 See, for example, Peter Lake, 'The moderate and irenic case for religious war: Joseph Hall's *via media* in context', in Susan D. Amussen and Mark A. Kishlansky (eds), *Political culture and cultural politics in early modern England* (Manchester, Manchester University Press, 1995).

38 Tyrrell, *PNM*, preface.

39 Locke, *Political writings*, pp. 83–9.

40 For the defence of Filmer against the charge of extremism, see Bohun, *PP*, I.5, I.12.

41 Tyrrell, *PNM*, p. 44.

42 James Tyrrell, *Bibliotheca politica; or, a discourse by way of a dialogue, whether monarchy be jure divino ... Dialogue the first*, (Richard Baldwin, 1691/2) p. 44.

43 *Ibid.*, p. 44.

44 Tyrrell, *PNM*, p. 41.

45 *Ibid.*, p. 31.

46 *Ibid.*, p. 23.

47 *Ibid.*, p. 27.

48 *Ibid.*, p. 110.

49 *Ibid.*, p. 111.

50 *Ibid.*

51 *Ibid.*, p. 28.

52 Bohun, *PP*, II.47.

53 Tyrrell, *PNM*, p. 26.

54 *Ibid.*, pp. 234–5; see also p. 26.

55 *Ibid.*, pp. 26–7.

56 *Ibid.*, p. 26.

57 Slaves and servants are discussed in Tyrrell, *PNM*, pp. 102–9; wives are discussed on pp. 109–13.

58 Margaret Sommerville, *Sex and subjection: attitudes to women in early-modern society* (Arnold, 1995), pp. 79–84.

59 Tyrrell, *PNM*, p. 14.

60 *Ibid.*, pp. 13–14.

61 *Ibid.*, pp. 14–15.

62 *Ibid.*, p. 13. The passage to which Tyrrell refers is in *Patriarcha*, pp. 138, 145.

63 Tyrrell, *PNM*, p. 13.

64 *Ibid.*, pp. 14–15.

65 *Ibid.*, p. 22.

66 *Ibid.*, p. 106.

67 *Ibid.*, p. 105.

68 *Ibid.*, p. 107.

69 *Ibid.*, p. 110.

70 *Ibid.*, p. 113.

71 *Ibid.*, p. 41.

72 Locke, *TT*, II.67.

73 Jean Bodin, *Six books of the commonwealth* [1576, French edn], in Eric Cochrane *et al.* (eds), *Early modern Europe: crisis of authority* (University of Chicago readings in western civilization 6) (Chicago, University of Chicago Press, 1987), p. 234.

74 Locke, *Political writings*, pp. 49–64. On the exclusion crisis context of the *Two treatises*, and their precise dating, see also John Locke, *Two treatises of government*, ed. Peter Laslett [1960] (Cambridge, Cambridge University Press, repr. 1991), Introduction; Richard Ashcraft, *Revolutionary politics and Locke's Two treatises of government* (Princeton, Princeton University Press, 1986); John Marshall, *John Locke: resistance, religion and responsibility* (Cambridge, Cambridge University Press, 1994).

75 Tyrrell, *PNM*, pp. 15–16.

76 Locke, *TT*, II.67.

77 *Ibid.*, I.88.

78 See *ibid.*, II.45–50.

79 *Ibid.*, II.182.

80 *Ibid.*, I.93.

81 *Ibid.*, I.114–15.

82 Tyrrell, *PNM*, pp. 18–20.

83 Locke, *TT*, II.58.

84 *Ibid.*, II.55.

85 See, for example, Gordon Schochet, 'The significant sounds of silence' in Hilda L. Smith (ed.), *Women writers and the early modern British political tradition* (Cambridge, Cambridge University Press, 1998), p. 229.

86 Locke, *TT*, II.52 (and see also I.55).

87 *Ibid.*, II.65.

88 *Ibid.*, II.65.

89 *Ibid.*, I.47. It is worth recalling that Locke was a professional physician.

90 *Ibid.*, I.47.

91 *Ibid.*, I.48.

92 *Ibid.*, II.82.

93 *Ibid.*, II.58, II.59, II.61. On this, see Brennan and Pateman, 'Mere auxiliaries to the commonwealth'.

94 Locke, *TT*, II.67. Italics mine.

95 *Ibid.*, II.66.

96 *Ibid.*, II.2.

 97 *Ibid.*, II.77.
 98 *Ibid.*, II.83.
 99 *Ibid.*, II.83.
100 *Ibid.*, II.82.
101 *Ibid.*, II.82.
102 *Ibid.*, II.81.
103 *Ibid.*, II.81.
104 *Ibid.*, II.82.
105 Tyrrell, *PNM*, pp. 112–13.
106 Locke, *TT*, I.61.
107 Mary Shanley, 'Marriage contract and social contract'.

Part II

The Revolution of 1688 and
the politics of gender

Chapter 3

The politics of legitimacy: women and the warming-pan scandal

In 1703, the anonymous Jacobite author of a manuscript pamphlet made a subversive comparison between the events of 1688 and those of 1649. Speaking of the allegations that the son born in 1688 to James II and his consort, Mary of Modena, was supposititious, he ridiculed the claims of sceptics that the birth of the Prince of Wales had not been well enough witnessed by reducing their position to an absurdity. 'I cannot imagine what you would have', he wrote, 'unless you would either have had the queen delivered, as her father-in-law [i.e. Charles I] was beheaded, at her palace gate on a scaffold, or else have had her discharge all her ladies of honour and persons of quality and send for the good women out of St. James's market to come to her labour'.[1]

This striking image of the queen's body being exposed to public view came uncomfortably close to the truth. The warming-pan scandal (so called because the supposititious Prince of Wales was alleged to have been smuggled into the queen's bedchamber in a warming-pan as she pretended to give birth) became the subject of numerous rumours, pamphlets and satirical lampoons in the summer and autumn of 1688. These played an important role in the propaganda campaign leading up to the Glorious Revolution, and brought the physical details of the queen's pregnancy and labour into the public eye.[2] But did this public scrutiny of the queen's body constitute, as the Jacobite author implied, a desecration of the dignity of monarchy, a breach of social hierarchy, and a metaphorical regicide? Or did it represent the triumph of the rule of law and of the principle of hereditary succession to kingdoms and property? Implicit in this question were the issues that lay at the heart of the debate over the birth of the Prince of Wales: could the legitimacy, or authenticity, of heirs be proven? Who had the authority to decide? How public or private should a birth be? The debate about the warming-pan affair was different from the debate that occurred in the exclusion crisis. It concerned not the rights and powers of subordinates within the family, but the problem of access to knowledge. At issue was not just the power of women within the family, but their power to influence affairs of state.

Historians have finally begun to recognize that women were not entirely excluded from the political arena prior to the advent of women's suffrage: a growing body of studies has examined the roles of queens, consorts, royal mistresses, women petitioners and rioters.[3] The warming-pan affair, however, offers a unique angle from which to look at the question of women's political participation, since the mechanism of that participation was unusual and anxiety-provoking. The debate over the birth of the Prince of Wales involved questions about the birth and legitimacy of children, matters about which women were traditionally thought to know more than men. For this reason, it gave women a chance to speak authoritatively on a matter of political importance. It also raised questions in the minds of contemporaries about the power that this privileged knowledge about legitimacy and childbirth gave to women to interfere with men's political and property rights. This chapter will look at how the warming-pan scandal both reflected and shaped contemporary understandings of women's relationship to political life.

THE USES OF THE WARMING-PAN MYTH

The announcement of Mary of Modena's pregnancy in January 1688 touched off a crisis that had been brewing for years between James II and his Protestant subjects. If the child were male, he would take precedence in the line of succession to the throne over the staunchly protestant Mary of Orange, James's eldest daughter by his first marriage. The queen's pregnancy thus raised the spectre of a Catholic heir to the throne. It was at this moment, William Speck has argued, that the 'Orangist conspiracy' was born — and so was the warming-pan legend.[4] Rumours of a fraud began to circulate almost immediately. Henry Hyde, the Earl of Clarendon, noted on 15 January that 'the queen's great belly is everyhere ridiculed, as if scarce anybody believed it to be true'.[5] Satirical lampoons on the royal pregnancy appeared by the beginning of March.[6] *Mr Partridge's wonderful predictions, pro anno 1688* predicted that 'there is some bawdy project on foot either about buying, selling, or procuring a child, or children, for some pious use', and that 'some child [is to be] topt upon a lawful heir to cheat them out of their right and estate'.[7]

Rumours about the possible fraudulence of the queen's pregnancy also featured in the messages which Protestant politicians sent to the Prince and Princess of Orange. The Earl of Devonshire, writing to William on 13 March, reported ominously that 'the Roman Catholics incline absolutely that it should be a son', and that 'it is certain, that we expect great extremities'.[8] The next day, Princess Anne wrote to her sister Mary that 'her [the queen's] being so positive it will be a son, and the principles of that religion being such, that they will stick at nothing ... give some cause to fear there may be foul play intended'.[9] She drove the point home a week later, telling Mary that there was 'much reason to believe it a false belly. For methinks, if it were not, there having been so many stories and jests made about it, she should, to convince the world, make either me, or some of my friends, feel her belly'.[10] Anne's sentiments were echoed by Thomas Osborne, the Earl of Danby, who wrote William on 29 March that 'many of our ladies say that the queen's great belly seems to grow faster than they have observed their own to do'.[11] When the queen gave birth to a son on 10 June, suspicions had already been planted.

While gazettes and newsletters were 'stuffed with nothing but rejoicings from towns for the birth of the Prince',[12] and the government set off fireworks to celebrate the happy event,[13] rumours and lampoons continued to circulate. 'People give themselves a great liberty in discoursing about the young Prince, with strange reflections on him, not fit to insert here', Narcissus Luttrell noted.[14] In a mock dialogue, the Prince of Wales's nurse told the papal nuncio, 'O Lord, sir, now the whole kingdom laughs at the sham; and there's never a joiner in town but has a pattern of the bedstead; nay, the next Bartholemew Fair they intend to have a droll called "The tragedy of Perkin Warbeck".'[15]

Some writers accepted the authenticity of the queen's pregnancy but suggested that the father of the child was not James II but the papal nuncio himself, whose very name, Ferdinand D'Adda, lent itself to an incriminating pun. This theme was taken up in a satirical poem that purported to offer childless Catholics the opportunity to purchase a miracle:

> You men have help too, there's nothing more asked
> Though your reins have grown weak and are soundly clapped
> Our Lady can do it if you purchase her will
> And a priest swive your wives to colour her skill
> She'll give you a nod
> To show she's a God
> And you must believe it though never so odd
> Then down on your knees and forever adore
> The Church that got heirs and I doubt she's a whore[16]

Satirical medals struck at the time in both England and Holland often displayed windmills, a reference to the rumour that the child's father was a miller. Others, less specific, showed a priest pulling a baby from a set of panniers, or depicted the Prince of Wales as a chameleon (that is, a changeling).[17] There was not a single story about the birth, but many.

By October, the government was forced to respond. The king called a meeting of the Privy Council on 22 October, at which forty-two men and women gave depositions that they believed the Prince of Wales to be the king's son. These depositions were given quasi-legal status by being enrolled in the court of Chancery, and were then printed by royal authority.[18] By this time, it was too little and too late. William's invasion of England was under way. Among other reasons for his actions, William's *Declaration* cited 'the just and visible grounds of suspicion' that 'the pretended Prince of Wales was not born by the queen'. He promised to refer to Parliament 'the enquiry into the birth of the pretended Prince of Wales, and of all things relating to it and the right of succession'.[19]

William believed that the birth was a fraud, in spite of the testimony of forty-two people, because it provided him with an excuse to invade England in defence of the hereditary right of his wife. The importance of this as an excuse was emphasized in the 'invitation' sent by the 'immortal seven' on 30 June, in which William was chided for having congratulated James II on the birth of his son:

> We must presume to inform your Highness that your compliment upon the birth of the child (which not one in a thousand believes to be the queen's) hath done you some injury. The false imposing of that upon the princess and the nation, being not only an infinite exasperation of the people's minds here, but being certainly one of the chief causes upon which the declaration of your entering the kingdom in a hostile manner must be founded on your part, although many other reasons are to be given on ours.[20]

William was further encouraged to make use of the rumours about the birth by his agent, James Johnstone, who suggested that he secretly sponsor the publication of a pamphlet, purporting to be written by a private citizen, that would air suspicions about the Prince of Wales's authenticity and call on the Prince of Orange to intervene.[21] Whether William believed the rumours or not, he was persuaded to appear to believe them.

It is, moreover, possible that William and other opponents of James II did not simply exploit rumours which already existed but actually created and promoted them. Some Jacobites were later to charge that there was a premeditated plot by James's enemies to cast doubt on the queen's pregnancy even before she became pregnant. One writer quoted a letter from one 'E. S'. which contained information about a cabal of English gentlemen in Holland two years before the Revolution who 'resolved not to attempt anything upon England, till they should hear of the queen's being delivered of a son; and then to proceed upon that point of its being a suppositious child'. The same writer also recalled the remark made by Roger L'Estrange in the *Observator*, after the birth of a daughter to Mary of Modena in 1682, that the whigs had tried to cast suspicion on the then Duchess of York's pregnancy and only desisted when the child proved to be a girl. 'We must expect', L'Estrange had prophesied, 'that the same flam shall, at any time hereafter, be trumped up again upon the like occasion'.[22] These bits of information may suggest that there was a predisposition on the part of James's opponents to believe that Mary of Modena might fake a pregnancy. As evidence of a premeditated conspiracy to discredit her pregnancy before the fact, however, they should be taken with several grains of salt, as they come from biased sources.

We can, however, establish that if protestant politicians did not actually invent rumours themselves they did, from the early days of the queen's pregnancy, help to create the conditions under which it would be easy for people to believe them. The role of Princess Anne was especially important in this respect, and a study of it reveals something about how the strategy of James's opponents worked. As already noted, Anne passed the rumours about the fraudulence of the queen's pregnancy to Mary as early as March. But despite having given the impression in her letters that she had tried hard to find out if the pregnancy was real but had been rebuffed by the queen, Anne did not remain on call to witness her stepmother's lying-in. When the queen gave birth on 10 June, Anne was at Bath taking the waters for her health.[23]

Anne's absence from the birth of the Prince of Wales lends (and lent) itself to some intriguing speculations. Writing to Mary on 18 June, Anne appeared apologetic and defensive about her lost opportunity: 'My dear sister cannot imagine the concern and vexation I have been in, that I should be so unfortunate to be out of town when the queen was brought to bed, for I shall never now be satisfied whether the child be true or false'. She then, however, used this circumstance to cast suspicion on the queen for having deceived the world about the date of her reckoning and 'chosen' to give birth while Anne was away: 'But that, which seems to me the plainest thing in the world, is, her being brought to bed two days after she heard of my coming [back] to town [London], and saying that the child was come at full term, when everyone knows, by her own reckoning, that she should have gone a month longer'.[24] One of the earliest pamphlets stating the case against the authenticity of the birth, *An account of the pretended Prince of Wales*, developed this theme, charging that Anne had been sent away 'on purpose to keep her at a sufficient distance till the scene was over', for fear that she would be a 'vigilant observer'.[25]

It is quite possible that Anne deliberately absented herself from the birth in order to avoid being called upon as a witness if the pregnancy proved to be real, and to make it look as though the queen had tried to exclude her. Not surprisingly, this argument can be found in Jacobite literature. For example, James Montgomery suggested in *Great Britain's just complaint* (1692) that Anne had sought physicians who would advise her to go to Bath although her physicians in ordinary were against it.[26] This interpretation of Anne's behaviour is also accepted by Anne's most recent biographer, Edward Gregg.[27] We will never know whether Anne deliberately stayed away or whether she genuinely did not expect the queen to give birth so soon. This in itself may be a tribute to her cleverness in covering her tracks. The important point is that, with or without premeditation, Anne found or put herself in the convenient position of not being able to confirm the authenticity of the birth.

Anne took further advantage of her own ignorance in a letter to her sister on 24 July. Mary had presented Anne with a list of questions about the circumstances of the queen's pregnancy and lying-in. Although these questions can only be described as 'leading' (Mary asked, for example, 'whether in any former labour the queen was delivered so mysteriously, so suddenly, and so few being called for'),[28] Anne's replies failed to add up to a convincing case against the Prince of Wales. To Mary's question about the queen's former labours, for example, Anne gave the surprisingly un-ominous and insignificant answer that her labour 'never used to be so long'.[29] When Mary asked 'Whether the treating of the queen's breasts for drawing back the milk [during her pregnancy], and the giving her clean linen, has been managed openly or mysteriously', Anne responded with third-hand and inconclusive information: 'All I can say is that once in discourse, Mrs Bromley told Mrs Roberts, one day Rogers's daughter came into the room, when Mrs Mansell [the queen] was putting off her clothes, and she was very angry at it, because she did not care to be seen while she was shifting'.[30] All of this proved nothing. However, like her absence from the birth, Anne's responses made it possible for Mary to believe that the authenticity of the Prince of Wales had not been sufficiently established.

This was, of course, precisely the point. Anne's strategy, and that of other promoters of the warming-pan myth, was simply to give people (in this case, her sister) a reason to continue believing what they wanted to believe. James Johnstone's letter of advice to William brilliantly if unintentionally captured the essence of this technique. He did *not* say that a pamphlet about the Prince of Wales's birth would persuade neutral observers that the boy was supposititious. Rather, his language suggests that the goal was to preach to the converted in order to help them sustain their position. '[E]ven those that believe that there is a trick put on the nation', he wrote, 'will be glad to know why they themselves think so, and those that only suspect the thing, will be glad to find reasons to determine them'.[31] By keeping the burden of proof on those who said the birth was real rather than on those who said it was false, promoters of the warming-pan myth were able to make every inconclusive detail look like a damning indictment.

The warming-pan myth was thus valuable and effective as a justification for William's invasion in 1688. But it later became inconvenient for William and his supporters for precisely the same reasons that it had previously been useful. The rumours about the false birth were effective only as long as their promoters were able to insist that the birth had not been sufficiently proven to be real. Not even they, however, could definitively prove that a fraud had occurred, and by continuing to use the warming-pan myth they would have shifted the burden of proof onto themselves. Moreover, as we shall see in the next chapter, William did not mean merely to protect Mary's right as hereditary monarch, but to sit on the throne himself.

For reasons of expediency, then, the warming-pan story was dropped as an official justification for the Revolution. Not surprisingly, the promised parliamentary inquiry into the birth of the Prince of Wales never materialized. During the Sacheverell trial, an event that became in effect a trial of the Revolution itself, the spokesmen for the whig ministry publicly admitted that the birth of the Prince of Wales had been genuine. As contractarian views of the Revolution became more accepted, the warming-pan story came to be seen as an embarrassment. As John Dalrymple put it almost one hundred years later, 'to defend the Revolution upon a pretended supposititious birth, is to affront it; it stands upon a much nobler foundation, the rights of human nature'.[32]

Nonetheless, the truth or falsehood of the warming-pan story remained an important issue for many people. Queen Anne herself never lost interest. When her physician, David Hamilton, told her in 1712 that he believed 'the Pretender was not the real son of King James, with my arguments against it', the queen 'received this with cheerfulness, and by asking me several questions about the thing'.[33] The debate also remained alive in the popular press. In 1696, for example, the notorious informer William Fuller published *A brief discovery of the true mother of the pretended Prince of Wales*; the book was re-issued in increasingly elaborate versions at least eight times between 1696 and 1702.[34] Among the clergy, the warming-pan story remained the subject of passionate debate. William Lloyd, the Bishop of Worcester, devoted himself to finding new evidence that the Prince of Wales was supposititious, despite the fact that he had already argued in print that William had established his right to the throne by 'conquest'. In 1703, his evidence was summarized in a widely circulated manuscript, and found its way into Gilbert Burnet's *History of my own time*.[35] Lloyd's opponents, a circle of non-juring clergymen that included George Hickes and George Harbin, responded by interviewing some of the original witnesses to the birth. An extensive body of correspondence survives in which Hickes and Harbin strive to bolster the confidence of a wavering comrade, Robert Jenkin, in the authenticity of the Prince's birth.[36] The warming-pan story was also kept alive through fears of a Jacobite invasion, and many of the earlier pamphlets were reprinted in 1715 and 1745.

The persistence of the warming-pan story suggests the tenacity of the doctrine of hereditary succession. It allowed those who could not accept William as the 'elected' monarch at least to accept Mary as the hereditary one, and later provided a reason for some non-jurors who had resisted allegiance to William III to accept Anne as the legitimate Stuart monarch.[37] However, the myth also undermined the principle of hereditary succession by magnifying the problem that lay at its heart: how is one to know who the heir is? Ironically, the arguments made to prove that the Prince of Wales was a fraud bore a strong resemblance to arguments which (as discussed in Chapter 2) were made during the exclusion crisis by Algernon Sidney and William Lawrence. Whether they intended, like Sidney, to challenge the principle of hereditary succession or – like Lawrence – to institute it in a more pure form, the whig exclusionists had called attention to the fact that paternity and legitimacy were difficult to prove. In this context, it is not surprising that the warming-pan story seemed plausible and important. It touched on matters that, as far as pamphleteers on both sides of the question were concerned, should interest any man hoping to pass his estate to his legitimate heirs. The debate about the birth of the Prince of Wales was about who had the authority to determine matters relating to marriage, childbirth or legitimacy. It was also a debate about the power and trustworthiness of women. As a result, it made women both the subjects and objects of political discourse.

VERIFYING CHILDBIRTH

At one level, the warming-pan affair created an opportunity for women to take part in political debate. It opened up a space where women's presumably superior knowledge about pregnancy and childbirth gave them the authority to speak on a matter of political importance. The roles of Princess Anne and Mary of Orange (which were available to them only because they were women) have already been discussed, and it is obvious that they had the most to gain from the story. In addition, a number of women from a variety of social classes and occupations expressed opinions on both sides of the issue. These included the poet Aphra Behn and the midwife Elizabeth Cellier, who both hazarded predictions in print that the queen's child would be a boy;[38] the witnesses who gave depositions before the Privy Council; Lucy Armstrong, who approached the Earl of Nottingham in March 1689 with a story that the midwife had confessed the fraud to a woman of her acquaintance;[39] Isabella Wentworth and Margaret Dawson, who provided George Hickes and his non-juring colleagues with further evidence concerning the birth;[40] and Frances Shaftoe, who in 1708 published a narrative claiming that Sir Theophilus Oglethorpe was the true father of the Prince of Wales.[41]

But if the warming-pan affair put women in a privileged position to speak about political events, it also made women the objects of suspicion. Some writers appealed to male paranoia over paternity by suggesting that Mary of Modena was not the only woman in the world to have foisted a supposititious child on an unwitting husband. One pamphlet cited an account of 'a woman who pretended to be delivered in bed by a midwife, but the imposture was discovered afterwards by the said midwife and the true mother'.[42] Edward Fowler, Bishop of Gloucester, wrote of 'a trial here in England within the memory of man wherein the father and mother and midwife have all sworn to the truth of the birth of a son, and yet the jury upon hearing the whole evidence have given judgment that it was supposititious'.[43] Robert Jenkin, the wavering non-juror, reminded George Hickes that a supposititious birth had occurred 'but a few years ago in a private family, unknown to the supposed father'.[44] David Hamilton suggested that such events were common when he told Queen Anne, 'I have been witness to the same imposition amongst persons of a far less degree, and to answer a far less design'.[45]

These fears about women's control over childbirth and legitimacy probably seemed reasonable in part because they were linked to a widely held set of assumptions about the sexual ethics of the Catholic Church. An account of Mary Tudor's false pregancy was issued in 1688 with the motto from *Ecclesiastes*, 'there is no new thing under the sun'.[46] The warming-pan myth itself uncannily echoed William Lawrence's complaint that conspiracies of women and priests could alter the succession of kingdoms. Catholicism, in warming-pan literature, was associated with a kind of monstrous motherhood that deprived men of their paternal rights. It was common, for example, for writers to take a jab at Mariolatry through an ironic identification of Mary of Modena's 'miraculous' conception with that of the Virgin Mary. Sixteen-year-old Abraham de la Pryme, upon learning of the queen's pregnancy, wrote in his diary, 'they say that the Virgin Mary has appeared to her, and declared to her that the holy thing that shall be born of her shall be a son. They say likewise that the Pope has sent her the Virgin Mary's smock, and hallowed bairn clothes'.[47]

A full answer to the depositions (1689) employed almost identical imagery:

> Some of the popish party ... tell a blasphemous and wicked invention (if true) that the holy ghost was to appear to her [Mary of Modena] and make her conceive, when she put on the pretended smock of the Virgin Mary, which apparition, they say, was in the likeness of the Pope's nuncio, and so by innuendo give us to understand that he got it on the queen.[48]

The image of Mary of Modena as a pseudo-Virgin, miraculously begetting heirs without the aid of a husband, was even more intimately associated with the Catholic Church in 'The triumphs of fire on the stage of water', a mock court masque presented 'in honour of the mother of the P. of W'. The obscenely fertile 'mother' turns out to be the Church herself:

> This deity (for we ne'er deal with other)
> Is fertile call'd, t'imply a fruitful mother;
> Around her naked sprawling infants cling,
> And at her feet are hares engendering

> This is the nursing mother, th'infants we
> Who the true heirs to all her whoredoms be.[49]

Promoters of the warming-pan story thus created a strong emotional impact by invoking a rich set of associations between the pseudo-miracles of the Roman Church and the 'miraculous' birth of the Prince of Wales, between Mary of Modena and the Church of Rome as apparent 'mothers' who are really whores, and between the birth of the Prince of Wales, other fraudulent births, and Catholic sexual ethics in general.

In addition to casting suspicion on scheming wives and mothers, promoters of the warming-pan story tried to construct a standard by which births could be proven and which this particular birth had failed to meet. This raised the question of whether women could speak, and with what authority, about the birth of the Prince of Wales. *An account of the reasons of the nobility and gentry's invitation* and *A full answer to the depositions ... concerning the birth of the Prince of Wales*, the two most important pieces of warming-pan propaganda published in 1688 and 1689, express the conviction that births must be 'public' and subject to strict standards of evidence. Let us briefly look at how the testimony of women as witnesses to the birth was treated in these tracts.

An account of the reasons focused on the question of who was present at the birth rather than on the details of what they saw. The gist of the argument was that the queen, once aware of the suspicions surrounding her pregnancy, should have taken steps to assure that the birth be properly witnessed and proved 'beyond all possible contradiction'.[50] Her failure to do this was itself in violation of the law. To make this point, the author invoked the sanctity of 'our English laws' which 'abhor any entry upon the apparent legal right of another', in this case the right of Princess Mary to her father's throne. For anyone to do this 'without sufficient manifestation of their own greater or better rights, is directly contrary to God's eternal law, and that of all righteousness amongst men'.[51]

This appeal to ancient principles of common law and eternal principles of divine and natural law allowed the author to treat the allegedly supposititious birth as yet one more instance of James II's threats to the rights and liberties of Englishmen, and to cast himself as a defender of the unalterable principle of hereditary succession to the throne.[52] As legal scholarship, however, it left much to be desired. In an effort to show that those who had been present in the queen's bedchamber were not eligible witnesses, and that those who had not been there should have been, the author cited precedents from common law, canon law, civil law, and the custom of 'all the civilized kingdoms in the world'.[53] These, alas, either had no basis in fact, or were based on precedents that had been stretched beyond recognition.

When, for example, the author claimed that 'our common law abhors all appearance of fraud about inheritances, and hath appointed twelve of the most able neighbours to judge of all the signs and appearances of fraud, and setting up counterfeit heirs', he may have been thinking of a procedure whereby a presumptive heir could obtain a writ *de ventre inspiciendo* in cases where his inheritance was threatened by the pregnancy of a widow of a recently deceased man. This writ entitled him to have the widow examined by matrons or midwives to see if she was really pregnant, and to keep her under restraint until she was delivered. However, the author stretched the precedent beyond recognition by applying it in a case where the husband was still alive.[54] Equally dubious was the author's claim that it was the custom of all 'civilized kingdoms' that royal births be witnessed by a host of dignitaries, including 'the princes of the blood, the chiefest men of religion, and the greatest nobles and officers ... and the ambassadors and ministers of foreign kingdoms'.[55] The only precedent – for who should be present at a royal birth – which has surfaced contradicts this assertion: in the reign of Henry VII, only women were admitted to the queen's bedchamber.[56]

It is significant that although the author of *An account of the reasons* produced reasons to exclude those who had been present at the birth on the grounds that they were Roman Catholics, courtiers dependent on royal favour, persons not well known in the kingdom or foreigners, he never tried to exclude the female witnesses on grounds of their sex.[57] On the contrary, his elaborately constructed vision of who should have been present at the birth gave women a significant role. Only women (noble Protestant matrons, of course) were suited to witness the child emerge from the queen's body. These women were to be possessed of 'sufficiency of knowledge and understanding in matters of child-bearing, such as knew by experience all those works of nature;' they were to be matrons 'whose gravity and sobriety were fit to attract some decent reverence from the men of like quality;' they should be aristocrats, so that they would 'have more audacity and confidence to make such near approaches to the queen in her travail and bringing forth, as are necessary, that they may be ocular witnesses that they have see the child in its very birth'.[58] The presence of men would give the birth its public character, that of women would guarantee its authenticity.

In theory, then, *An account of the reasons* acknowledged the authority of women. Its point was simply to show that instead of the noble Protestant matrons who should have witnessed the birth, the bedchamber had been filled with foreigners, papists, and courtiers.[59] *A full answer to the depositions*, a work published in early 1689 in response to the Privy Council hearing, used a different tactic. Although the author never explicitly said that women were not sufficient witnesses to the birth of a child, he defined the nature of 'proof' in such a way as to make the testimony that the women (noble Protestant matrons included) actually gave look insufficient.

The differences between *An account of the reasons* and *A full answer* can be seen if we consider how they used the term 'public'. The birth, declared the author of *A full answer*, should have been 'public to extremity, but on the contrary it was private to a nicety'.[60] The meaning of 'public', however, was somewhat different from what it had been in the earlier tract. In *An account of the reasons*, a 'public' birth meant one witnessed by the representatives of the public. The author of *A full answer*, although he grappled with the meaning of 'publicness', never defined it in terms of a list of proper witnesses. Instead, he stressed the importance of legal and medical standards of evidence, especially physical details that could only be provided by doctors. Had man-midwives been present at the birth, they would not have been 'so easily cheated as other men, nay, as women, for being doctors they could have distinguished the very cries, whether true or counterfeit'.[61] The authority of doctors over midwives and women was further asserted in a gratuitous attack on Elizabeth Cellier, the 'popish midwife' who was known not only for her political intrigues but also for her efforts to raise the professional status of midwives; readers were further warned that 'the wife's word, or [that of] only a profligate midwife', would not be considered sufficient evidence that a birth had occurred.[62] The pamphlet should be placed in the context of a professional struggle between midwives and 'man-midwives' that lasted into the eighteenth century.[63]

The author of *A full answer* thus used his faith in the medical verifiability of childbirth in order to expose what he saw as a crucial lack of detail in the depositions. Since 'child births are obvious, and things the most capable of a plain testimony and explanation ... of any human affair whatsoever', the witnesses ought therefore to have given 'incontrovertible proofs', if they had any, as to the authenticity of the birth.[64] Based on that standard, he found the testimony inadequate. For example, when Penelope, Countess of Peterborough deposed that she saw the queen's belly 'so as it could not be otherwise but that she was with child', he pointed out that the countess had not said whether she saw the queen's belly clothed or naked.[65] When Mrs Mary Crane, a gentlewoman of the bedchamber to the queen dowager, stated that she had stayed with the queen after she was delivered and saw 'all that was to be seen after the birth of a Child', he complained that this phrase was 'not well expressed', for Mrs Crane had not specified whether the 'all that was to be seen' had come out of the queen's body.[66] He then interpreted this lack of detail in the witnesses' testimony as a sign of their acquiescence in the plot. The one exception to this method was his reading of the testimony of Thomas Witherly, a Protestant physician who deposed that he 'was present in the queen's bedchamber when the Prince of Wales was born'. This time, the lack of specific detail was interpreted as Witherly's clever way of letting his audience know that he himself thought that the birth was a fraud but was afraid to say so in public.[67]

A full answer sought to discredit the testimony of forty-two witnesses by exploiting the gap that existed between what the deponents considered to be sufficient testimony and what the author led his readers to consider 'incontrovertible proof'. Most of the deponents seem to have thought it was enough to state their own belief. For some, this meant stating their own belief while admitting that they saw nothing at all, which made giving a deposition something like taking a loyalty oath.[68] But some of the women meant their statements of belief to carry evidential weight. When the Countess of Lichfield said that she was 'sure she could not be deceived but that the queen was with child', or when Elizabeth Bromley said that she had 'observed the bigness of her Majesty's belly, which could not be counterfeit', they were not being vague or evasive.[69] Rather, they were speaking with an authority that they thought should be acknowledged by virtue of their experience. They assumed that matrons familiar with pregnancy and childbirth did not need to give clinical details in order to claim to be 'certain'. The success of *A full answer* thus lay in the author's ability to define a standard of proof different from the one used by the witnesses.

It was precisely on the question of what constituted adequate evidence that the defenders of the Prince of Wales took issue with these and other pamphlets. They criticized the entire business of 'proving' the birth, pointing out that there was not 'one subject in any of the three kingdoms that can prove his own birth so well as the Prince of Wales'.[70] It was ridiculous to call this birth into question unless one was prepared to do the same for all others. This would, as the non-juror Thomas Wagstaffe put it, 'fill the world with confusion' and 'at this rate make supposititious not only all princes, but all men in the world'.[71] Similarly, George Hickes outlined the dire consequences that would follow if fathers were to disown their sons simply for lack of absolute certainty as to their birth or identity, and he asserted that 'no suspicions or presumptions, how great soever, would defeat the title of a child owned [that is, admitted to be their own] by private parents'.[72]

The defenders of the Prince of Wales thus dealt with the uncertainty at the heart of hereditary succession not by looking for better 'proofs' of the Prince's authenticity but by accepting uncertainty as inevitable. In this they closely followed Robert Filmer, who had argued (see Chapter 1) that the social acknowledgement of parental identity was enough: 'No child naturally or infallibly knows who are its true parents, yet he must obey those that in common reputation are so'.[73]

In other words, the literal truth of the birth was not worth prying into. This attitude towards 'evidence' caused supporters of the Prince of Wales to adopt a different attitude towards the testimony of women. Thomas Wagstaffe observed that there was 'scarcely a woman in England, who ever had any children', who did not know that it was impossible to hide a baby in a warming-pan! 'Why should the Prince of Orange have so mean an opinion of us, that we would sit down and give up our faith to such pretences as every midwife and every woman can confute?'[74]

Ultimately, however, the reason Jacobites and non-jurors did not subject women to scrutiny and suspicion was not – or not only – their trust in female credibility, but their trust in paternal instinct. It was impossible, they argued, for James to have done anything to disinherit his daughters, or any children that he might have in the future, in favour of a stranger. Paternal love was elevated to the status of a natural law: 'Nature and the law which is copied from nature abhors' the thought that a father would prefer a 'brat' to his own children.[75] Wagstaffe asked,

> Will any man adopt an heir when he does not know but he may have one of his own? Much less will he pick up one from a dunghill to inherit the glory of his ancestors, when his own loins may afford him many branches to support it. Let all married men and women, who have any sense of children, consult your own bowels, and then let them believe this if they can.[76]

We must not, therefore, leap to the conclusion that the defenders of the Prince of Wales were also the champions of women. The faith of Jacobites and non-jurors in the testimony of women was grounded on an even greater faith in the power of men's paternal affections for their own children.

The warming-pan affair sheds light on the social meaning and political location of the doctrine of indefeasible hereditary right to the throne. It is often assumed that this doctrine was part and parcel of 'patriarchalism'. However, as illustrated in Chapter 1, it was not of particular importance to Filmer. But it was strongly tied to the anti-exclusionist tory cause by the particular circumstances of the exclusion crisis. Therefore, anti-exclusionist tories who eventually supported the Glorious Revolution, and those who did not, had to reconcile the positions that they took on the Revolution of 1688 with adherence to that doctrine. Each side did do by telling a story about the authenticity of the Prince of Wales.

Whigs, who did not regard hereditary succession as indefeasible, had less invested in the outcome of the debate. They may, however, have responded to elements within it. Given their preoccupation with the sanctity of property, for example, they may have found the notion that William had intervened to protect the property of his wife compelling as a justification for the invasion. Moreover, many of the anxieties about the capacity of women to undermine the succession of property through the male line were expressed (as exemplified in Chapter 1) in whig rather than tory writing during the exclusion crisis. Nonetheless, whig's acceptance of the Revolution did not stand or fall on the truth or falsehood of the warming-pan story.

The most dramatic gender-political differences in the warming-pan debate emerged not between whigs and tories, but between Williamite tories (hereafter referred to simply as 'tories') and Jacobites. Jacobite narratives about the birth were more friendly toward the authority and trustworthiness of women. They dismissed the fears of their opponents about the capacity of women to foist bastards or supposititious children as heirs upon unwitting husbands. They insisted that the female witnesses to the birth could be trusted.

Tories, by contrast, collected stories of scheming women who conspired with priests and midwives to deprive men of the right to pass on property to the children of their own loins. In this respect, they harped upon the same question that some whigs had raised during the exclusion crisis: how can a father know that he is a father? They did not, however, follow that line of reasoning in the same way as the whigs had done. That is, they did not call the doctrine of hereditary succession to the throne itself into question. They committed themselves to the position that births could be proven, but that this one had not been. The tory position implies a rather jaundiced view of women's trustworthiness. The author of *A full answer* – and the many writers who claimed that the warming-pan story was credible because fraudulent births had happened so many times before – maintained that births could be more reliably proven if the whole process were taken out of the hands of women.

Yet, women had something to gain on the tory side of the debate as well. The warming-pan story did, after all, uphold the claims of a woman, Mary of Orange, to the throne. Moreover, some women used their access to feminine gossip and their privileged knowledge of childbirth to claim that the birth was fraudulent. Tories had no *a priori* objection to believing their testimony. Moreover, as we saw, the author of *An account of the reasons* did not condemn the witnesses to the birth as women *per se*, but as the wrong kind of women.

The doctrine of indefeasible hereditary right opened a space for women to speak with authority about a matter of political importance. But it also made that speech itself a matter of concern. The warming-pan affair thus raised questions about the power of women in the political sphere, without resolving them. Neither side had a monopoly on the claim to be the party of female empowerment. Indeed, neither side would have been grateful to receive the title! But that did not preclude women from taking advantage of the incident to make their voices heard. They did so, moreover, on both sides of the debate.

A study of the warming-pan debate does not, then, allow us to claim that the doctrine of hereditary succession (or, for that matter, either of the competing narratives about the birth of the Prince of Wales) can be characterized as inherently empowering or disabling for women. But it says much about the opportunity that some political debates provided for gendered individuals to negotiate their place in the world *as* gendered individuals. It also reveals the permeability of the line separating the realm of political affairs from that of the family. That line was made even more elusive by the settlement of the crown upon a married couple, the implications of which will be explored in the next chapter.

NOTES

1 BL Additional MS 33286, fol. 20.

2 A warming-pan is a covered metal container in which hot coals are placed; it is then put in between covers to warm up a bed before it is slept in. The only previous article devoted to this affair is J. P. Kenyon, 'The birth of the Old Pretender', *History Today* 13 (1963). For the wider propaganda context see Lois G. Schwoerer, 'Propaganda in the Revolution of 1688–89', *American Historical Review* 82 (1977). Works on the Revolution of 1688 are too numerous to cite, but a relatively recent overview is William A. Speck, *Reluctant revolutionaries: Englishmen and the Revolution of 1688* (Oxford, Clarendon Press, 1988).

3 It is a sign of progress on this front that a recent survey text, Sarah Mendelson and Patricia Crawford, *Women in early modern England* (Oxford, Clarendon Press, 1998), devotes a substantial chapter to 'politics'; see works referenced in that chapter for recent bibliography on the subject of women's political activity.

4 W. A. Speck, 'The Orangist conspiracy against James II', *Historical Journal* 30 (1987).

5 [Earl of Clarendon], *The correspondence of Henry Hyde, Earl of Clarendon*, ed. Samuel W. Singer, 2 vols (Henry Colburn, 1828), 2:156.

6 Dates can be determined from the 3 March 1688 entry in Roger Morrice's 'Entr'ing book, being an historical register of occurrences', 4 vols, Dr Williams' Library, Roger Morrice's historical MSS, 2:239.

7 *Mr Partridge's wonderful predictions, pro anno 1688* [1688], pp. 6, 13.

8 John Dalrymple, *Memoirs of Great Britain and Ireland*, 2nd edn, 2 vols (W. Strahan & T. Caddell, 1771–73), 2:218–19 (part 1).

9 Princess Anne to Mary of Orange, 14 March 1688, in Dalrymple, *Memoirs* 2:300 (part 1).

10 Princess Anne to Mary of Orange, 20 March 1688, in Dalrymple, *Memoirs* 2:300–1 (part 1).

11 Andrew Browning, *Thomas Osborne, Earl of Danby and Duke of Leeds, 1632–1712*, 3 vols (Glasgow, Jackson, Son & Co., 1944–51), 2:120.

12 Narcissus Luttrell, *A brief historical relation of state affairs, from September 1678 to April 1714*, 6 vols (Oxford, Oxford University Press, 1857), 1:444 (18 June 1688). See also pp. 448, 450, 452, 454.

13 Morrice, 'Ent'ring Book', 2:284 (14 July 1688).

14 Luttrell, *Brief historical relation*, 1:449 (7 July 1688).

15 *The sham prince expos'd. In a dialogue between the Pope's nuncio and a bricklayer's wife* (1688).

16 'Loretta and Winifred, or the new way of getting children by prayers and presents', Bodl. Douce MS 357, fol. 152.

17   *A catalogue of prints and drawings in the British Museum, division I: political and personal satires*, vol. 1 (Trustees of the British Museum, 1870), pp. 711–16. Visual satires and medals are described in Schwoerer, 'Propaganda'.

18   The forty-two testimonies were published as *The several declarations, together with several depositions made in Council on Monday, the 22nd of October, 1688. Concerning the birth of the Prince of Wales* [1688].

19   *The declaration of his Highness William Henry, by the grace of God Prince of Orange, &c. of the reasons inducing him to appear in arms in the kingdom of England* (The Hague, Arnout Leers, 1688). The Declaration, dated 30 September 1688, was printed with a postscript dated 24 October.

20   *Calendar of state papers domestic, 1688*, no. 1236. The signatories were the Earls of Devonshire, Danby and Shrewsbury, Baron Lumley, the Bishop of London, Admiral Russell and Henry Sidney.

21   Lois G. Schwoerer, *The declaration of rights, 1689* (Baltimore, Johns Hopkins University Press, 1981), pp. 107, 111. The letter from James Johnstone is reprinted in N. Japikse (ed.) *Correspondentie van Willem III en van Hans Willem Bentinck ... het archief van Welbeck Abbey*, 2 vols (The Hague, Martinus Nijhoff, 1927–28), 2:603.

22   BL Add. MS 33286, fols 30–1. The passage from L'Estrange is reprinted in Dalrymple, *Memoirs*, 2:313 (part 1).

23   In 1701, Margaret Dawson, a former gentlewoman of the bedchamber to Mary of Modena, told a group of non-jurors that Anne had never expressed any interest in examining her stepmother's belly or being admitted to her bedchamber: 'Deposition of Margaret Dawson', BL Add. MS 26657.

24   Dalrymple, *Memoirs*, 2:303 (part 1).

25   *An account of the pretended Prince of Wales, and other Grievanses, that occasioned the nobilities inviting, and the Prince of Orange's coming into England* (1688), pp. 15–16. More fully developed versions of this pamphlet were published under two other titles, *An account of the reasons of the nobility and gentry's invitation to the Prince and Princess of Orange* (N. Ranew & J. Robinson, 1688) and *A memorial from the English protestants for their Highnesses the Prince and Princess of Orange* (1689). The similarities between Anne's letters to Mary in June and July of 1688 and these tracts are worth noting.

26   [James Montgomery], *Great Britain's just complaint* (1692), p. 21.

27   Edward Gregg, *Queen Anne* (Ark, 1984), pp. 53–8; see also his 'Was Queen Anne a Jacobite?', *History* 57 (1972).

28   Dalrymple, *Memoirs*, 2:306 (part 1).

29   *Ibid.*, 2:309 (part 1).

30   *Ibid.*, 2:305, 2:307 (part 1).

31   Japikse, *Correspondentie*, 2:603.

32   Dalrymple, *Memoirs*, 2:314 (part 1).

33   *Hamilton diary*, pp. 44–5.

34   These later versions of Fuller's work include *A further confirmation* (1696); *Mr William Fuller's third narrative* (1696); *A plain proof* (1700); *Twenty-six depositions* (A. Baldwin, 1702). For a full list, and more on Fuller's career, see George A. Campbell, *Imposter at*

the bar: *William Fuller, 1670–1733* (Hodder & Stoughton, 1961).

35 'An account of the birth of the pretended Prince of Wales, as it is delivered by the lord Bishop of Worcester', BL Add. MS 32096; Burnet, *HOT*, 3:245–63.

36 Bodl. English history MS b. 2; BL Add. MS 33286; BL Add. MS 32096.

37 The point is made in J. C. D. Clark, *English society, 1688–1832* (Cambridge, Cambridge University Press, 1985), pp. 126, 163.

38 Aphra Behn, *A congratulatory poem to her most sacred Majesty* (Will. Canning, 1688); Elizabeth Cellier, *To Dr. —— an answer to his queries* [1688].

39 Lucy Armstrong to Nottingham, 14 March 1689, Historical Manuscripts Commission, *Report on the manuscripts of the late Allan George Finch*, 4 vols (HMSO, 1913–65), 2:195–6.

40 'Deposition of Margaret Dawson', 13 February 1701, BL Add. MS 26657; 'Conference with the Lady Wentworth', 22 April 1702, BL Add. MS 33286 fols 3–4.

41 *Mrs Frances Shaftoe's narrative* (1707).

42 *A compleat history of the pretended Prince of Wales* (1696), p. 12.

43 [Edward Fowler], *An answer to the paper delivered by Mr Ashton at his execution* (R. Clavell, 1690), p. 15. A note in the margin identifies the incident as 'the case of Robin's child at Hereford Assizes about an[no] 1668'.

44 Jenkin to George Hickes, 7 October 1701, Bodl. Eng. Hist. MS b. 2, fols 188–9.

45 *Hamilton diary*, p. 45.

46 *Idem iterum: or, the history of Q. Mary's Big-Belly* [1688]. For a lurid rendition of anti-Catholic sexual stereotypes, see [David Clarkson], *The practical divinity of the papists discovered to be destructive of Christianity and men's souls* (T. Parkhurst & N. Ponder, 1676), pp. 337–60.

47 *The diary of Abraham De la Pryme, the Yorkshire antiquary*, ed. Charles Jackson, Surtees Society publications vol. 54 (Durham, Andrews, 1870), p. 11.

48 *A full answer to the depositions; and to all the pretences and arguments whatsoever, concerning the birth of the Prince of Wales* (Simon Burgis, 1689), p. 4.

49 Bodl. Rawlinson poetry MS 159, fols 15–18.

50 *Account of the reasons*, p. 11.

51 *Ibid.*, p. 11.

52 *Ibid.*, pp. 16–17.

53 *Ibid.*, p. 11.

54 *Ibid.*, p. 21. On writs *de ventre inspiciendo*, see William Blackstone, *Commentaries on the laws of England*, 12th edn, 4 vols (T. Cadell, 1793), 1:456 (book 1, ch. 16); *Baron and femme*, 2nd edn (John Walthoe, 1719), pp. 11–16; James Oldham, 'The origins of the special jury', *University of Chicago Law Review* 50 (1983), pp. 171–5. *A full answer* also cites this precedent. *De ventre inspiciendo: or, remarks upon Mr Ashton's answerer, in a letter to a friend* [1691], a printed paper found in George Harbin's manuscripts (BL Add. MS 32095) discusses the non-applicability of the writ *de ventre inspiciendo* to the Prince of Wales's birth.

55 *Account of the reasons*, p. 11.

56 Society of Antiquaries of London, *A collection of ordinances and regulations for the government of the royal household, made in divers reigns* (John Nichols, 1790), p. 125.

57 *Account of the reasons*, pp. 14, 15, 12.

58 *Ibid.*, pp. 12–13.

59 In fact there were a number of Protestant women present, including Anne, Countess of Arran; Penelope, Countess of Peterborough; Anne, Countess of Sunderland; Isabella, Countess of Roscommon; Susanna, Lady Bellasis; Henrietta, Lady Waldegrave; Dame Isabella Wentworth; Mrs Margaret Dawson; Anne, Countess of Marischall; and Elizabeth Bromley.

60 *A full answer*, p. 9.

61 *Ibid.*, p. 7.

62 *Ibid.*, pp. 3, 10.

63 Jean Donnison, *Midwives and medical men* (Heinemann, 1977).

64 *A full answer*, p. 13.

65 *The several declarations*, pp. 8–9; *A full answer*, p. 19.

66 *The several declarations*, p. 14; *A full answer*, p. 17.

67 *The several declarations*, p. 35; *A full answer*, pp. 19–20.

68 See, for example, the deposition of Alexander, Earl of Moray, *The several declarations*, p. 28. In some cases, the testimony was so sparse and non-committal as to suggest that the speaker was hedging his bets. Sidney Godolphin's testimony, in *The several declarations*, pp. 31–2, invites such speculation.

69 *The several declarations*, pp. 23, 17.

70 [George Hickes?], *The pretences of the Prince of Wales examined and rejected* [1701?].

71 [Thomas Wagstaffe], 'Innocence protected' [1692?], Bodl. English history MS d. 1, pp. 3–4. This pamphlet seems to exist only in manuscript.

72 Hickes to Robert Jenkin, BL Add. MS 33286, fols 11–12.

73 'Observations concerning the original of government' [1652], in *Patriarcha*, p. 192.

74 Wagstaffe, 'Innocence protected', p. 4.

75 'Out of a MS. by Sir George Mackenzie', BL Add. MS 33286.

76 Wagstaffe, 'Innocence protected', p. 4.

Chapter 4

'Strange paradox of power': images of Mary II

The relationship between political and familial authority was nowhere more intimate or problematic than in the newly installed monarchy. The Glorious Revolution created an unprecedented constitutional settlement by bestowing the crown jointly upon William and Mary. For the first time in English history, the 'king' literally had two bodies. The political question of where authority lay within the joint monarchy was also a question about authority in marriage. This chapter examines the representations of Mary II found in political poetry and propaganda, especially in the sermons and elegies published after her death in 1694. These reveal how pro-court propagandists manipulated gender ideology in order to resolve (or to create the illusion of having resolved) the political questions confronting the new regime.[1]

THE PROBLEM OF JOINT MONARCHY

The first of these concerned the settlement of the crown. As indicated in Chapter 3, William justified his invasion of England as an attempt to protect the hereditary right of his wife to the throne. Once James II had fled England, however, a split developed between those who would put Mary on the throne as James's legitimate heir, and those who supported William's claims as an elected monarch.

The gender dimension of the debate between 'Williamites' and 'Maryites' is evident in *A brief justification of the Prince of Orange's descent into England*, published at the time of the Convention. The author argued that the choice of William, who had no immediate hereditary claims to the throne, would both affirm the right of Parliament to dispose of the crown as it pleased, and avoid the embarrassing necessity of exposing King James to ridicule by revealing the true scandal of the warming-pan. Moreover, the author declared, the Princess of Orange, 'being the best woman as well as the best wife', would never accept the crown, as this would 'both be a detracting from the glory of her husband, and to the damage and prejudice of the community'.[2] Similarly, the author of *Reasons for crowning the Prince and Princess of Orange jointly, and for placing executive power in the prince alone* pointed to the need for a 'vigorous and masculine' administration, and argued that 'a man, by nature, education, and experience, is generally rendered more capable to govern than the woman', and therefore 'the husband ought rather to rule the wife, than the wife the husband'.[3]

There was also, however, strong sentiment in favour of Mary. Elinor James, a printer's widow turned prophetess, wrote in an open letter to the members of the Convention that 'nobody can condemn [William] for looking after the right of his wife; but all the world will highly condemn you to give, or him to receive, the right of the king'.[4] The author of *Reflections on the present state of the nation* argued that the immediate recognition of Mary as James's heir was the only way to 'preserve ancient and hereditary monarchy' from 'republican principles'; and went on to ask, 'will not the declaring her royal highness Queen of England, as next in succession, be the surest and best foundation to begin our settlement upon, rather than upon the groundless conceit of the government being devolved to the people, and so they proceed to elect a king?'[5]

When the Convention met in February, the Maryite position was taken up by a small group led by the Earl of Danby.[6] In the House of Lords, supporters of Mary joined with those who favoured the establishment of a regency (a scheme that would avoid the necessity of deposing James) to twice defeat the Commons' motion that the throne was 'vacant'. The Lords' rejection of the vacancy motion sprang from their desire to preserve the principle of hereditary succession. As Nottingham explained to the Commons, 'because, by the constitution of the government, the monarchy is hereditary, and not elective', and 'because no act of the king alone can bar or destroy the right of his heirs to the crown', the throne could not possibly be vacant because 'if the throne be vacant, of King James the Second, allegiance is due to such person [Mary], as the right of succession does belong to'.[7]

The Commons again debated the question of vacancy, and Mary received some support. The tory Sir Joseph Tredenham, for example, spoke of female monarchy and Mary's rights in terms reminiscent of Elinor James:

> As for [Mary] being a woman, Queen Elizabeth was so, and reigned gloriously. I would be grateful to the Prince of Orange, for the great things he has done for the nation; but is this the way to erect a throne, to the ruin of the Princess? ... His matrimonial right was the argument that brought him over; and therefore whilst we compliment him, I would not put a disreputation upon what he has so generously done, to put the crown singly upon this noble prince's head.[8]

On the other side, a number of speakers defended the necessity of regarding the throne as vacant, and opposed the expedient of crowning Mary as the lawful heir. The principle articulated by Nottingham (that allegiance was 'due to the next heir') left England vulnerable. Although the Maryites who opposed the vacancy motion meant that the throne was not vacant because Mary was already the lawful successor, a denial that the throne was vacant also opened the way for the 'pretended Prince of Wales' (or any future heir born to James II) to claim the throne by hereditary right. As Colonel Birch pointed out, 'there's a Prince of Wales talked of; and if he be not so, you will never want a Prince of Wales'[9] – even if this prince's authenticity were denied, the way would still be open for another pretender to claim the title. At a more practical level, to deny William the crown simply because the throne was not vacant would leave William with no incentive to defend England against her enemies, especially France.

Supporters of William also invoked the need for male authority within marriage. As Henry Pollexfen put it,

> And does any think the Prince of Orange will come in to be a subject of his own wife in England? This is not possible, nor ought to be in nature. If you stay till the princess please to give the government to the prince, you gratify the prince, by taking away his wife from him, and giving her the kingdom. If we are for unity and the protestant interest, I hope this marriage was made in heaven, and I hope good effects of it. That marriage, thus made, shall never be separated by my consent.[10]

Pollexfen's argument carried the day, and the House of Commons voted again, 282–151, that the throne was vacant.[11] The deadlock thereby created between the Commons and the Lords was broken only when William, declaring himself unwilling to be his wife's 'gentleman usher', threatened to withdraw his forces from England. Not surprisingly, the Lords soon brought themselves to agree to the Commons' formulation that James had abdicated and the throne was vacant.[12] On 13 February 1689, the crown was presented jointly to William and Mary, with the crucial provision that the administration of the kingdom be vested in William alone, and that William be able to remain on the throne should he survive his wife.

If the establishment of a joint monarchy was a tribute to the principle of male authority in marriage, it ultimately raised more questions than it answered. The problem became obvious in May 1690, when William proposed to lead his troops against the Jacobites in Ireland and to leave Mary to govern as regent in his place. The debate in the House of Commons on this Regency Bill reveals that Mary's status within the constitutional settlement was extremely difficult to define. The seemingly straightforward Regency Bill from the House of Lords, providing that in the king's absence 'the regal government of England, and dominions thereunto belonging, shall be in the queen', proved legally and constitutionally indigestible, though politically unavoidable. There had always, of course, been provisions made for a monarch to appoint a *custos regni* to govern in their absence. This involved merely the delegation of authority to a subordinate. In this case, however, Mary could not be regarded as a *custos regni* because she was already queen. Nor could anyone else have the job, for, as Heneage Finch pointed out, "tis impossible there should be [a regent] so long as the queen is here'.[13]

To confer the exercise of regal power upon the queen raised a host of questions. Did 'transferring the administration' imply that the crown had 'descended' to Mary?[14] How was William to resume his 'regal power' upon his return? What if the two powers should clash? Worse, what if the queen should die? Worse yet, 'what if, out of duty to her father, if he land, she should not oppose him?'[15] Finally, was it appropriate for Parliament to create a statute of this sort, or did this amount to yet another instance of Parliament divesting the king of his power? Members of the House of Commons expressed the feeling that the bill, as it stood, would 'downright depose the king', 'make the king no king and the queen no queen', and 'put the king upon another abdication'.[16]

How, then, in the accurate but hardly legalistic language of Sir Christopher Musgrove, was the Parliament to 'let the queen into some of that regal power now in the king; and ... how to let the queen into more than she has already' without taking it away from the king?[17] A few, like Robert Sawyer, saw little problem with the bill. Sawyer maintained that putting the administration in the queen was to 'make the great seal speak', that is, to recognize the joint sovereignty already established in the Revolution settlement.[18] Nuanced changes of language designed to protect William's power were offered by Heneage Finch, John Lowther and George Hutchins, who proposed (respectively) 'that the queen's act in the king's absence shall be valid in all cases except where the king directs the contrary'; that 'all the queen does in the absence of the king shall be of the same force as if the king had executed it'; or that 'the government may be exercised in the name of the king and queen'.[19]

Even by the standards of the time, these distinctions were hairsplitting. Thomas Littleton complained that 'a thousand things may be said, able to make a man's head ache'.[20] It was pointedly remarked 'Thomas Aquinas brought religion to nothing by nice distinctions'.[21] 'The more I hear the debate, the less I am able to resolve myself', sighed John Hampden, 'you are got into a labyrinth by this discourse'.[22]

But beneath the hairsplitting lay a strong sense of urgency and danger. The Revolution was only a year old, and the prospect of 'unsettling' a government that had been so recently settled seemed to open up the possibility of more political upheaval. 'Your government is not strong enough to try experiments upon', Littleton warned.[23] Sergeant Maynard was more explicit: 'Many hold themselves not at all bound to King William'.[24] John Somers pointed out that "'tis discoursed abroad of a commonwealth, and we should be very considerate in divesting and divesting'.[25] Somers went to the heart of the problem when he added that the 'nice distinction' between 'regal power' (in one person) and 'authority' (in both William and Mary) was open to a subversive interpretation: since 'there are some opinions in the world, that the king is only *de facto*', the removal of William's 'regal power' could be received as an open invitation to consider William's title void.[26]

The debate also exposed the ambiguity of Mary's position. What did it mean to have an equal share of royal 'authority' but lack the right to exercise 'regal power?' 'This doubt, whether the queen is not so amply and fully queen as in the Act of Settlement, may be of dangerous consequence', observed Hutchins.[27] Sir Joseph Williamson thought that the 'inconveniences' (in the sense of absurdities or lack of internal agreement) in the bill 'may be such as may dissolve the frame of government that you have taken so much pains to settle'. This led him to dub the entire joint sovereignty arrangement 'impracticable' and to suggest that Mary's status as monarch be ignored so that a traditional regency could be established.[28]

In the end, pragmatism rather than logic led to the adoption of the Regency Bill as the least of all possible evils. Fortunately, Mary's lack of interest in testing the constitutional limits of her power made the many subsequent transitions in and out of the the regency flow smoothly, so justifying the judgements of the members of Parliament that she was the 'best woman in the world'.[29] However, the dilemmas exposed by the regency debate re-emerged as themes in political poetry. A study of representations of Queen Mary, both in occasional verse and in funeral elegies and sermons, suggests that the problems posed by Mary's possession of regal 'authority' without regal 'power' could be resolved more easily in poetic conceits than in legal terms.

THE SYMBOLIC USES OF MARY II

As Lois Schwoerer has pointed out, Mary was the most eulogized monarch of the seventeenth century. But whereas Schwoerer interprets this fact as evidence of Mary's political skills, this chapter will emphasize Mary's usefulness as a symbol for propagandists for the Williamite regime, regardless of her virtues as a ruler.[30] Indeed, Mary was a useful symbol even before she had a chance to prove herself as regent. The flood of elegies upon her death only intensified a dynamic already at work in her life.

Mary's usefulness lay in the ambiguity of her constitutional position. She was a 'paradox' both in the sense that she had regal 'authority' without regal 'power', and in that she was both a wife and a ruler. This made it uniquely possible for Mary to be imagined as a figure who straddled and transcended the very conceptual categories that were central to the construction of political arguments on such controversial topics as allegiance and political virtue. The concept of political 'virtue', which played an important role in the political conflicts of the 1690s relied heavily on distinctions between public and private; the distinction between monarch and subject was central to any notion of political authority in this period. The fact that these distinctions could be blurred in the figure of Mary proved politically useful to the new regime. By creating an image of Mary that was both private and public, monarch and subject, political propagandists could create an illusion of consensus by rendering the grounds for political controversy obsolete.[31]

The usefulness to Williamite propagandists of Mary's boundary-straddling qualities can be seen in the court's responses to 'country' claims about virtue and corruption in the 1690s. The debate over virtue reflected the new political divisions of the post-revolutionary era. Although the fear of a corrupt and overpowerful executive had motivated both the exclusionist movement and the Glorious Revolution, William as king naturally sought to expand his influence and prerogative. As a result, old alignments broke down. The whig–tory conflict was partly replaced, or at least complicated, by a new division – between 'court' and 'country'.[32] As the court sought to increase its control of Parliament by appointing complaisant members (known as 'placemen') to lucrative government offices, the 'country' opposition responded by reviving the republican rhetoric of 'virtue', by which they defined themselves as altruistic servants of the public good and their court opponents as seekers after private interest. But 'virtue' could also be used by the court against the country: insofar as 'virtue' connoted martial prowess, the court could claim to be 'virtuous' in its support of William's foreign policy, while tarring the country with the brush of softness and effeminacy (the opposite of virtue) for its isolationism. The court and country parties, then, could each claim a monopoly on virtue, but each meant something different by it.

Mary was the court's answer to the country critique. Court propagandists celebrated her personal piety and chastity in order to defend the court from any association with 'corruption'. Sexual and political corruption had been metaphorically linked in the pornographic satire of Charles II's reign.[33] The tradition continued into the 1690s when, as David Hayton has argued, members of the House of Commons who took stands against placemen and standing armies tended also to support bills against blasphemy, vice, immorality and atheism.[34] A pamphleteer writing from a country perspective on *The dangers of mercenary Parliaments* blamed such parliaments for 'the progress of all sorts of debauchery ... in short, a general depravation of manners, and almost utter extirpation of virtue and moral honesty'.[35] In this context, representations of Mary as *sexually* virtuous helped the court to steal, or at least mute, the moral thunder of its country opponents.

When it came to public-spiritedness, Mary was portrayed as if anything more virtuous than it was possible for William to be. This was proven by her lack of personal political ambition. William Walsh, in *A dialogue concerning women* (1691), compared the joy with which Mary relinquished her authority as regent upon William's return to the joy with which Cincinnatus, the Roman general and model of republican virtue, returned after the wars to his humble plough.[36] James Abbadie thought that Mary's humility was a virtue for sovereigns because it 'teached the prince to despise himself in the midst of that crowd of flattering admirers, who adore his faults and prostrate themselves before his fortune'.[37] Mary, being immune from flattery, would never give out patronage except to men of merit.

Better yet, Mary uniquely reconciled the two otherwise irreconcilable meanings of virtue – public-spiritness and martial-spiritedness – in her very person, and allowed the court to claim both. At the same time as her much-touted lack of ambition and her wifely humility made her into a model of public-spiritedness, her public-spiritedness was expressed in her co-operation with William's foreign agenda.

The conflation of the two types of virtue was most apparent in a set of poems written on the occasion of William's voyage to Holland in 1691. The royal trip was potentially controversial because it symbolized the king's continuing attachment to his native land, and exacerbated anxiety about whether his foreign policy was more in the Dutch than in the English interest. Court propagandists used the figure of Mary to dramatize the shift that they hoped to bring about in the hearts of the English audience. Two of the most interesting pieces, both written by women, portrayed Mary as a passionate wife who is at first unwilling to let her husband leave the safety of her arms but is eventually persuaded to let him go.

Alicia D'Anvers cast her poem on the subject of William's voyage in the dramatic form of a quarrel between Brittania, William's young bride, and Belgia, his mother. Brittania begins with a lament that pits the importance of her private feelings against the trivialities of politics and diplomacy:

> Shall a curst nicety of honour's law
> Tug from these fondling arms my dear Nassau?
> Councils, or hated business, call thee hence!
> To love, and me, nothing's a just pretence.

It is left to the wiser Belgia to remind Brittania of the importance of William's honour, and to chastize her for her 'effeminacy'.

> You Brittania have been found of late
> Soft to a scorn, nice, and effeminate,
> From your brave ancestors degenerate.[38]

The poem *Maria to Henric and Henric to Maria: or, the queen to the king in Holland*, written by 'a young lady', follows a similar trajectory. Maria chides Henric for being away so long in the wars, bemoans her misery, and asks if men ever really love women as much as women love men. This time it is Henric himself who recalls her to a sense of political responsibility, and reminds her of the importance of his honour. 'My vows are jointly made to love and war', he asserts, and adds a dose of guilt: 'you seem to wish me as my Gallic foe/ He'd have me always stay at home with you'[39] The poem ends by emphasizing Mary's power and responsibility as a ruler in William's absence.

These poems worked brilliantly as propaganda in favour of William's foreign policy. By deliberately combining Britain and Mary in the single figure of Brittania (or Maria), they suggested that the English people should go through the change of heart experienced by the female protagonist. This had the effect of discrediting legitimate opposition to the war effort by reducing it to merely selfish personal feeling. It equated isolationism with the effeminacy and self-interestedness of the jealous bride, while associating support for the war with the ability to renounce personal interests. By combining both kinds of virtue in the figure of Mary, court propagandists cut the grounds of critique out from under the opposition by claiming for Mary the qualities that the opposition claimed for itself.

The Williamite regime's needs were served in yet another way by the capacity of Mary to stand as both monarch and wife, a political and a sexual figure. One of the most frequently repeated conventions was that Mary governed by her 'looks' alone. It meant that Mary could command simply by looking (as opposed to ordering, coercing, doing, and so on), and that Mary's physical appearance was the source of her authority. In *Henric to Maria*, for example, Mary is described as having a face that can tame 'mad-brained multitudes', strike malefactors dead, and make even enemies obey her will. 'Your eyes are both our sceptres', Henric tells her.[40] Similarly, Henry Park treated Mary's physical aspect as a transparent indication of her authority:

> A female sweetness, courage masculine
> Majestic dread, yet free address
> Awe, without superciliousness
> Kind clemency, and bright imperial meen
> All these united in her looks were seen.[41]

The identification of Mary's power with her looks placed its source outside the sphere of politics (where it might be the subject of controversy) and defined it in purely personal, even sexual terms. Given the fact that the precise grounds of William and Mary's claims to the throne, and the grounds on which subjects were expected to swear loyalty to the new regime, were fiercely debated in this period, this construction worked to mystify political authority.

The emphasis on Mary's 'looks' also made it possible to identify loyalty to Mary with sexual desire for her. 'A crown adds nothing to your power/ For you were chosen queen of hearts before', wrote Thomas Rogers in a coronation poem.[42] At the end of *Maria to Henric*, Henric wishes that Maria could appear before his troops

> Like some auspicious star
> And by her glories cheer the men of war
> Which all in ecstasy, when e'er thou art seen
> With eager voices cry, 'long live the queen'[43]

All of this, of course, recalls Elizabeth Tudor's exploitation of codes of chivalry and conventions of courtly love in order to inspire political loyalty.[44] Unlike Elizabeth, however, Mary was a married woman; indeed, the depiction of her as an erotic object for the masses sits rather oddly with the praise of her love for William. An interesting tension emerges in many of the poems between the poet's attempt to inflame the reader with desire for Mary, and the cele-bration of the passion between the royal spouses. A romantic triangle is established between the subject (or reader), William and Mary. But this triangle proves to be politically efficacious. It does not make the subject into William's rival. Rather, it lays the groundwork for transforming the subject's love for Mary into allegiance to William. This transformation can occur, however, only because Mary can be represented as wife, queen, and subject at once.

Colley Cibber's funeral elegy provides a particularly revealing example of how Mary's multiple status can allow a poet to eroticize her, and then turn that eroticization to politically useful ends. After describing those virtues of Mary that were 'obvious to each common eye', the poet invites our 'dazzled fancy' to imagine the 'secret' virtues reserved for William alone:

> Though heaven no offspring from her bed designed,
> But bade her live the phoenix of her kind,
> Her love was fruitful still: for love's in the mind.
> Her soul was married to her monarch's will,
> Which he could scarce declare, she would so soon fulfil,
> Desire of pleasing, as the child of love,
> They both, like tender parents did approve.[45]

At one level, this passage purports to show us the unambiguously private side of William and Mary's relationship. In fact, however, private sexuality is politicized in several ways.

First, the allusion to Mary's lack of reproductive fruitfulness raises the question of political continuity: what will Mary 'leave' us after her death? The answer, literally, is that her 'offspring', the product of her marriage bed, is her 'desire of pleasing' William, which we will now inherit. At this point, another slip occurs which transforms Mary's wifely and sexual 'desire of pleasing' William into our political 'desire of pleasing' William. Cibber states that Mary's soul was 'married to her monarch's will'. By using 'monarch' instead of 'husband', Cibber changes Mary from a wife into a political subject, and confuses erotic pleasure with political obedience. This also has the effect of putting Mary in the same category as the reader who (after Mary's death especially) will relate to William as a monarch. In other words, we are slipped into Mary's shoes (or nightgown) just as she is slipped into ours. This confusion is underscored later in the poem, where Mary is praised for having, 'while her absent hero led the war/ Taught us the pleasure of obedience here'. The 'pleasure of obedience' in this case can refer to both the pleasure we feel in obeying Mary during her regency, and the pleasure of obedience to William that Mary has taught us by her own example. By linking political obedience and sexual pleasure, Cibber solves the problem of political continuity after Mary's death by persuading us to transfer our affection to William.

Persuading subjects happily to transfer their affection from Mary to William was not necessarily easy. Nonetheless, while Mary's death for this reason posed a potential threat to the security of the Williamite regime, it also gave propagandists an opportunity to strengthen it. The numerous sermons and poetic elegies that poured from the presses after Mary's death can best be seen as a form of political therapy. Writers and poets took the opportunity to define where the political divisions lay, invent a crisis around them, and then resolve that crisis imaginatively.

It is particularly telling in this respect that the deceased Mary was praised for virtues that pertained to areas where the government had conspicuously failed to draw praise. The controversial appointments of latitudinarian bishops and the failed attempts to achieve toleration or comprehension in the early years of the reign had pleased neither Anglicans nor dissenters. Yet Mary was continually celebrated for her piety and love of the Church. In fact, the only cantankerous poem I have found on the death of Mary accuses the tory Anglicans of trying to appropriate the late queen as their patron saint, when she ought to be recognized as a supporter of Protestantism, toleration and the whigs.[46] However, in its exposure of the conflicts underlying the unanimous praise of Mary, this poem seems to have been unique.

Most poems, by contrast, work to create a sense that unity is urgently needed. They dwell at length on the grief of the nation and William at Mary's death, and express the fear that her untimely departure will open up the floodgates that hold back political discord, divine punishment, and perhaps the French as well. In John Dennis's *The court of death*, for example, death is pictured as an absolutist ruler who bears a striking resemblance to Louis XIV. The expedient of killing Mary with smallpox is proposed by a character called 'Discord'. Furious that she has been cast out of England, which in Mary's reign was filled with 'perpetual concord and fraternal love', Discord promises the tyrant that in 'that hour in which you pierce Maria's heart/ William and Europe tremble at thy dart'.[47] Another image frequently used to dramatize the potential political consequences of Mary's death is that of the queen as another Josiah, the virtuous king whom God removed from earth so that he would not have to witness the divine punishment of his sinful subjects.[48] If Mary's subjects are to avoid such a fate, the elegists suggest, they must transform grief for Mary into loyalty to William.

The funeral elegies also facilitated that transfer by deflecting the more egregious criticisms of the post-1688 regime and obscuring the contradictions of the joint settlement. Poems on Mary's death neatly resolved the anxieties expressed in the regency debate through the promulgation of two closely related ideas. First, Mary's relationship to William was said to be so close that their very wills were united; or that she, at least, had no desire of her own except to do his bidding. As we have seen, Colley Cibber made this claim in the poem discussed above. James Abbadie, 'minister of the Savoy [Chapel]', portrayed Mary as one who 'set [William's] will before her, as the rule of her life'. 'Her love and admiration for him made her submission a delight to her', he continued, 'the king did nothing without the queen's consent: And the queen never attempted anything, even during the time of her administration, but by the inspiration of her absent lord'.[49] Gilbert Burnet asserted that William and Mary were united in their thoughts as well as their persons, and that their complementary virtues constituted one whole.[50]

Second, it was universally asserted that Mary, while more than competent as a ruler, was completely lacking in political ambition. As the Dean of St Paul's put it in her funeral sermon, 'Never was there a greater skill in government, with less fondness for it ... she was always grieved at the occasion of taking the government, and as glad to resign it'.[51] John Glanville contrasted Mary to Semiramis, who 'when regnant made/ advanced to rule, th'advancer she betrayed'.[52] The image of Mary joyfully relinquishing the reins of power was a favourite theme of the poets:

> In thee alone, in wondrous thee
> Contrasting contrarieties agreed,
> Humble submission and supremacy,
> Tempering their opposite extremes so well,
> Empire and duty did together dwell,
> And from their fierce antipathies were freed!
> Empire disdains a partner in the throne,
> Duty implies humble subjection,
> Yet both in thee combining were but one!
> In foreign fields, while our heroic lord,
> 'Gainst th'oergrown French drew his undaunted sword;

> Secure the sceptre rested in thy hand,
> Yet though accomplished for the high command;
> The martial monarch, above empire dear
> Though absent, still commanded here:
> Strange paradox of power, by love allayed,
> While the queen governed, still the wife obeyed!
> How didst thou pray against a long campaign?
> How often wish to interrupt thy reign?
> How didst thou fly to meet him on the shore?
> Ambitious only to give oer,
> At his return, thy undervalued power?[53]

In addition to allaying the fears raised by the regency debate, these images helped to clear Mary of patricidal guilt. Opponents of the Glorious Revolution had depicted her as an 'unnatural daughter', likening her to Lear's 'cruel, lustful Goneril' and to the Roman Tullia, who had driven her chariot over her father's bleeding corpse.[54] A Jacobite mock-elegy had hilariously excoriated her as 'poor Moll who stole her father's crown/for terror of her husband's frown'.[55] By emphasizing Mary's lack of personal political ambition, propagandists for the new regime could show that she had only reluctantly rebelled against her father but for higher principles; by emphasizing her joyful compliance with William's will they could suggest that one of those higher principles was, indeed, the duty of wives to obey their husbands, which trumped the duty of children to obey their fathers. This depiction of Mary as a paragon of wifely obedience had the further advantage of reassuring readers that, despite the alarmist warnings of the Jacobites, the Revolution of 1688 would not have the effect of undermining the hierarchy within marriage by introducing sexual contractarianism. It also, perhaps, constituted a response to the ubiquitous jibe that William was either impotent or homosexual.[56]

The qualities for which Mary was praised as a queen were essentially those of a good wife: lack of personal ambition, loyalty to William, and the ability to govern by love rather than by coercion. But because Mary's public and private identities were fused into one royal body, writers could identify wifely submission with an ideal of political virtue or political obedience, without acknowledging the difference between the public and private contexts in which these qualities existed.

Thus, Mary's efficacy as a symbol lay in the fact that she straddled and even muddied the boundary between public and private, not that she was confined to one side of it. This observation should cause us to question the truism that women were relegated to the private side of a public/private dichotomy that arose sometime over the long eighteenth century and for which the Glorious Revolution and John Locke might be particularly blamed. But it also confirms the insight of feminist scholars that such a dichotomy was of central importance to political discourse in this period. Any account of women's relationship to political life, and of the significance of the presence of a female ruler for that relationship, must recognize both the importance with which contemporaries invested the boundary between public and private, and the elusiveness and malleability of that boundary. This book will later examine how the categories of public and private affected, and were manipulated by, women far more ambitious than Mary II.

NOTES

1 For a different interpretation of some of this material, see Lois G. Schwoerer, 'Images of Queen Mary II, 1689–95', *Renaissance Quarterly* 42 (1989). The image and reality of Mary II is also discussed in W. A. Speck, 'William — and Mary?' in Lois G. Schwoerer (ed.), *The Revolution of 1688–89: changing perspectives* (Cambridge, Cambridge University Press, 1992), and Melinda Zook, 'History's Mary: the propagation of Queen Mary II, 1689–94', in L. O. Fradenburg (ed.), *Women and sovereignty* (Edinburgh, 1992); Tony Claydon, *William III and the godly revolution* (Cambridge, Cambridge University Press, 1996), ch. 3.

2 *A brief justification of the Prince of Orange's descent into England* (Richard Baldwin, 1689), p. 36.

3 *Reasons for crowning the Prince and Princess of Orange jointly* (1689).

4 Elinor James, untitled broadside beginning 'My Lords you cannot but be sensible' [1688].

5 *Reflections on the present state of the nation*, printed in *A collection of scarce and valuable tracts*, ed. Walter Scott, 13 vols, 2nd ed. (T. Cadell & W. Davies, 1809–15), 10:203–4. This tract was also published as *Proposals humbly offered on behalf of the Princess of Orange*.

6 For accounts of manoeuvring in the Convention on the question of the succession, see Andrew Browning, *Thomas Osborne, Earl of Danby and Duke of Leeds, 1632–1712*, 3 vols (Glasgow, Jackson, Son & Co., 1944–51), 1:419–33; Henry Horwitz, *Revolution politicks: the career of Daniel Finch, second Earl of Nottingham, 1647–1730* (Cambridge, Cambridge University Press, 1968), pp. 70–82; Henry Horwitz, 'Parliament and the Glorious Revolution', *Bulletin of the Institute of Historical Research* 47 (1974); Eveline Cruickshanks, David Hayton and Clyve Jones, 'Divisions in the House of Lords on the transfer of the Crown and other issues, 1689–94: ten new lists', *Bulletin of the Institute of Historical Research* 53 (1980); Howard Nenner, *The right to be king: the succession to the crown of England, 1603–1714* (Chapel Hill, University of North Carolina Press, 1995), ch. 7. On the Convention generally, see Lois Schwoerer, *The Declaration of Rights, 1689* (Baltimore, Johns Hopkins University Press, 1981).

7 *Journals of the House of Commons*, 9:19–20 (5 February 1689). See Horwitz, *Revolution politicks*, pp. 77–9 for the temporary alliance between the advocates of regency and the Maryites.

8 Anchitell Grey (ed.), *Debates in the House of Commons, from the year 1667 to the year 1694*, 10 vols (D. Henry & R. Cave, 1763), 9:56.

9 *Ibid.*, 9:59. See also remarks of Henry Pollexfen, in *ibid.*, 9:64.

10 *Ibid.*, 9:64.

11 *Journals of the House of Commons*, 9:20.

12 Danby himself was instrumental in bringing about the agreement between the Houses on whether the throne was vacant. See Browning, *Thomas Osborne*, 1:430–1.

13 Grey, *Debates*, 10:127.

14 *Ibid.*, 10:101.

15 *Ibid.*, 10:108.

16 *Ibid.*, 10:122, 99, 108.

17 *Ibid.*, 10:117.

18 *Ibid.*, 10:100, 105.

19 *Ibid.*, 10:124, 104, 118.

20 *Ibid.*, 10:123.

21 *Ibid.*, 10:106.

22 *Ibid.*, 10:118.

23 *Ibid.*, 10:122.

24 *Ibid.*, 10:106.

25 *Ibid.*, 10:102.

26 *Ibid.*, 10:103.

27 *Ibid.*, 10:118.

28 *Ibid.*, 10:117–18.

29 *Ibid.*, 10:103. Mary ruled as regent on six separate occasions for a total of about 33 months. See Schwoerer, 'Images of Queen Mary II'.

30 Schwoerer, in 'Images of Queen Mary II', counts 110 elegies for Mary against about 30 each for the other seventeenth-century monarchs. Claydon's approach, in *William III and the godly revolution*, ch. 3, is closer to my own view that these poetic effusions reflect Mary's usefulness as a symbol.

31 Insofar as the political affiliations of the writers discussed below can be established, they were whigs and in some cases allied with the court. According to Stanley J. Kunitz and Howard Haycraft (eds), *British authors before 1800: A biographical dictionary* (New York, H. W. Wilson, 1952): Colley Cibber was a 'stout whig', John Dennis was 'in favour with the government', William Walsh was 'a protestant and a whig'. James (Jacques) Abbadie, a Huguenot, defended the Revolution and William in *Défense de la nation Britannique* (The Hague, 1692) and *History of the late conspiracy* (1696). Deull Pead preached sermons with a pro-whig, pro-William slant. Henry Park and John Glanville both wrote panegyrics on William as well as Mary.

32 Mark Goldie, 'The roots of true whiggism, 1688–94', *History of Political Thought* 1 (1980); Tim Harris, *Politics under the later Stuarts: party conflict in a divided society 1660–1715* (Longman, 1993), ch. 6; Dennis Rubini, *Court and country, 1688–1702* (Rupert Hart-Davis, 1967); David Hayton, 'The "country" interest and the party system, 1689–c.1720', in Clyve Jones (ed.), *Party and management in parliament, 1660–1784* (Leicester, Leicester University Press, 1984). The significance of place bills is discussed in Cruikshanks, *et al.*, 'Divisions in the House of Lords'.

33 Rachel Weil, 'Sometimes a sceptre is only a sceptre: pornography and politics in Restoration England' in Lynn Hunt (ed.), *The invention of pornography* (New York, Zone Books, 1993).

34 David Hayton, 'Moral reform and country politics in the late seventeenth-century House of Commons', *Past and Present* 128. It should be noted, however, that most of Hayton's data come from the period after Mary's death. For a different reading of Mary's virtue, cf. Claydon, *William III*, ch. 3.

35 *The danger of mercenary parliaments* (1690), quoted in Hayton, 'Moral Reform', p. 85.

36 William Walsh, *A dialogue concerning women* (1691), pp. 31–2.

37 James Abbadie, *A panagyrick on our late sovereign lady Mary* (Hugh Newman, 1695), p. 10.

38 Mrs. [Alicia] D'Anvers, *A poem upon his sacred Majesty, his voyage for Holland* (Thomas Bever, 1691), p. 3.

39 *Maria to Henric and Henric to Maria* (Joseph Knight, 1691), p. 10.

40 *Ibid.*, p. 11.

41 Henry Park, *Lachrymae sacerdotis* (John Dunton, 1695), p. 4.

42 Thomas Rogers, *Lux occidentalis: or providence displayed in the coronation of King William and Queen Mary* (Randall Taylor, 1689), p. 14.

43 *Maria to Henric*, p. 12.

44 See Louis Montrose, 'Shaping fantasies: figurations of gender and power in Elizabethan culture', *Representations* 2 (1983).

45 Colley Cibber, *A poem on the death of our late soveraign lady Mary* (1695), p. 11.

46 *A poetical elegy devoted to the glorious memory of our late queen, occasioned by a number of poems and sermons on her death* (1695).

47 John Dennis, *The court of death* (James Knapton, 1695).

48 Deull Pead, *A practical discourse upon the death of our late gracious queen* (Abel Roper, 1695), p. 18; Andrew Barnett, *A just lamentation for the irrecoverable loss of the nation* (Thomas Parkhurst, 1695), pp. 2–3.

49 Abbadie, *A panagyrick*, pp. 3, 21.

50 Gilbert Burnet, *An essay on the memory of the late queen* (Richard Chiswell, 1695), pp. 36–8.

51 Quoted in *The life of that incomparable princess Mary* (Daniel Dring, 1695), pp. 59–60. For the same sentiment, see James Perizonius, 'A funeral encomium upon the Queen', printed in *A collection of funeral orations pronounced by publick authority in Holland* (John Dunton, 1695), p. 38.

52 John Glanville, *A poem dedicated to the memory and lamenting the death of her late sacred Majesty of the small pox* (John Newton, 1695), p. 6.

53 [Mr Hume], *A poem dedicated to the immortal memory of her late Majesty* (Jacob Tonson, 1695), pp. 6–7.

54 'The female parricide', in *POAS*, 5:157; 'Tarquin and Tullia' in *POAS*, 5:47–54. See also 'The late duchess of York's ghost', *POAS*, 5:298–302; poem beginning 'In vain the Bourbons and Plantagenets', BL Harley MS 7314, fol. 108v.

55 'Epitaph on ABC or elegy on M.P.O.', Bodl. Rawlinson poetry MS 181, fol. 16.

56 Ralph Gray, 'The coronation ballad', *POAS*, 5:39–45; 'The reflection', *POAS*, 5:57–61; 'Jenny Cromwell's complaint against sodomy' (poem begins, 'In pious times e're Bug[gin]g did begin'), Bodl. English poetry MS c. 18, fols 132–135*v*; Poem beginning 'Declining Venus has no force o'er love', Bodl. English poetry MS c. 18, fols 130*v*–131*v*; 'The ladies complaint' (poem begins 'Since ladies were ladies I dare boldly say'), Bodl. English poetry MS c. 18, fols 180*v*–181; poem beginning 'Is Wolly's wife now dead [and] gone?', Bodl. Rawlinson MS D.361, fol. 263.

Chapter 5

───────◆───────

The politics of divorce

In the aftermath of the Glorious Revolution, Parliament considered private bills to dissolve the marriages of the Duke and Duchess of Norfolk, and of the Earl and Countess of Macclesfield. Unlike the divorces *a mensa et thoro* granted by ecclesiastical courts – separations 'from bed and board' which released the parties from the obligation to cohabit but prohibited remarriage by either party during the other's lifetime – these private bills gave the Earl of Macclesfield and the Duke of Norfolk the right to remarry, and recognized the children of future marriages as legitimate. In Macclesfield's case, children that the Countess of Macclesfield had borne to her adulterous lover were delegitimated in order to prevent them from inheriting the Earl's estate.

The Macclesfield and Norfolk divorces were not entirely unpredecedented. Parliament had passed similar private legislation for the Marquess of Northampton in 1552 and for Lord Roos in 1670. But the question of parliamentary divorce was debated with a new intensity in the 1690s. In addition to the Norfolk and Macclesfield bills, Parliament considered the cases of the Countess of Anglesea (who petitioned to have her physically abusive husband forced to settle a maintainance allowance on her), of one Mr Lewknor (who claimed his wife had deserted him), and of Mrs Wharton (who asked for a dissolution of her marriage on the grounds that she had married before the age of consent).[1] These cases were well publicized through satires, transcripts of proceedings, and short tracts and broadsides; they inspired some authors to write general treatises on marriage, divorce, adultery and fornication.

The fact that the Norfolk and Macclesfield divorces, and the wider debate about them, occurred in the decade or so after the Glorious Revolution raises intriguing questions about the relationship between politics and views of marriage. Lawrence Stone has speculated that 'in the 1690s, whig political radicalism about the dissolubility of the contract between king and people and moral radicalism about the dissolubility of the contract between man and wife came together'.[2] Gilbert Burnet, the whig Bishop of Salisbury, also made the connection between support for the Revolution and support for divorce when he described everyone who opposed the Duke of Norfolk's bill as a Jacobite or crypto-Jacobite.[3]

But Burnet's account should probably be taken with several grains of salt. Although the divisions in the Norfolk case fell out roughly along party lines (whigs voting for the divorce, tories against), the reasons for this were quite specific to that case.[4] It did not necessarily follow that the same pattern applied to other cases, or to divorce in general. The non-juror George Hickes, for example, accepted the permissibility of divorce of grounds of adultery.[5] Unfortunately for Stone's hypothesis, the association of marital and political contractarianism was generally made by opponents rather than supporters of the Glorious Revolution. Nonetheless, the fact that Burnet, himself an important propagandist for the new regime, chose to link the question of divorce to the question of the Revolution is itself a starting point for an analysis. What political issues were thought to be at stake in the question of whether a divorce could be obtained by private bill in Parliament? The connections between debates about divorce and debates about politics in the 1690s and early 1700s are explored in this chapter.

FAMILY AND STATE, DIVORCE AND REVOLUTION

As we have seen, analogies between the family and the state had a powerful hold on the minds of late Stuart people. Even Locke could not entirely free himself from such comparisons. Analogical thinking was, as Susan Staves has shown, ubiquitous on the English stage, where protests against political and familial tyranny became increasingly popular in English drama in the years before 1688.[6] After the Glorious Revolution, works by women were laced with references to the 'rights of freeborn Englishwomen' and complaints about the 'Turkish despotism' of husbands and the 'passive obedience' expected of wives. Elizabeth Johnson's preface to the poems of Elizabeth Rowe compared the poet to William III, restoring the liberties of the oppressed sex.[7] The author of *The female advocate*, writing in response to the notoriously sexist sermon by John Sprint, accused her opponent of preaching in favour of absolute tyranny, slavery, and passive obedience.[8]

Whig writers after 1688 were well aware that setting limits on royal power might raise questions about the limits on men's power in the family. In his popular series of sermons on *The relative duties of parents and children, husbands and wives, and masters and servants* (1705), the radical whig clergyman William Fleetwood laid out the natural, customary and scriptural grounds for male authority in the home. He also, however, added some important caveats: 'Where men's commands are evidently unreasonable, shamefully indiscreet, unusual and unheard of, infamous or unbecoming their age, their credit, quality, and condition, they may be safely passed by; omitted rather than neglected or despised'.[9]

Gilbert Burnet's *Enquiry into the measures of submission*, his first and most radical defence of the Revolution, also made room for exceptions to the rule that wives and children must be obedient. Although he began with the premise that 'the law of nature has put no differences nor subordination among men, *except* it be that of children to parents, or wives to husbands' (italics mine),[10] he also claimed – in a later section arguing that the maxim that 'the king can do no wrong' should not be taken literally – that

> all general words, how large soever, are still supposed to have a tacit exception, and reserve in them, if the matter seems to require it. Children are commanded to obey their parents in 'all things': Wives are declared by the Scripture to be subject to their husbands in 'all things, as the Church is unto Christ': and yet how comprehensive soever these words may seem, there is still a reserve to be understood in them.[11]

Burnet went on immediately to explain that 'though by the form of our marriage, the parties swear to one another, "till death do them part", yet few doubt but that this bond is dissolved by adultery, though it is not named'.[12]

Burnet's fast move away from the thorny question of when disobedience is justifiable and into an endorsement of divorce on grounds of adultery (and only on such grounds) should be regarded as a strategically wise leap onto safer terrain. Acceptance of divorce on grounds of adultery was a far less radical or subversive position than the one that critics were prone to assign to supporters of the Revolution. The writers who made an analogy between a people's right to depose a ruler and a wife's right to 'depose' a husband were generally opponents of the Revolution who wanted to illustrate the dangerous consequences of political contractarianism. Thus the prophetess Elinor James, in her 1688 *Letter to the convention*, likened the English people to a wife and James II to an errant husband. Even if it were legal to divorce such a husband, she asserted, it would be immoral:

> And though there may be many things said against the king ... consider that he has been misled by strangers, as many men have been misled by strange women, yet they are not willing their wives should turn them out of doors and take other husbands, though they might do it by the law, yet people would think such to be bad women.[13]

Similarly, a savage lampoon directed against Gilbert Burnet and John Tillotson, two of the whig bishops appointed in 1688 to replace the deprived non-jurors, satirized their support for the Norfolk divorce in a way that linked it to the Revolution of 1688:

> Our master and dame we shall please with this thing
> And ourselves justify; for spouse, bishop and king
> All used to be made with the help of a ring
> Which nobody can deny.
>
> Parting kings and their crown abdication we call
> For supplying full sees, we new bishops instal
> Yet both's but divorcing, when all comes to all
> Which nobody can deny.[14]

Virtually all defenders of the Revolution were eager to distance themselves from the notion that marriage (or even government) could be dissolved so casually. Within that framework, their positions on divorce varied. Burnet and Fleetwood both deemed divorce allowable on the limited grounds of adultery.[15] Other writers defending the Revolution avoided even this limited justification of full divorce.

White Kennett's *Dialogue between two friends*, written as an exchange between a Williamite and a Jacobite, illustrates one way in which a defender of the Revolution could avoid questioning the limitations of existing canon law (which did not permit divorce even on grounds of adultery) and thereby free himself from any taint of sexual unorthodoxy. Kennett introduces the problem of divorce by having his Jacobite speaker suggest that the principles justifying the revolution would also allow wives to divorce their husbands at will:

> When once the act [of choosing a king] was done and allegiance sworn, the people have no more reason or pretence to revoke or annul that election, than a wife (who has chosen her husband, promised him her obedience, joined herself to him in marriage) has to put away her husband, and to say that the people may depose their king if there be a bargain or contract between them is to affirm the wife may divorce her husband because she chose him.[16]

The Williamite immediately rejects this analogy, declaring that 'the wife after marriage may not put away her husband that lives with her as an husband: Nay, though a very ill husband, [that] turn non-thrift, spend his estate, abuse her person, prove unnatural to her children; notwithstanding all this she is obliged to obedience'. *But,*

> if her husband prove tyrannically cruel; so far prosecute the wicked councils and designs of her enemies, as to give signal and evident demonstrations that he intends her ruin, destruction and death; if he be himself insufficient (as in the case of the Countess of Essex by her husband Devereux) the law allows relief to such a distressed wife ... In short, though the wife cannot put away her husband because she chose him; yet the cruelties, injustice, violence and irregularities of the husband may be such as to give just cause for divorcement.[17]

The 'just causes of divorcement' that Kennett's Williamite speaker names are meant to call to mind the behavior of James II. It is important to note, however, that they are also exactly the ones sanctioned by existing ecclesiastical law. Church courts would grant a woman a separation *a mensa et thoro* on grounds of cruelty, and declare marriages null in cases where the husband was impotent. Thus, Kennett allowed for a comparison to be made between the Revolution of 1688 and a divorce, but not in a way that would grant women any more rights than they already had by law.

Significantly, Kennett had his two speakers cease their pursuit of the analogy between divorce and revolution immediately after the passage quoted above. Having taken the 'wife' (England) to the point of preserving herself against threats to her life, the Williamite did not go on to explain how she could get herself a new 'husband' (William and Mary). It is easy to see why Kennett stopped where he did. Were the analogy to be pursued any farther, the Williamite would have been on less safe ground. There was no way that the existing canon law could be interpreted to sanction a wife taking a new husband, even if she had justly separated from the old one on grounds of cruelty.[18] Kennett introduced and pursued the analogy between revolution and divorce as long, and only as long, as he could use it to show himself to be an upholder rather than a destroyer of the existing familial order.

The author of *Letter to a gentlewoman concerning government* (1697) offered a much more detailed consideration of the analogy between wives and subjects, husbands and kings, and of its limitations. Approaching the problem of 'divorce' from a different angle than Kennett, the writer ultimately displayed the same commitment to the principle of familial order. They found the appropriate analogy for the events of 1688 not, as had Kennett, in a wife's right to separation *a mensa et thoro* from a dangerous husband, but rather in the absolute right of any person to self-defence from rape or murder: 'a woman may kill any man that offers to ravish her, if she can no other way avoid the rape'.[19] Having put self-defence in cases of extremity under a rubric that had nothing to do with divorce, the writer could argue that revolution and divorce were completely unconnected.

The author explained that a king's right was not 'indefeasible' in the way that a husband's was, and enumerated the differences between kings and husbands. A king could be deposed, for example, 'when he loses his intellectuals, either by simpleness or total distraction'; however, 'the distraction or imbecility of a husband does not defeat his right to his wife, his wife being as firmly tied to him while he lives in frenzy or imbecility as if he were in his right senses'.[20] Moreover, kings could abdicate their thrones, whereas 'no father can resign to another man his rights over his child, so as to have no paternal power over him; no husband can lawfully leave his wife, and in his lifetime resign her to another'.[21] Finally, the author considered the case of a wife who was completely abandoned by her husband. It was true, he acknowledged, that a woman in this position was after a certain amount of time entitled by law to consider her husband dead and remarry. But here, the author emphasized the difference between such a woman, and the nation: 'it is not absolutely necessary that a woman should marry', but a nation must be governed.[22]

The author of *Letter to a gentlewoman* thus drew the line between the family and the state much more sharply than had Kennett in his *Dialogue*. Where Kennett had played, albeit in a limited way, with the notion that abused wives (or wives with impotent husbands) were in the same position as the subjects of James II, the author of *Letter to a gentlewoman* sidestepped the analogy completely:

> I have heard you compare a king to a father and to a husband, and subjects to children and to a wife. These comparisons may be used in a moral sense, to press the moral duties between them. But in a strict sense, such as we are upon now, they are false.[23]

There are some important variations, then, in how authors defending the Revolution handled the divorce metaphor, which reflect different attitudes toward the existing ecclesiastical laws. Burnet and Fleetwood implicitly suggested the laws should be changed, while Kennett showed no sign of wanting this. There were also significant differences in what each author considered a legitimate justification for the events of 1688. But the similarities between these authors are more important the the differences. All of them wanted to defend the Revolution, and to close off any possibility that justifications of the Revolution would also justify marital contractarianism.[24]

It is not surprising, then, to find defenders of the Revolution taking advantage of an opportunity to show that it was their opponents, not themselves, who were guilty of extending contract theory into the family. Such an opportunity arose in a bizarre form in 1697, when John Butler, a non-juring clergyman, published *The true state of the case of John Butler*. The pamphlet told a tale of ordinary marital woe and an extraordinary response to it. Butler had been sued in the Court of Arches by his wife, Martha, because he had been sleeping with his servant, Mary Tomkins, for the last ten years. Butler did not deny the liaison, but offered a unique justification for it. Martha, he claimed, had refused to sleep with him: it was she, therefore, who had ended the marriage because she had 'clearly divorced herself from this respondent's bed by a malicious and obstinate desertion, having utterly dissolved all bonds of wedlock between this respondent and herself by her own authority, by breaking her conjugal vows in wilfully denying the duties of marriage required in holy writ'.[25]

Regarding himself as divorced, and being one of those men who could not 'contain himself', of whom Saint Paul said 'it is better to marry than to burn', he considered his relationship with Mary Tomkins as 'lawful concubinage in a case of necessity'.

> This respondent pleads that his present bedding with Mary Tomkins is a bed undefiled, and therefore lawful and honourable even as the marriage bed, being made at a time when lawful marriage could not be conveniently had; for he having taken onto his bed an honest woman and no whore, and this without offence to God or any man breathing, not for the satisfaction of unclean lust, but to avoid fornication.[26]

Butler's pamphlet provoked the wrath of the grand jury of London, which presented him in December 1697 'for writing and publishing a wicked pamphlet, wherein he maintains concubinage to be lawful, and which may prove very destructive to divers families, if not timely suppressed'.[27]

Butler's arguments also provoked a response, *Concubinage and poligamy disproved*, issued by the whig publisher, Richard Baldwin. The anonymous author could not resist the temptation to make political hay from the spectacle of a sexually libertine non-juror. In his 'epistle dedicatory', he pointed to the inconsistency of Butler's political stance as a non-juror and his argument about marriage, parodying Butler's views by phrasing them in the language of contract theory. Butler, he wrote, had 'vindicated the original right of mankind' to 'the liberty of polygamy or concubinage'. It seemed a 'paradox'

> that a man should pretend to so much conscience in keeping an oath to a temporal prince, from which his abdication and the causes of it absolved him in the opinion of both church and state, and yet make no scruple of breaking his marriage vow to God and his wife ... That he himself should take it upon himself to be the judge in his own cause, and yet not allow the supreme power of the nation to be the judge in theirs against a prince, whom he owns to have acted tyrannically ... That Mr. Butler should allow desertion in his own wife to be a sufficient cause of marrying another, and yet scruple to own that tyranny and desertion are not sufficient to dissolve the contract betwixt king and people, and to set another upon the throne.[28]

By associating Butler with sexual contractarianism, the whig author was able to tie the threat of sexual anarchy to the old regime and its Jacobite or non-juring supporters, rather than to the whigs. Significantly, one of the polygamists mentioned in *Concubinage and poligamy disproved* was Charles II.

Sexual contractarianism was at issue once again in the controversy surrounding the divorce of the Earl and Countess of Macclesfield in 1697–98. In this case the argument was not about whether the marriage should be dissolved, but about whether the countess had a right to a refund of her marriage portion. According to the summary in Cobbett's *Parliamentary history*, the Countess petitioned Parliament to restore her fortune. Claiming that her adultery was caused by her husband's having 'maliciously secluded her from bed and board', she argued that if the Lords thought fit to pass this bill of divorce, she demanded her fortune be refunded, both because a divorce dissolves the whole frame of the marriage contract, and because it were the highest injustice that a man who was guilty of making his wife commit adultery should be rewarded out of the same wife's fortune.[29]

The response of the earl and his supporters can be gleaned from *Further considerations on the Earl of Macclesfield's bill*, which expressed outrage at the idea that the earl's behavior could 'dissolve the whole frame of the marriage contract' and thus leave his wife with the same property that she would have had if she had never married. The author asserted in strong terms that a wife had a duty patiently to suffer even malicious seclusion from bed and board: 'if she had been without cause secluded ... she ought by her virtuous and retired life, to have endeavored to regain her husband's esteem'.[30] To refund her fortune would be to reward her for committing adultery. Indeed, the provisions which the bill already made for her 'is more than consists with the Jewish law, and the laws of other nations, by which all adulteresses ought to be put to death'.[31]

The political dimensions of the Macclesfield case were less clear-cut than those of either the Norfolk divorce or the furore surrounding John Butler. Individuals who in the Norfolk case opposed the dissolution of the marriage (like Thomas Powis, Bartholemew Shower, and Dr Pinfold) supported Macclesfield in his efforts to rid himself of his wife.[32] The inconsistency can be explained in part by the fact that Macclesfield's bill was easier to swallow than Norfolk's. Unlike Norfolk, Macclesfield had at least begun proceedings in the church courts before introducing his bill in Parliament; the fact that the ecclesiastical suit was not yet concluded was widely blamed on Lady Macclesfield's delaying tactics. The fact that the countess had already born two children by her lover, who stood to inherit the earl's estate unless Parliament delegitimated them, also weighed in the earl's favour.

For this reason, the Macclesfield case matched well with whig efforts to purge themselves from any taint of sexual contractarianism. Macclesfield's credentials as an ardent whig were evident in the fact that he had been accused of complicity in the Rye House plot in Charles II's reign. The response that he offered to the countess's petition carried with it an implicit political meaning. Against her vaguely contractarian justification of her adultery and of her demands, he affirmed the duty of wives to submit even to unjust treatment from their husbands. The case thus offered whigs an exceptional opportunity to demonstrate that even the most radical of them supported hierarchy in the family.

THE NORFOLK DIVORCE, 1692–1700

Of all of the cases considered by Parliament in the 1690s, the Norfolk case went on the longest, was the most obviously politicized, and generated the greatest public interest. The Duke of Norfolk first introduced a bill to dissolve his marriage into the House of Lords in 1692, but it was turned down. He tried again later that year, having in the intervening time won an action for criminal conversation against his wife's lover John Germain. Again he lost, this time by 6 votes (in January 1693). His bill finally passed both houses in 1700.

The public had ample opportunity to witness the spectacle. Publishers sold printed transcripts of the parliamentary proceedings and of the criminal conversation trial in the court of King's Bench. Both sides issued broadsides summing up their positions. Satires and lampoons on the subject can be found in a number of manuscript collections. Exactly what the public thought of the affair is harder to determine. Satirical commentary that circulated in manuscript often damned both sides equally, and was directed at the petty and self-serving squabblings of the members of the House of Lords or the arrogance and debauchery of the aristocracy in general.[33] Both the duke and the duchess were clearly guilty of adultery, and neither one inspired a great rush of public sympathy. It is telling, for example, that when the non-juring lawyer Roger North wrote up arguments against the allowability of parliamentary divorce, he identified the victim of injustice in the case not as the duchess but as the duke's collateral heirs, who would lose a chance to inherit the estate if the duke had children by a second marriage.[34]

How, then, did contemporaries attribute political meaning to this unedifying event? Supporters of the Glorious Revolution who also supported the Norfolk divorce deemed their positions on these two matters to be consistent for a number of reasons. That political contract theory could be applied to marriage was not one of them. But the divorce could be linked to the rejection of 'popery' (in several senses), to claims about the debauchery of the old regime, and to the defence of property.

Popery was an issue at a very practical level. The Duke of Norfolk was the only Protestant in his family. His collateral heirs were Catholic, as was the duchess. The political implications were obvious. Roger North noted that it was alleged on the duke's side that 'it will be for a public service to restore a protestant succession to such a noble family, and to defeat that of a papist least the government which is Protestant should at length suffer by it'.[35] In his presentation of the case in 1700, the duke alluded explicitly to the desirability of keeping his great estate out of Catholic hands.[36] It is very possible that by this time, the duchess's involvement in the Jacobite Fenwick conspiracy encouraged him to press the point. Norfolk's cause, then, could be linked to that of the Revolution of 1688.

Norfolk's cause (and the question of parliamentary divorce in general) also became politicized because it played into already existing struggles over the nature of the English Church, and over the relationship between church and state. Supporters of the divorce often made the argument that the fact that English canon law permitted divorce only *a mensa et thoro* was a remnant of popery, a symptom of the incompleteness of the reformation in England. In his account of the Norfolk divorce in *History of my own time*, Gilbert Burnet explained that he and the other new bishops appointed by William had regarded divorce on grounds of adultery as 'lawful and conformable, both to the words of the gospel, and to the doctrine of the primitive church'; he also thought that the contrary doctrine (that not even adultery could break the bond of marriage) was a popish invention.[37] Protestant churches on the continent permitted full divorce (divorce *a vinculo*) in cases of adultery. The argument that divorce in cases of adultery had been permitted by Christ in *Matthew* 5:32 had been made by Bishop Cosin during debates on the Roos divorce in 1669; his argument was cited by the Earl of Macclesfield in 1696, and by Norfolk in 1700.[38]

Why this line of argument should spark political controversy requires some explanation. Its provocativeness lay not in what was said but in who said it: in effect, it meant something different coming from Cosin than it did coming from Burnet. Cosin possessed solid credentials as a high-church Anglican; Burnet, on the other hand, was tainted by association with Dutch Calvinism, Scottish presbyterianism, dissent and latitudinarianism. Thus, when Burnet and the new whig bishops appointed by William upheld the position that English canon law was popish, it was taken as a threat to the high-church Anglicans who made up the bulk of the tory party. While every Protestant in England was, of course, in favour of the gospel and against popery, high-churchmen took it as a given that people who criticized the Church of England for not being sufficiently reformed were really seeking to overthrow both church and state, just as they had in 1641. The fact that Burnet was a bishop did not exempt him from the charge; it merely demonstrated that closet presbyterians had been promoted by William into the upper ranks of the Anglican hierarchy.

Parliamentary bills for divorce also reinforced already existing anxieties about the proper relationship of church and state. William's deprivation of the bishops who for reasons of conscience had refused to take an oath of loyalty to the new regime was, from one point of view, an encroachment on the autonomy of the Church.[39] But one did not have to be a non-juror to dislike the intervention of the Williamite state in Church affairs. The king had pushed (successfully) for a Toleration Bill and (unsuccessfully) for the 'comprehension' – or inclusion – of dissenters within the Church; he had presided over the abolition of episcopacy in Scotland; and he foiled the plans of the high-church sympathizers who formed the majority in the lower house of Convocation by preventing Convocation from meeting. Although, given his Calvinist background, William proved more conciliatory towards the Anglican Church establishment than one could have expected, he was unable to defuse the rising level of resentment among the lower clergy towards his regime.[40]

In this context, the idea that Parliament could unmake a marriage was yet another encroachment by the state upon the Church. Even the Earl of Macclesfield's bill (which was introduced when proceedings in church courts had already begun) was the occasion for a lampoon on the outrageous pretensions of Parliament to undo a holy sacrament.

> It is an old saying that the House called Common
> Can all things perform but of man make a woman
> But although they can't that, yet this they can do
> What today heaven made one they can tomorrow make two
> In spite of the priest and his spiritual glue
> In vain with old texts our new casuists bustle
> To an Act of the House what are those of the Apostle?[41]

Norfolk's bill threatened the Church more profoundly than Macclesfield's, since Norfolk had not bothered with the church courts at all. He gave as his explanation the fact that these courts could not give him what he wanted. In reality, his own adultery would probably have barred him from obtaining a separation by canon law. His contempt for what he dubbed an 'inferior court' was a further blow to a Church percieved by tories to be already in danger. The fact that Norfolk's bill for divorce was supported by all of the new bishops – whom William had appointed to replace the deprived non-jurors – only added fuel to the fire.

Gilbert Burnet's *History of my own time* provides further insight into the ecclesiastical politics of the Norfolk case. As could be expected, Burnet eagerly denied that contract theory could be applied to marriage, and explained that he and his fellow whig bishops supported the Norfolk bill because they regarded divorce on grounds of adultery as 'lawful and conformable to the words of the gospel'. He accompanied this assertion with a peculiar historical account of the 1669 debates in the House of Lords over the Roos divorce bill. Its thrust was that even though most of the bishops had opposed the Roos bill in 1669, the Church of England had not really changed its position! Rather, the bishops had opposed the Roos bill only out of fear that it would encourage the libertine Charles II to divorce his wife, Catherine of Braganza. In Charles II's reign, he explained,

> a sceptical and libertine spirit prevailed, so that some began to treat marriage only as a civil contract, in which parliament was at full liberty, to make what laws they pleased; and most of King Charles' courtiers applauded this, hoping by this doctrine

that the king might be divorced from the queen. The greater part of the bishops, apprehending the consequences that Lord Roos' act might have, opposed every step that was made in it; though many of them were persuaded, that in the case of adultery, when it was fully proved, a second marriage might be allowed.[42]

Archbishop Tillotson, identically, claimed during the 1692 debates on the Norfolk bill that the bishops who voted against Lord Roos's divorce in 1669 did so 'not out of conscience but prudential consideration, lest King Charles II's divorce should be brought before them'.[43]

Burnet's and Tillotson's strange accounts of the Roos case helped them to define the nature of the Williamite church of England. Their goal was to surround the Revolution and the new ecclesiastical establishment with an aura of providential blessing and godly reformation, without proclaiming a radical break with the past. To this end, it was necessary to explain away the obvious difference between their own stand on divorce and that of bishops in previous reigns. Their version of history minimized the discontinuities between the new Williamite episcopal appointees and their predecessors. Implicitly, this meant that the fears of high-churchmen about the Calvinist, low-church, latitudinarian or even Socinian sympathies of the new bishops were unfounded. At the same time, the notion voiced by Burnet and Tillotson that the previous bishops had behaved out of 'prudential considerations' was double-edged. It carried with it a hint of disapprobation, if not of the bishops themselves, then of the regime and monarch that forced them to hide their true beliefs. Not surprisingly, Tillotson was (according to the manuscript account) 'immediately and severely reprimanded by [Compton, the tory bishop of] London and the [tory] Earl of Rochester. The latter of them said, that the bishops of that age were honest, brave, courageous, loyal prelates, and that he need have a commission from the dead that could enter into their thoughts, and durst charge them with dissimulation'.[44] The violence of the reaction underscores the narrowness of the line that the new bishops had to walk.

The story about the Roos case told by Burnet and Tillotson was also part of a narrative about the debauchery of the old regime. The Revolution of 1688 was regarded by many of its supporters not merely as a triumph of protestantism over popery but as a triumph of morality over debauchery. As Tony Claydon has shown, Burnet was at the centre of an effort to associate William and Mary with the reformation of manners.[45] The sexual libertinism of the court of Charles II was the theme of novels, histories, and collections of political poetry published in the aftermath of the Revolution.[46] William and especially Mary, by contrast, were represented as models of sexual virtue and marital fidelity. Burnet's account of the Roos divorce controversy thus exploited and amplified a familiar trope in Williamite political discourse. It allowed him, ingeniously, to dissociate from the Glorious Revolution the notion that marriage was a contract, and link it instead to the 'sceptical and libertine spirit' of the old regime. Moreover, Burnet used the occasion not only to vindicate the new bishops, but also to tar with the brush of sexual libertinism those who disagreed with them. Those who opposed Norfolk's bill for divorce, he claimed, did so out of popish and/or Jacobite sympathies (the Duchess of Norfolk herself being a Catholic and a Jacobite), or because they themselves were engaged in 'lewd practices'.[47] Although Burnet did not actually say that these were the same, one can imagine him thinking that they went together.

The defence of property rights provided one more axis along which support for the Norfolk divorce could be linked to support for the Glorious Revolution. Pamphleteers writing in support of the permissibility of full divorce in the case of adultery almost always made something of the fact that adultery was a particularly grievous crime in women because it deprived rightful heirs of their property and prevented men from passing on property to the children of their own loins.[48] For example, it was argued by the Earl of Macclesfield's supporters that it was unfair 'that for his wife's fault he should be deprived of the common privilege of every freeman in the world, to have an heir of his own loins, to inherit what he possessed, either of honour or estate'.[49]

Macclesfield's wife had already borne children to her lover. The Duchess of Norfolk, however, had not. This did not prevent the duke from claiming in 1700 that he was 'in danger of being succeeded by Sir John Germain's issue'.[50] In his arguments before the House on the duke's behalf, Serjeant Wright explicitly justified the sexual double standard. The duchess had complained that she had been given no chance before Parliament (as she would have been in ecclesiastical courts) to prove that the duke had committed adultery; Wright countered that such proof would have been irrelevant: the 'injury to families' was not equal in the case of male adultery, because 'a man by his folly of this kind, brings no spurious issue to inherit the lands of his wife, but the woman deprives her husband of any legitimate issue when she converses in this manner with another man'.[51] As a result, 'the estate does not go according to the law of God and nature, for everybody desires his own blood should succeed him'.[52]

We should not assume that such concerns about the sanctity of property were particular to whigs, or to supporters of the Revolution. There is no evidence that Jacobites, non-jurors or tories thought that women had a right to impose upon their husbands bastards begotten in adultery. Moreover, as Margaret Sommerville points out, the notion that the wife's adultery was particularly bad because it allowed another man's bastards to inherit from her husband had existed for a long time.[53] Nonetheless, it is fair to say that security of property was a fundamental building block of political argument in favour of the Revolution of 1688. The idea that the natural love of parents towards children would be expressed as a desire to pass on property to them was, as we have seen, already embedded in whig thought during the exclusion crisis. The capacity of women to interfere with this process had also been a concern of some whigs in 1680. Williamite tories had taken on the habit of expressing anxieties about the uncertainty of paternal identity in the context of the warming pan debate.

It is therefore not surprising that some post-1688 authors who emphasized the importance of making men secure that their children were their own tried to hitch their cause, at least loosely, to that of the new regime. The author of *Marriage promoted* (1690) expressed support for William and Mary, and tied the promotion of marriage to several goals that the new regime had declared desirable: larger population, greater military strength, flourishing industry, the reformation of manners, and 'a better obedience and conformity to the law of God, in matters of religion, and a greater contentedness and subjection to government'.[54] Moreover, he (assuming it *was* 'he') offered an account of the origins of political society vaguely reminiscent of Locke in the connections it made (or assumed) between property and social order, and between marriage and the care of offspring. There cannot be 'any true propagation of human nature', he argued, 'but by matrimonial contract',

> whereas were there a promiscuous use of women, the world must be peopled with mankind in the same confusion that the wilderness abounds with beasts; herds, not communities would inhabit the earth, and natural affection would hardly continue with such brutes, to rear up their increase till they had strength to provide for themselves; and then what inhuman violence these savages would mutually exercise uppon one another, it is not easy to imagine; but where there is a distinct property, it naturally creates love, and love maintains protection; so that if we run it up to the fountain, the whole band of civil society, and of a regular communion betwixt men in the world, proceeds from the succession of a lawful issue, which is the broadseal of heaven, and by which divine charter we hold all our earthly enjoyments and possessions whatsoever.[55]

The author of *Conjugium languens* (1700) was less explicit in his Williamite sympathies. Nonetheless, he invoked the Williamite narrative of the debauchery of the old regime, when 'the sins of C[harles] II ... made England to sin', and sounded familiar Williamite themes in his praise of 'martial English bravery' and England's flourishing commerce.[56] His call for Parliament to make divorce less tedious and expensive was expressed as a plea that the benefits of the Glorious Revolution be extended: 'Since therefore the happy constitution of our government takes care of all other proprieties [meaning both 'property' and 'what is proper'], it will not, I hope, suffer this which is most dear and tender, to be so easily invaded and ravished from us'.[57]

The ground was laid, then, for casting the Duke of Norfolk's bill as a defence both of the right to property and of the Revolution of 1688. The defence of property rights, however, could be a double-edged sword. The

Duchess of Norfolk's advocates deftly appropriated their opponent's concern with property rights, pointing out that the Duke of Norfolk's collateral heirs would be arbitrarily deprived by these 'summary proceedings' of the estate they otherwise stood to inherit if the Duke remained childless. Roger North, in a manuscript that may have been intended as advice to the duchess's lawyers, presented the divorce proceedings as an instance of arbitrary government that deprived subjects of the right to property and due process under the law. The proceedings punished people for violating laws that did not exist, they contravened the existing law of the land, they allowed the friends of the parties to sit in judgment upon them, they denied the defendants the right of appeal, they were conducted according to no existing precedent or procedure, they were not available equally to all subjects, and, he said, such an action 'depreciates the high court of Parliament, which is instituted for preservation of liberty and care of the public'. If the government thought that its security depended upon robbing Catholics of their estates, they would soon do the same to presbyterians, independents, and Quakers, so that the nation would become 'a desert of wolves'.[58]

By focusing on the unprecedented and unconstitutional nature of the proceedings, North could sidestep the charge that to oppose the divorce smacked of popery. He explicitly abstained from answering what he termed 'theological' questions. Some people, he acknowledged, 'say that the canon law hath not done right', but it was still the law, and if the canon law were to be judged wrong then the proper courts would have to do it. In the 1700 parliamentary proceedings, Thomas Powis made the same point, invoking Magna Carta's guarantee that no freeman could be punished except by the lawful judgment of his peers and the law of the land: 'Why, in this case, the ecclesiastical law is *lex terrae*. And if that is to be taken away without remedy, why may not the law in any other case'.[59]

There was a delicious irony for a tory like Powis and a non-juror like North in using the language of law, liberty and Magna Carta to defend a Catholic Jacobite.[60] The case gave them a chance to show that the Duke of Norfolk's supporters, and implicitly the new regime, were guilty of the very tyranny they had claimed to overthrow in James II. The defence of the Duchess of Norfolk was useful to non-jurors, Jacobites and tories because it allowed them to establish themselves, in this context, as the defenders of the liberties of the subject against arbitrary threats to life and property.

Significantly, their defence of the subject's liberties extended even to women. Although the Duchess of Norfolk was legally a *femme covert*, she defended herself as a freeborn English subject. Whereas the duke's advocates presented female adultery as a unique, and uniquely heinous, kind of crime, the duchess's supporters challenged the double standard. Powis argued that the adultery of the husband was as serious as the adultery of the wife, because such men brought home 'something to their wives ... [venereal disease] which stick by them longer than their children'.[61] Powis also presented the duchess's situation as analogous to that of a man attainted for treason:

> A bill of divorce of a woman in Parliament, without a legal trial [in the church courts], is just the same thing as a bill of attainder against a man for treason: the one forfeits the estate, corrupts the blood, and takes away his life, and the other does very little else: for I find according to the bill, 'tis to forfeit her jointure, defame her person, corrupt her reputation; and though it leave her life, it is left with infamy, which is worse than death.[62]

The only difference between attainders and these proceedings, he continued, was that subjects attainted for treason were given more opportunities to defend themselves than had been allowed to the duchess.[63] Powis was not, of course, setting out to make women the legal equals of men. He constructed this slightly strained analogy to highlight the arbitrary and unprecedented nature of the proceedings. But the consequence of his strategy was, in effect, to present the duchess as a person in possession of properties that were parallel to, albeit distinct from, properties possessed by men. A woman had a right to protect her reputation and jointure in the way that a man had a right to protect his life, lineage and estate. Thus, Powis had no difficulty using arguments and analogies that implicitly put the duchess in the position of a man. 'I need not take notice of what everybody knows, that we have a happy constitution, if we can keep it, every man can call his wife his own, and his estate his own, because it can't be taken away except by legal trial'.[64]

It is important to note, however, that if Powis and North were able to conceive of the duchess as a rights-bearing subject in spite of her gender, they were able to do so only – or largely – because of her class. The duchess and her supporters alluded frequently to the fact that she was a member of one of the oldest and greatest families in England. As the duchess put it in her reponse to the duke's first bill in 1692, 'I am not only the Duke of Norfolk's wife, but also born and descended from parents and ancestors of the ancient nobility'.[65] The duchess's aristocratic status was used by her advocates to construct a vision of order and disorder that rivalled the one presented by the duke. Whereas the duke appealed to the fear that women would overturn the proper order of the family, the duchess played to anxieties about the subversion of social hierarchy. The fact that the witnesses against the duchess were servants made this a powerful theme in her defence:

> Masters are already too much in the power of their servants, and if they charge their masters with adultery, felony or even treason, it is not easily in the power of the master to defend himself against downright swearing; servants having those opportunities of the knowledge of times and places and company, which cannot be denied or avoided, and which others have not, whereupon they may frame and build

false evidence, and many times are of ill principles and desperate fortunes, and of tempers very revengeful, so that whoever turns away a servant, he is in his power for his estate, honour, even life itself.[66]

The duchess's advocates were more willing than the duke's to view women as persons with rights but also more ready to distinguish between persons on the basis of social status.

Whether the alternative visions of order and rights that emerged in the debate reveal inherent differences in the gender politics of the two sides, or whether they were produced by contingency, is hard to say. The link between support for the Revolution of 1688 and support for the Duke of Norfolk's attempt to rid himself of his wife was forged along a number of axes, through circumstances that could easily have been different. Had the duke's collateral heirs been Protestant, had the duchess not been a Jacobite, or had the duke's own adultery not discouraged him from going first to the ecclesiastical courts, the sides might have fallen out differently. Had the household servants supported the duchess, her side might have praised the honesty of the lower orders rather than railed against their testimony.

But given that the circumstances were what they were, the debate about the Norfolk divorce provided an opportunity for each political group to create a unifying myth for itself, to fuse together disparate strands of self-justification or complaint. For whigs, support for the Norfolk divorce bill was a point around which a narrative of the Revolution as the triumph of a generalized moral reformation and rejection of popery could be brought together with a narrative of the Revolution as a triumph of a 'purer', continental (read: dissenting) protestantism; this in turn could be joined with a secular concern with the preservation of property. Jacobites and non-jurors made a different kind of sense out of the whole affair, seeing in the divorce a symbol of the new regime's disregard for sacred bonds, and for its disregard of the rights of its opponents. From the point of view of high-Anglican churchmen and their supporters, the role played by the new Williamite bishops in the affair became a focal point of resentment about a variety of different threats to the Church. On each side, disparate strands of ideological self-justification were brought together around the case and welded into a coherent whole.

What is interesting here, then, is not so much whether an individual's views on divorce rose organically out of their political beliefs, but how groups used the controversy over divorce as a way of legitimating themselves politically. In this process, the differences between parties may be less important to historians than the similarity of their aims. Whatever position they took on the allowability of parliamentary divorce, all parties (whig and tory, Williamites and Jacobites, high- and low-churchmen) used the debate on the Norfolk divorce as an occasion to present themselves as the defenders both of the familial order and of the rights of English subjects to have their most sacred property protected under the law. They had, of course, very different ideas of what this involved, but they played for the same ideological stakes: a chance to legitimate their political views in terms that were broadly acceptable to all members of the political nation.

This has mostly been a story about how people with political agendas used a debate about marriage and divorce to further those agendas. Did the process ever work in the other direction? The writings of the early 'feminist' and tory polemicist, Mary Astell, present us with an opportunity to explore the ways in which concerns about political power and about marriage could be brought together by someone who certainly cared deeply about the nature of relations between men and women.

NOTES

1 On the development of parliamentary proceedings on divorce, see Lawrence Stone, *The road to divorce* (Oxford, Oxford University Press, 1990), ch. 10. See also John F. MacQueen, *A practical treatise on the appellate jurisdiction of the House of Lords* (1842), pp. 550–76.

2 Stone, *Road to divorce*, p. 312.

3 Burnet, *HOT*, 4:226–9.

4 This is true at least for the 1692 votes. See Eveline Cruickshanks, David Hayton and Clyve Jones, 'Divisions in the House of Lords on the transfer of the Crown and other issues, 1689–94: ten new lists', *Bulletin of the Institute of Historical Research* 53 (1980), pp. 73–5.

5 George Hickes, *A word to the wavering* (1689), p. 5. I owe this reference to Alison Schulz, who generously shared her MA thesis.

6 Susan Staves, *Player's sceptres* (Lincoln, University of Nebraska Press, 1979).

7 Elizabeth Singer Rowe, *Poems on several occasions* (John Dunton, 1696), preface.

8 'Eugenia', *The female advocate; or, a plea for the just liberty of the tender sex. By a lady of quality* (Andrew Bell, 1700), pp. 13, 26, 28.

9 William Fleetwood, *The relative duties of parents and children, husbands and wives, and masters and servants* (C. Harper, 1705), pp. 176–7.

10 [Gilbert Burnet], *An enquiry into the measures of submission to the supream authority* [1688], p. 1.

11 *Ibid.*, p. 5.

12 *Ibid.*

13 Elinor James, *To the right honorable Convention* [1688].

14 'The divorce' (1692) – the poem begins, 'You Englishmen all that are under a curse' – printed in *POAS*, 5:316–22. See also 'On the promoted bishops' (1691) – the poem begins 'For the miracles done' – printed in *POAS*, 5:312–15, for the same analogy.

15 Fleetwood, *Relative duties*, pp. 177–8; Burnet, *Enquiry into the measures of submission*, and see below.

16 W[hite] K[ennett], *A dialogue between two friends, occasioned by the late revolution of affairs* (Richard Chiswell, 1689). p. 17.

17 *Ibid.*, pp. 17–18.

18 See note 22 below for a possible solution to the problem that husbands, unlike kings, could not be replaced.

19 *A Letter to a gentlewoman concerning government* (Elizabeth Whitelocke, 1697), p. 10.

20 *Ibid.*, p. 12.

21 *Ibid.*, p. 13.

22 *Ibid.*, p. 14. This is one way to fill the gap Kennett opened by failing to pursue his logic.

23 *Ibid.*, p. 13.

24 For a penetrating analysis of the tendency of eighteenth-century jurists to avoid letting contract theory be extended into the family, see Susan Staves, *Married women's separate property in England, 1660–1833* (Cambridge, Mass., Harvard University Press, 1990), esp. chs 5 and 6.

25 John Butler, *The true state of the case of John Butler* (printed for the author, 1697), p. 7.

26 *Ibid.*, p. 19.

27 *Proceedings of the Old Bailey, 8th–11th December* (1697).

28 *Concubinage and poligamy disproved* (Richard Baldwin, 1698), 'epistle dedicatory'.

29 William Cobbett, *Parliamentary history of England*, 36 vols (London, T. C. Hansard, 1806–20), 5:174–5. Cobbett's account is partly confirmed by *Further considerations on the Earl of Macclesfield's bill* [1697], in which the author responds to a 'mock-case' published by the countess which sounds much like the argument described by Cobbett. The 'mock-case' in printed form has not been found. See also *Lords Journals* 16, pp. 195, 197, 224, 235.

30 *Further considerations*, p. 3.

31 *Ibid.*, p. 4.

32 See Historical Manuscripts Commission, *Manuscripts of the House of Lords, 1697–99*, n.s., vol. 3 (HMSO, 1905), p. 58. Conversely, Sergeant Wright, who supported the Duke of Norfolk, supported Lady Macclesfield in this case.

33 'Resolutions of the house of ladies', Bodl. English poetry MS c. 18, fols 112v–113; 'Some observations touching the Duke of Norfolk's case in the House of Lords', Bodl. English poetry MS c. 18, fols 111v–112v. The first of these can be loosely described as lambasting the duchess rather than the duke.

34 Roger North, 'The case of divorce by act of Parliament', BL Add. MS 32523, fols 42–6. This paper addresses the question of whether the case should come before parliament or not. It was most probably written as advice to the duchess's lawyers. Although undated, it closely resembles arguments made for the duchess in the 1699/1700 debate.

35 *Ibid.*

36 *The Duke of Norfolk's case: with reasons for passing his bill* [1700], printed in *The proceedings upon the bill of divorce between his Grace the Duke of Norfolk and the Lady Mary Morduant* (Matthew Gillyflower, 1700), pp. 38–40. Interestingly, this was not given as a reason the first two times the duke presented his bill.

37 Burnet, *HOT*, 4:228. See his *Enquiry into the measures of submission*, p. 5, for the same argument.

38 The relevant gospel passage in the King James translation is, 'whosoever shall put away his wife, saving for the cause of fornication, causeth her to commit adultery'. Cosin's argument was widely circulated; see, for example, *Bishop Cozen's argument, proving that adultery works the dissolution of a marriage* [1669]. For Norfolk citing Cosin, see *The proceedings*, pp. 41–4.

39 That perspective is well described in Mark Goldie, 'The non-jurors, episcopacy, and the origins of the convocation controversy', in Eveline Cruickshanks (ed.), *Ideology and conspiracy: aspects of Jacobitism, 1689–1759* (Edinburgh, John Donald, 1982).

40 On William and the Church, see G. V. Bennett, 'King William III and the episcopate', in G. V. Bennett and John D. Walsh (eds), *Essays in modern English church history* (New York, Oxford University Press, 1966); G. V. Bennett, 'Conflict in the Church', in Geoffrey Holmes (ed.), *Britain after the Glorious Revolution* (Macmillan, 1969); Henry Horwitz, *Revolution politicks: the career of Daniel Finch, second Earl of Nottingham 1647–1730* (Cambridge, Cambridge University Press, 1968), ch. 6.

41 'Upon the divorces made by an act of Parliament especially the Earl of Macclesfeld' (poem begins, 'It is an old saying'), BL Harley MS 7319, fol. 387.

42 Burnet, *HOT*, 2:227. See also 4:226–9, 1:479–82.

43 'Some observations touching the duke of Norfolk's case', Bodleian English poetry MS c. 18, fols 111v–112v.

44 *Ibid.*

45 Tony Claydon, *William III and the godly revolution* (Cambridge, Cambridge University Press, 1996), especially ch. 3. See also Dudley W. R. Bahlmann, *The moral revolution of 1688* (New Haven, Yale, 1957).

46 These are discussed in Rachel Weil, 'Sometimes a sceptre is only a sceptre: pornography and politics in Restoration England', in Lynn Hunt (ed.), *The invention of pornography* (New York, Zone, 1993). Novels about the old regime include *The amours of the Sultana of Barbary* (Richard Baldwin, 1689); *The amours of Messalina, late Queen of Albion* (John Lyford, 1689), *The amours of the Duchess of Portsmouth* (Richard Baldwin, 1690).

47 Burnet, *HOT*, 4:228.

48 'Castamore', *Conjugium languens: or, the natural, civil and religious mischiefs arising from conjugal infidelity and impunity* (R. Roberts, 1700), pp. 16–17; *A treatise concerning adultery and divorce* (R. Roberts, 1700), p. 15. The second of these is printed again in Thomas Morer, *Two cases: the first of adultery and divorce* (Thomas Newborough, 1702).

49 Cobbett, *Parliamentary history*, 5:1174. See also *Reasons for the Earl of Macclesfield's bill in Parliament* [1697].

50 *Duke of Norfolk's case* in *The proceedings*, p. 2.

51 *The proceedings* (1700), p. 57.

52 *The proceedings* (1700), pp. 59–60.

53 Margaret R. Sommerville, *Sex and subjection: attitudes to women in early-modern society* (Arnold, 1995), pp. 141–50. Many of her citations, however, are from the late seventeenth century.

54 *Marriage promoted* (Richard Baldwin, 1690), pp. 29, 31, 62.

55 *Ibid.*, p. 9.

56 'Castamore', *Conjugium languens*, pp. 19, 2.

57 *Ibid.*, p. 28.

58 North, 'Case of divorce', fols 42–6. For similar statements in the 1700 proceedings, see *The proceedings* (1700), especially Mr Powis's presentation of the duchess's case, pp. 49–53. See also *A vindication of her Grace Mary Dutchess of Norfolk* (1693), p. 13.

59 *The proceedings*, p. 50. This stance allowed advocates of the duchess to take differing positions on whether the canon law was popish. Some of the duchess's supporters did make the argument that English canon law was already conformable to the gospel. See John Asgill, *A question upon divorce* (1717) for such a defence. See also the speech by Dr Pinfold, in *The proceedings*, pp. 54–5. Powis thought the Roos, Macclesfield and Northampton divorces were different from Norfolk's case because the church courts had been used first in the former.

60 Powis's relationship to Jacobitism is unclear. He was solicitor-general under James II; he lost his post after Anne's death in part because he was regarded as sympathetic to the pretender. See Edward Foss, *A biographical dictionary of the judges of England* (John Murray, 1870).

61 *The proceedings*, p. 60.

62 *Ibid.*, p. 50.

63 *Ibid.* Roger North, 'Case of divorce', also makes a comparison to attainder.

64 *Ibid.* It is possible that 'wife' is a misprint for 'life'. The latter makes more sense, but the slip is interesting.

65 *A vindication of her Grace*, p. 13.

66 *The case of Mary, Dutchess of Norfolk* [1700], in *The proceedings* (1700), p. 48.

Chapter 6

Mary Astell: the marriage of toryism and feminism

Mary Astell has been hailed as 'the first English feminist'. She was also a savage and effective tory polemicist. How she brought those two things together is the subject of this chapter.[1] Astell's commitment to tory politics does not in itself indicate that tory political ideology was more hospitable to some forms of 'feminism', however that is defined, than was whig ideology in the seventeenth century.[2] Such a claim would ignore the existence of whig women who were 'feminists', such as Elizabeth Rowe and Susanna Centlivre. Moreover, as few tory men showed marked sympathy for women's plight, Astell cannot be regarded as a typical tory. Rather, she provides a case study in how a woman could find meanings that she deemed relevant to her condition as a woman within the political discourses generated by men, and how she could modify those discourses accordingly. Astell's achievement, moreover, was not just to appropriate tory ideology for 'feminist' purposes, but to put her critique of gender relations and gender inequality to use *in* her tory polemic, constructing links between political and gender-political concerns.

ASTELL'S VIEW OF MARRIAGE

The nature of Astell's 'feminism' requires some clarification. Her most famous work, *Reflections on marriage* (1700), disturbs the modern reader with its ardent (it is tempting to say masochistic) appreciation of the value of suffering. The occasion for the work was the publication in English of the proceedings in the notorious case of the Duke and Duchess of Mazarin. Having been sold by her uncle into marriage to an insane and tyrannical husband, the duchess fled to England, where her wit, beauty and charm made her a great favourite at the court of Charles II. Astell, writing in the first edition anonymously and in a male voice, treated the case as an extreme instance of a common situation. Many husbands took advantage of their superior position to tyrannize over wives who were clearly their intellectual equals or superiors.

Nonetheless, Astell condemned the duchess's behaviour as being inconsistent with what Astell took to be a fundamental political injunction of the Christian religion (as established in Matthew 22:21, Ephesians 5:22 and Titus 3:1, for example) to 'obey the powers that be'.

> But this world being a place of trial and governed by general laws, just retributions being reserved for hereafter, respect and obedience many times become due for order's sake to those who don't otherwise deserve them.[3]

A right understanding of her duty to obey would enable even the most abused wife to turn her suffering into an opportunity for spiritual growth. Astell dwells lovingly on the process whereby an injured wife, 'if discretion and piety prevail upon her passions ... sits down quietly, contented with her lot'; refusing to take solace in crowds of admirers or frivolous entertainments, she finds that she was 'never truly a happy woman till she came in the eyes of the world to be rendered miserable'.

> Affliction, the sincerest friend, the frankest monitor, the best instructer, and indeed the only useful school that women are ever put to, rouses her understanding, opens her eyes, fixes her attention, and diffuses such a light, such a joy into her mind, as not only informs her better, but entertains her more than ever her *ruel* did though crowded by men of wit.[4]

Why, the reader might ask, is the work considered 'feminist' at all? Because the book deliciously skewers men's pretensions to inherent superiority. Astell makes gestures in the direction of proving that men deserve their right to govern women, only to undercut her praise and transform panegyric into mock-panegyric:

> But how can a woman scruple entire subjection, how can she forbear to admire the worth and excellency of the superior sex, if she at all considers it? Have not all the great actions that have been performed in the world been done by men? Have not they founded empires and overturned them? Do they not make laws and continually repeal and amend them? Their vast minds lay kingdoms to waste, no bounds or measures can be prescribed to their desires. War or peace depend on them, they form cabals and have the wisdom and courage to get over all the rubs which may lie in the way of their desired grandeur. What is it they cannot do? They make worlds and ruin them, form systems of a universal nature and dispute eternally about them; their pen gives worth to the most trifling controversy; nor can a fray be inconsiderable if they have drawn their swords in it.[5]

It is worth emphasizing that the two sides of Astell's view of marriage are tightly (if maddeningly) linked: her insistence on the duty of wives to obey is precisely what licenses her to demonstrate that the duty to obey does not arise from the fact that men deserve their power, but from the fact that they have it. For Astell it is only the person who understands the reason for obedience to authority — that it *is* authority — who will see through its pretensions clearly. Humility, Astell notes, 'does not put out our eyes':

> And when a superior does a mean and unjust thing ... and yet this does not provoke his inferiors to refuse that observance which their stations in the world require, they cannot but have an inward sense of their own superiority, the other having no pretence to it, at the same time that they pay him outward respect and deference, which is such a flagrant testimony of the sincerest love of order as proves their souls to be of the highest and noblest rank.[6]

We can better situate Astell's views of marriage by comparing her work with one of the best-selling pieces of advice literature of the day, the Marquess of Halifax's *Advice to a daughter*, first published in 1688 and reprinted numerous times throughout the eighteenth century. The comparison suggests that Astell's views ran counter to one significant and popular way, if not the dominant way, of conceptualizing the position of women in marriage.

Astell and Halifax have much in common. Halifax begins his discussion of marriage by acknowledging, like Astell, the contradiction between the inequality of men and women and a common-sense view of fairness. 'The laws of marriage', he admits, 'run in a harsher style towards your sex'.[7] He nonetheless asserts, like Astell, that law and custom cannot be changed. Halifax and Astell come to terms with this situation, however, in radically different ways.

Halifax's treatment of the problem of inequality between the sexes is highly equivocal. He appears at first to attribute it to men's superior reasoning ability, suggesting that God has arranged things for the best:

> You must first lay it down for a foundation in general, that there is inequality in the sexes, and that for the better economy of the world, the men, who were to be the lawgivers, had the larger share of reason bestowed upon them, by which means your sex is the better prepared for the compliance that is necessary for the better performance of those duties which seem to be the most properly assigned to it.[8]

This bland confidence in the natural foundation of inequality is belied, however, by the rest of the chapter on marriage, wherein the female reader is shown how, by a 'wise and dextrous conduct', she can protect herself in any situation, including that of having a husband stupider than herself! Some women, he acknowledges, do possess more reason than most men, and Halifax apparently expects his reader to be one of them.[9] He therefore walks a fine line between asserting a natural basis for inequality and showing that such a claim is absurd.

Halifax's real point, however, is not to make a judgement about the justice of the order of things, but to suggest a stance that one can take towards that order. His intellectual equivocation can be taken as a model for the approach that he invites his reader to take towards marriage. Just as he pays lip service to a view of the world which he then neglects to take seriously, so his reader, under the guise of deference to authority, can do as she pleases. Provided she doesn't challenge law and custom, she can manipulate it.

> You are, therefore, to make your best of what is settled by law and custom, and not vainly imagine it will be changed for your sake. But that you may not be discouraged, as if you lay under the weight of an incurable grievance, you are to know, that by a wise and dextrous conduct, it will be in your power to relieve youself of anything that looketh like a disadvantage in it.[10]

If a husband is ill-tempered, for example, 'a little flattery may be admitted, which, by being necessary, will cease to be criminal'.[11] If he is avaricious, watch for a fit of vanity, ambition, or drunkenness, and let not one of these critical moments 'slip without your making advantage of it'.[12] If he is foolish, 'do like a wise minister does to an easy prince: first give him the orders you afterwards receive from him'.[13]

For Halifax, lip service to male superiority is the price one pays for subverting male authority. Astell takes the opposite approach to the theory and practice of patriarchal marriage. For her, genuine obedience is the price one pays for the intellectual privilege of refusing to pretend that men are superior in an intellectual or spiritual sense. Moreover, Astell takes the rendering of obedience to authority as a sign of the superiority of the person who is willing to do it.

Consequently, the fact that some women (such as the Duchess of Mazarin) do make the mistake of withdrawing obedience from unworthy masters is for Astell a good argument in favour of educating women. 'Men never mistake their true interest more than when they endeavour to keep women in ignorance', because 'if man's authority be justly established, the more sense a woman has, the more reason she will find to submit to it'. Without education, 'can it be expected that she should so constantly perform so difficult a duty as entire subjection, to which corrupt nature is so averse?'[14] Paradoxically, the very act of submission becomes potentially embarrassing to the authority itself.

REFLECTIONS ON MARRIAGE AS A POLITICAL TRACT

Astell constantly plays in *Reflections on marriage* with analogies between the family and the state. The language of the text itself would thus seem to indicate that Astell's views on marriage have something to do with her political beliefs. But what? *Reflections on marriage* is unmistakably the work of a tory thinker committed to the principle of 'passive obedience'.[15] The political thrust of the work, however, is not to rehash arguments in favour of this principle.[16] Conspicuously absent from *Reflections on marriage* are the usual topoi of arguments on allegiance: the obligatory remarks on the origins of government, the indefeasibility of hereditary right, the Hanoverian succession, the truth or falsehood of the warming-pan story, and so on.

Astell approaches politics in a radically subjective manner: it is not about the rules governing relations between people in civil society, but about people's relationship to themselves and to God. It is the arena in which one comes to terms with powerlessness, or – if one is in a position of authority – restrains one's will to power. Her political universe is divided between two kinds of people, the egotistical and the pious: the former try to control the world in accordance with their own desires, the latter restrain their impulses in accordance with their duty. The dichotomy between the egotistical and the pious cuts across that between ruler and subject. A pious ruler is one who knows that he has no inherent 'right' to govern, and therefore rules for God rather than for himself. By the same token, an egotistical subject (who, for Astell, is the same as a seditious subject) is the moral equivalent of a tyrant.

Astell's strongest political commitment was to the Church of England, which she saw as being endangered by latitudinarians, dissenters, freethinkers, Socinians and atheists.[17] Her pamphlets attacking occasional conformity (the practice whereby dissenters annually took communion in the Church of England in order to fulfil the requirements for holding political office) provide the best example of how she deployed the moral categories of egotism and piety to vicious effect in the context of particular debates. A study of these pamphlets will also show how the dichotomy between the egotistical and the pious links her writings on politics to her writings on marriage.

Astell's critique of occasional conformity is based upon the understanding of passive obedience developed in her writings on marriage. As we saw, Astell believed that internal intellectual and spiritual freedom was the one consolation available to the obedient wife or subject. Occasional conformists, however, want internal *and* external freedom, conscience *and* political office. Astell finds this desire to have it both ways offensive and threatening.

Astell is careful to distinguish her attack on occasional conformity from an attack on dissent *per se*. People are entitled to have 'tender consciences', even if they are erroneous. Freedom of 'conscience', confined within the heads of individuals, is a fact of life, and the English state is sufficiently generous to consciences in that it permits dissenters freedom of worship. But, says Astell (quoting with approval the Elizabethan statesman, Frances Walsingham), 'when conscience exceeds its bounds, and grows to be faction, it loses its nature'.[18] This is the case with the occasional conformists, whom Astell presents as socially privileged and wealthy men envious of the preferments available to members of the Church of England. A true Christian, Astell argues, would be happy to be barred from political office: 'He will not therefore think himself injured but obliged by being disengaged from this world, and left at full liberty to pursue the great concerns of the next'.[19] The early Christians set a standard which puts the dissenters to shame: St Paul, 'a prisoner for the cause of Christ', warned against false teachers who instructed Christians 'how to avoid persecution'.[20] The sufferings of dissenters are trivial in comparison to those of the early Christians, and their very desire for worldly goods it itself proof of their lack of religious conviction.

It is not surprising that Astell would find the question of when 'conscience' is conscience, and when it is 'faction', compelling, even to the point of obsession. The issue was at the heart of the post-1688 debate on allegiance, during which whigs had depicted tory claims to conscience as a mask for Jacobitism. Astell's attack on the faction-masquerading-as-conscience represented by dissenters might well be seen as retaliation for whig attacks on the 'conscience' of tories who in the 1690s had difficulty taking oaths of allegiance, or who took those oaths on what whigs regarded as the wrong grounds; she would have seen those attacks as arising not from a justifiable fear of crypto-Jacobitism, but as a calculated strategy of politically crippling the tories by labelling them as crypto-Jacobites.

The debate on occasional conformity, then, was itself the result of an earlier debate over the proper grounds of allegiance, specifically, about whether the security of the government was threatened by the tory advocates of passive obedience and non-resistance. The stakes for tories in that debate were extremely high, since losing it would lead to being labelled crypto-Jacobites. And it was to that debate that *Reflections on marriage* was directed.

To understand how *Reflections on marriage* addresses and intervenes in the allegiance controversies of the 1690s requires some background. The Glorious Revolution posed a dilemma for people who believed, as Astell did, that the Bible and the teachings of the Church of England demanded passive obedience to established authority. If resistance to that authority was a heinous sin, how could pious Christians accept the new rulers when the rightful king still lived? In spite of this obvious difficulty, most people who believed strongly in passive obedience were able to find a way to reconcile that belief with an acceptance of the new regime. There were a variety of stories and arguments available for this purpose: James had 'abdicated', William was a conqueror in a 'just war', James was not in possession of the government and therefore could not offer his subjects the protection required by divine ordinance of rulers, God had indicated by way of William's providential victory that William was divinely anointed. None of these ways of understanding what had happened in 1688 required a belief that the people of England had done anything to *choose* William. For this reason, they appealed to tories, and to many people described as 'moderate whigs'.[21] Thus, most people eventually brought themselves to take the oath of allegiance to the new regime.

Controversy in the 1690s revolved not so much around whether people *should* swear allegiance to the new regime, but around the proper grounds for doing so. From the point of view of some whigs, tories who used arguments from conquest or possession to justify taking the oath of allegiance could not be trusted. The author of *The anatomy of a Jacobite tory: in a dialogue between Whig and Tory* (1690) lambasted the authors of two other tracts for advocating submission to William as the *de facto* (albeit not *de jure*) ruler of England. In doing so, he argued, they were encouraging their readers to obtain offices and preferment under the new regime while leaving them a loophole which enabled them to switch their allegiance back to James if he showed signs of being able to recover his throne by force.[22] The author of the imaginary dialogue had his whig speaker put pressure on his tory friend's principle of 'passive obedience' by testing it in hypothetical situations. If the tory knew, for example, that there was a Jacobite plot against William's life, would he warn William about it?[23] At the end of the dialogue the tory, who has taken the oath of allegiance, acknowledges that it is hypocritical to obey William as a *de facto* ruler without regarding him as a lawful one as well, and declares himself a full-fledged Jacobite. Clearly, a mere willingness on the part of some people to 'obey the powers that be' was not a reason to trust them! The only way to flush out crypto-Jacobites from office in church and state was to require more explicit and positive oaths of loyalty which would force those who took them to declare more openly the terms and grounds of their allegiance.

Accordingly, whigs throughout the 1690s made efforts to circumscribe the grounds upon which the swearing of allegiance was acceptable. In January 1693, Parliament ordered the public burning of both Gilbert Burnet's *Pastoral letter* (published 1689) and Charles Blount's *King William and Queen Mary conquerors* (1693) and passed a resolution defining any use of conquest-based arguments as 'highly injurious to their majesties' rightful title to the crown' and 'inconsistent with the principles on which this government was founded'. As Mark Goldie points out, both of the condemned books employed the Grotian *jus gentium* argument which sanctioned governments established by conquest, but only in the case of a 'just war'. Neither Burnet nor Blount, then, could fairly be accused of using the argument that William's title was established merely by force to cloak a crypto-Jacobite 'mental reservation'. The condemnation of these pamphlets must be seen, as Goldie says, as 'a victory for the whigs in their ideological campaign to limit the range of casuistical manoeuvre in the Revolution debate'.[24] The death of Mary II in 1695 further limited the range of manoeuvre for tories: there was now no legitimate heir to James II on the throne, and the fact that Mary had died young from a disfiguring disease did not say much for God's providential support of the Glorious Revolution.

The attempted assassination of William III in 1696 gave the whigs a further opportunity to constrict the definition of what might be properly thought to constitute allegiance. Both Houses of Parliament adopted, in slightly different forms, oaths of Association which raised the level of the ideological hurdle in much the way that the author of *The anatomy of a Jacobite tory* had recommended. Subcribers were bound to declare William a 'rightful and lawful' king and undertake 'revenge upon his enemies' should he die by violence. The country was swept by a wave of oath-taking; in some communities the entire adult male population, *and* some women, subscribed to the Association.[25] Although the Association was technically 'voluntary', it was administered publicly in ways that were meant to embarrass anyone who would not subscribe to it. For that reason, it provided the whigs with a weapon to use against the tories, some of whom, like the Earl of Nottingham, found the combination of new circumstances and tougher language a stumbling block to taking the new oath and consequently found themselves vulnerable to being labelled as Jacobites.[26] The process of defining the tory doctrine of passive obedience as a form of crypto-Jacobitism, which culminated in the 1710 trial of Henry Sacheverell,[27] was well underway by the time Astell wrote *Reflections on marriage* in 1700, and provides an important context for it.

Astell's view of the Revolution of 1688, and the justifiability of swearing oaths of allegiance to it, is hard to pin down precisely. We know that she had friendly relations with non-juring clergymen in Anne's reign, although she seems to have accepted, and helpfully amplified, Henry Dodwell's proposal that the non-jurors reunite with the rest of the Church of England once the original non-juring bishops had died.[28] After 1714, as Ruth Perry has demonstrated, she was closely connected to prominent Jacobites.[29] This does not mean, however, that she was actively plotting for a Jacobite restoration in the reigns of William or Anne. On the contrary, the title page to her *Fair way with dissenters* (1704) describes the pamphlet as 'not writ by Mr. L——y [Charles Leslie], or any other furious Jacobite, whether clergyman or layman; but by a very moderate person, and a dutiful subject to the Queen'.

The more important point is that whether secretly a Jacobite or not, Astell lived and worked under the shadow of suspicion that anyone who adhered to the doctrine of 'passive obedience' was insufficiently loyal to the government. As a passionate supporter of the high-church position in ecclesiastical matters, she was part of the group most vulnerable to Jacobite-baiting by whigs. Not surprisingly, she was an adept at the game of throwing the charge of disloyalty back. In *An Impartial enquiry into the causes of rebellion and civil war*, she suggested that just as the presbyterians in the 1640s had used the fear of popery to justify rebellion, so too the whigs and low-churchmen who charged their tory opponents with closet sympathy for the Pretender and the French were the real threats to the security of the government, and espoused 'some of the vilest Popish doctrines' (she meant regicide) themselves.

> Let them [the whigs] not upbraid any one, and much less the best patriots, and her
> Majesty's most dutiful and loyal subjects, with a design of bringing in the French
> and arbitrary power; since they themselves are zealous advocates, industrious and
> indefatiguable bustlers for principles that will bring in anybody: a Philip of Spain,
> or a Lewis of France, or the Great Turk himself, if he were near enough.[30]

Anyone who believed they had 'consented' to government might just as easily
consent to a different one'.

Echoes of the allegiance debate resonate in the text of *Reflections on
marriage*. By moving the argument about the proper grounds of allegiance
from the terrain of government to that of marriage, Astell made a powerful
case that those who obey a power simply because it is there (passive obedient
tories) are steadier in their allegiance than those who obey a power on grounds
that it is deserving of obedience (whigs). Such an argument was far easier to
make with reference to conjugal authority than to governmental authority
precisely because the claim that husbands should rule over their wives
whether they deserved to or not by their own merits was entirely uncontroversial. The brilliance of *Reflections on marriage* as a political work lies in how
Astell, shielding herself with the non-controversial claim, manipulates her
reader into accepting a far more subversive one.

Astell's complicated strategy requires she skirt the edge of sedition: 'If they
[men] have usurped, I love justice too much to wish success and continuance
to usurpations, which though submitted to out of prudence, and for quietness
sake, yet leave every body free to regain their lawful right whenever they have
power and opportunity'.[31] The presence in the text of such dangerous
statements (which play to whig fears about the untrustworthiness of tory
submission) may explain why Astell chose to publish anonymously, and to
distance herself from the argument by speaking through a persona that is
implicitly male. The important point, however, is that the suggestion that
usurpers will be overthrown is carefully framed by a declaration that those
who hold power (men, the Williamite regime) have nothing to fear if their
power is *not* usurped. Indeed, such fear is itself a sign of illegitimacy: in a
pointed reference to oaths of allegiance, she remarks that usurpers are 'always
most desirous of recognitions and busy in imposing oaths, whereas a lawful
Prince contents himself with the usual methods and securities'.[32]

A ruler confident of his 'lawful prerogative', moreover, will not expect the
flattery of being told he has deserved his lawful power by his own merits.
Answering the objection that men, imagining 'I have made some discoveries
which like Arcana Imperii, ought to be kept secret', will object to her frank
exposure of the fact that they are not morally or mentally superior, Astell
insists that 'in good earnest, I do them more honour than to suppose their
lawful prerogatives need any mean arts to support them'. She thereby creates a
space for loyal criticism, and shifts the blame for disloyalty to the efforts of

authorities to demand that their authority be accepted because of the sheer merit of those who wield it. Those who do fear criticism are implicitly acknowledging their own unlawfulness, and have only themselves to blame if they are discredited in the eyes of their subjects.

To underline the point, Astell introduces the figure of a female reader who might misinterpret what has been said, and conclude that 'if a man has not these qualifications [to govern] where is his right? That if he misemploys, he abuses it? And if he abuses it, according to the modern deduction, he forfeits it'.[33] We are meant to see that 'the modern deduction' is misguided. But the joke is that the erring female reader has only taken those who try to justify male authority at their word, and it is these justifiers rather than Astell who are to blame for the mistake:

> if he who is freely elected, after all his fair promises and the fine hopes he raised, proves a tyrant, the consideration that he was one's own choice, will not render [one] more submissive and patient, but I fear more refractory. For though it is very unreasonable, yet we see tis in the course of the world, not only to return injury for injury, but crime for crime; both parties indeed are guilty, but the aggressors have a double guilt, they have not only their own, but their neighbour's ruin to answer for.[34]

This is a brilliant turning of the tables. Astell has manipulated her reader into admitting that the apparently stronger claims offered by whigs for the legitimacy of the new regime may in fact be less conducive to loyalty than the tories simple, weaker one of 'passive obedience', and that the regime (not the tories) is responsible for any disloyalty that it incurs by failing to live up to its own inflated claims to legitimacy.

PATRIARCHY, SEXUAL DANGER, AND ASTELL'S ANTI-WHIG POLEMIC

The obedient wife who understands rightly the grounds of her duty to obey her husband is clearly a better model for the *political* subject than are the men who insist that their superiority entitles them to rule. This claim connects Astell's marital and political ethics. It also suggests that for Astell, the dichotomy between the egotistical and the pious was gendered in significant ways. This is not to say that she literally believed that all obedient subjects and caring rulers were women, or that all rebellious subjects and tyrannical rulers were men. But she did use the figure of the tyrannical husband to expose the hollowness of whig protests against tyranny. At the same time, she allowed the obedient wife to represent the ideal model for political behaviour in a subject.

The religious and political ideal presented in *Moderation truly stated* is closely related to that of the passive-obedient wife presented in *Reflections on marriage*. Women, being excluded from political society, are presented by Astell as the ideal political subjects because they are not tempted by the sins of faction and rebellion: 'Since we are not allowed to share in the honourable offices of the commonwealth', she wrote in *The Christian religion*, 'we ought to be ashamed and scorn to drudge in the mean trade of faction and sedition'.[35]

By the same token, it is no accident that Astell harps continually on the figure of the male subject who opposes tyranny in the state but exercises it in the home. 'How much soever arbitrary power may be disliked on a throne', she notes ironically in *Reflections on marriage*, 'not Milton himself would cry up liberty to poor female slaves, or plead for the lawfulness of resisting a private tyranny'.[36] Similarly, in the preface to the 1706 edition, she asked 'if absolute sovereignty be not necessary in a state, how comes it to be so in a private family?' and 'if all men are born free, how is it that all women are born slaves?'[37] The point for Astell is not that lovers of political liberty are contradicting themselves by failing to extend contract theory into the domestic sphere. Rather, it is that rebellious subjects are precisely the sort of people who fail to restrain their egotism. The conjuncture between political rebelliousness and domestic tyranny in such men is, for Astell, entirely predictable.

Astell's tendency to treat the behaviour of men in relation to women as a kind of political allegory is especially evident in her obsession with courtship and seduction. The vision of men as sexual predators and of women as victims who must be protected runs throughout Astell's work.[38] Her apparent obsession with the predatory aspects of male/female relationships allows her to rewrite an already existing tradition of anti-whig sexual polemic in a new way.

As we have seen in preceding chapters, whigs were eager to establish themselves as the party of sexual order, to deny the sexually subversive potential of contract theory, and to show that libertinism and debauchery were characteristic of the old regime, of Jacobites and of crypto-Jacobites. Tories and Jacobites conducted a similar campaign against the whigs. A key term in this campaign was 'libertinism'. As James G. Turner has pointed out, 'libertinism' had multiple and often contradictory social, religious, and political associations: it denoted drunkenness, sexual predation, irreligion and egotism.[39] Insofar as it could be linked to the flamboyance of the royalists in the civil war and the debauchery of the old regime, it was available to whigs for use against tories. But it could also be applied to the over-heated religious enthusiasm of Puritan and dissenting congregations; the wilful lawlessness of antinomian sectaries; the irreverent scepticism of deists, Socinians, and latitudinarian churchmen. As such it was equally available to tories for use against whigs.

The connection between the predatory sexuality of the (whig) libertine and his disrespect for the Church of England is made in the tory squib, written in 1705 on the occasion of 'the vote of the House of Lords that the Church was not in danger':

Good Halifax and pious Wharton cry
The Church has vapours and no danger's nigh.
To what we love not, we no danger see;
So were they hanged where would the danger be?
Hard that we must be silent midst our fears
And not believe our senses, but the Peers;
Just so a ravisher that's void of shame
First stops her mouth and then deflowers the dame.[40]

Like the author of this poem, Astell expresses her sense of outrage and danger by turning political dramas into sexual ones. For example, in the mock dedication to the whig Kit-Kat club in *Bart'lemy fair* (1709), she presents the whigs as libertine bullies who beat up fathers when they try to protect their innocent daughters from ruin.[41] Her *Impartial enquiry into the causes of rebellion and civil War* (1704), which draws explicit parallels between recent events and those of the 1640s, is littered with allusions to both licentiousness and seduction. The parliamentary army, for example, is characterized as so dissolute that its soldiers made 'Westminster Abbey, but even the very altar their brothel'.[42] The rebels of 1649 (and the whigs of 1704) are characterized as having 'depraved and boundless appetites': '"liberty of the people" in their language, signifies an unbounded licentiousness'.[43]

Moreover, the language Astell uses to describe how an evil faction persuades the rest of the nation to rebel against their rightful ruler bears a strong resemblence to the language she uses to describe seduction. She is fond of metaphors of hunting and trapping in both contexts. 'The encroachments are small at first, and industriously concealed', she writes in *An impartial enquiry* of the presbyterian fanatics of the 1640s, 'so advances are made by degrees, and the unwary people are trapped by them, without perceiving the snare, till they are entangled in the greatest crimes'.[44] The English people resemble an unwary young woman who, however well-meaning, has been insufficiently vigilant in guarding her virtue:

Far be it from us to think that the body of the nation ever concurred in that villainy we deplore ... any further than by a supine neglect of opposing it vigorously and in time. Wicked men are active and unwearied, they stick at no methods, use the vilest means to carry their point. They become the flatterers of men's follies, and the panders of their vices, to gain them to their party.[45]

The same language appears in *Reflections on marriage*, but it is used to describe courtship. A man, we are told, possesses a 'greater portion of ingenuity ... How deep is his policy in laying his designs at so great a distance and working them up by such little accidents'; 'it were endless to reckon up the divers strategems men use to catch their prey'; 'the steps to folly as well as sin are gradual, and almost imperceptible'. 'Can a woman be too much upon her guard?' The advice of well-meaning friends is futile once she is 'entangled in the snare'.[46]

The flattery of women by men in courtship is for Astell the classic example of the relationship between sexual seduction and contract theory. To flatter another person is to aggrandize oneself; men pretend to humble themselves before women but actually consider themselves women's superiors and intend to dominate them. Insofar as the flatterer's eloquence reflects more on the glory of the speaker than on the thing spoken about, flattery can also be considered a form of idolatry (the worship of oneself via the worship of one's own creation).[47]

> For nothing is in truth a greater outrage than flattery and feigned submissions, the plain English of which is this, 'I have a very mean opinion of both your under-standing and virtue, you are weak enough to be imposed on, and vain enough to snatch at the bait I throw ... I offer you incense, tis true, but you are like to pay for it .... If for nothing else, you'll serve at least as an exercise of my wit, and how much soever you swell with my breath, 'tis I deserve the praise for talking so well upon so poor a subject. We who make the idols are the greater deities; and as we set you up, so it is in our power to reduce you to your first obscurity, or to somewhat worse, to contempt.[48]

The relationship between the flatterer and the object of his flattery provides Astell with a model for the way that whigs understand the relationship of themselves as subjects to their sovereign. The passage quoted above ends with a sinister echo of the language of contract theory: 'you are therefore only on your good behaviour, and are like to be no more than what we please to make you'.[49] Flattering suitors, like whigs, pretend to submit to a figure of authority that they have created, in the full knowledge that they can reverse the relation-ship — depose their king — at will. The humble and admiring male suitor who becomes a despot at the moment of marriage is thus linked in Astell's mind with other subjects who, given a chance, will become tyrants: 'The scum of the people', she remarks of men who marry above their social station, 'are the most tyrannical when they get the power, and treat their betters with the greatest insolence'.[50]

In one sense, Astell's association of whiggery and men preying on women is entirely conventional. The link between 'liberty' and 'libertine' was a common tory trope. There is a crucial difference, however, between Astell's views of male predation and the conventional epithets hurled by tories at their oppon-ents. For Astell, to prey on a woman and to marry her are the same thing. She conflates seduction and courtship, treating both as based on contempt for women and resulting in a woman's ruin. It is interesting to compare *Reflections on marriage* to Halifax's *Advice to a daughter* in this respect. Astell and Halifax both use images of conquest and preying; both warn of the dangers to women of taking even 'innocent' liberties in their relations with men; both view the compliments paid by gallants as a form of self-aggrandizement; both are suspicious of platonic friendship between the sexes.

There is, however, a crucial difference between them. Halifax is clearly talking about the ruin of a woman's sexual reputation or her seduction. Astell uses identical language to explain how some women come to choose spouses badly, in particular how they come to make unequal matches: 'When once she admits a man to be her friend, tis his fault if he does not make himself her husband'.[51] Astell thus takes the language that Halifax used to describe the threat to the family order via seduction and applies it to the process by which the family order is constituted via marriage. She puts sexual libertinism and patriarchal marriage in the same category: both involve the abuse of power over women by men. By treating the two as the same rather than as opposites, she departs from the tory tradition of depicting the whigs as libertines because they *threaten* male authority.

Astell thus rewrote the sexual mythology of anti-whig polemic. Instead of attacking contract theory for undermining patriarchy, she attacked whigs for being contemptuous of women. We might further suggest that in branding whigs as patriarchs, Astell was not so much 'discovering' a hidden sexist strand in contract theory as inventing it. It is worth noting that Astell's picture of the attitudes of whig men towards the family was not an observation of reality but a deliberate distortion. As we saw, whigs did raise questions about the limits on patriarchal authority in the home. The answers that they gave to these questions were, granted, extremely vague, even deliberately so. It is, nonetheless, striking that Astell never acknowledged the fact that the questions were asked. This may have been in part because she tended to think about politics in terms of the subjective experience of obligation rather than the objective limitations on authority. But we may also see it as a deliberate manoeuvre to construct the whigs as more patriarchal than they really were in order to attack them as hypocrites. This mode of attack was perfect, moreover, because it could not be turned back against her: if anyone tried to point to a contradiction between her tory politics and her feminism, she could invoke her commitment to passive obedience in both the family and the state.

These polemical moves made it possible for Astell to render her own position as a tory and a feminist coherent rather than contradictory. By casting her political morality in terms of a dichotomy between egotism and piety, she could interpret both political rebellion and the tyranny of superiors (men) towards subordinates (women) as expressions of egotism. This in turn made it possible for her to imagine the whigs as both libertines and domestic tyrants: that is, to draw upon the tory tradition of casting whigs as threatening to the sexual order, but to portray this as a male threat to women's integrity rather than as a threat to patriarchy.

In finding the terms in which to reconcile toryism and feminism, moreover, Astell also found the terms in which to define her stance as an author and license herself to speak in public. The most admirable woman in her text is the one who refuses to sentimentalize the structures of power but nonetheless obeys them. It is tempting to identify that woman with Astell herself. The notion that intellectual freedom may be compatible with – or even dependent upon – political or familial subjection allows her to use her own lack of political power as a way of licensing herself to speak about politics.

We should be wary, however, in imagining that the web connecting Astell's gender politics, tory politics and authorial identity is completely seamless. There are at least two issues that complicate the picture drawn in the preceding paragraph. First, since Astell never married, there is a glaring gap between the elaborately imagined relationship of women to male authority, and her own experience. Would it have been as easy for Astell to develop a synthesis of toryism and feminism if she had spoken from the vantage point of an independent woman rather than the imagined ideal of the passive-obedient wife? Although she raised the question of the relationship of unmarried women to the structure of sexual hierarchy,[52] she significantly never answered it.

Second, the accession of Queen Anne in 1702 altered the terms of Astell's synthesis of feminism, tory politics, and authorial voice. Anne's presence on the throne facilitated Astell's task. Since the monarch was female, the denigration of women was in Astell's view seditious. In the preface to the 1706 edition, Astell wrote that, if one believed women to be naturally inferior, 'it would be a sin in any woman to have dominion over any man, and the greatest Queen ought not to command but to obey her footman, because no municipal laws can supercede or change the law of nature'.[53] It is only after Anne's accession that Astell outed herself as a female author. Significantly, she used Anne as the rhetorical occasion to reveal her sex in the preface to the 1706 edition, announcing the presence of a female ruler and a female author with the same phrase: 'the Reflector, who hopes Reflector is not bad English, now that Governor is happily of the feminine gender'.[54]

Moreover, in the final passage of the 1706 preface, Anne is hailed as a model of female excellence, the protector of her sex, and a figure who will preside over a new era of female achievement and sexual equality. Significantly, it is also the point at which Astell is most assertive about the 'unnatural' character of sexual hierarchy.

> To conclude, if that great queen, who has subdued the proud, and made the pretended invincible more than once fly before her ... will not think we need, or does not hold us worthy of, the protection of her ever victorious arms, and men have not the gratitude for her sake at least to do justice to her sex, who has been such a universal benefactress to theirs: Adieu to the liberties not of this or that nation or region only, but to the moiety of mankind! To all the great things that women might perform, inspired by her example, encouraged by her smiles, and supported by her

power! ... In a word, to those halcyon, or if you will millenium days, in which the wolf and the lamb shall feed together, and a tyrannous domination which nature never meant, shall no longer render useless if not hurtful, the industry and understandings of half mankind![55]

If Anne's presence makes a synthesis of toryism and feminism easier, however, it is important to recognize that it is a very different kind of synthesis from the one established in the original (1700) edition. As I argued above, the body of the text of *Reflections on marriage* hinges on the problem of obedience to an authority that has scant reason to justify its existence beyond the fact that it exists, and it draws from the tory response to William III. There is a disjunction between the idealized ruler presented in the 1706 preface and the attitude to authority implicit in the text. William's authority was seen as unnatural; this perception energized Astell's assault on the naturalness of men's right to govern women. Anne's authority, however, was presented as unproblematic. The feminism of the preface hinged on the legitimacy of Anne's authority, not its contingency. It would have been possible for Astell to reconcile toryism and feminism in both reigns, but the terms of the reconciliation, and the role that the monarch played in it, were different. Astell's synthesis of toryism and feminism was not a natural outgrowth of an inherent feminist subtext in tory ideology. Rather, it was hard won, requiring a particular construction of the self, which was made possible by particular historical circumstances.

English society after 1688 struggled not only to confer acceptable narratives (resistance, abdication, conquest, and so on) upon the events of the Glorious Revolution, but also to determine what the social and familial implications of each narrative might be. Contemporaries had diverse views of what the claim 'that people could choose their ruler' meant about the rights of women in the family. Tory propagandists discredited contract theory by claiming that it would lead to the erosion of patriarchal authority. Some of their opponents countered that contract theory would not lead to sexual anarchy because the state and family had nothing to do with one another. Yet others, with a 'feminist' agenda and from a whig perspective, used the analogy between the family and the state to call for an abolition of what they termed 'domestic tyranny'. Susanna Wesley, whom we met in the Introduction, opposed 'domestic tyranny' in practical terms by giving herself more leverage within her marriage, but she did so on the basis of the anti-contractarian theory that all bonds, political and marital, were unbreakable. Mary Astell represented a fifth alternative: sharing with 'whig feminists' a hatred of domestic tyranny, and with tory propagandists a desire to discredit contract theory, she invented an entirely new account of the gender-political implications of contract theory, arguing that rather than diminishing patriarchal authority contract theory licensed its worst abuses.

The evidence in this chapter, and the preceding ones, does not lend itself to stories of the natural unfolding of the logical consequences of political argument, nor to one about changes in the areas of politics and gender relations moving in tandem. Rather, it shows that people made the links between arguments about gender and arguments about politics in accordance with diverse agendas. An adequate account of the process by which this occurred will have to leave room for the role of human creativity and rhetorical strategizing.

NOTES

1 The most comprehensive discussion of Astell is Ruth Perry, *The celebrated Mary Astell: an early English feminist* (Chicago, University of Chicago Press, 1986). Other important critical discussion, particularly of *Reflections on marriage*, includes Joan Kinnaird, 'Mary Astell and the conservative contribution to English feminism', *Journal of British Studies* 19 (1979); Patricia Springborg's introduction to Mary Astell, *Astell: political writings*, ed. P. Springborg (Cambridge, Cambridge University Press, 1996); Bridget Hill's introduction to Mary Astell, *The first English feminist: reflections on marriage and other writings by Mary Astell*, ed. B. Hill (Gower/Maurice Temple Smith, 1986); Catherine Gallagher, 'Embracing the absolute: the politics of the female subject in seventeenth-century England', *Genders* 1 (1988); Ruth Perry, 'Mary Astell and the feminist critique of possessive individualism', *Eighteenth Century Studies* 23 (1990).

2 But cf. Gallagher, 'Embracing the absolute', and Perry, 'Mary Astell and the feminist critique of possessive individualism'.

3 Mary Astell, *Reflections on marriage* (1700), p. 112, printed in Astell, *The first English feminist*. All citations of *Reflections on marriage* are to this edition.

4 *Ibid.*, pp. 96–7.

5 *Ibid.*, p. 115.

6 *Ibid.*, p. 112.

7 George Savile, Marquess of Halifax, *Advice to a daughter*, printed in *The complete works of George Savile, first Marquess of Halifax*, ed. Walter Raleigh (Oxford, Clarendon Press, 1912), pp. 8–9.

8 Halifax, *Advice to a daughter*, p. 8.

9 *Ibid.*, p. 9.

10 *Ibid.*, pp. 9–10.

11 *Ibid.*, p. 14.

12 *Ibid.*, p. 16.

13 *Ibid.*, p. 17.

14 Astell, *Reflections on marriage*, p. 116.

15 For Astell's services to the tory party, see Perry, *The celebrated Mary Astell*, esp. chs 6–7.

16 Cf. *Astell: political writings*, p. xxviii, which argues that the target of *Reflections on*

marriage is 'the absurdity of voluntarism on which social contract theory is predicated'. Springborg is right that the book has a political point. That Astell intended it as a refutation of contract theory, however, is dubious. If Astell had wanted to invoke a non-voluntary relationship of subjection in the family to show the absurdity of voluntarism, she would have been better off using, as Filmer had, the example of children and parents. Marriage offered a flawed analogy with government for the anti-contractarian thinker: while it was divinely ordained that people have governments, women were free not to marry. Astell herself chose to remain single, and she speaks about celibacy as a legitimate and indeed wise option in *Reflections on marriage* and in her *Serious proposal to the ladies* (1694). There is no reason for Astell to have repeated Filmer's case against contract theory with a weaker example. I doubt that she meant to.

17 Her high-church sympathies are evident in her three polemical pamphlets of 1704 (*A fair way with dissenters*, *Moderation truly stated*, and *A modest enquiry into the causes of rebellion and civil war*) as well as her longer works, *The Christian religion* (1705) and *Bart'lemy Fair: or, an enquiry after wit* (1709).

18 Mary Astell, *Moderation truly stated* (Richard Wilkin, 1704), pp. 93–4.

19 *Ibid.*, p. 35.

20 *Ibid.*, p. 6.

21 Mark Goldie, 'The Revolution of 1689 and the structure of political argument', *Bulletin of Research in the Humanities* 83 (1980). My labels 'tory' and 'moderate whig' are drawn from the chart on p. 508 in Goldie's article. See also J. P. Kenyon, *Revolution principles: the politics of party, 1689–1720* (Cambridge, Cambridge University Press, 1977), which argues for the *prevalence* of non-contractarian argument; H. T. Dickinson, 'The eighteenth-century debate on the Glorious Revolution', *History* 61 (1976); Thomas P. Slaughter, '"Abdicate" and "contract" in the Glorious Revolution', *Historical Journal* 24 (1981).

22 *The anatomy of a Jacobite tory: in a dialogue between Whig and Tory* (Richard Baldwin, 1690). The pamphlets attacked were *A modest examination of the new oath of allegiance* (Randall Taylor, 1690) and *Reasons why the rector of P. took the oath* [1690].

23 *Anatomy of a Jacobite tory*, p. 10.

24 Mark Goldie, 'Edmund Bohun and *jus gentium* in the Revolution debate, 1689–93', *Historical Journal* 20 (1977), pp. 573–5.

25 David Cressy, 'Literacy in seventeenth-century England: more evidence', *Journal of Interdisciplinary History* 8 (1977), pp. 144–5.

26 On the political uses of the Association, see Henry Horwitz, *Parliament, policy and politics in the reign of William III* (Manchester, Manchester University Press, 1977), pp. 175–9. See also his *Revolution politicks: The career of Daniel Finch second Earl of Nottingham, 1647–1730* (Cambridge, Cambridge University Press, 1968), pp. 156–7.

27 Geoffrey Holmes, *The trial of Doctor Sacheverell* (Eyre Methuen, 1973).

28 See Astell's letter to Henry Dodwell (11 March 1706) printed in Perry, *The celebrated Mary Astell*, pp. 357–9. But cf. Perry, pp. 211–12, for a different interpretation of that letter.

29 Perry, *The celebrated Mary Astell*, pp. 172–80.

30 Astell, *An impartial enquiry into the causes of rebellion and civil war*, in *Astell: political writings*, pp. 163–4. All citations are to this edition.

31 Astell, *Reflections on marriage*, p. 131.

32 *Ibid.*, p. 109.

33 *Ibid.*, p. 132.

34 *Ibid.*, p. 131.

35 Mary Astell, *The Christian religion as professed by a daughter of the Church of England* (Richard Wilkin, 1705), section 329.

36 Astell, *Reflections on marriage*, p. 102.

37 *Ibid.*, p. 76.

38 See Perry, *The celebrated Mary Astell*, ch. 5.

39 James G. Turner, 'The properties of libertinism', in Robert P. Maccubin (ed.), *Unauthorized sexual behaviour during the enlightenment, Eighteenth-Century Life* 9 (1985). For a description of the sexual and religious dimensions of libertinism dating approximately from Astell's time, see *The rake: or, the libertine's religion. A poem* (Randall Taylor, 1693).

40 BL Lansdowne MS. 852, fol. 24. Wharton and Halifax were both members of the Junto, the most aggressive wing of the Whig party.

41 Mary Astell, *Bart'lemy fair: or, an enquiry after wit* (Richard Wilkin, 1709), p. 6.

42 Astell, *Impartial enquiry*, p. 190.

43 *Ibid.*, p 195.

44 *Ibid.*, p. 196.

45 *Ibid.*, p. 139.

46 Astell, *Reflections on marriage*, pp. 119, 120, 121.

47 See Astell's discussion of the dissenters' obsession with preaching, which she regards as a form of showing off, in *Moderation truly stated*, pp. 45–6.

48 Astell, *Reflections on marriage*, p. 100.

49 *Ibid.*, p. 100.

50 *Ibid.*, p. 106.

51 *Ibid.*, p. 124.

52 *Ibid.*, p. 85.

53 *Ibid.*, p. 71.

54 *Ibid.*, p. 90. For the empowering effect of Anne's presence for women writers, see Carol Barash, *English women's poetry, 1649–1714* (Oxford, Clarendon Press, 1996), ch. 5.

55 Astell, *Reflections on marriage*, p. 87.

Part III

———◆———

Women and political life
in the age of Anne

Chapter 7

'Queens are but women': images of Queen Anne

The good King Charles of modern fame
Was governed by two w[hore]s;
His brother Jemmy by two priests
Who turned him out of doors.

When Hogen Mogen William reigned
Two Dutchmen ruled the roost;
And soon these butter bores grew
Great lords to England's cost.

Two laundresses queen An[ne] did rule
Who lived by washing shirts;
And now King George to crown the jest
Is governed by two Turks.[1]

WHEN Anne Stuart was crowned in 1702, she was hailed as a Deborah or a second Elizabeth, a warrior queen who would defend England and protestantism from Louis XIV. Such images, it has been argued, not only empowered the queen, but enhanced the authority of women writers.[2] Yet by the time of her death in 1714, Anne had lost political credibility, and was regarded by whigs and tories alike as weak and pliable, in thrall to favourites and bed-chamber women. Negative perceptions of the queen were now connected to broader anxieties about the place of women in political life. Female favourites were blamed for the ills of the reign, and the enthusiastic participation of women in party politics was the butt of satire.

In their famous account of a night at the Haymarket opera, Addison and Steele ridiculed partisan passions by presenting them in female form.

> I could not but take notice of two parties of very fine women that had placed themselves in the opposite side boxes, and seemed drawn up in a kind of battle array one against another. After a short survey of them, I found they were patched

differently, the faces on the one hand being spotted on the right side of the forehead, and those of the other upon the left. I quickly perceived that they cast hostile glances upon one another, and that their patches were placed in those different situations as party signals to distinguish friends from foes ... upon inquiry I found that the body of amazons on my right hand were whigs, and those on my left tories.[3]

Women's presence as spectators at the trial of Henry Sacheverell in particular drew comment from all sides. John Perceval's letter to his brother Philip captures the flavour of both printed and manuscript accounts:

> Tuesday night we sat by two ladies at the trial, who fell out, being of different sides, and had certainly fought, but the mother of one of them pulled her daughter away and carried her home. She wondered how the other could justify so wicked a man; besides madam (said she), he is not a bit handsome ... My lady Rooke is a heroine in his [Sacheverell's] behalf. She was t'other day eating some chicken in the Hall, and gave a wing to a gentleman who sat by her. But it coming into her head to ask if he was for St. Cheveril, and he answering , no by G–d madam, then by G–d sir, said she, I will have my wing again, and snatch it out of his hands.[4]

In a fascinating comparison of Queen Anne and Elizabeth I, Toni Bowers links Anne's political failure to cultural changes with broader implications for women. Although Anne appropriated Elizabethan imagery – adopting Elizabeth's motto 'semper eadem' and like Elizabeth compensating for reproductive failure by portraying herself as mother to the nation – Bowers argues that the attempt was doomed to fail because of shifts in the status of motherhood, and of symbolic representation itself, between the sixteenth and eighteenth centuries. It was no longer possible for a female ruler in the eighteenth century to cast herself as a metaphorical 'mother of the people', Bowers argues, because women were becoming increasingly identified with the physical body; moreover, 'cultural ideals for virtuous motherhood were changing' to relegate maternity to a private sphere: 'motherhood was being reimagined as ... a symbolic activity without empirical significance in the public world'.[5] For Bowers, then, Anne's failures are intimately connected to a circumscription of women's authority in the public realm.[6]

This chapter and the next examine the relationship between perceptions of Queen Anne, the fact that she was female, and contemporary views of the place of women in political life. Although my treatment can complement Bowers', it departs from her argument in several respects. My aim, first, is to restore politics to the story. Views of Anne and of women in political life were in part products of immediate polemical necessity. A feminist critic who ignores politics ironically exaggerates the extent of Anne's political failure. Bowers, although acknowledging the partisan character of statements about Anne's weakness, cites them to legitimate her claim that 'Anne was virtually excluded from practical governance', a view no longer accepted by political historians.[7] Moreover, while Bowers emphasizes the importance of changing views of motherhood, I will try to show that contemporary notions about the vulnerability of women's sexual reputations were also at work in depictions of Queen Anne.

Finally, I part ways with Bowers in that I find that the most useful context for understanding the discourse surrounding Anne and her bedchamber favourites is not the eventual relegation of women to the 'private sphere' (which, if it happened at all, happened later than Anne's reign) but rather the political issues that Anne's contemporaries found difficult to resolve. The reign of the last Stuart monarch straddled the transition from a pre-modern to a modern political regime, combining elements of the two in ways that bewildered contemporaries. The new political institutions, practices, ideologies and mechanisms of the early eighteenth century – frequent and contested elections between parties with distinct platforms, the increasing power of Parliament in relation to the executive, the diminishing relevance of the monarch's person, preferences, reproductive capacity and bedchamber servants in relation to the important affairs of government – were steps on the road to political modernity. But we are not dealing with a textbook case of modern political society. In the first age of party, it was necessary for any politician hoping for the trust of the queen or even the electorate to claim to transcend party divisions. At a time when the bedchamber was less a source of political power than ever before, fantasies about the power of bedchamber women over the queen ran wild. 'Country' rhetoric flowed from the mouths of courtiers. The distinction between public and private was increasingly taken to be the basis for a healthful polity, yet the definition of the boundary between them was highly contested.

Discourses on Anne were not simply about women, or reflections of attitudes to women; they were ways of negotiating the challenges posed by a political life in which the rules were shifting, and practices and ideals were starkly at odds. Anne's sex may have made such problems more visible, but it did not cause them. Indeed, the role of Anne's sex as a causal factor in criticism of her is by no means self-evident. As the epigraph at the head of this chapter shows, much of what was said about Anne's pliability in the hands of favourites was said about male monarchs as well. But this is not to deny the significance of Anne's reign for women; its particular circumstances had a discernible effect upon the opportunities available for women to legitimate themselves as political writers and actors, and to find gender-political significance in political affairs.

This chapter begins with an analysis of what Geoffrey Holmes has characterized as the 'almost pathological' fears of Anne's contemporaries about the influence of bedchamber women on the queen.[8] I shall attempt to discover the role Anne's sex played in these, and other, perceptions of her. The second part presents a case study of the tory novelist, Delariviere Manley, as a step towards uncovering the meanings that Anne's female contemporaries might have found in the image of a weak, pliable and vulnerable female monarch.

WAS QUEEN ANNE A WOMAN?

Edward Gregg's definitive biography of Queen Anne provides a convincing explanation of why ministers, politicians and propagandists were so eager to regard the queen as a political cipher. Anne, Gregg notes, was particularly determined to keep herself free from domination by either the whig or the tory party, or by her own ministers. To this end, she habitually encouraged politicians who were not part of her ministry, or who belonged to the party out of power, to visit her in private. Insofar as Anne's secret dealings with these politicians took place in her bedchamber, and insofar as the meetings were facilitated by female servants who controlled access, there was some truth to the idea that bedchamber women were powerful. But it was the queen, and not the female favourites, who determined access.[9]

Thus, expressions of anxiety about the influence of a female favourite usually came from those currently in office who expressed frustration at their lack of more complete and secure control. Sarah Churchill, for example, was attacked at precisely the moment when Anne disappointed tory expectations that she would definitively suppress occasional conformity. As a tory ditty put it, 'No child ever stood in more awe of a rod/ than Nan does of Sarah's very looks or a nod'.[10] The roles were reversed in 1707 and 1708, when Anne's reluctance to appoint Junto whigs (Baron Somers and the Earl of Sunderland) to the cabinet, and her appointment of tory bishops over Godolphin's strenuous objections, caused Marlborough and Godolphin to wonder at her resistance. They concluded that she was subject to the 'secret influence' of her new favourite, Abigail Masham.

As Godolphin wrote to Marlborough on 16 August 1707, 'I reckon one great occasion of [Anne's] obstinacy ... proceeds from an inclination of talking more freely than usual to [Mrs. Masham]'.[11] In a similar vein, Marlborough wrote in July 1708 that he was sorry to hear the queen was 'fonder of [Masham] than ever. I am sure as long as that is, there can be no happiness'.[12] The tables were turned again by the appearance of a new whig favourite, the Duchess of Somerset, who, shortly after replacing Sarah Churchill as Groom of the Stole, was described by the tory Jonathan Swift in exactly the same terms as the whigs had used to describe Abigail Masham: she was 'a most insinuating woman, and I believe they [the whigs] will endeavour to play the same game that has been played against them'.[13] The political success of the tory ministers did nothing to allay Swift's fears. Even after the Duke of Marlborough had been deprived of his command in January 1712, Swift worried that 'The Duchess [of Somerset] is not out yet, and may cause more mischief'.[14]

Ministers and party politicians developed fantasies of the power of bedchamber favourites, because such fantasies allowed them to ignore the basic structural contradiction of their situation. It was essential for any politician hoping to gain the trust of the queen to proclaim his independence of party loyalty. But for reasons that will be discussed at greater length in the next chapter, all of the queen's ministers – Marlborough and Godolphin on the one hand, Harley and Bolingbroke on the other – were compelled to ally themselves with, respectively, whigs and tories. By exaggerating the influence of bedchamber women, the ministers resolved the contradiction between maintaining their own identities as virtuous and disinterested royal servants and yet engaging in precisely the kind of partisan politicking that they had promised to help the queen to stamp out. The belief in the influence of favourites also allowed them to avoid the truth that they did not want to admit: that Anne was herself trying to be independent of them.

How relevant was the fact that Anne was female to this story? The answer is complicated, because the relationship of female English monarchs to the female sex in the early modern period was always unstable. Queens were not simply women, any more than kings were simply men. The notion that the monarch possessed two 'bodies' mystically fused together in her person, her mortal body and the immortal body of the 'king-who-never-dies', was available to ensure that the weaknesses to which all mortal flesh was subject (including femaleness) did not diminish the aura of divine authority attaching to the ruler's person.[15] Thus, Elizabeth I was able to declare that she had 'the body of a weak and feeble woman, but I have the heart and stomach of a king'.

It would be unrealistic, however, to imagine that a queen's subjects failed to notice that their ruler was female. The mortal body of the queen (or king) was not trumped, pulverized, or rendered entirely irrelevant by its union with the eternal body of the sovereign. Its particular qualities were visible, and symbolically powerful. It could be detached from and re-attached to the monarch's political persona in complex ways, in accordance with political needs. Even Elizabeth I – who stands as the purest case of a queen who called herself 'king' – even she sometimes used her sex as an ideological and diplomatic tool.[16] Mary II's femaleness, as we have seen, was more central to representations of her, most of which stressed her status as a wife.

Anne makes for an interesting contrast to both her sister and to Elizabeth I. Although Anne was married, the political circumstances which had made it necessary for propagandists to stress Mary's wifely obedience in order to legitimate the Williamite regime did not apply at Anne's accession. The Revolution of 1688 was in less need of defense by 1702, and Anne's husband, George of Denmark, did not demand a share in the crown. We encounter, therefore, a greater range of representations of Anne, some of which moored her firmly in her female body and some of which did not. The choice depended upon what the creators of images were trying to achieve.

The range of possibilities can be established by a quick look at some works published early in her reign.[17] For some writers, Anne's sex was worth emphasizing in order to create an inspiring myth about England's struggle against France. God, predicted Nicholas Brady, would make the fall of that 'haughty monarch', Louis XIV, especially 'grating and uneasy' by 'providentially' reserving it 'for one of the weaker sex', so that

> we may all have reason to take up Judith's song of praise, when she frustrated the designs of such another oppressor ... 'the Almighty Lord has disappointed him by the hand of a woman'.[18]

By contrast, John Sharp's coronation sermon, on the text 'kings shall be thy nursing fathers, and their queens thy nursing mothers', conjured up nurturing rather than bellicose associations. Sharp was careful, however, to avoid biological essentialism: kings could nurse as well as queens, and nursing was not confined to biological parents:

> Let us take the terms in what sense we will; whether for natural parents, or for those that supply the place of parents in the taking care of children, that is to say, guardians or nurses; yet the relation in both these notions doth imply a wonderful trust reposed in Princes; and a wonderful care, and solicitude, and tenderness required of them, on behalf of their subjects.[19]

By treating Anne's status as nursing mother as metaphorical rather than literal, Sharp was able to invoke the traditional metaphor of the state as a family while dissociating himself from patriarchalist doctrines of legitimacy (which in this situation would have constituted Jacobite sedition). He may also have intended to soften the harsh irony that Anne had literally failed to become a mother (her last surviving child, the Duke of Gloucester, had died in 1700). Thus, while Sharp evoked 'feminine' images, he avoided attributing his description to the fact that Anne was female.

While Brady and Sharp constructed their diverse images of Anne in accordance with political agendas, the issue at stake for other writers was the nature of women. As already discussed in Chapter 6, Mary Astell in the 1706 preface to *Reflections on marriage* identified Anne with women as a group in order to question the moral superiority of men over women. Other writers treated Anne as the exception to the rule. The author of *The prerogative of the breeches* (1702), for example, described the queen as possessing 'a masculine spirit beneath the softer body of a woman; her natural endowments translate her from the rank of women'.[20] Anne's metaphorical masculinity could thus be invoked to justify the subordination of women in general.

So far, we have discussed positive images of the queen, in which Anne's femaleness was either denied or emphasized to a variety of ends. What, then, of negative images? Anne's sex could be used to undercut her authority, as it was in the remark of John Pencuik, one of the Scottish commissioners for the union in 1706, that 'nature seems to be inverted when a poor, infirm woman becomes one of the rulers of the world'.[21] But such statements are rare. It is significant that even in works criticizing Anne, the queen's sex was not unduly emphasized. There was a political reason for this silence. According to the Act of Settlement, the heir to the throne of England (until her death in 1714) was the Electress Sophia of Hanover. Any attack on a female ruler *as* a female ruler would therefore smack of Jacobitism.

This female succession helps to explain why, at moments when she was criticized for being in thrall to favourites, Anne was identified as a man. In Delarivière Manley's *Memoirs of Europe*, for example, Anne became the Emperor Constantine, Sarah Churchill became 'his' mother, and Masham appeared as both Constantine's wife and as his male friend Leonidas. In *Rufinus* (1712), a satire on the Marlboroughs, Sarah Churchill and Abigail Masham were cast as rivals for the heart of a male monarch. The gender-bending in these texts may also be explained by the need of authors to impose a heterosexual plot line on the story of Anne's relationships with other women. The important point, for our purposes, is that Anne's weakness as a ruler was not imagined to be the result of her sex.

John Dunton's *King Abigail* (1714) is the exception which proves the rule. Published after the deaths of both Sophia and Anne, it comes close to identifying Anne's sex with her political failure, but without doing so overtly. The pamphlet takes the form of a sermon on *Isaiah* 3.12, 'Women rule over them, and children shall be their oppressors'. It seems on the surface to be an attack on *all* women on top.

> Women ruled them ... finely governed! A woman ought to keep at home and mind the affairs of her own house, as the Apostle sayeth (*Titus* 2.5). Sarah was in her tent at home (*Genesis* 17.9) as the fittest place for such, but in church or state, it is both a sin and a judgement when women shall rule over them.[22]

But the word 'women', Dunton explains, does not refer to women possessed of regal authority, but to those that over-ruled those that should have ruled them, such as Athaliah, Brunhild, Catherine de Medici, and of course Abigail Masham.

The meaning of the term 'women' stretches even farther, however, to include male favourites, such as Gaveston, Wolsey, Harley and Bolingbroke. Rulers (like Anne) who are governed by favourites are identified as 'children'. Thus, the 'women' in this pamphlet who rule are sometimes women, and sometimes people (of whatever sex) who rule illegitimately over rulers. By sliding between literal and metaphorical meanings of gender, Dunton manages to convey the impression that Anne's reign was a worst-case scenario of inversion and misrule through the presence of women-on-top, and at the same time to avoid actually making anybody's sex (Anne's or Abigail Masham's) a causal explanation of anything.

Anne's sex is thus curiously present and absent in representations of her as a weak ruler. Nonetheless, writers who declined overtly to mention the fact that Anne was a woman to explain her weakness relied implicitly upon that fact to create meanings in a text; these, moreover, were more plausible and powerful than they would have been if Anne's sex had been overtly mentioned.

Such a rhetorical dynamic is visible in the flood of rival 'secret histories' of the court that poured forth upon Anne's death in 1714. These post-mortem accounts purported to offer a privileged insider's knowledge of what the queen had really felt about her various ministers and their policies, and what she would have done had she not died, in ways that vindicated the author's political friends and indicted his political enemies. Whigs took the opportunity to blame Harley for the dishonourable peace of Utrecht, while Harley maintained he had merely carried out the queen's will. Among the tories, the rivalry of Harley and Bolingbroke produced competing narratives about the inner workings of the court, with each camp accusing the other of negotiating with the Pretender. Harley's supporters, now scrambling for the favour of George I, insisted that Harley had always been a moderate who, had it not been for the evil influence of Bolingbroke and Masham, would have brought the whigs back into the ministry. Jonathan Swift, in a futile attempt to reconcile all tories, wrote (but did not publish) a pamphlet that blamed the queen's wilful caprice for frustrating the programme of any and all ministers.[23]

Despite their political differences, the writers of the post-mortem 'secret histories' shared a common dilemma. With the exception of Swift (whose failure to publish is significant), they all insisted on the queen's moral virtue and political wisdom: Anne, had she lived, would have done the right thing (however defined), and the writer's position somehow represented her true wishes (although these up to now had been invisible). At the same time, Anne's death had to be presented as a welcome relief, since it brought George I to the throne. Mourning the best of queens while cheering her demise was no easy task. Writers were able, however, to exploit the fact of Anne's sex to create narratives that obscured the contradictory nature of their claims.

Post-mortem accounts of Anne emphasized her 'tenderness', her willingness to please others, and the vulnerability of her 'reputation' during her lifetime. Although no one said that these characteristics were the result of her sex, the terms and concepts associated with Anne were in general associated with women, or in any case took on particular meanings when attached to women that they did not have when attached to men. Tenderness and reputation, moreover, were brought in contemporary conduct literature into a vexed, morally ambiguous relationship: the quality of tenderness (along with the desire to please, compliasance, compliance, patience and civility) was valorized, yet held to be dangerous to women's reputations. Political writers could exploit this understanding of desirable and dangerous feminine traits present in conduct literature in order to render Queen Anne simultaneously praise- and blame-worthy, to treat her death as both a tragedy and a relief.

The moral ambivalence surrounding the very qualities for which Queen Anne was famous is evident in the Marquess of Halifax's best-selling *Advice to a daughter*. Halifax cautions:

> Your civility, which is always to be preserved, must not be carried to a compliance, which may betray you into irrecoverable mistakes. This French ambiguous word *complaisance* hath led your sex into more blame, than all other things put together. It carrieth them by degrees into a certain thing called a good kind of woman, an easy idle creature ... She is a certain thing always at hand, an easy companion, who hath ever great compassion for distressed lovers; she censureth nothing but rigour, and is never without a plaster for a wounded reputation.[24]

Loss of reputation (one of the 'irrecoverable mistakes' to which Halifax refers), moreover, is not necessarily the result of sexual peccadillos *per se*, but of the excess of otherwise desirable qualities described above.

As Halifax further explains, civility and its attendant qualities are danger- ous for a woman, not because they lead to vice, but because they lead to the *appearance* of vice, or of tolerating vice.

> Therefore nothing is with more care to be avoided, than such a kind of civility as may be mistaken for invitation; and it will not be enough for you to keep yourself free from any criminal engagements; for if you do that which either raiseth hopes or createth discourse, there is a spot thrown upon your good name.[25]

Appearances, then, were bad enough. Herein lay the moral ambiguity of the concept of reputation. It was widely recognized that reputation was about public appearance and perception: a good reputation was not the same thing as true virtue and innocence. Yet, it was also recognized that the distinction was for all practical purposes moot. Women were responsible for reputations as well as actual behaviour. The penalty for losing one's reputation, even if innocent of actual wrongdoing (as Samuel Richardson's *Clarissa* was to show) was death.

Post-mortem narratives about Queen Anne eerily echo the cautionary tales presented in contemporary advice literature, and carry the same moral ambiguity. That Anne's reputation was in danger was acknowledged, and even emphasized, by commentators of all political stripes. Defoe, defending Harley in *The secret history of the white-staff,* lamented that 'the honour, dignity and reputation of the queen became a sacrifice in the hands of these men'.[26] Joseph Smith's sermon on Anne's death was organized around the notion that whereas the wicked were often honoured in their lifetimes, God sometimes allowed 'the corrupt passions and prejudices of mankind ... to vilify and abuse the reputation of the righteous on this side of the grave' so that the righteous would not be tempted to vanity; it was only now that Anne was dead that she was to be allowed her 'due share of veneration'.[27] Anne's ministers, according to the author of *King Abigail*, had 'taught their prince to break her word, to the great loss of her honour and credit in all christendom'.[28]

For her damaged reputation, moreover, Anne was simultaneously blame-worthy and innocent. The whig Charles Povey exploited the connection between lost reputation and death to convey a double message about the nature of the queen's guilt: although he affirmed her innocence, the innocence was only established by her death, which in turn was presented as an expiation of her sins. As Anne awoke to the 'ill prospect of affairs' she was

> taken with very violent fits that seized on her spirits and nerves; so that she could not live three months longer, to see herself betrayed and her kingdoms involved in civil war, and foreign troops ... coming over to engage in the grand combat.
>
> To prevent this, her Majesty's sacred life fell as a victim. For she is now stript into a naked spirit, and set on shore in the invisible world where that divine ray, I mean her soul, dwells in bright regions of light and glory, and is not to answer for the late, base treaty of peace ... though signed by her own hand.
>
> As the change is happy to the queen by being released from sighs, sorrows and tears; so I am sure the advantage is great to Europe.[29]

Thanks to the elusive nature of guilt when discussed within the framework of reputation, no one can be blamed for being glad Anne is dead or having feared her when alive, yet Anne can be mourned and exonerated.

Although, as we have seen, Anne was not seen as responsible for the loss of her reputation, the fact that she had lost it was associated in the minds of many writers with her solicitude for the wishes of others; that is, her tenderness or complaisance. As we would expect from reading Halifax, this quality was praiseworthy but problematic. It was also identified as feminine. Such a conclusion can be drawn from Bolingbroke's *Idea of a patriot king* (1749), a work written with Anne's troubles very much in mind. Bolingbroke praises Elizabeth I as being *not* 'womanish': 'Tho' a woman, she hid all that was womanish about her'.

> In her private behavior [Elizabeth] showed great affability, she descended even to familiarity; but her familiarity was such as could not be imputed to her weakness, and was, therefore, most justly ascribed to her goodness ... She had private friendships, she had favourites: but she never suffered her friends to forget she was their queen; and when her favourites did she made them feel that she was so.[30]

It is hard not to read this praise of the unwomanish Elizabeth as a comment on the problem with the womanish Anne. Bolingbroke's description of the problems that Elizabeth avoided closely matches contemporary accounts of the reasons for Anne's downfall. Joseph Smith described the queen as having 'tenderness to a fault' in relation to both her people and ministers. 'So far from invading the public rights of the community ... she seemed rather inclined to give up her own'. She was

> so far from avenging the injuries, indignities, and insults thrown upon her, that she rejoiced in the happiness and prosperity of all about her, even of those whose party prejudice, pride and ambition ... made them forget they were either servants, or subjects.[31]

The diary of Anne's whig physician, David Hamilton, showed a similar confusion about what to praise and what to blame. In the entry for 29 December 1711, Hamilton said that he had advised the queen to discipline her ministers and commented on the personality trait which inhibited her from doing so. Anne was

> a pattern of patience, and her bearing so much turned her into a subject to be afraid, instead of a queen to cause terror in others. This I can demonstrate by letting the whole world know, that she even denied her own inclinations, that she might not provoke those about her, and so by the provocations be made uneasy in her own mind.[32]

In a defense of Anne's character written after her death, Hamilton described her as possessed of 'civility and good breeding', having 'a mind pious towards God, willing to please all its fellow creatures', and desiring

> to make all her subjects easy, instead of reproaching them, as they have done her. I have stood in amaze myself, to hear her make excuses for others.[33]

Although the first passage was an analysis of the causes of Anne's political problems, while the second was meant as praise of her character, they said essentially the same thing. Anne's patience, her solicitude for others, was the quality that allowed the ministers to destroy her reputation; but it also vindicated her from whatever charge it was that was levelled at her in reputation-destroying fashion.

In this light, the one post-mortem narrative which attributed tenderness to Anne in an entirely positive way is worthy of note. *Memoirs of the conduct of her late Majesty*, purporting to be written by a lady of Anne's bedchamber, valorized tenderness by showing Anne weeping for the suffering of her war-torn subjects. Her 'disquiet was such, that it seized upon her vitals and affected her very constitution'. Her tears, which flow liberally through the pamphlet, are scornfully dismissed by her whig ministers as 'womanish tenderness' and 'vapours'. It is left to the heroic Harley to help Anne to change her ministry, and bring about the longed-for peace.[34] Harley, then, is vindicated by being shown to have done Anne's will, while the peace itself is vindicated as an act of compassion.

The status of femininity in *Memoirs of the conduct* is also worthy of comment. The pamphlet does not explicitly identify tenderness as a quality of women (since the only such identification is put in the mouths of the villains). Nonetheless, we are shown tenderness expressed in and confined to the female space of the bedchamber. The reason that we are hearing the story from a woman, we are told, is that only women were privy to the queen's true emotions. But the pamphlet's narrative celebrates the emergence of tenderness into the arena of politics; in a parallel fashion, the use of a female persona as narrator validates the political voice of women.

It is telling, therefore, that *Memoirs of the conduct* was attacked for making the queen appear 'womanish'. The whig author of *Queen Anne vindicated* objected vehemently to the image of the tearful queen; the author of *Memoirs of the conduct*, he said, had shown ignorance of the queen's true nature 'by making her descend to some weaknesses, as womanish tears, etc'.; no one who really knew the queen had ever seen her in 'so degenerate a condition as he places her'.[35] The 'vindication' of Anne from the charge of 'womanishness' proves upon closer scrutiny to be hardly a vindication, since the author's explanation of how the Treaty of Utrecht came about was even more unflattering to the queen. Surrounded by sycophants who put falsities into her head, Anne was misled and manipulated into a dishonourable peace. To 'vindicate' the queen meant to show that she was pliable and helpless in order to throw the blame for the Treaty of Utrecht onto Harley. The author of *Queen Anne vindicated* in effect substituted an image of Anne as excessively pliable for the image of Anne as womanishly tender.

The author of *Queen Anne vindicated* stands out for treating pliability (in the hands of subordinates) and womanish tenderness as mutually exclusive alternatives. Nonetheless, this exceptional example confirms our larger argument. The substitution of one quality (pliability) for another (tenderness) in *Queen Anne vindicated* was only possible because the two qualities were (as we saw in the cases of Joseph Smith and David Hamilton) often held to be closely related in and through women. Even as he expressed horror that his opponent could cast Anne as a mere woman, the author's rhetoric was underwritten by culturally well-established assumptions about women.

Although Anne's sex did not cause, and was not said to cause, either her political weakness or anyone's perception of it, it played a powerful and unacknowledged role in narratives about her. The work of the tory novelist, Delarivière Manley, however, seems to stand as a striking exception to the general trend. Manley's novels made strong connections between the queen's troubles, and the troubles of women in general. The relationship of public to private virtue, and of female vulnerability and public power, are at the centre of her work. Manley herself was a woman with a vulnerable reputation. She seems, moreover, to have regarded Queen Anne as another such woman. A reading of her work reveals the ways in which women might take the existing discourses on the problems with Anne and use them both to authorize their own political voices, and to comment on the condition of women.

DELARIVIÈRE MANLEY AND THE POLITICS OF SCANDAL

Manley's genre of choice was the scandal novel. Her *Secret history of Queen Zarah and the Zarazians* (1705), *The New Atalantis* (1709) and *Memoirs of Europe* (1710) all promoted the cause of the tory party by exposing the vices and peccadillos of prominent whigs.[36] In the dedication to the second volume of her *New Atalantis*, she compared herself to the Roman satirists and quoted Dryden at length to the effect that "tis an action of virtue to make examples of vicious men'.[37] But Manley's project of exposing vice was complicated by the fact that she hardly matched the image of a virtuous moral reformer. Her marriage at an early age to her cousin, John Manley, turned out to be bigamous. She then fell briefly under the protection of Charles II's ex-mistress, the Duchess of Cleveland. After that came several love affairs, including one with Richard Steele, as well as legal battles and financial intrigues. At the time *The New Atalantis* was written, she was living openly as the mistress of the London printer John Barber.

Manley handled her difficult relationship to the categories of virtue and vice by making the vulnerability of her own reputation part of her narrative. In volume II of *The New Atalantis*, for example, she incorporates herself as 'Delia', who tells the virtuous chaplain to the Duke of Beaumond [Beaufort, her literary patron, to whom the book is dedicated] how she was tricked into a bigamous marriage; the duke, she hopes, can help her to recover her good name. Manley's tattered reputation is also the subject of the dedication to volume I of *Memoirs of Europe* (1711). Addressed to Isaac Bickerstaffe [Richard Steele], it thanks him for having made her notorious by his attacks on her in *The Tatler*. Later in the novel, 'Sincerity' (one of the female allegorical figures who populate Manley's works) pointedly observes that poets who tell the truth about vice are always exposed to slander by mercenary pens. But truth is truth, Sincerity concludes, no matter who tells it.

By alluding to her own reputation in her work, Manley redefines the nature of 'reforming satire'. She does not claim to have been slandered, since she does not dispute the facts of her life. Rather, she shifts the reader's attention towards the politics of how reputations are made or destroyed. The targets of Manley's satire are not sexual acts, but the ways in which people maintain their own reputations by ruining those of others. People who can tell or collect stories of other people's vices without exposing themselves are always cast as the real villains. From this perspective, Manley's own tarnished reputation counts in her favour and lends her credibility.

Manley's work is thus much more about how stories about sex are told than they are about sex. An example of her technique can be seen in volume I of *The New Atalantis*, where Virtue, Intelligence and Astrea -- the divine beings who travel around the island of Atalantis to observe the generally unedifying doings of its inhabitants – witness a conversation between an unidentified lady, known only as 'the baroness', and the Count of Meilliers. The count asks for the baroness's hand in marriage; she responds that if he does not desist she will be forced to tell him a story that will destroy his good opinion of her, as there is no other way to explain her refusal to marry a man of his virtues. He insists on hearing the story.

It turns out that immediately after the death of the rich husband whom she had married only for money, she had been secretly wed by 'words and writing', though not by ceremony, to the Prince of Sira, with whom she had already committed adultery during her first husband's lifetime. The prince had shortly thereafter gone into exile, allegedly for political reasons but in reality to get away from her. As a result, she has been living in retirement and refusing all suitors. At this point, the count informs her that the Prince of Sira is returning to England with a new bride. The baroness, thirsting for revenge, wants to punish the prince without destroying her own reputation. The count points out that this is impossible, since the prince can only protect his own good name by slandering hers. There follows a long disquisition by the count on the fickleness of male desire; women are therefore to be blamed (and are blamed by the world) for trusting to false oaths and promises. The baroness should therefore, he concludes, consider herself happy that her secret is unknown, do nothing, and try to live a virtuous life.

This appears at first to be a simple tale of a woman insufficiently educated in the paths of virtue, who errs and suffers the consequences. The most interesting story, however, is not that of the baroness and the prince, but that of the baroness and the count. As the two figures pass out of sight, the three goddesses argue about the meaning of the conversation. Astrea opines that 'the count must himself have worth, that he can so worthily instruct and admonish her'. Intelligence, however, points out that the count has succeeded in extracting the baroness's secret, and can use it to force her to marry him, which he needs her to do because he is heavily in debt. Intelligence adds that despite the count's high moral tone, he has two mistresses already. The baroness has been rendered just as vulnerable by the surrender of her story as she would have been by the surrender of her body.[38]

The crimes in Manley's novels are not lust or lack of restraint, but ingratitude, disloyalty, hypocrisy, and the preservation of one's own good name at the expense of someone else's. Manley breaks down the barrier between sex and politics, not by making sex a metaphor for political power, but by making behaviour in sexual liaisons a test of character and political trustworthiness.

Ingratitude and disloyalty were particularly effective themes to invoke against John Churchill, the Duke of Marlborough. As the hero of the land campaign against Louis XIV, Marlborough was a difficult target. Manley wisely did not attack his public achievements. Instead, she told an old story. Both *Zarah* (1705) and volume I of *The New Atalantis* (1709) recount the affair which John Churchill, prior to his marriage to Sarah Jennings, had had with Charles II's mistress, the Duchess of Cleveland, whose generosity and favour had brought him rich rewards. Churchill had an ethical problem, since to be faithful to Cleveland was to cuckold the king. In a conventional story, we could look forward to watching our hero make a painful choice between sexual and political allegiance. But Manley has Churchill betray both king and mistress, while still retaining the great benefits he received from both. Having fallen in love with Sarah Jennings, John Churchill finds a way to direct blame at the Duchess of Cleveland for *her* ingratitude and disloyalty to the king, in order to justify his own disloyalty to her. This ingratitude to a benefactor foreshadows his later betrayal of James II during the Revolution of 1688, and suggests that he is a potential betrayer of Anne (who has also rewarded him richly).

The sexual double standard plays an important role in this narrative. In *Zarah*, Hippolito [Churchill] thinks that Clelia's [Cleveland's] betrayal of the king excuses his betrayal of her. As Zarah's [Sarah's] witch-like mother Jenissa puts it, 'Hippolito will scorn to be obliged long to a woman [Clelia] who having first forfeited her honour to her royal master, will cancel the obligations of honour he [Hippolito] otherwise owed to her', and that the king would be satisfied to have his rival married.[39] Manley, however, calls Jenissa's formulation of the issues of loyalty and betrayal in the situation into question by putting into the king's mouth a more complex response.

Congratulating Hippolito on his marriage to Zarah, the king refuses to view himself as injured. Instead, ironically justifying sexual infidelity in whig political language, he affirms the 'natural right' of men and women to 'bestow our affections where we please, and revoke them when we please: they are wretched who enjoy not that liberty'. Far from losing his authority by Clelia's infidelity, he is in fact the author of it:

> If Clelia had not been of my humour, I fancy I should not have loved her so well; and perhaps I love her for nothing more than that she loves inconstancy. I once endeavoured to engage her to be false to me, insomuch as I told her one day I dreamed I had seen her in your arms, and it was not long ere I found it true.[40]

Manley's treatment of this episode marks a significant departure from the political pornography of the Restoration. Whereas in Restoration satire Charles

II's sexuality signalled both his pretensions to absolutism and the fragility of his control,[41] Manley suggests that his equanimity in the face of cuckoldry is related to his kindness and generosity, and his lack of a double standard. His bountifulness triumphs, and even shines brighter, through the ingratitude of his subjects.

The New Atalantis offers an ironic twist on this story. This time, Fortunatus (John Churchill) acts as a pale imitation of the king, arranging for the Duchess de L'Inconstant (Cleveland) to be unfaithful to him by putting into her bed the gorgeous young cavalier, Germanicus; the duchess, mistaking Germanicus for Fortunatus, falls to rapturous lovemakng. At this point Fortunatus bursts in and feigns outrage at the duchess's infidelity. He deliberately cuckolds himself in order to preserve his honour and justify his own betrayal.[42] The superficial resemblance of Fortunatus' behavior here to that of the king in *Zarah* (both arrange for their mistresses to sleep with other men) serves to underscore the dramatic contrast between them. Fortunatus exploits rather than transcends the double standard; he is destroying his mistress's reputation rather than bestowing a gift on her. Perhaps, too, he is presuming to wield the power of a monarch, without being one.

The two versions of the Churchill–Cleveland story establish a rich set of connections. Generous and tolerant monarchs are pitted against ungrateful and hypocritical subjects who presume to exercise the powers of a king but do so for their own selfish ends. The central themes of Manley's work, the sexual double standard and the political ingratitude and duplicity of the whigs, are thus closely linked.

This insight gave Manley a powerful tool with which to defend Queen Anne's vulnerable reputation. Like the Duchess of Cleveland, Anne appears in Manley's work not as the embodiment of purity and innocence but as the victim of other people's attempts to preserve their own (undeserved) reputations. Significantly, lesbianism, or allegations thereof, is the subject of a passage in *The New Atalantis* at the very time when Anne's attachment to Abigail Masham was the subject of rumour and satire. Volume II, which appeared in October 1709, included a description of the 'new Cabal', a secret society of women devoted to the pursuit of passionate friendship with one another. It is, alas, impossible to establish a direct link between Sarah Churchill's innuendo about lesbianism made in private correspondence with the queen and Manley's discussion of it in volume II of *The New Atalantis*. Anne, Sarah, and Masham are not identified in any of the keys to the novel as characters named as members of the Cabal. But then again, we would not expect the allusion to be so obvious. It is virtually certain that Manley, who maintained close connections to Harley and to Swift, knew that the queen's relationship to Abigail Masham has become the subject of gossip; the novel itself contains references to the fall of Sarah Churchill and the rise of Hilaria [Masham] in Anne's affections.[43]

The most intriguing aspect of Manley's treatment of the new Cabal is her playful exploitation of the epistemological uncertainty at the heart of the 'scandal'. The segment is framed, like all stories in *The New Atalantis*, by a conversation among Astrea, Virtue and Intelligence; it is unusual, however, in that Intelligence, who acts as a tour guide for the others, is shown to be incapable of ascertaining the 'innocence' or 'guilt' of the Cabal. She begins with the assertion that its members are wrongfully accused of a detestable crime:

> [T]hese ladies are of the new Cabal; a sect (however innocent in itself) that does not fail of meeting its share of censure from the world. Alas! What can they do? How unfortunate are women? If they seek their diversion out of themselves and include the other sex, they must be criminal? If in themselves (as those of the new Cabal) still they are criminal? Tho' censurers must carry their imaginations to a greater length than I am able to do mine, to explain this hypothesis with success; they pretend to find in these the vices of old Rome revived; and quote you certain detestable authors, who (to amuse posterity) have introduced you lasting monuments of vice which could only subsist in imagination.[44]

Intelligence goes on to describe the Cabal's code of secrecy, which she juxtaposes with the male ethos of boasting about sexual conquests in coffee houses. Because, like Queen Victoria, Intelligence does not seem to believe that women could be guilty of anything with one another, she accepts the Cabal's combination of mysteriousness and innocence at face value.

The relationship of innocence and mystery is, of course, far more ambiguous than Intelligence assumes. As the next chapter will show, Manley wrote the new Cabal narrative just as Sarah Churchill was announcing that Anne's very desire to keep her relationship with Abigail Masham secure from public scrutiny was a sure sign that the queen had something to hide. The reader of *The New Atalantis*, moreover, has already been prepared to wonder if secrecy really indicates innocence. The account of the new Cabal is preceded in the text by a story about a puritanical but hypocritical young woman whose career of exposing the frailties of others ends when she herself becomes pregnant with an illegitimate child. Heterosexuality, then, is impossible to keep secret. It stands to reason that all we really learn from the Cabal's secrecy is that its activities are not heterosexual – which is, of course, precisely the accusation against it.

Not surprisingly, Intelligence's assertion that the Cabal is innocent is progessively undercut by the information she imparts. Not even the dichotomy between discreet women and boastful men is allowed to hold. In one story, the Marchioness of Lerma is exposed by her 'female favourite' who wants to preserve her honour in men's eyes; in another, women are shown boasting to one another about their heterosexual conquests. Intelligence's description of the Marchioness of Sandomire and Ianthe, members of the Cabal who dress up as men to pursue 'adventures' with prostitutes, demonstrates Manley's technique of undermining the narrator's certainty and moral authority.

But what adventures? Good Heaven! None that could in reality wound [the marchioness's] chastity! Her virtue sacred to her lord and the marriage bed, was preserved inviolable! For what could reflect back upon it with any prejudice, in the little liberties she took with her own sex? ... These creatures of hire, failed not to find their account, in obliging the marchioness's and Ianthe's peculiar taste, by all the liberties that belonged to women of their loose character and indigence. Though I should look upon it as an excess of mortification, were I the marchioness, to see the corruption of the sex, and to what extremes, vice may step by step, lead those who were born, and probably educated in the road of innocence. It may be surely counted an inhumane curiosity, and shows a height of courage, more blamable than otherwise, not to be dejected at the brutality, the degeneracy, of those of our own specie.[45]

Incredibly, Intelligence's only criticism of the marchioness is that she is not sufficiently horrified at the moral depravity of the prostitutes! To believe the ladies 'innocent' is, ironically, to accept the classic double standard which condemns prostitutes but not their customers.

Clearly, Manley does not want us to accept the claim that the Cabal is merely an innocent victim of slander. Astrea, the figure of justice, is understandably confused rather than assured by Intelligence's affirmations that the secrecy of the Cabal hides nothing'. 'It is something so new and uncommon, so laudable and blameable', she exclaims, 'that we don't know how to determine; especially wanting light even to guess at what you call the mysteries of the Cabal'.[46] Given that the Cabal's secrecy definitively indicates neither innocence nor guilt, Astrea makes a judgement which simultaneously draws upon contemporary moral conventions about sexual reputation while calling the justice of those conventions into question. She condemns the Cabal (à la Halifax) simply for having given grounds for suspicion, but also identifies the suspicion as a product of men's need to control women:

But when we look with true regard to the world, if [the Cabal] permit a shadow of suspicion, a bare imagination, that the mysteries they pretend, have anything in 'em contrary to kind, and that strict modesty and virtue do not adorn and support their conversation; 'tis to be avoided and condemned; least they give occasion for obscene laughter, new invented satire, fanciful jealousies and impure distrusts, in that nice unforgiving sex: who arbitrarily decide, that woman was only created (with all her beauty, softness, passions, and complete tenderness) to adorn the husband's reign, perfect his happiness, and propagate the kind.[47]

The final moment of the New Cabal narrative has been read by some critics as Manley's final assertion of the subversive or utopian character of separate female societies in what is otherwise an extremely ambivalent discussion of them.[48] There is truth in this. Presumably, Manley does not mean to endorse the 'arbitrary' male view dictating compulsory heterosexuality, the view explicated in the last sentence. But it also makes sense to read the last line as a way of focusing attention on the politics of scandal-making rather than the existence of a scandal. If we cannot know whether the Cabal is literally (in the sense of sexually) innocent or guilty, Manley seems to be saying, we can at least understand the motives which lie behind the accusations. This is far more effective as a response to the rumours about the queen and Abigail Masham than a straightforward assertion of the queen's innocence would have been.

Slander rears its ugly head once more in Manley's *A modest enquiry into the reasons of the joy expressed by a certain set of people upon the spreading of a report of her Majesty's death*, a pamphlet published on 4 February 1714 in the wake of the queen's near-fatal illness. Manley again employs the tactic of calling attention to the motives behind the slander rather than arguing about its truth or falsehood. Like the novels, the pamphlet links whig political ingratitude with the sexual double standard by casting Anne as a specifically female victim of gossip. The story Manley tells is set, significantly, in a coffee house, the very place where men in *The New Atalantis* were shown boasting about their sexual conquests.

A stranger enters, and concludes from the conversation he overhears that the queen must have been a tyrant 'who exceeded Nero and Caligula in acts of cruelty',[49] and that the queen's ministry will bring in a popish successor. Fortunately, a passer-by sets him straight. The 'common cant of the whole party, the fear of a Popish successor and Popery' demonstrates the whigs' lack of compassion for the queen's misfortune:

> The loss of the Duke of Gloucester [Anne's son, who died in 1702], and the want of hopes for posterity from her present Majesty, are misfortunes never enough to be lamented: But is it not a very ungenerous way of proceeding, instead of comforting and supporting their Prince under this calamity, to insult and despise her for it? To multiply their affronts and indignities, because she wants posterity, who might possibly revenge them?[50]

It seems odd that a tory like Manley would desacralize the person of the monarch by exaggerating her moral and physical vulnerability. However, if we look at the political circumstances surrounding the pamphlet, this representation of Anne can be read as a brilliant piece of obfuscation designed to promote the the cause of the Pretender, which Manley probably also saw as the cause of Robert Harley.

The fears expressed by whigs that the government planned to bring in the Pretender had a basis in the fact that Harley and Bolingbroke were both, independently of one another and without the queen's approval, negotiating with James Edward Francis Stuart, although (if Daniel Szechi is correct) less with the intention of restoring him than as a means of gaining leverage in dealing with domestic Jacobite tories and the French court.[51] What Manley knew of Harley's notoriously obscure intentions is uncertain. But she would certainly have been aware of rumours that Harley might restore 'James III' on the condition that he convert to protestantism, and it is likely both that she would both believe the rumours and approve the plan. Her novels, like much political writing from the period, reveal a deep ambivalence about the Revolution of 1688: expressions of loyalty to Anne and the protestant cause exist alongside glowing portraits of Jacobites and non-jurors as persons of rare integrity. Towards the end of Anne's reign, legitimist sentiment was growing amongst tories who had hitherto accepted the results of the Glorious Revolution, largely in reaction to the whiggish proclivities of the Hanoverian successor, the future George I.[52]

If we assume that – as a professional tory hack – Manley intended her pamphlet to please and defend Harley, we can see the difficulty of her task: she had to deny what she believed to be a true rumour that there were plans afoot to bring in the Pretender, while making those plans seem more acceptable. Manley's decision to put the vulnerable body and reputation of the queen at the centre of the pamphlet becomes explicable in this context. By treating what was really an attack on allegedly crypto-Jacobite ministers as an attack on the queen's person, she accomplished two things. First, she ruled out the possibility of any distinction being made between the ministers and the queen, thereby pre-empting criticism of Harley as an evil minister acting without the sovereign's knowledge or consent. Second, by treating the whig fears about the Pretender as a sign of their lack of compassion for Anne's womanly misfortune, Manley could suggest that the cause of Anne's political vulnerability was not her physical inadequacy to the task of reproduction but her subjects' disrespect for her person. This in turn implied that those who complained about the imminent arrival of the Pretender were not defenders of the constitutional monarchy, but rebels and potential regicides.

A modest enquiry can also be read as a subtle defense of the plan that Manley pretends does not exist. In view of the fact that the pamphlet was written when there was still hope that James Stuart would convert to protestantism (his announcement of his intention to remain Catholic came in March, a month after this pamphlet was published), it is significant that it mocks the whigs' fear of a popish successor but is silent about their fears of the Pretender. Moreover, it is full of allusions and metaphors which call attention to the familial bonds among the Stuarts and between the Stuarts and the British people. Anne is described as 'flesh of our flesh, bone of our bone'. She is a mother who has 'nourished and brought up children, but they have rebelled against her'. The Revolution of 1688 is treated as a family tragedy. Anne, we are reminded, showed her loyalty to the protestant cause by sacrificing 'what was perhaps dearer than her life', meaning her father. Manley's emphasis on Anne's physical vulnerability may itself be an expression of her legitimist views. The point of exposing Anne's mortal frailty is to demand that Anne's subjects defend and respect her person; it makes Anne herself, rather than the institution of monarchy or a particular set of policies, the proper object of her subjects' loyalty.

This insistence on loyalty to the mortal person of the monarch allowed Manley to acknowledge the significance of Anne's sex, and to put her story in the same category as that of other women. Anne was, she insisted, vulnerable to slander because women are vulnerable to slander. The radicalism of her approach to the problem lay in the fact that she defended the queen by exposing that double standard. Manley's defense of Anne thus became a defense of her own claims to virtue and authority.

Our discussions of Manley, and of Mary Astell, make it tempting to speculate that tory, Jacobite and crypto-Jacobite politics provided a natural home for persons with unconventional views of the gender order, at least in the reign of Queen Anne. The contrast between *Memoirs of the conduct*, with its valorization of female compassion and the privileged insider knowledge of bechamber women, and *Queen Anne vindicated*, with its frank avowal that to call the queen a woman was to insult her, lends force to such a conclusion. Moreover, it is undeniable that by the end of Anne's reign, the whigs came to express opposition to the regime in alarmingly misogynist terms. 'After Anne's death', notes Carol Barash, 'attacks on the female body that would have been indecorous at best – and treasonous at worst – during Anne's reign are unleashed full force'.[53] Dunton's *King Abigail* is a case in point.[54]

The argument that whigs tended toward misogyny, or that the whig triumph after Anne's death unleashed a flood of it, is valid, as long as it is remembered that the differences between whigs and tories did not spring full-blown from the theoretical principles of Locke and Filmer, but from contingent political circumstances. The tories had been as willing as whigs to decry the influence of female bedchamber favourites when the favourites in question were whigs, or when Anne favoured whig policies. But, as it happened, Anne tended in the latter part of her reign to please the tories. Moreover, because the conflict between whigs and tories came to revolve around questions of war and peace, the tories (as the pro-peace party) could place value on the stereotypically female quality of compassion. Finally, the death of Sophia of Hanover meant that whigs could look forward to a male successor known to be sympathetic to their party at the very moment when they were released via Sophia's demise from the obligation to avoid criticizing female rule.

Moreover, if Mary Astell and Delariviere Manley are taken to represent 'tory feminism', they represent very different forms of it. Indeed, one cannot imagine a tory more different from Manley in her attitudes toward sexual virtue than Astell herself, who would never invoke the hypocrisy of the sexual double standard to excuse the peccadillos of fallen women. The differences between them may be connected not only to their different sexual ethics, but to the fact that their work was shaped by different moments in toryism. Although Astell in the 1706 preface to *Reflections on marriage* briefly attached the cause of women to the cause of Anne, hoping that the queen's greatness would force men 'to do justice to her sex', she constructed her synthesis of toryism and feminism in the 1690s, at a time when tories confronted the problem of obedience to a ruler for whom they had no liking or attachment. It is the austere, sombre, self-denying subject of a tyrannical prince that provides the template for the virtuous woman in Astell's work.

Manley's synthesis of toryism and feminism, by contrast, is predicated on a fervent attachment to the person of the queen (the meaning of which was flexible enough to encompass Jacobitism but not require it). Just as toryism changed under the pressure of circumstances, so too did the possibilities for what women could make of it. Neither tory feminism nor tory ideology was monolithic; moreover, insofar as tory ideology provided a context in which individuals could express subversive ideas about the gender order, it was *only* a context. Manley and Astell found in tory ideology a resource for thinking about gender, but they had to manipulate it. Whig ideology might also, in some contexts, lend itself to manipulation by women.

To see what a woman could do with whig ideology, we turn to Sarah Churchill. She makes for a fascinating contrast with Manley. As will be obvious, she had very different ideas about sexual reputation. Although hers was, like Manley's, an object of public comment, she embraced the concepts of sexual virtue that Manley set out to dismantle. There were, in her view, two kinds of women (herself and Masham). There were two kinds of relationships, egalitarian friendships conducive to virtue on the one hand, and morally suspect secret intimacies between superiors and subordinates on the other. She thought that to lose one's reputation was equally bad, whether one were guilty or innocent. Her defenses of herself as a good favourite, her attacks on Abigail Masham as a bad one, and her efforts to coerce the queen by threatening to destroy her reputation, all relied on the basic assumptions that Manley attacked. But Sarah Churchill, too, was a woman trying to legitimate her own place in the political sphere, in the face of difficulties that were clearly related to her gender.

NOTES

1 'Epigram', Bodl. Firth MS b. 4, fol. 51.

2 Carol Barash, *English women's poetry, 1649–1714: politics, community and linguistic authority* (Oxford, Clarendon Press, 1996), p. 236.

3 Joseph Addison and Richard Steele, in *The Spectator* 81 (11 June 1711). Much of the satirical commentary on women's partisanship occurred around the Sacheverell trial.

4 John Perceval to Philip Perceval, 2 March 1710, BL Add. MS 47026, fol. 6. See also poem beginning 'Ye ladies and damsels pray why all this bustle' (May 1710) in BL Add. MS 40060 fol. 83; *The officer's address to the ladies* (Ann Baldwin, [1710]). See also Daniel Defoe's *Review* 6:19 (May 1710).

5 Toni Bowers, *The politics of motherhood: British writing and culture, 1680–1760* (Cambridge, Cambridge University Press, 1996), pp. 71–2; and see pp. 65–74.

6 Bowers, *Politics of motherhood*, p. 88. See also Barash, *English women's poetry*, p. 282, p. 290.

7 Bowers, *Politics of motherhood*, p. 87. Cf. Edward Gregg, *Queen Anne* (Ark, 1984), pp. 370–4, which is cited by Bowers but does not support the point.

8 Geoffrey Holmes, *British politics in the age of Anne*, revd edn (Hambledon Press, 1987), p. 213.

9 Gregg, *Queen Anne*, esp. pp. 181, 197–8, 403–4, and *passim*. See also Philip Roberts' introduction to [D. Hamilton], *The diary of Sir David Hamilton, 1703–14* (Oxford, Clarendon Press, 1975); Robert O. Bucholz, *The Augustan court: Queen Anne and the decline of court culture* (Stanford, Stanford University Press, 1993), pp. 156–88.

10 Poem beginning 'When first royal Nancy mounted the throne', Bodl. Rawlinson poetry MS 169, fol. 31.

11 Godolphin to Marlborough, 16 August 1707, MGC 880.

12 Marlborough to Sarah, 8 July 1708, MGC 1039. See also Marlborough to Godolphin, 28 August 1707, MGC 888; Marlborough to Sarah, 27 August 1709, MGC 1389; Godolphin to Marlborough, 24 December 1708, MGC 1198.

13 Letter 17, dated 4 March 1711, in Jonathan Swift, *Journal to Stella*, ed. Harold Williams (Oxford, Clarendon Press, 1948).

14 Letter 39, dated 25 January 1712 in Swift, *Journal to Stella*; see also letter 31 of 20 September 1711.

15 Ernst Kantorowicz, *The king's two bodies: a study in medieval political theology* (Princeton, Princeton University Press, 1957).

16 Commentaries on Elizabeth I and gender include: Louis Montrose, 'Shaping fantasies: figurations of gender and power in Elizabethan culture', *Representations* 2 (1983); Constance Jordan, 'Woman's rule in sixteenth-century British political thought', *Renaissance Quarterly* 40 (1987); Alison Heisch, 'Queen Elizabeth and the persistence of patriarchy', *Feminist Review* 4 (1980); Carole Levin, *The heart and stomach of a king: Elizabeth I and the politics of sex and power* (Philadelphia, University of Pennsylvania Press, 1994); Susan Doran, *Monarchy and matrimony: the courtships of Elizabeth I* (Routledge, 1996).

17 Much fuller discussions of representations of Anne may be found in Bowers, *Politics of motherhood*, and Barash, *English women's poetry*, ch. 5.

18 Nicholas Brady, *A sermon upon the death of King William; and her present Majesty's happy accession to the crown* (Joseph Wild, 1702), pp. 23–4. Similarly, amazon images were invoked during Anne's royal entry into the city of Bath in 1702, where she was met by 'about 200 virgins in two companies richly attired, many of them apparelled like Amazons with bows and arrows, and some with gilt sceptres and ensigns of regalia in their hands'. See *The queen's famous progress; or, her Majesty's royal journey to Bath* (J. W., 1702), p. 5.

19 John Sharp, *A sermon preached at the coronation of Queen Anne* (Walter Kettilby, 1702), p. 4. See Bowers, *Politics of motherhood*, pp. 50–65 for an extended analysis of the sermon.

20 *The prerogative of the breeches* (Ann Baldwin, 1702), p. 23.

21 Quoted in Gregg, *Queen Anne*, p. 231.

22 John Dunton, *King Abigail: or, the secret reign of the she-favourite* (John Dunton, 1715), p. 5.

23 Insightful guidance through the tangle of pamphlet literature can be found in J. A. Downie, *Robert Harley and the press: propaganda and public opinion in the age of Swift and Defoe* (Cambridge, Cambridge University Press, 1979), 'Epilogue'; Paula Backscheider, *Daniel Defoe: his life* (Baltimore, Johns Hopkins University Press, 1989), pp. 344, 353–6; Irvin Ehrenpreis, *Swift: the man, his works, the age*, 3 vols (Cambridge, Mass., Harvard University Press, 1962–83), 3:108–13; introduction to Jonathan Swift, *An enquiry into the behavior of the queen's last ministry* (Indiana University Publications in the Humanities Series no. 36, ed. Irvin Ehrenpreis (Bloomington, Indiana University Press, 1956).

24 Halifax, George Savile, Marquess of, *Advice to a daughter*, printed in *The complete works of George Savile, first Marquess of Halifax*, ed. Walter Raleigh (Oxford, Clarendon Press, 1912), p. 30.

25 Halifax, *Advice to a daughter*, p. 28.

26 [Daniel Defoe], *The secret history of the white-staff* (J. Baker, 1714), p. 44.

27 Joseph Smith, *The duty of the living to the memory of the dead* (Richard Smith, 1714), pp. 6–7.

28 Dunton, *King Abigail*, p. 14.

29 Charles Povey, *An inquiry into the miscarriages of the last four years reign* (Mr Robinson, 1714), pp. 7–8.

30 Henry St John, Viscount Bolingbroke, *The idea of a patriot king*, ed. Sidney W. Jackman (Indianapolis, Bobbs-Merrill, 1965), pp. 80–1.

31 Joseph Smith, *The duty of the living to the memory of the dead* (Richard Smith, 1714), pp. 13–14. I owe this reference to Toni Bowers.

32 *Hamilton diary*, p. 35.

33 *Ibid.*, p. 68.

34 *Memoirs of the conduct of her late Majesty and her last ministry, relating to the separate peace with France. By the right hononrable [sic] the Countess of ——* (S. Keimer, 1715), pp. 9–14. Cf. Backscheider, *Daniel Defoe*, p. 365 for a different reading.

35 *Queen Anne vindicated from the base aspersions of some late pamphlets* (John Baker, 1715), p. 23.

36 On Manley as propagandist, see Gwendolyn B. Needham, 'Mary de la Riviere Manley, tory defender', *Huntington Library Quarterly* 12 (1949). On her life and scandalous reputation, see Gwendolyn B. Needham, 'Mrs Manley: an eighteenth-century Wife of Bath', *Huntington Library Quarterly* 14 (1951); Fidelis Morgan, *A woman of no character: an autobiography of Mrs Manley* (Faber & Faber, 1986). Important critical discussions include Catherine Gallagher, *Nobody's story* (Berkeley, University of California Press, 1994), ch. 3; Ros Ballaster, *Seductive forms: women's amatory fiction from 1684 to 1740* (Oxford, Clarendon Press, 1992), ch. 4.

37 Manley, *Novels*, 1:527.

38 *Ibid.*, 1:405–20.

39 *Ibid.*, 1:10.

40 *Ibid.*, 1:33.

41 See Rachel Weil, 'Sometimes a sceptre is only a sceptre: pornography and politics in Restoration England', in Lynn Hunt, ed., *The invention of pornography* (New York, Zone Books, 1993).

42 Manley, *Novels*, 1:293–312.

43 Needham, 'Manley, tory defender'; Manley, *Novels*, 1:679–89.

44 Manley, *Novels*, 1:575. The following discussion of the new Cabal passage has benefited much from conversations with Carol Barash.

45 *Ibid.*, 1:581.

46 *Ibid.*, 1:589.

47 *Ibid.*, 1:590.

48 Ballaster, *Seductive forms*, pp. 140–2; see also her 'The vices of old Rome revived: representations of female same-sex desire in seventeenth- and eighteenth-century England', in Suzanne Raitt (ed.) *Volcanoes and pearl divers: essays in lesbian feminist studies* (Binghamton, Harrington Press, 1994). See also Janet Todd, *Women's friendship in literature* (New York, Columbia University Press, 1980), pp. 340–2, 346.

49 [Delarivière Manley], *A modest enquiry into the reasons of the joy expressed by a certain set of people upon the spreading of a report of her Majesty's death* (John Morphew, 1714), pp. 8–10.

50 *A modest enquiry*, p. 18.

51 Daniel Szechi, *Jacobitism and tory politics, 1710–14* (Edinburgh, John Donald, 1984). See also Gregg, *Queen Anne*, pp. 363–95, and Gregg, 'Was Queen Anne a Jacobite?', *History* 57 (1972).

52 Tim Harris, *Politics under the later Stuarts* (New York, Longman, 1993), pp. 219–20.

53 Barash, *English women's poetry*, p. 226.

54 See also Dunton, *The medal: or, a loyal essay upon king George's picture* (John Dunton [1715]), p. 27, for an attack on women authors usurping the prerogative of men. Compare Defoe, *Secret history of the white-staff*, p. 92, for derogatory references to men of state who 'plough with the heifers of the court'.

Chapter 8

Sarah Churchill;
or, virtue unrewarded

About six weeks before her dismissal from office, Sarah Churchill warned Queen Anne's physician, David Hamilton, that 'the town and country are very full of prints that do Mrs. Morley [Anne] great hurt because she has given so much ground for such papers'. The latest attacks on the queen, she suspected, were much like previous ones, especially the 'odious ballad to the tune of Fair Rosamond' which had ridiculed Masham 'very justly ... but that which I hated was the disrespect to the Queen and the disagreeable expression of the dark deeds of the night'.[1]

Sarah's concern for the queen's reputation should be taken with several grains of salt. While she assured Hamilton that 'I never see any of the papers till they are public', there is evidence from other sources that she actively promoted the circulation of satires and rumours attacking Queen Anne and her tory favourite, Abigail Masham. The 'odious ballad' which Sarah claimed to have hated was, in fact, one which she had possibly written and certainly sang for the entertainment of her friends.[2] Her letter to Hamilton was an attempt to distance herself from a campaign of slander that she herself had instigated in order to intimidate the queen into changing her policies and letting Sarah retain her office as Groom of the Stole.

Sarah Churchill appears here to be just the kind of person that Delarivière Manley so successfully dissected, whose pretensions to expose vice covered sins more vicious than the ones exposed. It is entirely possible, in fact, that the campaign of slander that she waged against Abigail Masham, the woman who appeared to replace her as royal favourite, was itself the inspiration for Manley's acute analysis of the politics of anti-lesbian innuendo in the New Cabal section of *The New Atalantis*. We do not have to prove that Sarah Churchill was the subject of Manley's account of the Cabal to know that, by her attempts to manipulate Queen Anne via threats to her reputation, she did herself more harm than good in the public eye. She is remembered in history as a 'termagant' and a woman scorned. In her lifetime, she was an easy and conspicuous target of tory propaganda, but was barely defended by the whigs. Represented as the archetype of all the disorder that women bring to politics, she was said to have exerted undue influence through her personal friendship with the queen. The Duke of Marlborough's friends blamed Sarah for his political troubles; to his enemies, she was a powerful symbol of the greed and corruption of 'the family'.

Public perception of Sarah Churchill, Duchess of Marlborough, and her largely unsuccessful attempts to control it, form the subject of this chapter. I hasten to say that my intention here is not simply to present her in a more sympathetic light.[3] She is interesting for the combination of the ideals she embraced, and how she tried to define herself in terms of those ideals. Sarah saw herself as a virtuous political actor, that is, as a person who put the good of the country ahead of private concerns. This fact in itself is worthy of comment. Many feminist historians suggested that political virtue, the capacity to devote oneself to the public good, came to be defined some time in the eighteenth century as a quality available only to men. Women were supposed to be concerned with *sexual* virtue, and to confine themselves to the private sphere.[4] As a woman, then, Sarah Churchill was an unlikely candidate for virtue. The doors through which she entered politics were opened by personal, intimate connections: her close friendship with Queen Anne, her standing as the highest-ranking official in the queen's bedchamber, and her marriage to the Duke of Marlborough. None of these roles involved service to the 'public good' in the abstract. She was, then, on the wrong side of the public–private dichotomy.

Sarah Churchill's experience with political virtue thus sheds light on the nature of the very nature of that dichotomy. It is taken as a given in modern political discourse that the maintenance of a proper distinction between the public and the private is the key to both the health of the polity and the liberty of individuals; the improper mixing of public and private was, conversely, considered the definition of corruption and tyranny. The distinction could be applied in multiple, overlapping contexts: from the motivations of individual political actors (those who sought the public good versus those who pursued private interest), to the person of the monarch (the king that never dies versus the king who does), to the identity of the person whom that king's servants should serve (the king as an individual versus the public good and fundamental law embodied in the king); to types of royal servants (the household versus the Council); and finally, to discourse itself (things that were proper subjects of discussion in the 'public sphere' versus things that could be kept secret). Most of these distinctions pre-dated the eighteenth century.

However, they were pushed to the centre of political argument by a number of developments: the limits placed on royal prerogative by the constitutional settlement of 1688, the accident of female monarchy, the desacralization of the royal body and the decline of court culture, and the appropriation of a classical rhetoric of virtue that had once been associated with classical republicanism by a variety of political groups, court whigs as well as country tories. But while the public–private distinction was deployed frequently in late Stuart political argument, its application was not consistent.[5] A close study of what contemporaries meant when they invoked the dichotomy suggests that the line between public and private was not clearly defined and subject to manipulation.

Sarah was able to portray herself as a disinterested servant of the public good only because the differences between the bedchamber and the government, the queen's person and the body politic, the Duke of Marlborough's private interest and the good of the nation were all open to interpretation. Conversely, it was the duchess's own ambiguous position in relation to the boundaries between the public and the private that made her versions of her story open to question, and made her a lightning rod for controversy. Her success and her failure at portraying herself as a virtuous political actor were both bound up with the instability of the public–private distinction. Together, they indicate the possibilities and limits of female agency in shaping contemporary discourses about women's place in political life.

This chapter is divided into five sections. The first two will deal with what Sarah and her close political associates meant by 'virtue', at the behaviour that their political ethics in theory demanded, and how the specific political situation in which they operated complicated those ideals. Most of what is said in this section regarding the difficulty of implementing ideals of virtuous behaviour applied equally to Sarah Churchill and to her husband, the Duke of Marlborough. However, the problem did not impinge on them in the same way, and gender was a significant part of the difference. Sections three and four will explore the campaign Sarah conducted against the queen and Abigail Masham (between 1708 and 1712) from Sarah's own perspective. My concern here is with how Sarah herself manipulated the lines between the public and private, in a way that allowed her to give a political dimension to what could otherwise have been regarded as a private matter, while at the same time appearing to respect the queen's right to privacy. The last section will look at how the 'battle of Abigail' was interpreted by other people. We shall ask why, despite Sarah's attempt to give that struggle a political meaning, it was treated by others as a purely private, emotional event.

VIRTUE AND THE POLITICS OF CREDIT

Gender did not matter to Sarah Churchill's construction of herself as a political actor. She shared with the duumvirs (Marlborough and his close political ally, the Lord Treasurer Sidney Godolphin) a code of political ethics that privileged 'virtue', defining it as the subordination of private interest and ambition to the public good. As the 'country' ideologue Charles Davenant put it in 1699, 'all thoughts, endeavours and designments [of the good citizen] should tend to the good and welfare of our country'.[6] The ideal of political virtue has been associated with both classical republicanism (strictly defined, the belief that monarchy is undesirable and unnecessary) and with English 'country' ideology (a distrust of the power of the executive, and a desire to limit it by frequent elections, the purging of placement from Parliament, limitations on royal prerogative, and a ban on standing armies).

By Anne's reign, however, the language of political virtue had become more commonplace and flexible.[7] We would be mistaken to assume that the Ducess of Marlborough or her husband, or Godolphin were either republicans or country politicians. None advocated the abolition of the monarchy. The duke's notorious bid to be named 'Captain-General for life' did not suggest an opposition to standing armies. Equally antithetical to country principles was the desperate fight that all three of them put up to prevent the parliamentary election of 1710, on the grounds that it would threaten political stability. They were more often found struggling to get their allies into the executive branch of the government than trying to limit the power of that branch.

But the ducesss and her associates retained much of the moral thrust of 'country' ideology. They expressed an ideal of self-discipline and self-denial, in which greed, ambition, pleasure, and even pride were to be suppressed for the sake of the public good. The Duke of Marlborough's letters were suffused with references to his lack of worldly ambition, his earnest desire to eschew the magnificence of courts and retire to a humble country life, and a weary resolution to continue serving out of love for queen and country. As he told his wife, 'I had much rather end my days quietly with my neighbours, than be great at Court, where I desire no more power, than that of being able to persuade 42 [the queen] not to hurt themselves'.[8] Godolphin's advice to Marlborough, upon informing him that his son-in-law (the Earl of Sunderland) had been dismissed from office, captures the ethic. Despite this insult to his family, Marlborough was 'not in this case to look upon himself as a private person, but that all he has done, and all he is doing for the public, sets him, in the opinion of the world, very much above these sorts of injuries and malice'.[9]

The Duchess of Marlborough similarly spoke of herself as having eschewed ambition and wealth for the sake of the public good. She circulated to her friends detailed explanations of her management of the queen's financial affairs during her tenure as Groom of the Stole in order to prove that she 'never got a shilling'.[10] In her belatedly published self-vindication, *An account of the conduct of the Dowager Duchess of Marlborough* (1742), Sarah asserted that she had always acted 'out of regard for the public welfare' and from a 'disinterested principle of action', having 'never considered myself on any occasion where her [the queen's] interest or glory was concerned'.[11] She wholeheartedly adopted the country critique of the court, that it was full of obsequious parasites who flattered princes in order to advance themselves. A courtier herself, of course, Sarah was the unique exception to the general rule. As her friend and self-styled 'secretary' Arthur Mainwaring put it, she was a 'courtier in the interest of the country'[12] and 'the only favourite that ever a sovereign was the better for'.[13]

Francis Hare, the Duke of Marlborough's chaplain, marvelled that Sarah, 'a lady that was almost born in a court, and the chief favourite of it, that has been exposed to receive so much flattery herself, and under such temptations to give it to her Prince', could resist its blandishments. Indeed, he continued with no apparent sense of irony, 'I can't forbear saying to one that loves so little what looks like flattery, that it is the truest instance of heroic virtue I have ever seen'.[14] In her *Account of the conduct*, Sarah presented herself as a favourite who, uniquely, told a ruler the truth.

> Young as I was, when I first became this high favourite, I laid it down for a maxim, that flattery was falsehood to my trust, and ingratitude to my greatest friend; and that I did not deserve so much favour, if I could not venture the loss of it by speaking the truth, and by preferring the real interest of my mistress before pleasing her fancy, or the sacrificing to her passion.[15]

If the Duchess of Marlborough shared her husband's ideal of selfless service to the country, she differed significantly from him in her attitude to party politics. Sarah was openly and ardently identified with the whigs, in particular with the aggressive, well-organized and uncompromising element in the whig party known as the Junto.[16] She maintained contact with this group through her son-in-law, the Earl of Sunderland, and through Arthur Mainwaring, a whig MP who (between 1707 and his death in 1712) provided Sarah with flattery, advice, gossip and extracts from classical and philosophical literature. The Duke of Marlborough's attitude to the whigs was quite different. He shared the queen's well known aversion to partisan politics, and won her trust in part on that basis. Marlborough and Godolphin both defined themselves, at least initially, as moderates (or even, in Marlborough's case, as tory-leaning moderates).[17] However, their attempt to form a 'moderate ministry' in alliance with Robert Harley collapsed in 1708; this in turn drove the duumvirs into a closer relationship with the whigs, upon whom they came to depend for support for the war effort and for protection from Harley's machinations.

Even after the collapse of the moderate ministry, however, Godolphin and Marlborough never entirely relinquished their anti-party stance. Their credibility with Anne still depended upon her belief that they could protect her from the demands of the whigs.[18] Consequently, the alliance between the Junto whigs and the duumvirs was an uneasy one on both sides. The Junto flexed its muscle by trying to force the queen to appoint its allies and associates to high offices in church and state, even when Anne's personal dislike of the candidate was well-known. In each case, Marlborough and Godolphin faced a dilemma: to co-operate with the Junto in pressuring Anne to accept unwelcome appointments might alienate the queen, while not to do so would alienate the Junto. In any case, the Junto was prone to blame them for the queen's refusal, even if it was not their fault.[19] Mainwaring, writing to the duchess, bemoaned the duumvirs' reluctance to 'put themselves at the head of a party, in which they may be safe and easy ... and all this out of a little narrow principle of being independent of a party, which in this case is really in effect being a slave without friends'.[20] Marlborough, understandably, was protective of his independence. Asking his wife to convey to her Junto friends 'that I will always be in the interest of 89 [the whigs]', Marlborough none-theless sternly told her to warn them that 'for their sakes and that of the public, as well as my own reputation, I must be master of judging my actions towards 239 [the Queen]'.[21]

Despite Sarah's reputation as a termagant she played an important, and often successful, political role as a mediator between the whigs and the duumvirs.[22] But the dynamics of the strained relationship between the whigs and the duumvirs put enormous pressure on her to remain at court, and to maintain the appearance of holding the queen's favour even after she had lost it; ironically, this effort was to ultimately cost her her influence with the whigs, as well as with the queen. As the preceding discussion suggests, Marlborough and Godolphin retained the support of the whigs only because the whigs believed that Marlborough and Godolphin had the support of the queen. This meant that their power was, in a sense, based upon the *illusion* of power.

The importance of appearances was exacerbated by the diplomatic politics of the War of the Spanish Succession. The unity of the anti-French alliance was jeopardized by the spread of rumours abroad about the strength of the tories and the precarious tenure of the Marlborough–Godolphin ministry. The Dutch worried that England might pull out of the war or that Marlborough might lose his command; the duumvirs feared in turn that the Dutch would be prompted by this worry to make a separate peace with the French. In fact, the spreading of negative information about the duumvirs' standing was used as a tactic to damage them. Thus, Marlborough reported from The Hague in April 1708 that 'there is care taken by letters writ from England to persuade these people that 42 [Queen Anne] has no kindness for 240 [Sarah], 38 [Godolphin] and 39 [Marlborough]. I take this to be a *pollatique* of 199 [Harley] for the inducing these people to a peace'.[23]

The importance which the duumvirs attached to perceptions of their standing with the queen is evident in the frequency with which the word 'credit' surfaced in their discussions. The establishment of the Bank of England and the stock exchange had made credit central to economic life in a new way at the beginning of the eighteenth century. It was now possible to build wealth upon the appearance of wealth. Political life ran as much on credit, the appearance of power and influence, as did the economy. Thus, Marlborough lamented that 'the credit of 256 [Masham] occasions a good deal of disagreeable discourse in the country [Holland]',[24] that the tories would control the queen 'as long as 256 [Masham] has credit',[25] and that 'It is most certain that 38 [Godolphin], 39 [Duke of Marlborough] and 240 [Duchess of Marlborough] have no real credit'.[26] And indeed, the 'credit' that the ministry was perceived to have with the queen literally affected the 'public credit', the willingness of investors to lend money to the government.

The duumvirs' need to maintain the appearance of 'credit' with the queen shaped Sarah Churchill's position in important ways. Because her long-standing friendship with Anne was thought to be the source and guarantee of the queen's trust in Marlborough and Godolphin, her place in the queen's affections was watched eagerly by observers of all political stripes. On the whig side, Horatio Walpole reported optimistically to James Stanhope on 20 April 1708 that Sarah 'is constantly again with the Queen at court ... all things will hold as well as they are, if not mend'.[27] A year or so later, Ann Clavering wrote in despair that Sarah 'never appeared [at court] but when sent for', while Masham was 'more and more in esteem'.[28]

The tories were equally obsessed. Peter Wentworth kept his brother, Lord Raby, up to date on the gossip. ''Tis said the Qu[een] has been so provoked as to declare to more than once she has been so slighted by the Duchess of M[arlborough] that she can't endure the sight of her', he wrote on 30 January 1710. Two weeks later, he found the queen's dislike of Sarah further confirmed by the fact that 'the Duchess did not make her appearance at chapel with the Queen on her birthday, which most ladies of the bedchamber did'.[29]

The pressure on the Duchess of Marlborough to prevent the knowledge of Masham's favour from spreading was exacerbated by Arthur Mainwaring. As we have seen, Mainwaring and the duchess shared a common agenda of uniting the duumvirs and the whigs. But because his own status amongst the whigs came from his close friendship with her, he had a particularly strong stake in maintaining the whigs' belief in her influence on the queen. For whatever reason, he could almost always be found pressing Sarah Churchill to put on a show, often by offering inflated estimates of what could be gained by it. 'Your staying away [from court] makes more people uneasy than I ever knew in my life upon one subject', he told Sarah in August 1709. 'People have really made me believe that everything will in a great measure turn upon it, whether whigs or tories shall be uppermost, that is, whether the nation shall be happy or undone'. Sarah's mere appearance in the vicinity of the queen would bring in a 'new golden age': 'you would see the business well carried on, the whigs always cheerful, and yourself at the head of them'.[30] It was from

Mainwaring that Sarah learned how far the stories of her 'terrible battles' had travelled.[31] It was also from him that she learned that the whigs credited her with their eventual success in getting the queen to accept their candidate for the Admiralty. 'See how little is necessary to make everybody think you are in favour', he crowed, 'the wonder is only on the other side, when anyone says you are not so'.[32]

The Earl of Sunderland, Sarah's son-in-law, also emphasized the dependence of the whigs on Sarah's standing with the queen, and therefore of the importance of public perceptions. In April 1710, he urged her at least to go through the motions of a reconciliation with the queen, 'the very appearance of which, though there were nothing more in it, is absolutely necessary to save them [the whigs], Lord Marlborough, Lord Treasurer and the whole from ruin'.[33] He therefore begged her to come to town, 'if it were only to stop the mouths and insolent pushing of your enemies against you and all your friends'.[34] The constant scrutiny to which the duchess's relations with the queen were subject explains why Sarah's biggest battles and longest-nursed grievances occurred over matters which, however trivial in themselves, could be taken to indicate the relative standings of Sarah Churchill and Abigail Masham in the queen's affection: such things as the salaries of royal laundresses, the apportionment of palace lodgings, or appointments to minor posts in the bedchamber.[35]

Sarah's territoriality in matters of household patronage can be glimpsed from the letters of Elizabeth Cotterell and her daughter, Jane, to William Trumbull, which describe in detail the women's efforts to get Jane a post in the queen's bedchamber. From their friend Lady Arundel, the Cotterells learned that 'Mrs. Scarborough the last maid was put in by Mrs. Masham, for which reason the Duchess must now have her turn'.[36] Although the Cotterells had been made to understand that Sarah probably lacked the inclination or even the power to help Jane, they nonetheless thought it crucial to avoid offending her:

> 'Tis certain the Duchess opposes Mrs. Masham in whatever she desires, and though perhaps she won't do any good yet they say would take it ill if application be not first made to her as being the superior lady.[37]

The consequences of being seen by Sarah Churchill to make court to Abigail Masham were apparently unpleasant. Lady Arundel was reluctant to accompany the Trumbull women on a visit to the new favourite 'for fear of doing herself an injury'.[38] The Duchess of Marlborough's desire to discipline those who made court to the wrong favourite can be documented from Mainwaring's correspondence. Going to see Somerset in June 1708, Mainwaring assured the duchess that he intended to 'give him a hint, if I can, about his courtesy to Abigail'.[39] In September, he reported to her on the Earl of Kent's pathetic efforts to excuse himself when he realized that he had incurred Sarah's displeasure because 'I'm civil to Mrs. Masham': 'Dey never let me into any of deir politics, and I must be civil to all the queen's servants'.[40]

Sarah's effort to keep up the appearance of having influence with the queen undoubtedly put a strain on herself and others. Whether it actually helped the relationship between the whigs and the duumvirs, as Mainwaring promised, is an open question. It is probably the case that Sarah's stubborn presence at court farther alienated the queen, although it may also have delayed public knowledge of this fact by a few years. Although the friendship between the two women was shaky as early as 1704, it was not until around 1710 that Sarah's loss of the queen's affection came to be regarded as irrevocable and was openly referred to in party propaganda. But even after her loss of favour was publicly known, Sarah still had a role to play in the maintenance of the ministry's political credibility: whether the Duchess of Marlborough was to be allowed to keep her office came to be seen as the litmus test of the Duke of Marlborough's standing with the queen.

The duchess was in fact not the first of the Duke of Marlborough's intimates and associates whose tenure in office, despite Anne's dislike of them, was taken as a sign of Anne's confidence in the duke. When, for example, Anne wanted in 1709 to fire Sunderland (who was both a member of the whig Junto and Marlborough's son-in-law) the duumvirs had begged her to refrain on the grounds that it would adversely affect confidence – of the allies abroad, and the whigs at home – in the longevity of the ministry. Godolphin suggested that Marlborough write to Shrewsbury (the queen's close confidant at the time), 'taking notice of the rumours that are on that side of the water concerning 6 [Sunderland], and how they do not only affect him [Marlborough himself] really so much, but are thought to do so to that degree, that whatever his own inclination might be, it must needs make him incapable of being any use afterwards, either where he is [Douai], or with 116 [Holland], who would presently not fail to take care of themselves and by making their own terms [of peace with France]'.[41] Significantly, Godolphin went on in the same letter to suggest just how precarious the ministry's credit was made by these rumours, noting that many of the whigs 'are so uneasy, that they are ready to make their court to 199 [Harley]'. Similarly, Marlborough begged the queen to let his wife retain her offices in January 1710.[42]

THE MARLBOROUGHS AND THEIR CRITICS

The struggles of the Marlboroughs to appoint and keep friends and relatives in office shows how their rhetoric of disinterested virtue ran up against the need to maintain the appearance of having influence with the queen. The acquisition of honours, wealth and offices for their camp was a mark of the queen's favour, and hence, for reasons discussed above, a political necessity.

This muddied the clear boundary between public and private interest that the rhetoric of virtue was meant to protect. Predictably, both of the Marlboroughs were attacked as greedy and ambitious. The very honours that symbolized the queen's confidence in them became liabilities. Tory propagandists gleefully dwelt on what the Marlboroughs had gained: the grounds and funds to build the magnificent Blenheim Palace, a pension, offices at court for Sarah and her daughters, and a place in the Privy Council for their son-in-law, the Earl of Sunderland. The things that Marlborough was known to want but did not receive (the title of Captain-General for life, complete control of appointments in the army) were also harped upon by propagandists to illustrate his self-aggrandizing ambition. Swift's devastating article in *The Examiner* of 23 November 1710, entitled 'British ingratitude', brilliantly pitted the duke against his own classical models of virtue by comparing the duke's rewards to the modest amounts that the ancient Romans had spent when thanking their victorious generals.

This criticism affected the duke and duchess differently. The duke came to the problem from the position of indispensibility. There was no doubt that, as the commander of the queen's forces in Europe, he had served the public good. The fact that he had risked his life for the queen made his claims to be disinterested hard to challenge. However, it also meant that he could be virtuous only if he stayed in office, no matter what 'mortifications' he suffered. Ironically, this deprived him of the bargaining power that his obvious talents should have given him, a fact which Anne could exploit. When she finally dismissed Sunderland in June 1710, the queen pointedly remarked to Godolphin that 'it is true indeed, that the turning a son-in-law out of his office may be a mortification to the Duke of Marlborough; but must the fate of Europe depend on that, and must he be gratified in all his desires?'[43] The duke did not resign. Nor did he resign when Godolphin was dismissed in August, nor when all the remaining whig ministers resigned in protest over Anne's dissolution of Parliament. Likewise, although the Marlboroughs and Godolphin spoke throughout 1710 as if Sarah's dismissal from office might be the one 'mortification' that would render Marlborough unable to carry on with his command, the duke compliantly delivered the duchess's resignation to the queen when she demanded it.

Sarah had a different relationship to the problem of reconciling credit and virtue. The importance of credit had made her role more important, politicizing issues and activities that would otherwise have been trivial. But she had few claims, by virtue of office, to serve the 'public good'. In so far as her continuance in office could be said to promote the public good, it was because she was a sign of her husband's credit. This was not a strong claim. As events were to prove, she was expendable. Moreover, her right to her offices was challenged in the name of the very distinctions between public and private interest, between service to the nation and service to the monarch, between virtue and corruption, that she herself took to be axiomatic. The duke's desire not to be mortified by having his wife lose her places was over-ridden by his desire to appear so virtuous that he could bear the mortification of seeing his wife removed from office. As Sarah explained, John Churchill was brought to acquiesce in her dismissal in order that 'that people might not say he quitted upon the account of my places, which many thought was wrong'. She added sourly, 'I confess I thought using his wife so ill was as great [grave?] an affront as any, but wiser people had other notions'.[44]

Sarah Churchill was also both an earlier and an easier target than her husband for tory propagandists. As early as 1702 she was blamed by the high-church tories for Anne's betrayal of their cause.[45] Her intervention in the parliamentary elections of 1705, in which she allegedly pressured voters by telling them that the queen herself favoured the whigs, was subject to an inquiry by the House of Commons, during which (according to Burnet) the tory William Bromley 'compared her to Alice Piers, in King Edward the Third's time, and said many other virulent things against her'.[46]

In 1707 and 1708, the years of the 'battle of Abigail', a number of satirical poems were circulated in manuscript which were directed specifically at Sarah. One of these, 'A Visit to Duke Humphrey's Tomb', is worth quoting at length as a succinct summation of the charges against Sarah in which, significantly, the Duke of Marlborough is mentioned only as a military hero. Sarah is shown exulting at the grave of Duke Humphrey, who stands as a genuine example of a 'good' royal favourite (and thus revealing herself to be the opposite):

> Her crown shall be the footstool of my name
> Her sceptre but my hobby horse to fame
> Her court with pimps and parasites I'll fill
> Slaves to my pride, and creatures to my will
> Her bearded bench shall know no law but mine
> By fancy punish and by pique shall fine
> Nor shall she dare at my directing nod
> To own her kindred, friends, her church, her God
> And whilst my hero does her foes pursue
> My moderation shall her friends subdue
> Thus I the height of glory will obtain
> Anna shall wear the crown, but Sarah reign.[47]

The Duke of Marlborough was, by contrast, protected by his undoubted military accomplishments, at least until about 1711. This is not to say that he was immune from criticism. Early in Anne's reign, tory satirists suggested that he had used his good looks (or those of his wife and sister) to curry favour with monarchs and their favourites, that his military accomplishments were much exaggerated, and that his propensity for betraying monarchs, which had led him to abandon James II in 1688, would now lead him to join the Jacobites or in any case to usurp Anne's throne.[48] But even Delarivière Manley's vicious *The secret history of Queen Zarah and the Zarazians* (1705), which makes all of the charges listed above, was primarily an attack on Sarah, and paid at least lip service to the idea that 'none [of the duke's honours] could be too great for his services ... he merited a just esteem both from the court and the country'.[49]

The most damning charge against the duke, that he was prolonging the war in order to aggrandize and enrich himself, was slow to surface. It was first made in 1708 in a pamphlet attributed to Robert Harley, entitled *Plain English*, which suggested that

> victories obtained are employed for their [the Marlboroughs'] private advantage and profit, and not to the end designed for obtaining a safe and honourable peace, but to aggrandize themselves and prolong the war by which they get such vast wealth, and secure themselves so much power.[50]

Jonathan Swift in *The Examiner* made similar charges in late 1710 and early 1711.[51] But these are relatively isolated instances: Harley's pamphlet remained in manuscript, and Swift, when first making the charges, was associated with Henry St John's October Club and therefore something of a renegade in Harley's propaganda machine.[52] It was not until later in 1711, when Harley was openly lobbying for peace, that the tories united behind a full-fledged attack on Marlborough. The duke's dismissal in January 1712, and the parliamentary investigation into his alleged embezzlement of funds, opened the floodgates to hundreds of pamphlets, lampoons and thinly veiled historical allegories lambasting his war-mongering, greed, ambition and corruption.[53]

The duchess remained a special target of satire even after the duke had lost his relative immunity. She was almost invariably included in attacks directed at her husband, and sometimes singled out for special treatment. The central charges against her were, in essence, the same as those against her husband: greed, ambition, ingratitude to the queen, and occasionally Jacobitism. Some sins, however, were Sarah's alone. The alleged witchcraft of Sarah's mother, Frances Jennings, and the possibility that Sarah had inherited her talents, was mentioned more than once:

> No wonder magic art surrounds the throne
> Old Mother Jennings in her Grace is known
> Old England's genius rouse, her charm's dispel
> Burn but the witch, and all things will go well.[54]

The sexual slander directed at Sarah also differed in an interesting way from the sexual attacks on her husband. It was he, rather than she, who was portrayed as using his sexual attractiveness to get power. The suggestion that the duke rose by prostituting both himself and his sister, was made in the Jacobite poem, 'The false favourite's downfall', in 1692, the chorus of which ran : 'Ah Churchill! How much better might'st thou prevail/Wouldst thou hang up the sword and stick to thy tail'.[55] The story that John Churchill rose to power by seducing and then exposing Charles II's mistress, the Duchess of Cleveland, which had featured in Delarivière Manley's *Zarah* and *The New Atalantis* volume I, was repeated in the anonymous *Oliver's pocket looking-glass* (1711) and *The perquisite-monger* (1712).

Sarah Churchill, by contrast, was not shown to use sex to gain power. At first glance this is surprising. Given the fact that she was notorious for using accusations of lesbianism against Abigail Masham and Queen Anne, one might expect to find the same charge levelled against her. One could argue that such a charge was implicit in the comparison made by William Bromley between Sarah and Alice Piers, or in the comparisons sometimes made between Sarah and 'fair Rosamond', the mistress of Henry II, who had met her death very near Sarah's own country seat at Woodstock.[56] But the precise source of Sarah's power over Anne was, perhaps out of respect for the queen herself, always either left mysterious or attributed to Anne's youthful *naïveté* at the time she fixed her affections on Sarah (who then, as Manley put it, 'stuck to her like a burr to a garment').[57] In so far as Sarah's sexuality was discussed in hostile satires, it was not the source of her power. Rather, she was shown to use power to get sexual favours. In Manley's *Zarah* (1705), for example, she uses her absolute control over the disposal of state patronage to obtain the sexual favours of a host of men, in particular Godolphin.[58]

The most important difference, however, between negative images of Sarah Churchill and negative images of her husband was that the former were more intense and powerful. It is instructive to compare the tone of Harley's attack on John and Sarah Churchill as a couple in *Plain English* (quoted above) to a nearly contemporary portrait of Sarah alone, for which Harley was also responsible. In a thinly veiled allegory, Sarah appears as

> an oldish woman of a fair countenance, in youthful dress; her chin and nose turning up, her eyes glaring like lightning, blasted all she had power over with strange diseases. Out of her nostrils came a sulphurous smoke, and out of her mouth flames of fire. Her hair was frizzled and adorned with the spoils of a ruined people; her neck bare, with chains about it of dice, mixed with pieces of gold; which rattling, made a horrid noise, for her motions were all fierce and violent, her garment was all stained with tears and blood ... She cast her eyes often with rage and fury on that bright appearance I have described [the Queen], over whom having no force, she tossed her head with disdain.[59]

No description of John Churchill quite matched this. Sarah took on superhuman, mythical or allegorical qualities in a way that her husband did not. Whereas John Churchill was even by his enemies acknowledged to be handsome, Sarah's physical characteristics, such as her famous upturned nose and habit of tossing her head, were turned into visible signs of her moral condition. She was not portrayed merely as greedy and ambitious, but as a witch, a fury, and a Medusa, the literal embodiment of wrath, malice, envy and overweening pride. In 'Duke Humphrey's answer', (the sequel to 'A visit to Duke Humphrey's tomb'), Gloucester's ghost rises to predict Sarah's doom, painting her as a monster whose head breeds 'poisonous vipers' and whose bloodline carries a 'black contagion'.[60] In George Sewell's *Epistle of Sempronia to Cethegus* (1713), she is likened to Frances Howard, the Duchess of Somerset, who was convicted in James I's reign for the murder of Thomas Overbury and widely reputed to be a witch:

> Such eyes as Somerset's imperious dame!
> With mocked ambition fierce, and red with shame
> Her murders, poisons, and intrigues displayed
> And all the sorceries of her arts betrayed
> Cast on that court, where once she shone in state
> And what she could not rule resolved to hate.[61]

Sarah was attacked, then, with a particular intensity. But precisely because her political identity was so multifaceted, it is hard to determine whether she was being attacked as the royal favourite, as a whig, as a stand-in for her husband, or as a political actor in her own right. Her attackers were vague on this score. In fact, the vagueness might have been deliberate. To understand its usefulness, it is necessary to recall the political differences between John Churchill and his wife. The extent of Sarah's influence on her husband was, at the time, an open question. It was known that while she passionately espoused the whig cause, he maintained (at least in public) a moderate, anti-party stance. Before 1712, many tories and self-styled 'moderates' hoped not so much to purge the duke, but to separate him politically from the duchess, the Junto, and Godolphin. Some historians have suggested that Harley himself hoped to obtain Marlborough as an ally.[62] The duchess, although perhaps unreasonably anxious, regarded *rapprochement* between Marlborough and Harley as a real possibility as late as October 1710.[63]

In this context, it made sense for tory propagandists to focus on the Duchess of Marlborough. She was useful as a representation of the politics which the Duke of Marlborough was in danger of embracing but might be encouraged to reject. The sexual relationship that Sarah was frequently imagined to be having with Godolphin could be taken as a metaphor for the political alliance between them, based upon whig principles. Such was the message of the rather graphic stanza that literally tied Sarah's whig politics and sexual adultery to the Lord Treasurer (here in the guise of Volpone):

> Oh were the sage Volpone bound
> His head her thighs betwixt, sir
> To suck from thence his notions sound
> And savoury politics, sir[64]

And if we take Sarah as the embodiment of whiggery and its attendant evils (as she literally is here), an attack on her in the form of a fantasy about a sexual relationship between her and Godolphin may have been a way to exert pressure on the duke to separate himself from the politics of his wife and the Lord Treasurer.

At the same time, attacks on the duchess could be used to tar the duke as well. Her function as a symbol for tory propagandists was flexible, and it was in their interest to keep their options open by leaving it ambiguous which aspect of Sarah's identity they were assaulting. The particularly intense quality of the attacks on Sarah may also reflect the fact that her political battles were widely perceived to be mixed up with personal ones. If Sarah was shown not merely to covet wealth and power but positively to spit venom, it was in part because the story of her failed friendship with Anne and her unsuccessful rivalry with Abigail Masham was widely known. Sarah appeared, in the eyes of tories and also, eventually, of whigs as well to display the classic fury of a woman scorned. But how did this perception arise?

BEDCHAMBER NARRATIVES

Sarah Churchill's assault on Abigail Masham can best be understood in the context of the ambiguity surrounding personal service to the monarch in this period. The queen's personal life and her bedchamber were, on the face of it, increasingly depoliticized in the early eighteenth century. Gone were the days, described by David Starkey, when the performance of intimate physical service to the monarch brought with it a piece of the numinous royal charisma and made the Groom of the Stole a legitimate bearer of royal authority.[65] As Robert Bucholz has argued, Anne asserted her right to a private life and strove to make her bedchamber a personal rather than a political space. Appointments to positions in the queen's household were defined as matters of Anne's personal preference, cordoned off from the politics of party struggle.[66] Even Sarah Churchill had to acknowledge in theory Anne's right to 'love whom you please'.

Anne's reign did not, however, represent a complete depoliticization of the monarch's mortal body, personal feelings, and private space. The queen's choice of body servants was read like tea leaves as indirect evidence of her political intentions, and her health and happiness were readily conflated with those of the nation.[67] Moreover, it was impossible to prevent body servants from discussing politics with the queen. The line between public and private service therefore was not easy to draw; people in Anne's reign continued to confer political meanings on the monarch's mortal body and its doings, but did so in a way that appeared to respect her privacy.

As a Groom of the Stole who claimed to be concerned only for the public good, Sarah Churchill felt acutely the ambiguities surrounding the nature of bedchamber service. But she was not alone in confronting them. For purposes of comparison, it may be useful to take a brief digression into the writings of David Hamilton, the queen's physician. Between 1710 and 1714 Hamilton kept a diary in which he described the queen's physical health, her political decisions, and his own attempts to intervene in both for her benefit. David Hamilton and Sarah Churchill had much in common: a commitment to the whig party, a rhetoric of disinterested service to queen and country, and an official position as a body servant to the queen. Like Sarah, David Hamilton used his privileged knowledge about the queen's private body and its doings to construct narratives that would explain her political behaviour and justify his own. He came to the task, however, from a different position than Sarah, and accordingly he understood the relationship between the 'private' and 'public' dimensions of the queen's life rather differently than she did.

Hamilton was, from the whig point of view, a key player at court. After the fall of the Marlborough–Godolphin ministry, he was one of the few whigs who had access to the queen. He used his position to encourage Queen Anne's friendship with the (whig) Duchess of Somerset, and acted as a go-between for the queen and Lord William Cowper, one of the former whig members of the Privy Council, to whom the queen continued to turn for advice. Sarah herself used him to communicate with Anne, writing him letters that purported to be for his eyes only but that were meant to be shown to the queen. Hamilton's loyalties in this were somewhat ambiguous. To be an effective agent for Sarah, he had to win Anne's trust. It was for this reason that he pretended to Anne that Sarah didn't know he was showing the queen her letters. But Sarah herself was never sure whose side he was really on. Her uncertainty testifies to the contradictory nature of his position.[68]

The contradictions, and Hamilton's handling of them, are worth exploring. As Anne's physician, Hamilton saw it as his duty to 'make the queen easy', as this was in his view essential to her health. He was therefore willing to carve out a space for the queen to have a 'private' life. He insisted, for example, that the queen's affections should dictate her choice of personal servants. It was precisely this respect for the autonomy of the queen's emotional life that made Sarah Churchill distrust him. But, as will be seen, Hamilton's position was a convenient one for a whig to take during the period when Sarah had already lost Anne's affections. Depoliticizing the queen's feelings was a way for whigs to construe Sarah's imminent dismissal from office as a result of the queen's displeasure with Sarah, rather than the queen's displeasure with the party as a whole. Moreover, privileging the queen's personal happiness, and cordoning off her private life from party politics, allowed Hamilton to support Anne's efforts to retain her whig favourite, the Duchess of Somerset, at a moment when the tories wanted to drive her out. Losing the Duchess of Somerset, Hamilton insisted, would disquiet her Majesty and injure her health.[69]

On the surface, then, Hamilton drew a sharp line between the queen's public and private life, treating her personal health and happiness as something separate from politics. But this was itself a way for Hamilton to legitimate his own form of political intervention. He was quick to identify those political decisions that he thought the queen should not have made as the cause of her disquiet, and assumed that her ease and good spirits could only be restored if she reversed them. In September 1710, for example, after Anne had provoked the remaining whig members of her council to resign by calling for new elections in spite of their vehement objections, Hamilton told the queen to go to to the country to ease her mind, 'for it must needs be a great uneasiness to a person of so good a disposition as Her Majesty, to put people out, when anger and rage were not the motives, but supposed prudential reasons, and the strong solicitations of those [Harley *et al.*] confided in'.[70]

Hamilton's diagnosis of the cause of the queen's death reveals his tendency to conflate the health of the queen's body and the health of the body politic. Anne died, he explained, because the 'gouty humour' located in her knee and foot was 'translated' to her brain. This 'translation' was made possible by the 'preparatory sinking of her spirits and weakness of her nerves' that had, apparently, been brought about by political events. At the beginning of the reign, Anne's health had been good, he considered, because a 'succession of pleasures' had 'undoubtedly refreshed her mind, and strengthened her spirits'. These pleasures included the union of England and Scotland, the victories against Louis XIV, and her 'universal fame for piety' which engaged 'the love of her subjects and the admiration of all Europe'.

But in the last seven years of the reign (1707 onwards) 'there happened a succession of disquiets, which by grieving her mind, made her less able to resist outward impressions and importunitys, a compliance with which has loaded the latter part of her life, with reflections, and her memory with reproaches; and by impairing her health and weakening her nerves, rendered them less able to resist this last translation of the gout, which was the cause of her sudden death'.[71] The disquiets were both personal and political: the death of Prince George, the falling out between Anne and Sarah, the rise of Harley, the fall of Marlborough and Godolphin, and Anne's loss of her subjects' love through the shameful Peace of Utrecht and her tory ministers' flirtation with the Pretender. Anne's physical, personal and political troubles were closely related and mutually reinforcing: her ill health led her to abdicate responsibility to evil advisers, which in turn led her to make bad political decisions, thereby damaging her health.

'Making the queen easy' did not, then, mean helping her to get what she wanted. Indeed, Hamilton justified his own pressure on her by painting the queen as someone who was *so* susceptible to pressure that she needed to have counter-pressure applied in order to make her do what she had really wanted to do all along. When Anne told David Hamilton that Godolphin was 'as hot as the rest' [of the whigs], he took it as evidence that the queen had been under pressure from the tories. It was, he wrote,

> a plain demonstration, of the success of outward endeavour to impress the queen against him [Godolphin] and that though there had been a great disquieting struggle between her own inclinations, and the force of outward pressure, yet she was a yielding. For to my own personal knowledge, her natural calmness, was such, that a continued teasing, as she termed it herself, would make her yield, unless she stood in the middle between the teasings of two different sorts, and then her affection and personal respect would cast the balance between the two advisers, as is the common temper of a good natural disposition.[72]

Hamilton's elaborate narrative about the queen's health and emotions reconciled a number of contradictions. He could distinguish between those who 'made the queen easy' and those who 'teased and pressured her', while justifying the pressure he himself exerted. He could devote himself to the welfare of the queen's private body, appearing to cordon it off from the hurly-burly of party struggle, while following a party agenda in the queen's bedchamber.

Hamilton found a way to reconcile serving the monarch's private pleasure and the public good. His manipulation of the boundaries between the private and public made it possible for him to construe himself, as Sarah construed herself, as a 'courtier in the interest of the country'. Even behaviour on Hamilton's part which, in classic accounts of corruption, smacked of secrecy and manipulation (the fact that Hamilton would meet the queen incognito, for example) could be construed as patriotic. The language of political virtue, although consistent in its vocabulary, was manipulable: it could be used by those whose political influence was based on intimacy, even secret friendship, with the queen, as well as those outside of the court.

Sarah Churchill grappled with all of the same issues as David Hamilton. Like him, she had to legitimate her own influence on the queen while excoriating Anne's susceptibility to pressure from favourites. But the differences are instructive. Sarah faced constraints that came from both her sex and her personal history with the queen. It was arguably more dangerous for a woman than for a man to engage in bedchamber narratives. Sarah was more vulnerable to having the charges that she made about the power of female favourites boomerang against her, and less protected by an aura of professional authority. Moreover, whereas Hamilton was legitimating the influence of people who successfully engaged in the project of 'making the queen easy' (himself and the Duchess of Somerset), the Duchess of Marlborough had to explain why she had failed and lost the queen's friendship.

We shall now turn to the 'bedchamber narratives' that Sarah Churchill created. What is analysed here under the rubric of bedchamber narrative is in fact a diverse body of material which, taken together, allows us to see how

Sarah explained to herself and others the extraordinary 'change' that had occurred in Anne's heart and bedchamber. This material includes letters from Sarah to Anne, correspondence with friends (particularly Arthur Mainwaring and Lady Mary Cowper) about Abigail, letters Sarah sent to David Hamilton in the hope that he would show them to Anne, printed and manuscript propaganda that Sarah either wrote or helped to circulate (or referred to in correspondence), and her subsequent narratives of events, many of which were circulated to her friends long before her *Account of the conduct of the Dowager Duchess of Marlborough* was printed in 1742. The value of this material lies mostly in what it tells us about what Sarah told herself. As an attempt to manipulate Anne, her narratives were a failure. What is interesting here, however, is their internal logic.

Unlike David Hamilton, Sarah Churchill did not equate the queen's legitimately private space with the queen's bedchamber. Anne certainly had a right to 'privacy' with respect to her choice of friends, but not necessarily in her choice of bedchamber servants. Sarah saw her capacity to control household patronage and retain her court offices as a sign of the Marlborough–Godolphin ministry's 'credit', and therefore as a political rather than a personal matter. She made the distinction between friendship and office-holding clear when describing a letter that Anne had written after one of their famous quarrels: Anne had said 'that it was impossible for me to recover her former kindness, but that she would always behave herself to me as the D[uke] of Marlborough's wife and as her Groom of the Stole'.[73]

Thus, the queen's bedchamber (in Sarah's eyes) was not a space which Anne Stuart, in her mortal person, could order according to her pleasure, but one in which Sarah had 'rights of office' which could be defined in quasi-legal terms. When the queen ignored her recommendation of Mary Fane as a new bedchamber woman in favour of Masham's candidate, Isabella Danvers, Sarah reminded Anne of household protocol: 'when a place is vacant under any of your other officers, tho' your Majesty does not allow them immediately to fill it, yet some regard is had to them and their recommendation'.[74] She likewise challenged Anne's right to raise the salaries of the royal laundress without her permission.[75] In October 1709, she battled with Anne over the right to appoint a new seamstress. Again, Sarah cited precedent in defence of her rights: 'that place is in the disposal of my office as much as a footman [is] in the Duke of Somerset's [disposal]'.[76]

Anne's emotions, by contrast, were (in Sarah's eyes) beyond politics, even beyond understanding. Although Sarah had initially tried to restore her intimacy with the queen, it was fairly certain by 1708 that those efforts were futile. This view was shared by the Duke of Marlborough, who wrote to his wife in July 1708 that the queen 'will not be made sensible or frighted out of this passion'.[77] Mainwaring encouraged Sarah to adopt a stance of indifference, almost contempt, for the royal heart she had lost. He indulged himself in the fantasy that Sarah, at some future date, would be able to use the queen in a 'jocose manner': 'And then, for that noble treasure, her heart, I would tell her, that since she has given it to so worthy an object as fair-faced Abigail, I would never think of regaining it, nor of disturbing what is so very well placed'.[78] In keeping with his agenda of getting Sarah to go to court, he encouraged her to make the distinction between favourites and bedchamber officers. 'Remember that you are Groom of the Stole', he admonished, 'without the odious name of favourite'.[79] He promised that her mere presence at court would make her 'greater than you could ever have been as a favourite'.[80]

At one level, Sarah Churchill and Arthur Mainwaring were simply defining a boundary in a particular way. The distinction between public and private was no longer marked by the line between Anne Stuart's bedchamber and the queen's ministry, but between Anne's emotions (private) and Anne's bed-chamber (public). But even this line was not as clear-cut as it seemed. If Sarah's only goal had been to keep her offices, then such categories would have been adequate and appropriate for her argument. But she wanted to do more. She was not interested in offering Anne a private life. Rather, she was interested in using Anne's need for privacy as an indictment of that private life, and in using the threat of exposing it as a way to pressure Anne politically. Sarah was not drawing a sharp line between what was considered public and what was considered private; rather, she was linking them in complex ways.

These links were established through a complicated, elusive rhetorical strategy that Sarah used in her exchanges with Anne and with people close to Anne. The keystone was an elaborate but double-edged expression of concern about Anne's reputation. When she broached the topic of Abigail Masham to the queen, she usually did so by reporting what other people thought, sometimes 'helpfully' enclosing extracts and summaries of satires and pamphlets already in circulation. Her letter to David Hamilton quoted at the beginning of this chapter is one example of this tactic. Similarly, she wrote:

> You cannot but remember ... how many affronts King Charles had, that was a man, upon account of the Duchess of Portsmouth; and I think I need not say a great deal to show how much worse it is for your Majesty, whose character has been so different from his, to be put in print and brought upon the stage perpetually for one in Abigail's post'.[81]

The beauty of this concern for 'reputation' was that it absolved Sarah from having to say whether she thought or knew that the rumours were true. As illustrated in Chapter 7, it was a commonplace in contemporary advice litera-ture that when it came to women's reputations, appearance was more impor-tant than truth. By harping on Anne's vulnerable reputation, Sarah licensed herself to discuss the queen's relationship with Masham without claiming to know anything about it.

Moreover, while Sarah consistently spoke of Anne as a person in danger of exposing herself and ruining her reputation, she conspicuously refused to say what it was that Anne was exposing. She often made an elaborate show of veiling the identity of her subject and/or the content of what she was reporting, but did it so transparently that the reader could not fail to fill in the blank. Abigail was referred to with phrases like 'one who I am ashamed to name'[82] or 'another person ... whom I believe the queen is enough concerned for, to wish they might be well spoken of'.[83] Sarah's delicate refusal to explain what she was talking about heightened the scandalousness of a book which (she told Anne) contained 'stuff not fit to be mentioned of passions between women'[84] and printed sheets which (she told Hamilton) 'which they said were not fit for me to see, by which I guessed they are upon a subject that you [Hamilton] may remember I complained of to you'.[85]

These rhetorical techniques had several purposes. First, they allowed Sarah to distance herself from the source of the rumours. This was necessary because Sarah was vulnerable to the very insinuations she was making about Abigail Masham: after all, she herself had risen by winning the queen's heart. If Abigail was compared to the Duke of Buckingham and the Duchess of Portsmouth, Sarah had been likened to Alice Piers and 'fair Rosamond'. To assert definitively that Abigail had seduced the queen would have laid her open to the inevitable *tu quoque*. It was safer to cultivate a stance of epistemological uncertainty and outsiderhood in relation to the facts of the queen's personal life. Her suspicions of Anne and Abigail, she insisted, were the same as those of any other concerned citizen. 'To show you I am not alone in this opinion', she wrote to Anne in November, 1709, 'if I should ask the first ordinary man I met what had caused so great a change in you, he would say that the reason was because you had grown very fond of Mrs. Masham, and were governed by those that govern her'.[86]

If one of Sarah's purposes was to establish her status as something other than a spurned and jealous ex-lover, her other goal was to put pressure on the queen to change her policies. It was because of these policies, Sarah insisted, that the world knew about Abigail in the first place. Abigail Masham would not have been 'named or so much [as] thought of if it were not for her friendship with the enemies of the government and your Majesty's unaccountable averseness to so many reasonable things'.[87] Anne could have privacy, if she behaved. Thus, in a letter of 26 July, Sarah pointedly gave Anne's infatuation with Abigail her blessing: Anne had told Sarah 'you thought you might love whom you pleased ... And indeed, if she had no influence over your affairs, and did not make your ministers useless, you might make her as dear to you as you pleased'. As long as Anne refused to take the advice of her ministers, ''tis certain your people will not long bear the ills that arise from such a passion'.[88] What would make Anne's private life truly private would be a change in her policies: 'The queen has but one way to secure Masham, which will secure all, and that is to do what is right and be advised by those that she owns to be her council'. Then the queen and Abigail could be 'happy for ever in one another'.[89]

THE POLITICS OF PRIVACY

There is still a missing piece to this puzzle. Sarah claimed to draw, along with the rest of the world, the inevitable conclusions about Abigail Masham's influence from the queen's political behaviour. But what served to connect the political behaviour to Abigail? Since Sarah claimed ignorance of the queen's private life, and deferred elaborately to the queen's right to privacy, establishing this connection presented something of a hurdle. How could Sarah respect Anne's privacy and at the same time explain Anne's bad politics by reference to her bad personal life? The solution lay in her treatment of privacy.

Sarah's declared willingness to offer Anne (if she behaved) a private life free from scrutiny was actually a veiled accusation. Real virtue needed no privacy; or so Arthur Mainwaring had suggested in one of his philosophical letters when he recalled Drusus the Roman, who wished his house to be made of glass so that everyone could see into it.[90] Arthur Mainwaring and Sarah Churchill often imagined Anne and Abigail, by contrast, retreating into enclosed, hidden spaces as if they were ashamed of themselves. 'I will vex her so much as to convince even her stupid understanding that she has used me ill', Sarah declared of Anne, 'and then I will let her shut herself up with Masham'.[91] Mainwaring compared the queen to the Emperor Tiberius, hiding out with his favourite, Sejanus, on the island fortress of Caprese, which was

> enclosed by craggy rocks of a vast height, and a very deep sea at the bottom of them. So that it was very difficult for anyone to come thither and disturb their happiness. 'Tis pity this kingdom has no such delicious retreat near it.[92]

If Anne wanted to shield her private life from scrutiny, it was because there was something about it that would not bear scrutiny.

The secret, obscure and mysterious nature of Anne's relationship with Abigail Masham was made much of in the ballad to the tune of 'Fair Rosamond', which Arthur Mainwaring probably wrote and Sarah certainly helped to circulate in 1707.

> Whenas Queen Anne of great reknown
> Great Britain's sceptre swayed
> Besides the Church she dearly loved
> A dirty chambermaid.
>
> O Abigail that was her name
> She starched and stitched full well

But how she pierced this royal heart
No mortal man can tell.

However for sweet service done
And causes of great weight
Her royal mistress made her, Oh!
A minister of state.

Her secretary she was not
Because she could not write
But had the conduct and the care
Of some dark deeds at night.[93]

Exactly what the dark deeds were is an interesting question. Most modern historians take it as given that Sarah was accusing Anne of lesbianism. As was so often the case, the very vagueness of Sarah's language frustrates, and was designed to frustrate, simple assertions of this nature. But the elusiveness of the accusation made it more rather than less powerful.

There are numerous references to Anne's relationship with Masham both in Sarah's private correspondence and in propaganda that Sarah may have helped to write and circulate. They all came within the vicinity of accusing Masham of lesbianism without actually getting there. The lyrics to 'Fair Rosamond' were about as direct as published writing got. There was a more explicit reference to lesbian sex in *The rival dutchess; or, the court incendiary* (1708), an attack on Abigail Masham written in the form of a mock dialogue between Mrs Masham and Louis XIV's mistress, Madame de Maintenon. Here, too, however, a direct accusation of Masham is avoided, albeit so narrowly that it is hard not to think the anonymous author was gesturing at it. When Maintenon asks Masham about her romantic affairs, Masham responds that 'especially at court I was taken for a more modish lady, [who] was rather addicted to another sort of passion, of having too great a regard for my own sex, insomuch as few people thought I would ever have married'. When Maintenon asks if 'that female vice, which is the most detestable in nature, reign among you as it does with us in France', Masham tells the story of a 'lady of fashion' who attempted to ravish another woman.[94] The point of this discussion, however, seems to be that despite appearances Masham is heterosexual, since she goes on to tell the story of her affair with a man.

The language of Sarah's correspondence with both Anne and Arthur Mainwaring was equally elusive. It is important to remember that a vocabulary did exist in the late seventeenth century for describing sex between women; it is reasonable to assume that Sarah, coming of age in the court of Charles II, would have heard of the 'game at flats', of 'tribads', and of the many uses to which Englishwomen were thought to put the newfangled French or Italian import, the dildo.[95] That Sarah did not use that vocabulary with reference to Anne is therefore significant.

Sarah's letter of 26 July 1708 displays the ambiguous vocabulary that she did employ. Sarah asked Anne how she hoped to preserve her reputation

> after having discovered so great a passion for such a woman, for sure there can be no reputation in a thing so strange and unaccountable, to say no more of it, nor can I think the having no inclination for any but of one's own sex is enough to maintain such a character as I wish may still be yours.[96]

Sarah also described the queen as having a 'very strange passion',[97] an 'extravagant passion'[98] and 'exposed to be the talk of all courts and countries, for so wrong a thing, as having such a fondness for a bedchamber woman, and being so much governed by her'.[99] Mainwaring referred to the relationship with Mrs Masham with an assortment of similar terms: 'an inclination that is shameful, and that must be concealed and denied',[100] 'unnatural, a senseless, stupid, odious passion'.[101] She was 'abandoned to a shameful passion'[102] and had a 'stranger inclination' than even Charles II had when as a boy he was 'so strangely bewitched to be in love with an ugly crooked billet and cried if they put him to bed without it'.[103]

These terms and phrases can easily be taken as euphemisms for what we would today call lesbian desire. However, the strangeness, odiousness and shamefulness of Anne's passion for Abigail seem to have derived in Sarah's mind as much from Abigail's class as from her sex. Sarah repeatedly harped upon the lowliness of Masham's origins and occupation. She described her as 'low and inconsiderable in all things',[104] and as 'a dresser unknown to everybody but those she has betrayed' who is 'but just worthy to touch your limbs'.[105] 'Many people', she told Anne, 'have liked the humour of their chambermaids and been very kind to them, but it is very uncommon to hold a private correspondence with them and put them upon the foot of a friend and support them in all things right or wrong'.[106]

Mainwaring concurred. Abigail was 'a stinking ugly chambermaid'.[107] 'It is children's play', he complained, 'for any men to hold the first posts in government and not have it in their power to remove such a slut as that'.[108] Abigail was lambasted as a 'dirty chambermaid' and 'slut of state'.[109] The author of *The history of Prince Mirabel's infancy, rise and disgrace* declined to

> descend so low as to trace her from the little servile offices she went through in several private gentleman's families, neither shall I lose my own time or the readers in dwelling upon the nature of her former employments. Let it suffice that she was made one of the madonnas that buttoned on the imperial robe upon the Empress's shoulders, and, by a fawning diligence, let into the most secret recesses of Palatine's [Anne's] soul.[110]

Masham's lowliness and servility were explicitly contrasted with the free and frank converse that marked Sarah's friendship with Anne.

As Sarah explained in her *Account of the conduct*, her relationship with Anne was based on equality. As young women, the two friends had resolved to eschew 'form and ceremony', or 'the sound of words which implied in them distance and superiority', and to address one another by the names of 'Mrs. Morley' and 'Mrs. Freeman'.[111] When in later years Sarah circulated copies of letters between herself and Anne to her friends, she often called the reader's attention to the 'familiarity' of her tone, asking them to remember that it reflected a lifelong history of friendship. Sarah pushed the class distinction between herself and Abigail Masham as far as possible. In fact, she exaggerated the distinction, both by conferring upon herself a fictive social equality with the queen and by obscuring the fact that Masham was, despite her relative poverty, a respectable gentlewoman.

We do not have to choose between Mrs Masham's class and Mrs Masham's sexuality as the target of the Duchess of Marlborough's accusations. The emphasis on Masham's low class may have been a form of sexual innuendo. If, as Emma Donoghue suggests, the social equality of 'Mrs. Morley' and 'Mrs. Freeman' made their romantic friendship respectable,[112] then the inequality might itself be a signifier of the sexual nature of Anne and Mrs Masham's relationship. The labelling of Abigail Masham as a 'slut' underscores this possibility, as the word 'slut' had connotations of prostitution as well as physical dirtiness and menial service: it is is defined in the *Oxford English Dictionary* as 'a woman of dirty, untidy or slovenly habits', 'a kitchenmaid' *and* 'a woman of a low or loose character; a bold or impudent girl; a hussy, jade'.

Sarah's emphasis on Masham's class does, however, suggest that she was trying to get at something bigger than homosexuality. Absurdity, and not just sexuality *per se*, seems to be at the centre of her discourse on the subject of Anne and Abigail Masham. Her innuendo gestured at a disorder of the soul, the abandonment of reason and self-restraint, which could include sexuality but was not confined to it. Sarah's succinct and vicious sketch of Anne's behaviour at the death of Prince George provides a telling example of how sexual and non-sexual allegations could be intertwined. In a few short sentences, Sarah managed not only to suggest that Anne's much-vaunted conjugal love for her husband was a sham, but also to convict Anne of gluttony, emotional shallowness and a bizarre obsession with ceremonial forms.

> She has the greatest memory there ever was, especially for such things as are all forms and ceremony, giving people their due rank at processions and their proper places at balls and knowing the right order at an instalment and funerals, at the last she showed her great talents when she regulated that of the Prince, passing many hours every day in approving what should be done, which one in some affliction could no more have endured than to have eaten three meals as she did the day he died.[113]

Insofar as Anne was understood to be what we would call a 'lesbian', that characteristic was inextricably connected with other political and spiritual failings. Anne had succumbed to the classic vice of princes, whose 'passion is to be admired and feared, to have subjects awfully obedient, and servants blindly obsequious to their pleasure'.[114] Anne's fondness for Abigail was repeatedly connected, by both Sarah and Arthur Mainwaring, to Abigail's propensity to flatter her. As Mainwaring explained,

> If any body has one faithful servant, that tells nothing but truth, and endeavours only to do good, and to serve right; and afterwards takes a liking to some little servant, that always takes care to say what will please, and to humour the inclination, and to give into any wrong turn and measure; Tis certain that if this person has not a very extraordinary understanding, the wretched low servant will grow by degrees to be the better received, and the more hearkened to, than the faithful one.[115]

In rejecting the forthright Sarah for the flattering and servile Masham, Anne had rejected her political salvation. 'What a sad case is 42 [Queen Anne] in', Mainwaring exclaimed, 'surrounded by flatterers and liars, and at perfect enmity with the only person that ever told her truth'.[116]

Mainwaring provided Sarah with hosts of classical topoi supporting the proposition that (citing Plato here) 'the best possession a prince can have is the familiarity of those that will not flatter'.[117] Princes were, according to Mainwaring, 'not accustomed to hearing the truth, 'for what has truth to do with sceptres?' Princes were good for nothing but to ride on horseback, because only horses were ignorant of the difference between them and other men. He told her the story of the senator who flattered Tiberius by telling him his great fault was 'you neglect too much your own sacred person and take too much care of the public'.[118]

It was no wonder, then, that flattered princes so often became tyrants. Sarah suggested as much in a letter to David Hamilton. She urged him to show to Anne a description of Marcus Antoninus, who was meant to stand as a model of the virtuous ruler, and thus as Anne's antithesis. According to Sarah, Antoninus was, among other things, 'deaf to the charms of vanity and flattery, never swayed by passion;' He defended liberty and property, and preferred the public to his private good. Moreover, Sarah told Hamilton, 'I have not found in all the book one word of indefeasible unalterable divine right, destructive of all liberties and laws, to be disputed upon no account'. Masham was likened to the biblical Jezebel, who seduced King Ahab into tyranny and idolatry.[119]

Anne's relationship with Abigail, according to Sarah, also discredited the queen as an Anglican, the head of the Church of England. This too had a political dimension. It was Anne's pretensions to piety that, for Sarah, lay at the heart of her detestable kow-towing to the tories. Sarah tried to impress upon the queen the fact that her behaviour made a mockery of her pretensions to piety, and put her into spiritual danger. In October 1709 she sent the queen a long 'history' (known as the 'St. Alban's narrative') which described the course of their friendship, culminating in the harsh and unjust treatment Sarah had suffered at the queen's hands. Her intention, as she explained to Mainwaring, was to get Anne to read the narrative before taking the holy sacrament.[120] She enclosed with it extracts from Dr Taylor's sermons and the *Book of common prayer* that were meant to impress the queen with the spiritual danger she was in should she take communion without making amends to those she had injured (that is, Sarah). She helpfully provided guidelines for Anne to use when examining her behaviour towards her friends, derived from the Anglican spiritual handbook, *The whole duty of man*; these guidelines would prompt Anne to consider, among other things, whether she was guilty of neglecting lovingly to admonish a friend, forsaking friendship for slight or no cause, unthankfulness to those that admonish, or being angry at them, failure to make satisfaction for any injuries done her.[121]

Similarly, Sarah emphasized Anne's religious failings in a series of letters that she sent to David Hamilton in 1710. In a last-ditch attempt to hold on to her office, she threatened to print letters from the queen that she had in her possession. The letters she had in mind were passionate declarations of Anne's friendship, written at a time when the princess was under pressure from William and Mary to dissociate herself from the Churchills. It is unclear whether Sarah considered the extravagant gushy passion of the letters themselves to be embarrassing. She was more explicit about the threat that letters posed to Anne's reputation for piety.

Specifically, the queen had uttered oaths that she was now, by dismissing Sarah, about to break. Among other things, Anne had told Sarah, 'if you should ever do so cruel a thing as to leave me, from that moment I shall never enjoy one quiet hour. And should you do it without asking my consent (which if I ever give, may I never see the face of heaven) I will shut myself up'.[122] Now, Sarah asked David Hamilton, 'how can a religious person be easy in their own mind in putting out a woman in such a manner, even though she committed a fault, after such an oath written and sealed under her own hand'.[123] Accordingly, it was with her spiritual danger that Hamilton tried to impress the queen: 'I was at some pains to read the Annotations on the fifteenth Psalm, and on Ezekiel about an oath, in order to convince her of the danger of breaking it'.[124]

If Hamilton thought that the letters also damaged Anne's sexual reputation by showing she had 'no inclination for any but her own sex', he did not say so. Only Anne's reputation for piety was overtly mentioned as being in danger.[125] But then again, Hamilton and Sarah may have stressed the religious issue because they feared that an open discussion of Anne's youthful infatuation with Sarah would put Sarah on the defensive about her own status as a favourite. We do not, however, have to choose between religious and sexual dimensions of the threat to Anne's reputation. In fact, the distinction may not be appropriate. As historians of sexuality have noted, homosexuality was, in the early modern period, not a distinct crime or identity, but a subset of heresy and blasphemy.[126]

Sarah's failure to specify what was wrong with Anne's relationship with Abigail Masham made the wrongness loom larger. It turned the relationship into a cause of, and also a powerful metaphor for, all that was wrong with Anne as a monarch. Abigail's flattery of Anne was conflated with Anne's alleged fondess for divine right ideology, which was also a form of flattery to princes. The free scope Anne gave to her disordered passions for Abigail (whatever their nature) called to mind the tyrannical hedonism of Roman emperors such as Tiberius and Nero. It made a mockery of Anne's pretensions to piety, pretensions which themselves were at the centre of Anne's wrongheaded tory leanings. Anne's private passion and Anne's public policy thus discredited one another in a circular fashion.

Despite the lip service she paid to Anne's right to 'love whom you please', Sarah did not see Anne's choice between herself and Abigail Masham as a matter of mere personal preference; she strove to give it a larger political meaning. Her task was complicated by the fact that she had to respect the boundary between private and public. Not surprisingly, her own accounts were fraught with inconsistencies and contradictions. Anne's love for Abigail Masham was treated as extremely secret (a 'dark deed at night') but also as already completely exposed to the general public through the 'prints that do Mrs. Morley great harm'. Anne was admonished to change her policies in order to keep her dirty secret; yet the dirty secret itself (the relationship with Masham) was portrayed by Sarah as the very thing that made the tory politics inevitable. Sometimes, Abigail was portrayed as having tory principles, and using her iron grip on Anne to sway the Queen in the tory direction. At other times, Abigail was portrayed as a 'wretch for interest' who had no principles, but had simply flattered Anne's already existing inclinations for the tories in order to win Anne's heart, at a time when the principled Sarah had argued with the queen. Sometimes, Anne was said to have embraced tories and even crypto-Jacobites because they had offered to protect Abigail. Although Sarah told different stories at different moments, each version of the narrative served to link the public and the private, to show that Anne's rejection of Sarah and embrace of Abigail was a matter of national rather than personal concern.

Nonetheless, historians writing on the subject of Sarah, the queen and Abigail Masham have tended to become fascinated by the psychological rather than the political and rhetorical dynamics at work in it. Attention is focused, with varying degrees of sympathy, on the feelings and personalities of the subjects (especially Sarah).[127] Although the political consequences of Sarah's falling out with Anne are widely discussed (Sarah is given much of the blame for her husband's fall),[128] the structural political conditions that caused the quarrel to take the form it did are not discussed. This is all, alas, precisely the opposite of how Sarah Churchill herself wanted her story told.

It is worth asking why this is the case. The easy answer may be that historians are sexist, or that they assume that what happens between a female monarch and a woman of her bedchamber belongs in the category of emotional rather than political experience. A more interesting answer is that the coding of Sarah's story in this way was the result of the processes and struggles occurring around 1710–12, which are described in the next section.

A TALE OF JOHN AND SARAH; OR, BOTH TURNED OUT OF COURT AT LAST

The political fates of the Duke and Duchess of Marlborough were closely intertwined, but not identical. Exactly how they were related, and how they were thought to be related at the time, is the question that drives this next section, which looks at how the drama of Sarah's fall from Anne's affections came to be understood by other people after 1710. As things turned out, tories and whigs came to tell the story in precisely the way that Sarah herself did *not* want it to be understood, as a personal, emotional event. Anne's rejection of Sarah was seen (depending on the needs of the teller) either as irrelevant to the political story of the fall of the Marlborough–Godolphin ministry, or as an event that had political consequences but only personal causes (that is, it was all Sarah's fault). Ironically, there were political reasons for constructing Sarah's story as a purely personal one.

The process whereby the 'battle of Abigail' came to be defined as a personal and emotional drama involving Sarah alone, rather than a political struggle involving Sarah, the duumvirs and the whigs, begins with the failure of the Duke of Marlborough's attempt to eliminate Masham in 1710. This was precipitated by the death of the Earl of Essex in January 1710. The queen bestowed Essex's now-vacant post as commander of a regiment of dragoons upon Colonel Jack Hill, the brother of Abigail Masham. Marlborough, who had already (in a private letter to Anne) declared himself 'mortified' by 'your Majesty's change from Lady Marlborough to Mrs. Masham, and the several indignities Mrs. Masham has made her suffer'[129] took Jack Hill's appointment as a further mortification.

Marlborough retired angrily from the court to Windsor, and from there drafted (though he did not yet send) a letter to the queen. Hill's appointment was the result of

> Mrs. Masham's having assured Mr. Harley that I should receive such mortifications as should make it impossible to continue in your services ... the extraordinary methods she takes of making her husband and brother talk very impertinently and her pretensions to prefer officers in the army has already caused great disorder, and if not checked may unavoidably increase to such a degree as will make it impossible to have success in the next campaign. Her behaviour to me and mine has been such that it has brought that extremity upon me that I hope your Majesty will be pleased to dismiss her or myself, for I think I can neither with honour nor safety head the army without this mark of your protection to me.[130]

There followed a flurry of meetings between the queen and various whig ministers trying to avert the crisis. The case that was made to Anne centred not so much on the duke's hurt feelings as on the need for discipline within the army: the duke's authority would be undermined if everyone knew it was possible to get an appointment by going around him and straight to the Queen.[131]

Anne was finally pressured to rescind Jack Hill's appointment, and John Churchill for his part was persuaded to modify his letter to the queen so that it no longer contained a threat to resign unless Abigail Masham was dismissed. But apparently he had changed his methods rather than his goals. The next week, rumours were flying that the duke and his allies were lobbying to have Parliament demand Masham's removal and, as a bonus, to have the duke given the title 'Captain-General for life'. Support for this motion, however, did not materialize, especially once the queen lobbied vigorously against it. Neither the motion to impeach Abigail nor the one to give the duke a life appointment was ever introduced. Shortly thereafter, the duke was denying that either goal was ever intended.

From the Duke of Marlborough's perspective, the entire incident both crystallized and demonstrated the limits of the rhetoric of virtue. Marlborough had repeatedly contrasted himself with Masham in language that pitted service to the nation against 'lowly' service to the queen's private body, and left the judgement in the nation's hands. 'I must humbly submit to your Majesty's consideration what judgment the nation and the whole world will make of my services and Mrs. Masham's', he wrote to Anne.[132] The same contrast was articulated in his remark to Lord Cowper, 'I can't but think that the nation would be of opinion that I have deserved better than to be made a sacrifice to the unreasonable passion of a bedchamber woman'.[133] Mainwaring, similarly, invoked the nation's judgement in a letter to Sarah. If Anne remained stubborn, he wrote, it would be left to 'the nation and the Parliament' to 'enquire into the reasons for his absence and call him back by removing all those that obstruct and prevent his services'.[134] However, Marlborough's strategy of threatening to resign unless Masham were removed had a by now familiar fatal flaw: his only bargaining chip was the threat of going, yet by going he would seriously damage his claim to be the selfless servant of the public good. This explains why he backed down.

The important consequence of the episode was that Anne won the rhetorical battle over her right to privacy. Ironically, the distinction between servants of the queen's public body and servants of the queen's private body, which Marlborough and his allies had used to glorify the duke and denigrate Masham, was turned against them. Anne assured the whig notables who came to her on the duke's behalf that Masham was indeed only a dresser, who 'never meddled in business'.[135] Once Anne had repaired the only concrete injury she had done to Marlborough by rescinding Jack Hill's appointment, her position was hard to refute.[136] From that perspective, the demand that Abigail be removed looked like an intolerable intrusion on the queen's private life. As the tory *Letter to The Examiner* described it, the whigs and duumvirs had attempted to 'take that privilege from her [Anne], which the meanest of her subjects enjoy, and slavery was to pursue her even to her bedchamber'.[137]

The episode had devastating consequences for Sarah, Duchess of Marlborough. Although she did not instigate or even approve of the duke's actions,[138] she was blamed for the affair by both whigs and tories, whose narratives about the competition between Sarah and Abigail began to converge. Both groups, for different reasons, treated the abortive parliamentary address against Masham as the result of Sarah's insane jealousy of her successful rival. Simon Clement's tory pamphlet, *Faults on both sides*, attributed the address against Masham to the 'private animosity of a ministerial lady', for whom 'the thoughts of any competition in the Queen's favour, though in a degree much inferior to what she herself continued to enjoy, could not be borne'.[139] Sarah's jealousy was treated in this pamphlet as a particularly absurd symptom of a larger disease. The author described the address against Masham as an assault on the queen herself, who was 'disrespectfully treated through her sides'. This enabled him to link it to other attacks on legitimate royal authority by the whigs, and especially by the Duke of Marlborough; these included the persecution of Sacheverell, Marlborough's request of the title 'Captain-General for life', and the attempts of the duke to get the Dutch to interfere in English politics. For the tories, then, Sarah could function as an easily attacked symbol for the duke's 'private body': she represented his greed, ambition, and private interest, as distinct from his unquestionable military accomplishments.

Whigs, too, had reason to emphasize Sarah's role in the affair. Once the Duke of Marlborough decided not to resign, it was to his advantage to downplay the precariousness of his own standing with the queen. It became convenient to treat the continuing coldness of the queen to Sarah *not* as a sign that the queen was out to humiliate the duke in order to force his resignation, but as an isolated, personal issue between Anne and Sarah. The fact that Anne had won the battle to define her private life as private forced the whigs and duumvirs to change their strategy. There were to be no more attempts to get rid of Masham. The goal became, instead, the protection of their political interests in spite of Masham's presence in the bedchamber, and in spite of the now public falling-out between the queen and Sarah. Abandoning their earlier understanding that Anne's affection for Abigail and her bad political behaviour were somehow connected, they now constructed narratives that cordoned off the personal drama of Anne, Abigail and Sarah from the political one.

Thus whigs as well as tories blamed Sarah for the failed attempt to impeach Masham. As one whig observer put it, 'It was impossible for any man of sense, honour or honesty to come into an address to remove a dresser from the Queen ... only to gratify my lady Marlborough's passions'.[140] We cannot, unfortunately, know how many whigs shared this view of the source of the attack on Masham. It is telling, however, that several months later, Sarah was put under pressure by her political allies to offer Anne an assurance that such an attempt would never occur again. The logic behind this request was explained to Sarah by Mainwaring, who also thought she should comply. Anne would embrace any group that offered to protect Masham; she had already gathered around herself a 'third party for Masham', to 'oppose any other attempt of the like nature [that is, attacking Masham]'. The only thing the whigs could do was to eliminate the necessity for such a party by having Sarah assure Anne that Masham would be safe. Such an assurance would help persuade Anne to delay the dismissal of the Earl of Sunderland.[141]

The whigs' embrace of this logic left the Duchess of Marlborough isolated. For her to adopt it would require the rewriting of history. During the January 1710 crisis she, as well as Mainwaring and the duke, had invoked the judgement of the nation as a whole about the relative value of Marlborough's services and Masham's, and had implicitly assumed that it was the *nation*, in the form of Parliament, that would correct the wrong. To now give the queen assurances that Masham would be safe would be tantamount to admitting that the duchess alone, and not the nation, had been responsible for the attack on Masham in the first place. Moreover, as was seen earlier, Sarah had insisted that Anne would have to change her political behaviour in order for Abigail to be safe, since it was Abigail who had somehow caused and was somehow exposed by that behaviour. To believe, as the whigs now did, that that the protection of Abigail could come first, that the queen's bad political behaviour came not from Abigail's influence but from Anne's fear of losing her, was to repudiate Sarah's construction of the story.

Sarah reiterated her own version in her reply to Mainwaring: the queen could be safe only by listening to her ministers, that if the queen did so then she and Abigail could be 'happy forever in one another', that those who offered to protect Abigail were Jacobites and enemies to the government, and that if the queen continued to make the patriots who had her true interest at heart 'uneasy and unsafe, they will not bear it long but will talk upon what will give her the most trouble, which it seems is the person who puts on her clothes'. Sarah denied that she had instigated the attack. Assurances to the Queen would have to come from the whigs themselves, as 'I suppose she will not imagine that like Duke Trinkelow I can make a rebellion by myself'.[142]

Thus, while Sarah continued to insist that the question of Masham concerned the entire whig party (or all right-thinking individuals who wished well to the government), the whigs preferred to treat it as an issue that primarily involved Sarah alone. Sarah eventually did buckle under and sent a letter to Anne promising never to meddle with Masham. But although she denied that she ever had taken, or would take, action against Masham, she threatened that the whigs might.[143] It was not exactly the palliative the whigs had in mind.

The next few months put Sarah and the whigs even more at cross-purposes. By this time Sarah's hold on her bedchamber office was in jeopardy. The fact that she had not yet been dismissed, in spite of Anne's well-publicized alien-ation, was due to her status as the Duke of Marlborough's wife. On his last departure from England, the duke had begged Anne to let Sarah keep her office.[144] The duchess's dismissal was still a 'mortification' that he might not be able to bear. But Sarah's voluntary resignation was becoming a bargaining chip that the whigs might be able to offer to the queen. In a letter of 20 April 1710, for example, Godolphin reported that Shrewsbury had tried to convince him that 'the only sore place was the difference betwixt [Sarah and the queen], and that all the rest might presently be set right'.[145] Although Marlborough and Godolphin rejected this advice at the time, the situation had changed by January 1711. In an effort to save his own political career, the Duke of Marlborough, upon his return to London, made a show of surprise and anger at his wife's behaviour.[146] On 18 January 1711, Marlborough secured his wife's resignation and delivered her key of office to the queen.

As already indicated, Sarah Churchill viewed her position in the queen's bedchamber as a guarantee and sign of the Duke of Marlborough's standing with the queen. It is not surprising, then, that she viewed her dismissal as the first step in a deliberate plan to remove all whigs from office. This was the meaning of her complaint to David Hamilton, on the eve of her dismissal: 'Give me a reason or a precedent where a man's service has been regarded as useful to the queen and nation, and his wife put out of service ... There's nothing like this in Turkey, in Nero's time, or in any history'.[147] But once the duchess had been dismissed, it was clearly in the whigs' interest to have the duke stay in his command. Accordingly, they downplayed the magnitude of the insult to the general. Immediately after Sarah's removal, for example, Hamilton can be found telling the queen that 'it was expected some after

favour, should be shown to my Lord Marlborough (1st) to prevent the sur-
mises that the [Harley] ministry will not suffer him to continue, (2ndly) that
he may have the more honour and credit abroad; and so be capable to do the
more service for your Majesty'.[48] The queen's willingness to keep Sarah in
office had previously been regarded as the litmus test of her respect for the duke.
But the whigs now denied that Sarah's dismissal had any political implications.

The cruellest irony for Sarah was that her rhetoric gave her few resources
with which to combat the whigs' logic. Having maintained that her position in
the bedchamber was a guarantee and sign of the duke's prestige with the
queen, the fact that the duke could retain his position after her dismissal left
her high and dry. Moreover, the duke's decision to stay in his command was
necessitated and legitimated by ideals of self-sacrificing public service with
which Sarah herself had identified: she could not justify asking John Churchill
to resign just because of an affront to his wife.

Whig propagandists did little to support Sarah's contention that her
dismissal was intended to pave the way for other changes. This marked a
change from past thinking. Prior to Sarah's dismissal, whig pamphleteers had
occasionally suggested that attacks on Sarah were really directed at her
husband:

> So subtle canting knaves who would defame
> A powerful foe they know not how to blame
> They blacken those in whom he most confides
> And wound the man they fear through his companions' sides.[49]

But after Sarah's dismissal, whig writers seemed to blame her for her troubles
with the queen. In *He's welcome home* (1711), Sarah is shown chiding her
husband for his willingness to tolerate the queen's ingratitude, while humbly
acknowledging that she herself deserved the treatment she got:

> Go then, and make a fair retreat
> Be thanked as if you had been beat
> For me, I plead none of these ties
> I was perhaps more rash than wise
> And I can with patience bear my shame
> But 'twill not well become your name.[50]

The history of Prince Mirabel's infancy, rise and disgrace, a whig defence of the
duke, is notably non-committal in its account of Sarah's loss of office. The fact
that Sarah became 'not so pleasing to the Empress, as he [Marlborough] could
have wished' is chalked up to 'some indiscretion in [Sarah's] conduct or
proceedings, that were reputed as such by his and her enemies at court'. Upon
Sarah's resignation, the duke is shown writing to Anne that 'he will always
make it his business to atone for anything that may have been done [by Sarah]
or taken amiss on her part by constant obedience'. Marlborough's 'voluntary

sacrifice of a person so dear to him, but who had the misfortune to incur the Empress' displeasure' is presumably meant by the author to show his loyalty to the queen.[151]

Whigs were inclined, then, to separate the fate of Sarah from that of her husband. What happened to her was acceptable, what happened to him was outrageous. After the Duke himself was dismissed, some people went even farther, attributing his political problems to his wife. As the tory Peter Wentworth put it when commenting on the probability that the Duchess of Somerset would lose her position because of the queen's hostility towards her husband, 'Their [the Somersets'] case is the reverse of the Duke and Duchess of M[arlborough], in the eye of the world 'tis she [Sarah Marlborough] has been the ruin of him [John]'.[152] Similarly, *Memoirs of the conduct of her late Majesty* attributed the fall of the Marlborough–Godolphin ministry to Sarah's 'imprudent conduct' and 'excess of rudeness', which 'begot by degrees a confirmed aversion ... and made the men, as well as the women, become intolerable to the Queen'. 'Had [Sarah] thought proper to have preserved her interest in the Queen's affection', the author concluded, 'that ministry could never have fallen'.[153]

Neither whig nor tory accounts – of the relationship between Sarah's falling-out with the queen and the fall of Marlborough and Godolphin – adopted Sarah's version of the story. They either reversed the causal relationships that Sarah wanted to establish, or they treated the dismissals of the Duchess and Duke of Marlborough as two separate phenomena. Despite Sarah's best efforts to describe her dismissal in political terms, it was treated by others as a purely personal and emotional event.

It is telling in this respect that representations of Sarah after her dismissal, both positive and negative, tended to stress her private and domestic roles. The pro-Marlborough broadside entitled *He's welcome home* (1711) presents Sarah only as a wife. It opens with Sarah welcoming John home to her 'longing Arms'; the chance to 'love at home' is his compensation should the queen decide to fire him. Attacks on Sarah also emphasized the domestic, focusing on her lust for wealth rather than her lust for power. The process whereby the story of the Duchess of Marlborough's relationship with the queen became defined as *non*-political also made her particularly open to charges of greed and theft. Just as her amassment of office, reward and patronage had once been a sign of the Duke of Marborough's standing with the queen, now that it was divorced from the question of the duke's standing with the queen, it was simply a sign of the lack of the Marlboroughs' public-spiritedness, their use of office for personal aggrandizement.

Whereas earlier attacks had assimilated Sarah to other royal favourites (such as Alice Piers or the mistresses of Charles II) who in some way dominated monarchs, she was now presented as the archetypal political spouse who wants her husband in office so that the family can get the financial and social benefits of it. In a satire entitled *The petticoat plotters, or the D——ss of M——h's club* (1712), the wives of displaced whig politicians gather to mourn their loss of status. They complain that they are forced to cut back on footmen, coaches and jewels, that no one courts their daughters, and so on. They rail at the upstart wives of the new officeholders, resolving that 'their discourse [will be] to scandalize and rail at all in places'. They make their patron saint the Duchess of Marlborough.[154] Similarly, a ballad on the fall of the Junto painted Sarah as interested in clothes:

> Dame Za—h's fine clothes I will sell ye
> Ye shall have them both great and small
> And very cheap too I must tell ye
> For the queen has paid for 'em all.[155]

Public perceptions of Sarah Churchill were sadly at odds with her self-image. She would have been horrified to think of herself merely as a jealous ex-favourite or a politician's wife. In that sense, Sarah Churchill did find herself relegated to the 'private sphere' in ways that undermined her claims to virtue.

Sarah Churchill lends herself to somewhat contradictory narratives about the relationship of women, 'virtue' and political life over the long eighteenth century. From the perspective of a later era, the fact that she was so comfortably involved in political affairs is startling. If we think of the Revolution of 1688 as a stage in a modernizing process whereby the public was cordoned off from the private, and women consequently excluded from political life, her case shows that this did not happen immediately or even inevitably. While it is true that ultimately not even her own party took seriously her claim to be a virtuous political actor, this was surely not because they assumed women should be relegated to a private sphere. Although the public–private dichotomy was a feature of political discourse, it was there to be muddied and manipulated; in Sarah Churchill's case, it licensed rather than prohibited certain kinds of political interventions. Moreover, it is significant that Sarah's claims to political virtue and political relevance never involved an identification of herself as metaphorically masculine; they were often tied, rather, to her standing as the Duke of Marlborough's wife. We seem to have recovered a moment in history when what 'political modernity' would mean to or for women was an open question.

It is necessary, however, to analyse the terms on which women constructed a political voice, and not just rest content with the fact that they did it. What definition of femininity did they rely on? What were the gender politics of their efforts? Once those questions are asked, we have to acknowledge that there is a dark side to Sarah Churchill's story. After all, she reconciled the contradiction between being virtuous and being a royal favourite by distinguishing herself sharply from Abigail Masham, whom she cast as a slut; to pressure Anne, she exploited the double standard which made women's reputations their greatest point of vulnerability. There are equally dark sides to the discussion in the two previous chapters of Delarivière Manley (who did, after all, attack her enemies' sexual reputations, even if she framed that attack by a critique of the concept of reputation) and Mary Astell (who could only cast women as politically virtuous because she believed they were divinely commanded to obey their husbands). However adept women were at the rhetorical games that licensed their political voices and actions, they did not make the rules.

NOTES

These abbreviations are used for correspondence:
SM Sarah Churchill, Duchess of Marlborough
JM John Churchill, Duke of Marlborough
QA Queen Anne
SG Sidney Godolphin
DH David Hamilton
AM Arthur Mainwaring

1 SM to DH, 6 December 1710, BL Add. MS 61423, fols 35–7.

2 SM to Mary Cowper, 18 July 1708, HRO Panshanger MS D/EP F228, fol. 27; SM to Mary Cowper, 31 August 1710, HRO Panshanger D/EP F228, fol. 35.

3 For a sympathetic but balanced account, see Frances Harris, *A passion for government: the life of Sarah, Duchess of Marlborough* (Oxford, Oxford University Press, 1991).

4 The related (albeit not identical) themes of the expulsion of women from the 'public' sphere, the gendering of virtue and the definition of political (as opposed to sexual) virtue as an exclusively male quality has been a prominent theme in the feminist historiography of the French Revolution. See, for example, Joan Landes, *Women in the public sphere in the age of the French Revolution* (Ithaca, Cornell University Press, 1988); Dorinda Outram, '*Le langage male de la vertu*: women and the discourse of the French Revolution' in Peter Burke and Roy Porter (eds), *The social history of language* (Cambridge, Cambridge University Press, 1987). Compare, for the American Revolution, Ruth Bloch, 'The gendered meanings of virtue in revolutionary America', *Signs* 13 (1987). On the antithesis of women and virtue in a 'classical republican' tradition, see Hannah Pitkin, *Fortune is a woman: gender and politics in the thought of Niccolo Machiavelli* (Berkeley, University of California Press, 1984); J. G. A. Pocock has interesting suggestions on the 'masculine' nature of virtue in Pocock, *Virtue, commerce and history* (Cambridge, Cambridge University Press, 1985), ch. 6. For a nuanced discussion which proposes, importantly, that 'virtue' in eighteenth-century England was not always conceived in terms of a fierce antithesis of 'public' and 'private', see Shelley Burtt, *Virtue transformed* (Cambridge, Cambridge University Press, 1992).

5 This point – about inconsistent use of the public–private distinction – is best articulated by John Brewer, 'This, that and the other: public, social and private in the seventeenth and eighteenth centuries', in Dario Castiglione and Lesley Sharpe (eds), *Shifting the*

boundaries: transformation of the languages of public and private in the eighteenth century (Exeter, University of Exeter Press, 1995).

6 Charles Davenant, *Political and commercial works* (1771), quoted in Burtt, *Virtue transformed*, p. 18.

7 David Hayton, 'The country interest and the party system, 1689–c.1720', in Clyve Jones (ed.), *Party management in parliament, 1660–1784* (Leicester, Leicester University Press, 1984); Burtt, *Virtue transformed*; Mark Goldie, 'The roots of true whiggism, 1688–94', *History of Political Thought* 1 (1980).

8 JM to SM, 8 March 1710, *MGC* 1467. The Marlboroughs and their close associates used a numerical cipher system so their letters, if intercepted, could not be interpreted.

9 SG to JM, 15 June 1710, *MGC* 1567.

10 SM to Mary Cowper, February 1712, HRO Panshanger MS D/EP F228, fol. 78. See also Frances Harris, 'Accounts of the conduct of Sarah, Duchess of Marlborough, 1704–1742', *British Library Journal* 8 (1982).

11 Sarah, Duchess of Marlborough, *An account of the conduct of the Dowager Duchess of Marlborough, from her first coming to the court, to the year 1710* (George Hawkins, 1742), pp. 21, 12.

12 AM to SM, 6 April 1708, BL Add. MS 61459, fol. 16.

13 Draft of letter or pamphlet meant to be shown to Queen Anne (dated 13 March 1708), existing in hands of both SM and AM, BL Add. MS 61417, fols 123–9.

14 Frances Hare to SM, 1 December 1711, Sarah, Duchess of Marlborough, *Private correspondence of Sarah, Duchess of Marlborough*, 2 vols (Henry Colburn, 1838), 2:25, 27. See also 2:24 (on Sarah's 'just sense of the public good'), 2:27 (on her 'exalted pitch of disinterested virtue').

15 Duchess of Marlborough, *Account of the conduct*, pp. 11–12. For other references to flattery and the court, see AM to SM, 26 September 1709, BL Add. MS 61460, fol. 43.

16 Harris, *Passion for Government*. What follows here is deeply indebted to this work.

17 J. R. Jones, *Marlborough* (Cambridge, Cambridge University Press, 1993), pp. 202–6.

18 SG to JM, 27 August 1708, *MGC* 1086.

19 The paradigmatic case study is Henry L. Snyder, 'Queen Anne versus the Junto: The effort to place Orford at the head of the Admiralty in 1709', *Huntington Library Quarterly* 35 (1972).

20 AM to SM, 15 June 1708, BL Add. MS 61459, fol. 54.

21 JM to SM, 22 July 1708, *MGC* 1052; similarly, see *MGC* 1042, *MGC* 1067. Examples of Marlborough using Sarah to communicate with the whigs are in JM to SM, 24 May 1708, *MGC* 996 (regarding whig objections to seating Queensberry in the House of Lords), JM to SM, 25 July 1709, *MGC* 1358. Henry Snyder, 'Godolphin and Harley: a study of their partnership in politics', *Huntington Library Quarterly* 30 (1966–67), p. 261, n. 62 cites Godolphin complaining to Sarah in November 1706 about Junto intransigence over Sunderland's appointment.

22 Harris, *Passion for government*, pp. 142, 150–1, 158–78. Snyder, 'Queen Anne vs. the Junto', pp. 227–8 shows the whigs soliciting Sarah's aid and opinions by way of Mainwaring.

23 JM to SM, 25 April 1708, *MGC* 965.

24 JM to SM, 11 April 1708, *MGC* 952.

25 SG to JM, 30 July 1708, *MGC* 1059.

26 JM to SM, 25 July 1909, *MGC* 1358.

27 Horatio Walpole to James Stanhope, 20 April 1708, quoted in Gregg, *Queen Anne*, pp. 273–4.

28 Ann Clavering to John Clavering, 2 June 1709, quoted in Harris, *Passion for government*, p. 156.

29 Peter Wentworth to Thomas Wentworth, 30 January 1710, *The Wentworth papers, 1705–39*, ed. J. J. Cartwright (Wyman & Sons, 1883), pp. 105–6. see also p. 108.

30 AM to SM, August 1709, BL Add. MS 61460, fol. 3. For whig fears about Sarah's quarrels with Anne, see AM to SM, 8 August 1709, BL Add. MS 61459, fol. 183, reporting Halifax's remark that 'if [Sarah] and [Queen Anne] were not soon upon better terms, [Marlborough and Godolphin] would be ruined'.

31 AM to SM, 11 September 1708, BL Add. MS 61459, fol. 101.

32 AM to SM, 7 October 1709, BL Add. MS 61460, fol. 77.

33 Sunderland to SM [April 1710], BL Add. MS 61443, fol. 48.

34 Sunderland to SM, 29 April 1710, BL Add. MS 61443, fol. 50.

35 Gregg, *Queen Anne*, p. 291. Robert O. Bucholz, *The Augustan court: Queen Anne and the decline of court culture* (Stanford, Stanford University Press, 1993), pp. 76–8.

36 Elizabeth Cotterell to William Trumbull, 9 December 1709, BL Add. MS 72517, fol. 106. For a full account, see Frances Harris, '"The honourable sisterhood": Queen Anne's maids of honour', *British Library Journal* 19 (Autumn, 1993).

37 Jane Cotterell to William Trumbull [1710?], BL Add. MS 72518, fol. 100.

38 Jane Cotterell to William Trumbull [1710?], BL Add. MS 72518, fol. 101.

39 AM to SM, 15 June 1708, BL Add. MS 61459, fol. 54.

40 AM to SM, 11 September 1708, BL Add. MS 61459, fol. 101.

41 SG to JM, 29 May 1710, *MGC* 1545.

42 Harris, *Passion for Government*, p. 166.

43 QA to SG, 13 June 1710, in Anne, *The letters and diplomatic instructions of Queen Anne*, ed. Beatrice Curtis Brown, (Cassell, 1935), p. 303.

44 Account dated 1710/11, BL Add. MS 61422, fols 115–23.

45 Poem beginning 'When first royal Nancy was mounted the throne', Bodl. Rawlinson poetry MS 169, fol. 31. See also poem beginning 'No wonder winds more dreadful are by far', BL Harley MS 6914, fol. 106v (1703?).

46 *Commons Journals* 15, pp. 37–9 (24 November 1705). The incident is discussed in Harris, *Passion for government*, p. 117, and W. A. Speck, *Tory and whig: the struggle in the constituencies* (Macmillan, 1970), p. 58. For Bromley, see Burnet, *HOT*, 5:230.

47 Poem beginning 'When Sarah led by fancy, fate or scorn', BL Lansdowne MS 852, fols 22v–23.

48 Poem beginning 'The glory of the English arms retrieved', BL Harley MS 6914, fol. 107 (1704?); see also 'Epigram on the duke of Marlborough', beginning 'When whores ruled Charles those whores my beauty ruled' [1715], Bodl. Firth MS b. 4, fol. 51. For the Jacobite view, see 'The false favourite's downfall', beginning 'Deserted and scorned the proud Marlborough sat', *POAS*, 5:328–33. Jacobitism is hinted at (from an anti-Jacobite perspective) in *The beasts in power* (1709), pp. 6–7.

49 Manley, *The secret history of Queen Zarah and the Zarazians* (1705), in Manley, *Novels*, 1:103.

50 *Plain English* quoted in J. A. Downie, *Robert Harley and the press: propaganda and public opinion in the age of Swift and Defoe* (Cambridge, Cambridge University Press, 1979), p. 105.

51 See especially Swift's contribution in *The Examiner* 28 (8 February 1711).

52 On Swift in relation to Harley and St John, see Downie, *Robert Harley and the press*, pp. 130–8.

53 Swift (now in tune with Harley) published *The conduct of the Allies* (John Morphew, 1712), the keystone of the attack, on 27 November 1711. Other titles include *Oliver's pocket looking-glass* (1711); [William King], *Rufinus* (1711); *The land-leviathan; or, modern hydra* (John Morphew, 1712); *The perquisite-monger; or, the rise and fall of ingratitude* (1712); [William Wagstaffe], *The story of the St. Alban's ghost* (1712). For a full bibliography, see Robert D. Horn, *Marlborough, a survey: panegyrics, satires and biographical writings, 1688–1788* (New York, Garland, 1975).

54 Poem beginning 'No wonder winds more dreadful are by far' [1703?], BL Harley MS 6914, fol. 106v. See also [Wagstaffe], *Story of the St. Alban's Ghost*.

55 'The false favourite's downfall'. This poem can also be taken as a dig at William's alleged homosexuality.

56 'Duke Humphrey's answer', printed in *POAS*, 7:330–7, ends with a fantasy that Sarah will be murdered like Rosamond.

57 Manley, *Zarah* II (1705) in Manley, *Novels*, 1:135; *The Beasts in Power* (1709).

58 Manley, *Novels*, 1:142–6.

59 *An account of a dream at Harwich* (B. Bragg, 1708), p. 12. For the attribution to Harley, and a discussion of contemporary interpretations of the allegory, see Downie, *Robert Harley and the press*, pp. 106–11. Delarivière Manley's article in *The Examiner* 51 (19 July 1711) has a strikingly similar description.

60 'Duke Humphrey's answer', in *POAS*, 7:330.

61 [George Sewell], *An epistle from Sempronia to Cethegus* (John Holmes, 1713).

62 Geoffrey Holmes, *British politics in the age of Anne*, revd edn (Hambledon Press, 1987), pp. 189–92; G. Holmes and W. Speck, 'The fall of Harley in 1708 reconsidered', *English Historical Review* 80 (1965). But cf. Henry Snyder, 'Godolphin and Harley'.

63 Mary Cowper to SM, 25 October 1710 (passing on William Cowper's assurance that there is no need for Sarah to fear her husband would yield 'to the temptations before him'), BL Add. MS 61463, fol. 77.

64 Poem beginning 'All things went well in church and state', BL Add. MS 40060, fol. 71 (1708). See also poem beginning 'The glory of the English arms retrieved' for Sarah sleeping with Sidney Godolphin.

65 David Starkey, 'Representation through intimacy: a study in the symbolism of monarchy and court office in early-modern England', in Ioan Lewis, *Symbols and sentiments* (Academic Press, 1977).

66 Robert O. Bucholz, *The Augustan court: Queen Anne and the decline of court culture* (Stanford, Stanford University Press, 1993), esp. pp. 77–82.

67 See William Oldisworth, *The loyal mourner* (John Morphew, 1716), pp. 13–14; see also below on David Hamilton.

68 On Hamilton's role, see Philip Robert's introduction to *Hamilton diary*.

69 See *Hamilton diary*, pp. 37–40, 45–50, and *passim* on the Duchess of Somerset.

70 *Ibid.*, pp. 16–17 (21 Sept. 1710).

71 *Ibid.*, pp. 3–4; see also p. 67.

72 *Ibid.*, p. 7 (31 March 1710).

73 SM to SG, 27 October 1709, quoted in Harris, *Passion for government*, pp. 160–1.

74 SM to QA, 29 July 1709, quoted in Bucholz, *The Augustan court*, p. 77.

75 Bucholz, *The Augustan court*, p. 77.

76 *Ibid.*, pp. 77–8; Gregg, *Queen Anne*, p. 294. See also narrative beginning 'When Mrs. Morley first came to the Crown', 29 October 1709, BL Add. MS 61418, fols 36–43.

77 JM to SM, 26 July 1708, *MGC* 1056.

78 AM to SM, November 1709, BL Add. MS 61460, fol. 109.

79 AM to SM, 4 November 1708, BL Add. MS 61459, fol. 142.

80 AM to SM, August 1709, BL Add. MS 61460, fol. 3.

81 SM to QA, 26 July 1708, printed in David Green, *Sarah, Duchess of Marlborough* (New York, Scribner's, 1967), pp. 318–21.

82 SM to QA, *circa* 16 August 1708, *MGC* 1072A.

83 SM to DH [January 1711?], BL Add. MS 61423, fols 87–8. This was meant to be shown to the queen.

84 SM to QA, 1709, in Duchess of Marlborough, *Private correspondence*, 1:244.

85 SM to DH, 6 December 1710, BL Add. MS 61423, fols 35–37.

86 SM to QA, [7 November?] 1709, in Duchess of Marlborough, *Private correspondence*, 1:240–6; see *MGC*, p. 1403, note 6, for date.

87 *Ibid.*

88 Printed in David Green, *Sarah*, pp. 318–21.

89 SM to AM, 28 April 1710, BL Add. MS 61461, fol. 22. See also fol. 18 for the letter to which this responds.

90 AM to SM, [June 1710], BL Add. MS 61461, fol. 60.

91 SM [to SG?], 27 October 1709, BL Add. MS 61434, fol. 93.

92 AM to SM, 26 July [or 9 August] 1709, BL Add. MS 61459, fol. 185.

93 *A new ballad. To the tune of Fair Rosamond* [1707], also printed in *POAS*, 7:706–11. Sarah offered to sing this ballad for her friend, Lady Mary Cowper; see SM to Mary Cowper, 18

July 1708, HRO Panshanger MS D/EP F228, fol. 27.

94 *The rival dutchess; or, the court incendiary* (1708), pp. 8–9.

95 See Emma Donoghue, *Passions between women: British lesbian culture 1668–1801* (Scarlet Press, 1993), for an argument that late Stuart people were aware of such things. See also Lillian Faderman, *Surpassing the love of men* (New York, Morrow, 1981).

96 SM to QA, 26 July 1708, printed in Green, *Sarah*, pp. 318–21.

97 SM to QA, 29 October 1709, BL Add. MS 61418, fols 36–43.

98 *Ibid.*

99 'Account of what passed between the Queen and Lord Marlborough concerning Mr. Hill', dated 14 February 1710, BL Add. MS 61422, fols 45–8.

100 AM to SM, April 1708, in Duchess of Marlborough, *Private correspondence*, 1:129.

101 AM to SM, 15 May 1711, BL Add. MS 61461, fol. 131.

102 AM to SM, 30 April 1710, BL Add. MS 61461, fol. 27.

103 Fragment in Mainwaring's hand [1710?], BL Add. MS 61461, fol. 88.

104 SM to QA, 7 July 1708, printed in Green, *Sarah*, pp. 313–14.

105 SM to QA, *circa* 16 August 1708, MGC 1072A.

106 SM to QA, 7 July 1708, in Green, *Sarah*, pp. 313–14.

107 Mainwaring's hand (undated), BL Add. MS 61461, fol. 66.

108 AM to SM, 19 January 1710, BL Add. MS 61460, fol. 165.

109 *A new ballad. To the tune of Fair Rosamond* [1707]. This is the ballad that Sarah offered to help Mary Cowper sing.

110 *The history of Prince Mirabel's infancy, rise and disgrace* (J. Baker, 1712), pp. 22–3.

111 Duchess of Marlborough, *Account of the conduct*, pp. 13–14.

112 Donoghue, *Passions between women*, p. 164.

113 'Some hints towards a character [of Queen Anne]', BL Add. MS 61422, fols 199–201.

114 Duchess of Marlborough, *Account of the conduct*, p. 13.

115 AM to SM, 6 April 1708, BL Add. MS 61459, fol. 16.

116 AM to SM, 22 June 1710, BL Add. MS 61461, fol. 62.

117 *Ibid.*

118 AM to SM [November 1709], BL Add. MS 61460, fol. 110.

119 SM to DH, 1710, BL Add. MS 61423, fols 30–1.

120 SM to AM, 3 November 1709, BL Add. MS 61460, fols 99–100.

121 SM to AM, 29 October 1709, BL Add. MS 61418, fols 36–43.

122 Printed in Duchess of Marlborough, *Account of the conduct*, pp. 75–6. Paraphrased in *Hamilton diary*, p. 26 (10 January 1711).

123 *Hamilton diary*, p. 26 (10 January 1711).

124 *Ibid.*, p. 27 (12 January 1711); see also p. 12 (10 June 1710), where Sarah claimed the letters 'contained what would reflect on her Majesty's piety, such as breaches of

promise and asseverations'.

125 The only mention of Anne's sexual reputation I can find is Sarah's remark that the letters, if printed, will 'bring such reflections upon her Majesty as I wish never to see, besides that it will be a stain upon another person that can never be washed off, and for whom I believe the Queen is enough concerned for, to wish they might be well spoke of'. BL Add. MS 61423, fols 87–8: SM to DH [January 1711]. Note also that there were allusions to lesbianism in Sarah's letter to Hamilton of 6 December 1710.

126 See Alan Bray, *Homosexuality in Renaissance England* (Gay Men's Press, 1988).

127 See, for example, Virginia Cowles, *The great Marlborough and his duchess* (Macmillan, 1983), pp. 295–6; Iris Butler, *The rule of three: Sarah, Duchess of Marlborough and her companions in power* (Hodder & Stoughton, 1967), p. 191; Sir John Fortescue, *Marlborough* (New York, D. Appleton, 1932), p. 162. These portray Sarah as out of control and hysterical.

128 See, for example, J. R. Jones, *Marlborough* (Cambridge, Cambridge University Press, 1993), pp. 208–10; Gregg, *Queen Anne*, p. 181. Harris, *Passion for government*, pp. 164–5, is unusual in suggesting that the duke may on occasion have been more hysterical than his wife on the subject of Masham.

129 JM to QA, 29 September 1709, printed in Henry Snyder, 'The Duke of Marlborough's request of his Captain-Generalcy for life', *Journal of the Society for Army Historical Research* 45 (1967), pp. 73–4, 129. The following owes much to this article.

130 *MGC* 1447A (18 January 1710).

131 See Lord Cowper to JM, 17 Jan. 1710, *MGC* 1446A; Sarah's account is in BL Add. MS 61422, fols 41–4.

132 *MGC* 1447A (18 January 1710).

133 JM to Cowper, 18 January 1710, *MGC* 1447B.

134 AM to SM, 16 January 1710, BL Add MS 61460, fol. 154.

135 See, for example, Cowper to JM, 17 January 1710, *MGC* 1446A.

136 It was indeed accepted by the whigs. See Henry Boyle to JM, 22 January 1710, *MGC* 1451A.

137 [Henry St. John], *Letter to The Examiner* (1710), p. 13.

138 Harris, *Passion for government*, pp. 164–5 argues that Sarah was not behind the attempt. AM to SM, 22 April 1710, also takes this line, BL Add. MS 61461, fol. 18. Sarah thought the duke would have done better to publicize his grievances formally to the council; see SM [to AM?], [19?] January 1710, BL Add. MS 61460, fol. 168.

139 [S. Clements], *Faults on both sides* (1710).

140 Lord Coningsby, quoted in Gregg, *Queen Anne*, p. 303.

141 AM to SM, 22 April 1710, BL Add. MS 61461, fol. 18.

142 SM to AM, 28 April 1710, BL Add. MS 61461, fol. 22.

143 Harris, *Passion for government*, pp. 172–3.

144 *Ibid.*, p. 166.

145 SG to JM, 20 April 1710, *MGC* 1504; see also SG to SM, 29 April 1710, *MGC* 1517.

146 *Hamilton diary*, p. 24 (6 January 1711); see also Gregg, *Queen Anne*, p. 328.

147 *Hamilton diary*, p. 26 (10 January 1711). Her point was that Anne therefore meant to dimiss the duke as well.

148 *Ibid.*, p. 29 (22 January 1711). This is also the gist of Lord Cowper's remark, reported by Hamilton to the queen, that 'the Queen's known favour for the Duke was one great occasion for his success', *ibid.*, p. 29 (20 January 1711).

149 *Belisarius a great commander and Zariana his lady. A dialogue* (J. Morphew, 1710), p. 8. See also *The age of wonders* (n.p., 1711): The Duke of Marlborough to requite/For retrieving English honour/ His D——s shall have all the spite/ That fools can put upon her.

150 *He's welcome home: or, a dialogue between John and Sarah* [1711].

151 *The history of Prince Mirabel's infancy, rise, and disgrace*, 2nd edn (J. Baker, 1712), part III, pp. 58–9.

152 See 1 January 1712, *Wentworth papers*, p. 235.

153 *Memoirs of the conduct of her late Majesty and her last ministry ... by the right Hononrable [sic] the Countess of*—— (S. Keimer, 1715), pp. 15–16.

154 *The petticoat plotters; or, The D——ss of M——h's Club* (T. Wellard, 1712).

155 *An excellent new ballad made at the restauration of K. Charles II, with a second part to the same tune by a modern hand* [1712]. See also *Examiner* 17 for charges of greed.

Conclusion

———◆———

Political arguments in late Stuart England were closely intertwined with claims about gender and the family, but not in a way that neatly fits either Stonian or anti-liberal feminist narratives about the relationship of gender and politics at the dawn of political modernity. Indeed, this study has destabilized the conceptual foundations of both of those narratives. Where previous historians have debated the relative advantages of whig or tory ideologies of gender for women, we have shown that there were multiple ideologies of gender in both whig and tory camps. Where other historians have asked whether women were included in the 'public' sphere, we have emphasized the shifting, manipulable nature of the boundary between public and private, which made exclusion or inclusion a matter of perspective. What can the failure of our material to fit existing paradigms tell us about politics, gender, and the relationship of the two in the late Stuart period?

Somewhat paradoxically, gender was both expelled from and re-included in political argument during this period. As is well known, whig theorists loudly proclaimed that the family and state were distinct. But Lawrence's interest in the family is obvious; Locke and Tyrrell both made the notion that the family exists for the purpose of raising children central to their argument; Sidney's view of the state was built on and energized by an idealized vision of fraternal love and equality. In reality, whigs did not remove the family from political thought but incorporated it in a different way than Filmer had. Similarly, the public–private dichotomy was often invoked in political debate; this invocation did not, however, prevent stories about the private relationships and emotions of political figures from being told in the course of political argument, but it was used to confer political meanings on those stories in particular ways.

Why, then, were notions about gender deployed so frequently in political argument? The presence of gender was less a product of a late Stuart crisis in gender relations than of the divisions and uncertainty of political life.[1] As feminist scholars have pointed out, one reason the sex–gender system is so intractable is that it does important 'work' in justifying other hierarchies and relationships which otherwise have little to do with gender.[2] Susan Amussen has argued, along these lines, that the ubiquitous concern with 'well-ordered families' as the basis of a well-ordered state in early seventeenth-century England had more to do with social and political conflict rather than familial conflict. Defenders of the beleaguered social and political *status quo* likened it to a seemingly natural patriarchal order in order to make it appear inevitable.[3] Appeals to notions about gender and family buttressed arguments that would have been more questionable or controversial if stated plainly.

We have encountered many cases where the apparent obviousness of the familial order was used to resolve a less than obvious political problem. The invocation of Mary II's wifely obedience allowed Parliament to minimize the constitutional ambiguities created by the 1688 settlement. Tyrrell treated the family as a model for the 'moderate' exercise of power that he wanted to endorse but could not clearly define with respect to a state. Queen Anne's womanhood helped writers to make improbable but politically convenient stories about her weakness more convincing. A society that was confused about the precise line between public and private (as it bore on the allocation of money, the openness of political institutions to scrutiny, and access to the monarch) found it easier to attack a woman (like Sarah Churchill) who crossed that line, thereby affirming the line's existence, than explicitly to define it.

Following the trail of 'gender and politics' has led us to the issues which generated discomfort in late Stuart society. And it has revealed that, in spite of the claims of revisionist political historians, there was a lot of discomfort about. That discomfort sprang both from the fact that the Revolution of 1688 occurred at all, and also from the transitional character of the quasi-modern political culture that developed in its wake. There is no doubt that the Glorious Revolution was widely accepted, but such acceptance must have come with great psychic cost to people who had spent the previous quarter-century dwelling on the evils and horror of rebellion. The fact that questions of individual virtue loomed so large in political argument after 1688 suggests that consistency of character had to substitute for consistency of political principle. Yet, as we saw, in so far as claims to virtue rested upon the maintenance of a boundary between public and private, the very instability of the distinction made such claims inherently contestable. Morality in political life was a particularly vexed matter, and political argument was conducted in an atmosphere of moral danger.

The resulting anxiety accounts for the story-telling impulse present in much of late Stuart political discourse. It is not an accident that novels emerged as a form of political writing in this period.[4] Many people responded to morally ambiguous political situations not by applying abstract principles to fixed and known events, but by shaping their stories about what happened in ways that allowed them to feel that their actions suited their principles. As Mark Goldie puts it, 'it was not the events themselves but the interpretations of the participants and onlookers which would determine future generations' understanding of the Revolution'.[5] Tropes and situations drawn from the real or imagined experience of family life, because they invoked strong emotions, became a resource in constructing these stories: political dilemmas could be better dealt with when recast as dramas about daughters torn between wifely and filial duty, heirs cheated of their due, ambitious wives ruining their husbands on purpose or by accident.

That story-telling impulse explains not only why gender was present in political argument, but also why it is so hard to systematize its role. This study has not only emphasized the contingent and varied character of the ways in which ideas about gender and ideas about politics were connected, but also suggested that this variety and contingency were themselves the result of dynamics of political argument specific to the late Stuart period.

In asking the question of how gender became entangled in political debates, the particularities of context and strategy may tell us more than the fundamental principles of the parties. Gender did not enter into whig and tory argument at the level at which ideologies can be distilled to an essence, or of 'pure theory'. Rather, whigs and tories took ideas about gender on board as part of their argument in concrete, specific situations. Thus, the distinctions that did exist between whig and tory discourses on the family, while significant, were muted and muddied by events.

To illustrate the point, we can take the differences outlined in Chapter 1 between Filmerian/tory and whig approaches to the family, and see what those differences can and cannot predict. Tories tended to talk about order and authority, while whigs tended to talk about property and reproduction. We could expect, then, that an heir to the thinking of Robert Filmer would be quick to see the analogy between divorce and revolution (and despise both), to reject the idea that women and children have rights, and to assimilate the Revolution of 1688 to a story about children rebelling against fathers. A whig would be more upset about women foisting bastards or supposititious heirs on their property-owning husbands, thereby compromising the husband's control of his property and defeating the purpose of the family as a child-rearing institution.

These tendencies, however, did not translate into clearly distinct views of family and gender relations. There was no inherent conflict between these two approaches: they did not constitute opposing arguments about the family, but two different registers in which the family could be discussed. Moreover, there was room for play within the basic orientations. A whig might emphasize the right of every man to pass his property on to the children of his own loins (and therefore be upset by the capacity of women to deprive men of that right), or she might point to the fact that sometimes men adopt children but are still obliged to care for them. A whig might also propose that bastards should be able to inherit from their fathers, or she might assume that no society can exist without the 'security of the marriage bed'.

The tory approach to the family also contained internal ambiguities. If someone thought that the family existed to preserve order, then he might stress the authority of fathers, or he might stress the authority of husbands.

He might see the absolute authority of fathers as something that must be preserved in the present, or he might see it as only having been relevant in the early stages of human history. The internal ambiguities within whig and tory ways of talking about the family, and the fact that they did not directly contradict one another, meant that there never existed a monolithic, coherent ideology of gender, either whig or tory.

Moreover, the basic frameworks altered under the pressure of events, and in the context of particular debates. Jacobites, for example, were tories whose habit of thinking of the family as a site for the exercise of *both* husbandly and fatherly authority was put under pressure by events. The familial drama of the Revolution of 1688 made it obvious that obedience to fathers was not the same as obedience to husbands. In condemning Mary of Orange as a bad daughter (albeit a good wife), they chose obedience to fathers as the more important obligation. This is not to say that people became Jacobites *because* they thought obedience to fathers trumped obedience to husbands. Although one can speculate that people with strongly anti-contractarian political views were predisposed to think of politics in terms of father–child rather than husband–wife relationships, because the latter contained an unavoidable element of contract,[6] Jacobite assertions of the priority of filial over conjugal duty were certainly made inevitable by the circumstances of the Revolution. The Jacobites became thereafter the political group least committed to the praise of husbandly authority, at a moment when – and because – the new regime was being justified in terms of husbandly authority.

In the hands of the Jacobites, the Filmerian concern with order acted as an antidote, and counter to, the whig concern with property. The warming-pan affair and the Norfolk divorce case put them in the position of having to deny that men's concern to pass on property to their biological offspring was of paramount concern. Jacobites and non-jurors were less disturbed than either whigs or tories by the uncertainties surrounding biological paternity, and therefore least obsessed with the need to control women and punish adulteresses. It would be a mistake, however, to cast them as anti-capitalists unconcerned with property rights. The particular property rights of the Duke of Norfolk's collateral heirs loomed large in their defense of the duchess. They did not, then, develop a critique of how the family produced children and organized property at the expense of the rights of women! It would also be wrong to imagine that Jacobites were tolerant of female adultery. It was, after all, a form of disobedience. However, the fact that Jacobites were driven under particular circumstances to the positions they took on Mary's wifely obedience, on the warming pan affair, and on the Norfolk divorce, made Jacobitism a site where some people, if so inclined, could criticize the sexual double standard, the ideal of wifely obedience, or the male usurpation of authority over childbirth in ways that might today be considered 'feminist'.[7]

Tories were less consistent than Jacobites in maintaining a 'Filmerian' approach to the family. Mary Astell (if she can be considered a non-Jacobite) stands as an important exception to this rule: she was oblivious to the fact that people have children, and talked about the family in a rigorously authority-centred manner. How typical Astell is of tories remains, however, an open question. Even before 1688, tories had shown concern with property rights; this was even more the case after 1688, when for political reasons the tories adopted the warming pan story and its attendant 'whig' concerns about the inheritance of property and women's capacity to interfere with it.

Whigs after 1688 also altered their earlier stance. In the exclusion crisis, some (though not all) whigs challenged what they took to be a tory belief in the absolute authority of fathers and husbands directly, by talking about the right of wives and children to resist abuse. But because they invoked extreme examples (child-eating and wife-murder), it was easy for them to evade specificity about what the proper limits of male authority in the family should be. Thus, we should not exaggerate the extent to which whigs ever challenged male authority in the family in a significant way; arguably, they merely set up a monstrous tory straw-man to make themselves look sweetly reasonable. But whigs before 1688 certainly did not celebrate the authority of husbands in the way they did afterwards. The reasons for their new enthusiasm for husbandly authority lay in the need to justify Mary's rebellion against her father, and in the pressures put upon them by their opponents' argument that sexual contractarianism was the logical result of the Revolution, of government by consent, or even of any theory of legitimate resistance.

Arguably, then, there was a certain homogenization of whig and tory discourses on gender and the family after the Revolution of 1688. Both groups wanted to associate themselves with the maintenance of hierarchy and order in the family, and to cast their opponents as subverters of that order.[8] Moreover, tories and whigs were more similar than different in their attitudes towards female favorites and female political authority during Anne's reign; the well-known whig anxieties about Masham and whig anger at Anne over the Treaty of Utrecht are more widely known than tory fears about the Duchesses of Somerset and Marlborough or Anne's 'abandonment' of the Church, but that is because the whigs were the losers in the partisan struggle, not because they were more ideologically prone to misogyny.

Despite the basic similarities of whigs and tories, the interesting thing about the period is not the consensus around but rather the instability of, notions about gender and the family. Individual whigs, tories and Jacobites drew morals about gender from stories about politics in a kaleidoscopic variety of ways. As a result, conflict over gender did not divide into whig and tory sides, but took place within each camp. The picture that emerges here of gender ideology and its political usefulness is therefore in one important respect different from the one that Amussen has drawn for the early seven-teenth century. Whereas she emphasizes the stability of notions of gender and family in that period, they seem a bit more flexible in the latter part of the seventeenth century.

This might indeed mean that such notions became more contested and less stable as the seventeenth century progressed. It is significant if frustrating in this respect that Margaret Sommerville, whose magisterial *Sex and subjection* identifies a coherent ideology of gender existing in early modern Europe, ends her account in 1700.[9] Whether the fact that this present study has found far less coherence can be attributed to the difference between my microscopic case-study method and Sommerville's synthetic approach, or whether the late Stuart period represents some sort of break between early modern and modern configurations of the sex–gender system, will have to be determined by further research.

It is worth suggesting for now that the very frequency with which notions of gender and family were deployed in political debate may have made them more contestable. The dynamics of political argument which frustrate the search for clear whig–tory differences on the subject of gender also opened up numerous possibilities for individual whigs and tories to construct stories about how political events or axioms of political argument might be given meanings relevant to the politics of gender. In some cases, political debate provided an arena for people who genuinely had something to say about gender and family relations; examples include William Lawrence, John Butler, Mary Astell, Delarivière Manley, perhaps the Wesleys. In other cases, the obviousness of what constituted proper gender and family relations dissolved when those relationships were invoked in a failed attempt to force political consensus. The trajectory of Tyrrell's thinking is a case in point: he started by using the family to solve a problem in his political argument, but in the end he raised more questions about the family than he could answer.

Thus we see that political history must be treated as a part of the history of gender. Notions of gender, while not infinitely malleable, were subject to modification in the context of political debates. The fact that those who lived through the reigns of Mary II and Anne saw in so short a time such different representations of female royalty, each of which was presented as compatible with the 'natural' roles and characteristics of women, must have unsettled any idea that women had natural roles or characteristics. The boundaries between, and meanings of, virtue and corruption, public and private, family and state, and ruler and subject – all of which were integral to the construction of gender – were continually re-invented in the heat of political debate. Understanding the process by which gender was invoked and reshaped in the context of political argument gives not only a richer account of the construction of gender, but also of the nature of English political culture in a crucial period of transition.

NOTES

1 The 'gender crisis' paradigm is suggested in Anthony Fletcher, *Gender, sex and subordination in England 1500–1800* (New Haven, Yale, 1995), especially ch. 20; however, he acknowledges that gender systems may be constantly in crisis. David Underdown has suggested a crisis in gender relations in *early* Stuart England, in Underdown, 'The taming of the scold: the enforcement of patriarchal authority in early modern England', in A. Fletcher and J. Stevenson (eds), *Order and disorder in early modern England* (Cambridge, Cambridge University Press, 1985); cf. Martin Ingram, '"Scolding women cucked or washed": a crisis in gender relations in early modern England?', in J. Kermode and Garthine Walker (eds), *Women, crime and the courts in early modern England* (Chapel Hill, University of North Carolina Press, 1994).

2 Joan Scott, *Gender and the politics of history* (New York, Columbia University Press, 1988); Mary Poovey, *Uneven developments: the ideological work of gender in mid-Victorian England* (Chicago, University of Chicago Press, 1988).

3 Susan Amussen, *An ordered society: class and gender in early modern England* (Oxford, Basil Blackwell, 1988).

4 See Catherine Gallagher, *Nobody's story* (Berkeley, University of California Press, 1994).

5 Mark Goldie, 'Edmund Bohun and *jus gentium* in the Revolution debate, 1689–93', *Historical Journal* 20 (1977), p. 586.

6 This argument is suggested by Belinda Peters, '"That immaculate robe of honour": marriage in seventeenth-century English political thought' (Ph. D. dissertation, University of California at Irvine, 1996).

7 The subject of women and Jacobitism still awaits systematic study; the propensity of *anti*-Jacobite literature to associate Jacobitism with women is worth further analysis: examples include *Letter to a gentlewoman concerning government* (E. Whitelocke, 1697), p. 27; *The character of a Jacobite* (1690), pp. 20, 23–5; *Ancient and modern idolatry paralleled* (J. Roberts, 1716). For some interesting suggestions, see Paul Monod, 'The politics of matrimony: Jacobitism and marriage in eighteenth-century England', in Eveline Cruikshanks and Jeremy Black (eds), *The Jacobite challenge* (Edinburgh, John Donald, 1988).

8 Susan Owen has noted a similar phenomenon in whig–tory dramatic polemic in the exclusion crisis. See Owen, *Restoration theatre and crisis* (Oxford, Clarendon Press, 1996).

9 Margaret R. Sommerville, *Sex and subjection: attitudes to women in early-modern society* (Arnold, 1995).

Select bibliography

The place of publication is London, unless otherwise specified.

MANUSCRIPT SOURCES

BODLEIAN LIBRARY, OXFORD (BODL.)

Douce MS 357 (political poetry).

English history MS b. 2 (Papers relating to the birth of the Prince of Wales).

English history MS d. 1 (Papers relating to the birth of the Prince of Wales).

English poetry MS c. 18 (political poetry).

Firth MS b. 4 (political poetry).

Rawlinson poetry MSS 159, 169 (political poetry).

BRITISH LIBRARY (BL)

Additional MSS 26657, 32095–96, 33286 (papers relating to the birth of the Prince of Wales).

Additional MS 32523 (papers of Roger North).

Additional MS 40060 (political poetry).

Additional MS 47026 (Perceval correspondence).

Additional MSS 61417–18, 61422–3, 61434, 61459–63 (papers and correspondence of Sarah Churchill).

Additional MSS 72517–18 (Cotterell papers).

Harley MSS 6914, 7314, 7319 (political poetry).

Lansdowne MS 852 (political poetry).

DR WILLIAMS' LIBRARY, LONDON

Roger Morrice's historical MSS (Roger Morrice's 'Entr'ing book, being an historical register of occurrences,' 4 vols).

HERTFORDSHIRE RECORD OFFICE

Panshanger MS D/EP F228 (Cowper family correspondence with Sarah Churchill).

PUBLISHED SOURCES

PRIMARY PUBLISHED SOURCES

Abbadie, James, *A panagyrick on our late sovereign lady Mary*, Hugh Newman, 1695.

An account of a dream at Harwich, B. Bragg, 1708.

An account of the pretended Prince of Wales, and other grievanses, that occasioned the nobilities inviting, and the Prince of Orange's coming into England, 1688.

Addison, Joseph, and Richard Steele, *The Spectator*, S. Buckley & A Baldwin, 1711–14.

Addison, Lancelot, *The present state of the Jews*, William Crook, 1676.

The age of wonders, 1711.

The anatomy of a Jacobite tory: in a dialogue between Whig and Tory, Richard Baldwin, 1690.

Ancient and modern idolatry paralleled, J. Roberts, 1716.

[Anne, Queen of Great Britain], *The letters and diplomatic instructions of Queen Anne*, ed. Beatrice Curtis Brown, Cassell, 1935.

An answer to Pereat Papa [1681].

Asgill, John, *A question upon divorce*, 1717.

Astell, Mary, *Astell: political writings*, ed. P. Springborg, Cambridge, Cambridge University Press, 1996.

— *Bart'lemy Fair: or, an enquiry after wit*, Richard Wilkin, 1709.

— *The Christian religion as professed by a daughter of the Church of England*, Richard Wilkin, 1705.

— *The first English feminist: reflections on marriage and other writings by Mary Astell*, ed. B. Hill, Gower/Maurice Temple Smith, 1986.

— *Moderation truly stated*, Richard Wilkin, 1704.

Barnett, Andrew, *A just lamentation for the irrecoverable loss of the nation*, Thomas Parkhurst, 1695.

Baron and femme, 2nd edn, John Walthoe, 1719.

The beasts in power, 1709.

Behn, Aphra, *A congratulatory poem to her most sacred Majesty*, Will. Canning, 1688.

Belisarius a great commander and Zariana his lady. A dialogue, J. Morphew, 1710.

Bodin, Jean, *Six books of the commonwealth* [1576], repro. in Eric Cochrane *et al. (eds)*, *Early modern Europe: crisis of authority* (University of Chicago readings in western civilization 6), Chicago, University of Chicago, 1987.

[Bohun, Edmund], *A defence of Sir Robert Filmer against the mistakes and misrepresentations of Algernon Sidney, esq.*, Walter Kettilby, 1684.

Bohun, Edmund, 'Preface,' in Robert Filmer, *Patriarcha: or the natural power of kings*, R. Chiswell, 1685.

Bolingbroke, Henry St John, Viscount, *The idea of a patriot king*, ed. Sidney W. Jackman, Indianapolis, Bobbs-Merrill, 1965.

Select bibliography

[Bolingbroke, Henry St John, Viscount], *Letter to the Examiner*, 1710.

Brady, Nicholas, *A sermon upon the death of King William; and her present Majesty's happy accession to the crown*, Joseph Wild, 1702.

A brief justification of the Prince of Orange's descent into England, Richard Baldwin, 1689.

[Brydall, John], *The white rose: or, a word for the house of York*, 1680.

[Burnet, Gilbert], *An enquiry into the measures of submission to the supream authority* [1688].

Burnet, Gilbert, *An essay on the memory of the late queen*, Richard Chiswell, 1695.

— *History of his own time*, 2nd edn enlarged, 6 vols, Oxford, Oxford University Press, 1833.

Butler, John, *The true state of the case of John Butler*, printed for the author, 1697.

'Castamore,' *Conjugium languens: or, the natural, civil and religious mischiefs arising from conjugal infidelity and impunity*, R. Roberts, 1700.

Cellier, Elizabeth, *To Dr. —— an answer to his queries* [1688].

The character of a Jacobite, 1690.

Cibber, Colley, *A poem on the death of our late soveraign [sic] lady Mary*, 1695.

[Clarendon, Henry Hyde, Earl of], *The correspondence of Henry Hyde, Earl of Clarendon*, ed. Samuel W. Singer, 2 vols, Henry Colburn, 1828.

Clarke, Samuel, *A true and faithful account of the four chiefest plantations of the English in America*, Robert Clavel, 1670.

[Clarkson, David], *The practical divinity of the papists discovered to be destructive of Christianity and men's souls*, T. Parkhurst & N. Ponder, 1676.

[Clements, S.], *Faults on both sides*, 1710.

Cobbett, William, *Parliamentary history of England*, 36 vols, London: T. C. Hansard, 1806–20.

A collection of funeral orations pronounced by publick authority in Holland, John Dunton, 1695.

A collection of scarce and valuable tracts, ed. Walter Scott, 13 vols, 2nd edn, T. Cadell & W. Davies, 1809–15.

A compleat history of the pretended Prince of Wales, 1696.

Concubinage and poligamy disproved, Richard Baldwin, 1698.

Cosin, John, *Bishop Cozen's argument, proving that adultery works the dissolution of a marriage* [1669].

Dalrymple, John, *Memoirs of Great Britain and Ireland*, 2nd edn, 2 vols, W. Strahan & T. Caddell, 1771–73.

D'Anvers, Mrs [Alicia], *A poem upon his sacred Majesty, his voyage for Holland*, Thomas Bever, 1691.

De ventre inspiciendo: or, remarks upon Mr Ashton's answerer, in a letter to a friend [1691].

The declaration of his Highness William Henry, by the grace of God Prince of Orange, &c. of the reasons inducing him to appear in arms in the kingdom of England, The Hague, Arnout Leers, 1688.

[Defoe, Daniel], *The secret history of the white-staff*, J. Baker, 1714.

Dennis, John, *The court of death*, James Knapton, 1695.

Dunton, John, *King Abigail: or, the secret reign of the she-favorite*, John Dunton, 1715.

— *The medal: or, a loyal essay upon king George's picture*, John Dunton, [1715].

'Eugenia,' *The female advocate; or, a plea for the just liberty of the tender sex. By a lady of quality*, Andrew Bell, 1700.

An excellent new ballad made at the restauration of K. Charles II, with a second part to the same tune by a modern hand [1712].

F., E., *Letter from a gentleman of quality in the country, to his friend, upon his being chosen a member to serve in the approaching Parliament*, 1679.

[Ferguson, Robert], *A letter to a person of honour concerning the black box* [1680].

— *A letter to a person of honour, concerning the King's disavowing the having been married to the Duke of Monmouth's mother* [1680].

Filmer, Robert, *Patriarcha and other political writings*, ed. Johann P. Sommerville, Cambridge, Cambridge University Press, 1991.

Fleetwood, William, *The relative duties of parents and children, husbands and wives, and masters and servants*, C. Harper, 1705.

[Fowler, Edward], *An answer to the paper delivered by Mr Ashton at his execution*, R. Clavell, 1690.

A full answer to the depositions; and to all the pretences and arguments whatsoever, concerning the birth of the Prince of Wales, Simon Burgis, 1689.

Fuller, William, *A brief discovery of the true mother of the pretended Prince of Wales*, 1696.

Further considerations on the Earl of Macclesfield's bill [1697]

Glanville, John, *A poem dedicated to the memory and lamenting the death of her late sacred Majesty of the small pox*, John Newton, 1695.

Great and weighty considerations relating to the D. or successor of the crown, 1679.

Grey, Anchitell, *Debates in the House of Commons, from the year 1667 to the year 1694*, 10 vols, D. Henry & R. Cave, 1763.

Halifax, George Savile, Marquess of, *Advice to a daughter*, printed in *The complete works of George Savile, first Marquess of Halifax*, ed. Walter Raleigh, Oxford, Clarendon Press, 1912.

[Hamilton, David], *The diary of Sir David Hamilton, 1709–14*, ed. Philip Roberts, Oxford, Clarendon Press, 1975.

Harrington, James, *The commonwealth of Oceana* [1656], ed. J. G. A. Pocock, Cambridge, Cambridge University Press, 1992.

[Herbert, Thomas], *Some years travels into diverse parts of Africa and Asia the great*, 4th edn, R. Everingham, 1677.

He's welcome home: or, a dialogue between John and Sarah [1711].

Hickes, George, *A discourse of the sovereign power*, 1682.

— *A word to the wavering*, 1689.

[Hickes, George?], *The pretences of the Prince of Wales examined and rejected* [1701?].

The history of Prince Mirabel's infancy, rise and disgrace, J. Baker, 1712.

Select bibliography

Hobbes, Thomas, *De cive: the English version*, ed. Howard Warrender, Oxford, Clarendon Press, 1983.

— *Leviathan* [1651], ed. C. B. Macpherson, Penguin, 1985.

[Hume, Mr], *A poem dedicated to the immortal memory of her late Majesty*, Jacob Tonson, 1695.

Hunt, Thomas, *Mr. Hunt's postscript for rectifying some mistakes in some of the inferiour clergy*, 1682.

Idem iterum: or, the history of Q. Mary's Big-Belly [1688].

James, Elinor, untitled broadside beginning 'My Lords you cannot but be sensible' [1688].

—*To the right honorable Convention*, [1688].

Japikse, N. (ed.), *Correspondentie van Willem III en van Hans Willem Bentinck ... het archief van Welbeck Abbey*, 2 vols, The Hague, Martinus Nijhoff, 1927–28.

K[ennett], W[hite], *A dialogue between two friends, occasioned by the late revolution of affairs*, Richard Chiswell, 1689.

[King, William], *Rufinus*, 1711.

The land-leviathan; or, modern hydra, John Morphew, 1712.

[Lawrence, William], *Marriage by the moral law of God vindicated*, 1680.

L'Estrange, Roger, *The case put concerning the succession*, 3rd edn, Henry Brome, 1680.

A letter to a friend reflecting upon the present condition of this nation, 1680.

A letter to a friend. Shewing from scripture, fathers and reason, how false that state-maxim is, royal authority is ... in the people, 1679.

A letter to a gentlewoman concerning government, Elizabeth Whitelocke, 1697.

The life of that incomparable princess Mary, Daniel Dring, 1695.

Locke, John, *Political essays*, ed. Mark Goldie, Cambridge, Cambridge University Press, 1997.

— *Political writings of John Locke*, ed. David Wootton, New York, Mentor, 1993.

— *Two treatises of government*, ed. Peter Laslett [1960], Cambridge, Cambridge University Press, repr. 1991.

Lord, George de F., *et al.* (eds), *Poems on affairs of state: Augustan satirical verse, 1660–1714*, 7 vols, New Haven, Connecticut, Yale University Press, 1963–75.

Luttrell, Narcissus, *A brief historical relation of state affairs, from September 1678 to April 1714*, 6 vols, Oxford, Oxford University Press, 1857.

[Manley, Delarivière], *A modest enquiry into the reasons of the joy expressed by a certain set of people upon the spreading of a report of her Majesty's death*, John Morphew, 1714.

— *The novels of Mary Delarivière Manley*, ed. Patricia Koster, 2 vols, Gainesville, Florida, Scholars' Facsimiles and Reprints, 1971.

Maria to Henric and Henric to Maria, Joseph Knight, 1691.

[Marlborough, Sarah Churchill, Duchess of], *An account of the conduct of the Dowager Duchess of Marlborough, from her first coming to the court, to the year 1710*, George Hawkins, 1742.

— *Private correspondence of Sarah, Duchess of Marlborough*, 2 vols, Henry Colburn, 1838.

The Marlborough–Godolphin Correspondence, ed. Henry L. Snyder, 3 vols, Oxford, Clarendon Press, 1975.

Marriage promoted, Richard Baldwin, 1690.

Memoirs of the conduct of her late Majesty and her last ministry, relating to the separate peace with France. By the right hononrable [sic] the Countess of ——, S. Keimer, 1715.

Meriton, G., *A geographical description of the world*, 3rd edn, William Leake, 1679.

[Montgomery, James], *Great Britain's just complaint*, 1692.

Nalson, John, *The common interest of king and people*, Jonathan Edwin, 1678.

[Nalson, John], *The character of a rebellion, and what England may expect from one*, Benjamin Tooke, 1681.

—— *The complaint of liberty and property*, Robert Steele, 1681.

A new ballad. To the tune of Fair Rosamond [1707].

The officer's address to the ladies, Ann Baldwin [1710].

Ogilby, John, *Africa*, Thomas Johnson, 1670.

Oldisworth, William, *The loyal mourner*, John Morphew, 1716.

Oliver's pocket looking-glass, 1711.

Park, Henry, *Lachrymae sacerdotis*, John Dunton, 1695.

Mr Partridge's wonderful predictions, pro anno 1688 [1688].

Pead, Deull, *A practical discourse upon the death of our late gracious queen*, Abel Roper, 1695.

The perquisite-monger; or, the rise and fall of ingratitude, 1712.

The petticoat plotters; or, The D——ss of M——h's Club, T. Wellard, 1712.

Petty, William, *The economic writings of Sir William Petty*, ed. Charles H. Hull, 2 vols, Cambridge, Cambridge University Press, 1899.

—— *The Petty papers: some unpublished writings of Sir William Petty from the Bowood papers*, ed. Marquess of Lansdowne, 2 vols, Constable, 1927.

A poetical elegy devoted to the glorious memory of our late queen, occasioned by a number of poems and sermons on her death, 1695.

Povey, Charles, *An inquiry into the miscarriages of the last four years reign*, Mr. Robinson, 1714.

The prerogative of the breeches, Ann Baldwin, 1702.

Proceedings of the Old Bailey, 8th–11th December, 1697.

The proceedings upon the bill of divorce between his Grace the Duke of Norfolk and the Lady Mary Morduant, Matthew Gillyflower, 1700.

[Pryme, Abraham de la], *The diary of Abraham De la Pryme, the Yorkshire antiquary*, ed. Charles Jackson, Surtees Society publications vol. 54, Durham, Andrews, 1870.

Queen Anne vindicated from the base aspersions of some late pamphlets, John Baker, 1715.

The Queen's famous progress; or, her Majesty's royal journey to Bath, J. W., 1702.

The rake: or, the libertine's religion. A poem, Randall Taylor, 1693.

Reasons for crowning the Prince and Princess of Orange jointly, 1689.

Reasons for the Earl of Macclesfield's bill in Parliament [1697].

The rival dutchess; or, the court incendiary, 1708.

Select bibliography

[Robert, John ap], *The younger brother his apologie*, Oxford, Henry Hall, 1671.

Rogers, Thomas, *Lux occidentalis: or providence displayed in the coronation of King William and Queen Mary*, Randall Taylor, 1689.

Rowe, Elizabeth Singer, *Poems on several occasions*, John Dunton, 1696.

[St John, Henry], *Letter to The Examiner* (1710).

Scott, Walter (ed.), *A collection of scarce and valuable tracts*, 13 vols, 2nd edn, T. Cadell & W. Davies, 1809-15.

The several declarations, together with several depositions made in Council on Monday, the 22nd of October, 1688. Concerning the birth of the Prince of Wales [1688].

[Sewell, George], *An epistle from Sempronia to Cethegus*, John Holmes, 1713.

[Shaftoe, Frances], *Mrs Frances Shaftoe's narrative*, 1707.

The sham prince expos'd. In a dialogue between the Pope's nuncio and a bricklayer's wife, 1688.

Sharp, John, *A sermon preached at the coronation of Queen Anne*, Walter Kettilby, 1702.

Sidney, Algernon, *Discourses on government* [1698], 3 vols, New York, Richard Lee, 1805.

Smith, Joseph, *The duty of the living to the memory of the dead*, Richard Smith, 1714.

Swift, Jonathan, *The conduct of the Allies*, John Morphew, 1712.

— *An enquiry into the behaviour of the Queen's last ministry*, Indiana University Publications in the Humanities Series no. 36, ed. Irvin Ehrenpreis, Bloomington, Indiana University Press, 1956.

— *Journal to Stella*, ed. Harold Williams, Oxford, Clarendon Press, 1948.

Swift, Jonathan *et al.*, *The Examiner*, John Morphew, 1710-14.

A treatise concerning adultery and divorce, R. Roberts, 1700.

A treatise of feme coverts: or, the lady's law, 1732.

Two great questions determined by the principles of reason and divinity, Richard Janeway, 1681.

Tyrrell, James, *Bibliotheca Politica; or, a discourse by way of a dialogue, whether monarchy be jure divino ... Dialogue the first*, Richard Baldwin, 1691/2.

— *Patriarcha non monarcha. The patriarch unmonarch'd*, Richard Janeway, 1681.

A vindication of her Grace Mary Dutchess of Norfolk, 1693.

[Wagstaffe, William], *The story of the St. Alban's ghost*, 1712.

Walsh, William, *A dialogue concerning women*, 1691.

The Wentworth papers, 1705-39, ed. J. J. Cartwright, Wyman & Sons, 1883.

SECONDARY PUBLISHED SOURCES

Amussen, Susan D., *An ordered society: class and gender in early modern England*, Oxford, Basil Blackwell, 1988.

Appleby, Joyce, *Economic thought and ideology in seventeenth-century England*, Princeton, Princeton, New Jersey, University Press, 1978.

Ashcraft, Richard, *Revolutionary politics and Locke's 'Two treatises of government'*, Princeton, Princeton, New Jersey, University Press, 1986.

Backscheider, Paula, *Daniel Defoe: his life*, Baltimore, Johns Hopkins University Press, 1989.

Bahlman, Dudley W. R., *The moral revolution of 1688*, New Haven, Connecticut, Yale University Press, 1957.

Ballaster, Ros, *Seductive forms: women's amatory fiction from 1684 to 1740*, Oxford, Clarendon Press, 1992.

— 'The vices of old Rome revived: representations of female same-sex desire in seventeenth- and eighteenth-century England', in Suzanne Raitt (ed.), *Volcanoes and pearldivers; essays in lesbian feminist studies*, Binghampton, New York, Harrington Press, 1994.

Barash, Carol, *English women's poetry, 1649–1714: politics, community and linguistic authority*, Oxford, Clarendon Press, 1996.

Beddard, Robert, 'The unexpected whig revolution of 1688,' in Robert Beddard (ed.), *The revolutions of 1688*, Oxford, Clarendon Press, 1991.

Bennett, G. V., 'Conflict in the Church,' in Geoffrey Holmes (ed.), *Britain after the Glorious Revolution*, Macmillan, 1969.

— 'King William III and the episcopate,' in G. V. Bennett and John D. Walsh (eds), *Essays in modern English church history*, New York, Oxford University Press, 1966.

Bloch, Ruth, 'The gendered meanings of virtue in revolutionary America', *Signs* 13 (1987).

Bowers, Toni, *The politics of motherhood: British writing and culture, 1680-1760*, Cambridge, Cambridge University Press, 1996.

Bray, Alan, *Homosexuality in Renaissance England*, Gay Men's Press, 1988.

Brennan, Teresa, and Carole Pateman, '"Mere auxiliaries to the commonwealth": women and the origins of liberalism', *Political Studies* 27 (1979).

Brewer, John, 'This, that and the other: public, social and private in the seventeenth and eighteenth centuries,' in Dario Castiglione and Lesley Sharpe (eds), *Shifting the boundaries: transformation of the languages of public and private in the eighteenth century*, Exeter, University of Exeter Press, 1995.

British Museum, *A catalogue of prints and drawings in the British museum, division I: political and personal satires*, vol. 1, Trustees of the British Museum, 1870.

Browning, Andrew, *Thomas Osborne, Earl of Danby and Duke of Leeds, 1632–1712*, 3 vols, Glasgow, Jackson, Son & Co., 1944–51.

Bucholz, Robert O., *The Augustan court: Queen Anne and the decline of court culture*, Stanford, California, Stanford University Press, 1993.

Burtt, Shelley, *Virtue transformed*, Cambridge, Cambridge University Press, 1992.

Butler, Iris, *The rule of three: Sarah, Duchess of Marlborough and her companions in power*, Hodder & Stoughton, 1967.

Butler, Melissa, 'Early liberal roots of feminism: John Locke and the attack on patriarchy,' *American Political Science Review* 22 (1978).

Campbell, George A., *Impostor at the bar: William Fuller, 1670–1733*, Hodder & Stoughton, 1961.

Clark, Alice, *The working life of women in the seventeenth century* [1919], ed. M. Chaytor and J. Lewis, Routledge, 1982.

Clark, J. C. D., *English society, 1688-1832*, Cambridge, Cambridge University Press, 1985.

Clark, Lorenne M. G., 'Who owns the apples in the garden of Eden?' in Lorenne M. G. Clark and Lynda Lange (eds), *The sexism of social and political theory: women and reproduction from Plato to Nietzsche*, Toronto, University of Toronto Press, 1979.

Claydon, Tony, *William III and the godly revolution*, Cambridge, Cambridge University Press, 1996.

Colley, Linda, *In defiance of oligarchy: the tory party, 1714–1760*, Cambridge, Cambridge University Press, 1982.

Cowles, Virginia, *The great Marlborough and his duchess*, Macmillan, 1983.

Cox, Edward G., *A reference guide to the literature of travel: the new world*, Seattle, University of Washington Publications in Language and Literature, 1938.

Cressy, David, 'Literacy in seventeenth-century England: more evidence,' *Journal of Interdisciplinary History* 8 (1977).

Cruickshanks, Eveline, David Hayton and Clyve Jones, 'Divisions in the House of Lords on the transfer of the Crown and other issues, 1689–94: ten new lists,' *Bulletin of the Institute of Historical Research* 53 (1980).

Daly, James, *Sir Robert Filmer and English political thought*, Toronto, University of Toronto Press, 1979.

De Krey, Gary, S., 'The first Restoration crisis', *Albion* 25 (1993).

Desan, Suzanne '"War between brothers and sisters": inheritance law and gender politics in revolutionary France,' *French Historical Studies* 20:4 (1997).

Dickinson, H. T., 'The eighteenth-century debate on the Glorious Revolution,' *History* 61 (1976).

Dolan, Frances, *Dangerous familiars: representations of domestic crime in England, 1550–1700*, Ithaca, New York, Cornell University Press, 1994.

Donnison, Jean, *Midwives and medical men*, Heinemann, 1977.

Donoghue, Emma, *Passions between women: British lesbian culture 1668–1801*, Scarlet Press, 1993.

Doran, Susan, *Monarchy and matrimony: the courtships of Elizabeth I*, Routledge, 1996.

Downie, J. A., *Robert Harley and the press: propaganda and public opinion in the age of Swift and Defoe*, Cambridge, Cambridge University Press, 1979.

Ehrenpreis, Irvin, *Swift: the man, his works, the age* 3 vols, Cambridge, Mass., Harvard University Press, 1962–83.

Ezell, Margaret J. M., *The patriarch's wife: literary evidence and the history of the family*, Chapel Hill, University of North Carolina Press, 1987.

Faderman, Lillian, *Surpassing the love of men*, New York, Morrow, 1981.

Fletcher, Anthony, *Gender, sex and subordination in England 1500–1800*, New Haven, Connecticut, Yale University Press, 1995.

Fortescue, Sir John, *Marlborough*, New York, D. Appleton, 1932.

Fox-Genovese, Elizabeth, 'Property and patriarchy in classic bourgeois political theory,' *Radical History Review* 4:2 (1977).

Freist, Dagmar, 'The king's crown is the whore of Babylon: politics, gender and communication in mid-seventeenth-century England,' *Gender and History* 7:3 (1995).

Furley, W. O., 'The whig exclusionists,' *Cambridge Historical Journal* 14 (1957).

Gallagher, Catherine, 'Embracing the absolute: the politics of the female subject in seventeenth-century England,' *Genders* 1 (1988).

— *Nobody's story*, Berkeley, University of California Press, 1994.

Goldie, Mark, 'Contextualizing Dryden's Absalom: William Lawrence, the laws of marriage, and the case for King Monmouth,' in Donna B. Hamilton and Richard Strier (eds), *Religion, literature and politics in post-reformation England, 1540–1688*, Cambridge, Cambridge University Press, 1996.

— 'Edmund Bohun and *jus gentium* in the Revolution debate, 1689–93,' *Historical Journal* 20 (1977).

— 'John Locke and Anglican royalism,' *Political Studies* 31 (1983).

— 'The non-jurors, episcopacy, and the origins of the convocation controversy,' in Eveline Cruickshanks (ed.), *Ideology and conspiracy: aspects of Jacobitism, 1689–1759*, Edinburgh, John Donald, 1982.

— 'The Revolution of 1689 and the structure of political argument,' *Bulletin of Research in the Humanities* 83 (1980).

— 'The roots of true whiggism, 1688–94,' *History of Political Thought* 1 (1980).

— 'Tory political thought 1689–1714', Ph.D. dissertation, Cambridge University, 1977.

Goodman, Dena, 'Public sphere and private life: towards a synthesis of current historiographical approaches to the old regime,' *History and Theory* 31 (1992).

— *The republic of letters: a cultural history of the French enlightenment*, Ithaca, New York, Cornell University Press, 1994.

Gough, J. W., 'James Tyrrell, whig historian and friend of Locke,' *Historical Journal* 19 (1976).

Greaves, Richard L., 'The Restoration in turmoil', *Albion* 25 (1993).

Green, David, *Sarah, Duchess of Marlborough*, New York, Scribner's, 1967.

Greenfield, Susan, 'Aborting the "mother plot": politics and generation in *Absalom and Achitophel*', *ELH* [a journal of English literary history] 62 (1995).

Gregg, Edward, *Queen Anne*, Ark, 1984.

— 'Was Queen Anne a Jacobite?', *History* 57 (1972).

Habbakuk, H. J., 'Marriage settlements in the eighteenth century,' *Transactions of the Royal Historical Society*, 4th ser., 32 (1950).

— 'The rise and fall of English landed families,' *Transactions of the Royal Historical Society*, 5th ser., 29 (1979).

Hammond, Paul, 'The king's two bodies: representations of Charles II' in Jeremy Black and Jeremy Gregory (eds), *Culture, politics and society in Britain 1660–1800*, Manchester, Manchester University Press, 1991.

Hanley, Sarah, 'Engendering the state: family formation and state building in early modern France,' *French Historical Studies* 16 (1989).

— 'The monarchic state in early modern France: marital regime government and male right', in Adrianna Bakos (ed.), *Politics, ideology and the law in early modern Europe*, Rochester, New York, University of Rochester Press, 1994.

Harris, Frances, 'Accounts of the conduct of Sarah, Duchess of Marlborough, 1704–1742,' *British Library Journal* 8 (1982).

— *A passion for government: the life of Sarah, Duchess of Marlborough*, Oxford, Oxford University Press, 1991.

— '"The honourable sisterhood": Queen Anne's maids of honor,' *British Library Journal* 19 (Autumn 1993).

Harris, Tim, *London crowds in the reign of Charles II: propaganda and politics from the Restoration until the exclusion crisis*, Cambridge, Cambridge University Press, 1987.

— 'Party turns? or, whigs and tories get off Scott free,' in *Albion* 25 (1993).

— *Politics under the later Stuarts: party conflict in a divided society, 1660–1715*, London and New York, Longman, 1993.

Hayton, David, 'The "country" interest and the party system, 1689–c.1720,' in Clyve Jones (ed.) *Party and management in parliament, 1660–1784*, Leicester, Leicester University Press, 1984.

— 'Moral reform and country politics in the late seventeenth-century House of Commons,' *Past and Present* 128 (1990).

Heisch, Alison, 'Queen Elizabeth and the persistence of patriarchy,' *Feminist Review* 4 (1980).

Herrup, Cynthia, 'The patriarch at home: the trial of the second Earl of Castlehaven for rape and sodomy,' *History Workshop Journal* 41 (1996).

Hinton, R. W. K., 'Husbands, fathers and conquerors, part I.,' *Political Studies* 15 (1967).

Historical Manuscripts Commission, *Manuscripts of the House of Lords, 1697–99*, n.s., vol. 3, HMSO, 1905.

Holmes, Geoffrey, *British politics in the age of Anne*, revd edn, Hambledon Press, 1987.

— *The trial of Doctor Sacheverell*, Eyre Methuen, 1973.

Holmes, G., and W. Speck, 'The fall of Harley in 1708 reconsidered,' *English Historical Review* 80 (1965).

Horn, Robert D., *Marlborough, a survey: panegyrics, satires and biographical writings, 1688–1788*, New York, Garland, 1975.

Horwitz, Henry, 'Parliament and the Glorious Revolution,' *Bulletin of the Institute of Historical Research* 47 (1974).

— *Parliament, policy and politics in the reign of William III*, Manchester, Manchester University Press, 1977.

— *Revolution politicks: the career of Daniel Finch second Earl of Nottingham, 1647–1730*, Cambridge, Cambridge University Press, 1968.

Houlbrooke, Ralph, *The English landed family, 1450–1700*, Longman, 1985.

Houston, Alan C., *Algernon Sidney and the republican heritage in England and America*, Princeton, New Jersey, Princeton University Press, 1991.

Hughes, Ann, 'Gender and politics in Leveller literature,' in Susan Amussen and Mark Kishlansky (eds), *Political culture and cultural politics in early modern England*, Manchester, Manchester University Press, 1995.

Hull, Isabel V., *Sexuality, state and civil society in Germany, 1700–1815*, Ithaca, New York, Cornell University Press, 1996.

Hunt, Lynn, *The family romance of the French Revolution*, Berkeley, University of California Press, 1992.

Hunt, Margaret R., *The middling sort: commerce, gender and the family in England, 1680–1780*, Berkeley, University of California Press, 1996.

Ingram, Martin, '"Scolding women cucked or washed": a crisis in gender relations in early modern England?', in J. Kermode and Garthine Walker (eds), *Women, crime and the courts in early modern England*, Chapel Hill, University of North Carolina Press, 1994.

Jones, J. R., *The first whigs*, Oxford, Clarendon Press, 1961.

— *Marlborough*, Cambridge, Cambridge University Press, 1993.

Jordan, Constance, 'Woman's rule in sixteenth-century British political thought,' *Renaissance Quarterly* 40 (1987).

Kantorowicz, Ernst, *The king's two bodies: a study in medieval political theology*, Princeton, New Jersey, Princeton University Press, 1957.

Kenyon, John P., 'The birth of the Old Pretender,' *History Today* 13 (1963).

— *Revolution principles: the politics of party, 1689–1720*, Cambridge, Cambridge University Press, 1977.

Kerber, Linda, *Women of the republic: intellect and ideology in revolutionary America*, Chapel Hill, University of North Carolina Press, 1980.

Kinnaird, Joan, 'Mary Astell and the conservative contribution to English feminism,' *Journal of British Studies* 19 (1979).

Klein, Lawrence E., 'Gender and the public/private distinction in the eighteenth century: some questions about evidence and analytic procedure,' *Eighteenth Century Studies* 29 (1995).

Knights, Mark, *Politics and opinion in crisis, 1678–81*, Cambridge, Cambridge University Press, 1994.

Landes, Joan, *Women in the public sphere in the age of the French revolution*, Ithaca, New York, Cornell University Press, 1988.

Levin, Carole, *The heart and stomach of a king: Elizabeth I and the politics of sex and power*, Philadelphia, University of Pennsylvania Press, 1994.

MacQueen, John F., *A practical treatise on the appellate jurisdiction of the House of Lords*, 1842.

Marshall, John, *John Locke: resistance, religion and responsibility*, Cambridge, Cambridge University Press, 1994.

Maza, Sarah, 'The diamond necklace affair revisited', in Lynn Hunt (ed.), *Eroticism and the body politic*, Baltimore, Johns Hopkins University Press, 1991.

— *Private lives and public affairs: the causes celebres of prerevolutionary France*, Berkeley, University of California Press, 1993.

Mendelson, Sarah, and Patricia Crawford, *Women in early modern England*, Oxford, Clarendon Press, 1998.

Monod, Paul, 'The politics of matrimony: Jacobitism and marriage in eighteenth-century England,' in Eveline Cruikshanks and Jeremy Black (eds), *The Jacobite challenge*, Edinburgh, John Donald, 1988.

Montrose, Louis, 'Shaping fantasies: figurations of gender and power in Elizabethan culture,' *Representations* 2 (1983).

Morgan, Fidelis, *A woman of no character: an autobiography of Mrs Manley*, Faber & Faber, 1986.

Needham, Gwendolyn B., 'Mary de la Rivière Manley, tory defender', *Huntington Library Quarterly* 12 (1949).

— 'Mrs Manley: an eighteenth-century Wife of Bath,' *Huntington Library Quarterly* 14 (1951).

Nenner, Howard, *The right to be king: the succession to the crown of England, 1603–1714*, Chapel Hill, University of North Carolina Press, 1995.

Norton, Mary Beth, *Founding mothers and fathers: gendered power and the forming of American society*, New York, Alfred A. Knopf, 1988.

— *Liberty's daughters: the revolutionary experience of American women, 1750–1800*, Boston, Little, Brown & Co., 1980.

Oldham, James, 'The origins of the special jury,' *University of Chicago Law Review* 50 (1983).

Outram, Dorinda, *The body in the French revolution: sex, class and political culture*, New Haven, Connecticut, Yale University Press, 1989.

— '*Le langage male de la vertu*: women and the discourse of the French revolution' in Peter Burke and Roy Porter, (eds), *The social history of language*, Cambridge, Cambridge University Press, 1987.

Owen, Susan, *Restoration theatre and crisis*, Oxford, Clarendon Press, 1996.

Pateman, Carole, *The sexual contract: aspects of patriarchal liberalism*, Stanford, California, Stanford University Press, 1988.

— 'Women's writing, women's standing: theory and politics in the early modern period' in Hilda Smith (ed.), *Women writers and the early modern British political tradition*, Cambridge, Cambridge University Press, 1998.

Perry, Ruth, *The celebrated Mary Astell: an early English feminist*, Chicago, University of Chicago Press, 1986.

— 'Mary Astell and the feminist critique of possessive individualism,' *Eighteenth Century Studies* 23 (1990).

Peters, Belinda, '"That immaculate robe of honour": marriage in seventeenth-century English political thought', Ph.D. dissertation, University of California at Irvine, 1996.

Pincus, Steve, 'Neither Machiavellian moment nor possessive individualism: commercial society and the defenders of the English commonwealth,' *American Historical Review* 103:3 (1998).

Pitkin, Hannah, *Fortune is a woman: gender and politics in the thought of Niccolò Machiavelli*, Berkeley, University of California Press, 1984.

Plumb, J. H., *The growth of political stability in England, 1675–1725*, Macmillan Press, 1967.

— 'The new world of children in eighteenth-century England,' *Past and Present* 67 (1975).

Pocock, J. G. A., 'Machiavelli, Harrington and English political ideologies in the eighteenth century' in J. G. A. Pocock, *Politics, language and time*, New York, Atheneum, 1971.

— *The Machiavellian moment: Florentine political thought and the Atlantic republican tradition*, Princeton, New Jersey, Princeton University Press, 1975.

— *Virtue, commerce and history*, Cambridge, Cambridge University Press, 1985.

Pollock, Linda, *Forgotten children: parent–child relations from 1500 to 1900*, Cambridge, Cambridge University Press, 1983.

Poovey, Mary, *Uneven developments: the ideological work of gender in mid-Victorian England*, Chicago, University of Chicago Press, 1988.

Rubini, Dennis, *Court and country, 1688–1702*, Rupert Hart-Davis, 1967.

Rudolph, Julia, 'Rape and resistance: women and consent in seventeenth-century English legal and political thought,' *Journal of British Studies* (forthcoming).

— 'Revolution by degrees: the whig theory of resistance', Ph.D. dissertation, Columbia University, New York, 1995.

Schochet, Gordon, *Patriarchalism in political thought: the authoritarian family and political speculation and attitudes especially in seventeenth-century England*, New York, Basic Books, 1975.

— 'The significant sounds of silence: the absence of women from the political thought of Sir Robert Filmer and John Locke,' in Hilda Smith (ed.), *Women writers and the early modern British political tradition*, Cambridge, Cambridge University Press, 1998.

Schwoerer, Lois G., *The Declaration of Rights, 1689*, Baltimore, Johns Hopkins University Press, 1981.

— 'Images of Queen Mary II, 1689–95,' *Renaissance Quarterly* 42 (1989).

— 'Propaganda in the Revolution of 1688–89,' *American Historical Review* 82 (1977).

— 'Seventeenth-century Englishwomen: engraved in Stone?,' *Albion* 16 (1984).

— 'Women and the Glorious Revolution,' *Albion* 18 (1986).

Scott, Joan, *Gender and the politics of history*, New York, Columbia University Press, 1988.

Scott, Jonathan, *Algernon Sidney and the English republic, 1623–1677*, Cambridge, Cambridge University Press, 1988.

— *Algernon Sidney and the Restoration crisis, 1677–1683*, Cambridge, Cambridge University Press, 1991.

— 'England's troubles: exhuming the popish plot', in Tim Harris *et al.* (eds), *The Politics of religion in Restoration England*, Oxford, Basil Blackwell, 1990.

Shanley, Mary, 'Marriage contract and social contract in seventeenth-century English political thought,' *Western Political Quarterly* 32 (1979).

Shoemaker, Robert, *Gender in English society, 1650–1850: the emergence of separate spheres?*, Longman, 1998.

Slaughter, Thomas P., '"Abdicate" and "contract" in the Glorious Revolution,' *Historical Journal* 24 (1981).

Smith, Hilda, *Reason's disciples*, Urbana, University of Illinois Press, 1982.

Snyder, Henry L., 'The Duke of Marlborough's request of his Captain-Generalcy for life,' *Journal of the Society for Army Historical Research* 45 (1967).

— 'Godolphin and Harley: a study of their partnership in politics,' *Huntington Library Quarterly* 30 (1966–67).

— 'Queen Anne versus the Junto: The effort to place Orford at the head of the Admiralty in

1709,' *Huntington Library Quarterly* 35 (1972).

Sommerville, Margaret, *Sex and subjection: attitudes to women in early-modern society*, Arnold, 1995.

Speck, William A., 'The Orangist conspiracy against James II,' *Historical Journal* 30 (1987).

— *Reluctant revolutionaries: Englishmen and the Revolution of 1688*, Oxford, Clarendon Press, 1988.

— *Tory and whig: the struggle in the constituencies*, Macmillan, 1970.

— 'William — and Mary?' in Lois G. Schwoerer (ed.), *The Revolution of 1688–89: changing perspectives*, Cambridge, Cambridge University Press, 1992.

Spring, Eileen, 'The family, strict settlement, and the historians,' in G. R. Rubin and David Sugarman (eds), *Law, economy and society, 1750–1914*, Professional Books, 1984.

Starkey, David, 'Representation through intimacy: a study in the symbolism of monarchy and court office in early-modern England,' in Ioan Lewis, *Symbols and sentiments*, Academic Press, 1977.

Staves, Susan, *Married women's separate property in England, 1660–1833*, Cambridge, Mass., Harvard University Press, 1990.

— *Player's sceptres*, Lincoln, University of Nebraska Press, 1979.

Stone, Lawrence, *The family, sex and marriage in England 1500–1800*, New York, Harper & Row, 1977.

— *The road to divorce*, Oxford, Oxford University Press, 1990.

Szechi, Daniel, *Jacobitism and tory politics, 1710–14*, Edinburgh, John Donald, 1984.

Thirsk, Joan, 'Younger sons in the seventeenth century,' *History* 54 (1969).

Thompson, E. P., 'Happy families,' *Radical History Review* 20 (1979).

Todd, Janet, *Women's friendship in literature*, New York, Columbia University Press, 1980.

Todd, Janet (ed.), *Aphra Behn studies*, Cambridge, Cambridge University Press, 1996.

Tully, James, 'Rediscovering America: the *Two treatises* and aboriginal rights', in James Tully, *An approach to political philosophy: Locke in contexts*, Cambridge, Cambridge University Press, 1993.

Turner, James G., 'The properties of libertinism,' in Robert P. Maccubin (ed.), *Unauthorized sexual behavior during the Enlightenment, Eighteenth-Century Life* 9 (1985).

Underdown, David, 'The taming of the scold: the enforcement of patriarchal authority in early modern England,' in A. Fletcher and J. Stevenson (eds), *Order and disorder in early modern England*, Cambridge, Cambridge University Press, 1985.

Vaughn, Karen Iverson, *John Locke, economist and social scientist*, Chicago, University of Chicago Press, 1980.

Vickery, Amanda, 'From golden age to separate spheres?: a review of the categories and chronology of English women's history', *Historical Journal* 36 (1993).

Walmsley, Robert, 'John Wesley's parents: quarrel and reconciliation,' *Proceedings of the Wesley Historical Society* 29 (Sep. 1953).

Weber, Harold, *Paper bullets: print and kingship under Charles II*, Lexington, University of Kentucky Press, 1996.

Webster, Charles, *The great instauration: science, medicine and reform, 1626–1660,* Duckworth, 1975.

Weil, Rachel, 'Sometimes a sceptre is only a sceptre: pornography and politics in Restoration England,' in Lynn Hunt (ed.), *The invention of pornography,* New York, Zone Books, 1993.

Wiseman, Susan, '"Adam, the father of all flesh", porno-political rhetoric and political theory in and after the English civil war,' in James Holstun (ed.), *Pamphlet wars: prose in the English Revolution,* Frank Cass, 1992.

Worden, Blair, 'Classical republicanism and the puritan revolution,' in Hugh Lloyd-Jones *et al.* (eds), *History and imagination,* Duckworth, 1981.

— 'The commonwealth kidney of Algernon Sidney,' *Journal of British Studies* 24 (1985).

Zook, Melinda, 'History's Mary: the propagation of Queen Mary II, 1689–94,' in L. O. Fradenburg (ed.), *Women and sovereignty,* Edinburgh, Edinburgh University Press, 1992.

Zwicker, Steven, 'Virgins and whores: the politics of sexual misconduct in the 1660s' in Conal Condren and A. D. Cousins (eds), *The political ideology of Andrew Marvell,* New York, Scolar Press, 1990.

Index

Index

Index

Printed in October 2021
by Rotomail Italia S.p.A., Vignate (MI) - Italy